The Sustainable Enterprise Fieldbook

To all the children who will inherit the Earth
In the hopes that we bring them a few steps closer
To the horizon toward which we are journeying —
That constantly shifting time and place
When it all comes together

Advance praise for *The Sustainable Enterprise Fieldbook*

In the current groundswell of Earth community ideals and initiatives, *The Sustainable Enterprise Fieldbook* must surely count among the most realistic and practical. Its value will become apparent in the months and years ahead.

Thomas Berry, Historian, Geologian, and author of *The Dream of the Earth* and *The Great Work*

It is a magical moment, indeed, when a competency meets a true need. *The Sustainable Enterprise Fieldbook* has managed such a moment. The wide-gauge competency of Dr. Jeana Wirtenberg, William Russell, and Dr. David Lipsky weave a pragmatic "how to" for every manager now focused on creating and nurturing their own "sustainable enterprise." The "fieldbook" aspect assures the "how to do it" insights — easily accessed and understood — which will permit every caring manager to get it done in the name of "sustainable."

Bob Danzig, Former CEO, Hearst Newspapers; Author/Speaker/Professor

The bottom line and promoting a sustainable environment are no longer mutually exclusive. Sustainability is good business, but many do not know where to begin. *The Sustainable Enterprise Fieldbook* fills that gap and provides a clear and concise roadmap that will benefit any organization in meeting the challenges of getting to a more sustainable future.

Robert J. Garagiola, Maryland State Senator; recipient of awards from national organizations, including the Interstate Renewable Energy Council and the American Solar Energy Society, for his work on renewable energy and conservation efforts

"Sustainability" is not a familiar word or concept for Japanese companies yet, but I'm sure this book will raise the awareness of the importance of sustainability in Japanese society. As an HR manager in charge of leadership programs, I realized that I have missed some important points in planning and organizing the programs. I do hope the Japanese translation will be available soon so that many of my co-workers can study this important topic.

Ayako Hotta, Training and Development Manager, Sony Corporation, Tokyo, Japan

I love this book! This book, or rather this enterprise, is the fruit of a collaboration among dozens of practitioners, businesspeople, and scholars — no wonder it's so useful. Their holistic vision has produced a cornucopia of actionable tools and information for audiences in multiple contexts. And timely too! Generations of children to come, who will surely be educated beyond the old dichotomies of the industrial era, will thank these writers.

Hilary Bradbury-Huang, Editor in Chief, *Action Research*; and University of Southern California, Director, Sustainable Business Research Programs Center for Sustainable Cities

THE
SUSTAINABLE
ENTERPRISE
FIELDBOOK

WHEN IT ALL COMES TOGETHER

Edited by **Jeana Wirtenberg** PhD
with **William G. Russell** and **David Lipsky** PhD

in collaboration with

The Enterprise Sustainability Action Team

Greenleaf
PUBLISHING

American Management Association

New York • Atlanta • Brussels • Chicago • Mexico City • San Francisco
Shanghai • Tokyo • Toronto • Washington, D. C.

Special discounts on bulk quantities of AMACOM books are available to corporations, professional associations, and other organizations. For details, contact Special Sales Department, AMACOM, a division of American Management Association, 1601 Broadway, New York, NY 10019.
Tel.: 212-903-8316. Fax: 212-903-8083.
Website: www.amacombooks.org

This publication is designed to provide accurate and authoritative information in regard to the subject matter covered. It is sold with the understanding that the publisher is not engaged in rendering legal, accounting, or other professional service. If legal advice or other expert assistance is required, the services of a competent professional person should be sought.

ISBN: 978-0-8144-1278-7
Library of Congress Control Number: 2008927499

Printed in the UK on paper that is sourced and harvested from sustainable forests and is FSC-accredited

Published by AMACOM Books, a division of the American Management Association, in association with Greenleaf Publishing Limited, UK

Printing number
10 9 8 7 6 5 4 3 2 1

Contents

5 Employee engagement for a sustainable enterprise 141

Kent D. Fairfield, Richard N. Knowles, William G. Russell,
Jeana Wirtenberg, Sangeeta Mahurkar-Rao, and Orrin D. Judd

6 Sustainable enterprise metrics and measurement systems 162

William G. Russell, Shakira Abdul-Ali, Gil Friend, and David Lipsky

Part IV. Connecting, integrating, and aligning toward the future 203

7 Sustainable globalization: the challenge and the opportunity . 204

Victoria G. Axelrod, Joel Harmon, William G. Russell,
and Jeana Wirtenberg

Foreword

Georg Kell, Executive Head, UN Global Compact

Businesses are challenged as never before by the unrelenting and ever-increasing demands posed by the global economy and the marketplace to address the concerns of a wide range of critical stakeholders, including shareholders, customers, employees, and communities, both locally and around the world.

Technology and deregulation have unleashed an unprecedented expansion of business activities over the past quarter of a century. Many companies have gone global while governments have remained local. Businesses, large and small, are learning to integrate into a global marketplace that offers scale and efficiency gains.

New markets have been developed and much progress has been made in bringing hundreds of millions of people out of abject poverty. At the same time, poverty persists in many parts of the world, inequity has been on the rise, and the impact of human activities on the natural environment threatens our survival as a species.

We cannot predict the future, but the certainty of the major disruptive forces we are witnessing every day makes a compelling case for us to reexamine our fundamental values, shift our priorities, and shape a new strategic direction to create a more sustainable world.

How will we master this global transformation to a sustainable future? Where will leadership come from? Will we be able to extend the benefits of productivity gains to those who need them most while safeguarding our natural environment? Will openness as an economic and political idea prevail, or will we fall back into discriminatory behavior, building walls and creating enemies? Will we be able to provide stewardship that thrives on and cultivates the creativity of people and enterprises while safeguarding the common good? Are we willing — and are we capable enough — to change our patterns of consumption and lifestyles so that they meet our most basic human needs while considering those of future generations? Can we build incentive systems that reward and reinforce good environmental, social, and governance performance?

The stakes couldn't be higher. Never before have we been so dependent on each other.

There is always hope that policy-makers will eventually provide leadership. But all too often they are concerned with territorial constituency building or the sheer desire to maintain a hold on power. Few policy-makers are able, or willing, to take on global perspectives or a long-term vision that goes beyond election cycles.

Business can hardly afford to wait for this to happen. The changing landscape has made it imperative that business help architect and execute the solution. The notion and practice of business responsibility and the search for practical solutions has evolved over the past two decades. Business increasingly understands that the search for sustainability is not just about avoiding costs; it is increasingly about creating business value and inventing models that deliver societal and market success.

Clearly, the role of business is undergoing a profound transformation. The most obvious is the need to manage risks in an interdependent world. As business has become global, it can no longer take refuge behind one home government. It needs to learn to deal simultaneously with different regulatory and societal realities. At the same time, the pursuit of global integration and the sophistication of dispersed supply chains has created new vulnerabilities — as have the scarcity of natural resources and the unfolding of climate change–related regulatory and lifestyle changes.

New business models that understand how to build markets for the one billion people that remain excluded, that thrive on energy efficiency and environmental stewardship, and that build societal goodwill and support are likely to be the winning models of the future. Such enterprises will not only succeed in their own right, they will also make an enormously important contribution to the future of humanity.

We are called to support and promote business efforts that embrace sustainability strategies as a *modus operandi*. Many small and large innovations and alterations are needed to bring about a change on the scale required to safeguard our future. Human creativity and the will to shape the future are our best hope. This *Fieldbook* opens the door for business leaders and managers to the most appropriate and practical pathway for themselves and their enterprises to forge a more sustainable future. It takes us on a thoughtful journey through the eyes of 29 passionate, experienced practitioners inspiring us all to step up to the plate, create a plan, and move forward with velocity, intention, and commitment. It provides the tools, cases, best practices, learnings, and understandings — at once profound and practical — to equip and enable every manager and leader to play a role in the reinvention of the world.

Acknowledgments

The 29 members of the Enterprise Sustainability Action Team (ESAT) have so many people to acknowledge we hardly know where to begin and certainly have no place to end in our expressions of gratitude. We are grateful to our families. To our parents — those who are still with us, and to the memories of those who have passed — for bringing us into this world, raising us to value character and integrity, and supporting us in having our lives make a difference. We especially acknowledge Jeana's mother, Pearl Wirtenberg, for her selfless support of Jeana and the team. To our husbands, wives, and significant others who took care of life's many everyday challenges, and enabled us to spend the time following our calling and pursuing the work we are so passionate about.

We are grateful to our many mentors and teachers who inspired us. There are special acknowledgments from Jeana to Dr. Charles Y. Nakamura, Professor Emeritus in the Psychology Department at the University of California, Los Angeles (UCLA), who encouraged her to pursue her dreams and not succumb to those who told her that her vision was "too big." From Bill to Win Armstrong who set the example for him of how we all should be, believing in him and inspiring him during times of self-doubt to continue along his personal journey. From David to his wife Sharon and their precious children, Zachary, Jacob, Samantha, and Joshua, who demonstrate each day the simple and powerful principle of leaving everything a little better than they found it and inspiring him to do the same.

We are grateful to each other. The 29 contributors and co-authors who worked on this book will never be the same. We shared many experiences, learnings, epiphanies, challenges, shortcomings, occasional heartbreaks, and lots of good laughs. Amazingly, many of us have never met face to face. We came together out of a shared passion and vision of what is possible. We talked for over a year on teleconference calls before we ever wrote a word. We formed self-organizing teams. We re-formed our teams and made many changes along the way. We strove to live our values — and exhibited compassion, respect, generosity, concern, and awe at what incredible capabilities are represented on our team, knowing there are so many more people who would love to join our journey, if only we could offer them the opportunity.

We are especially grateful to our editor George-Thérèse Dickenson, who moved heaven and earth to help bring our words together into a common voice and vernacular. Her wisdom, generosity, capabilities, passion, and loyalty carried us all across the finish line.

We are grateful to our editors from Greenleaf Publishing, John Stuart and Dean Bargh, who exhibited great flexibility and support throughout the process. While many publishers said you cannot have 29 authors with one coherent voice, Greenleaf Publishing believed in our project from the start and guided us to translate our vision into reality.

Members of our team have forged a myriad of collaborative relationships and alliances with organizations and associations from all sectors who share our values and vision. We want to acknowledge two collaborative relationships in particular, which have played a pivotal and catalytic role for our work together.

The mission of the Institute for Sustainable Enterprise (ISE) at Fairleigh Dickinson University (FDU) is to "bring people together to learn how to develop and lead thriving, sustainable enterprises that are 'in and for the world.'" Consistent with its mission, the ISE helped bring us together as a loose-knit group of like-minded people, and supported us in a variety of ways throughout the process as we came together over the past three years.

The Global Community for the Future of Organization Development (GCFOD) is a global network whose vision is to bridge business leaders, organization development practitioners, and scholars committed to creating and nurturing sustainable, high-performing human enterprises. The GCFOD helped inspire and fuel our work, and provided ESAT with many of our extraordinarily talented and passionate members.

All that being said, we note that our gratitude extends far beyond the boundaries of those we personally know and with whom we have worked. We are grateful to the Earth and all living things, to the animal, plant, and aquatic species that have already become extinct and to those we are trying to save, so that we leave this world a little better than we found it.

To our children, and all children, grandchildren, and the children not yet born, the generations to come in the world who will inherit this beautiful Earth hopefully with a brighter and more sustainable future.

We are grateful for the indomitable spirit and magnificent possibilities of the people who inhabit this Earth, and hope that, in some small way, we are helping unleash this potential for the betterment of us all now and into the future.

Understanding reality: our context for *The Sustainable Enterprise Fieldbook*

Introduction and overview

Jeana Wirtenberg, William G. Russell,
and David Lipsky

> What changes in lifestyles, behaviour patterns and management practices
> are needed, and by when?
>
> *Intergovernmental Panel on Climate Change* (Pachauri, 2007, slide 15)

On October 17, 2005, a small group of like-minded committed practitioners convened at Fairleigh Dickinson University and began a conversation about the conditions in the world (the good, the bad, and the ugly) and what was needed to bring about large-scale transformation to a more sustainable world. We talked about what we could do individually and collectively to help people in organizations, especially leaders and managers, better appreciate the value they can bring to and the difference they can make in their organizations to help create more sustainable enterprises, and ultimately a more sustainable world. Over the next several years this team self-organized into a community of 29 diverse, experienced professionals and many additional collaborating friends and associates to discover and help breathe life into the missing ingredients of sustainability and to create a vision for the sustainable enterprise.

We began our journey with an eclectic group of people with diverse backgrounds, experiences, perspectives, and aspirations. Our shared commitment to creating a more sustainable world, especially ensuring that the world is livable for our children, grandchildren, and generations to come continues to fuel our passion and unite us. This is consistent with the basic and most widely used definition of *sustainable* drawn from the Brundtland Commission (World Commission on Environment and Development, 1987), "meeting the needs of the present without compromising the ability of future generations to meet their own needs."

This *Fieldbook* captures the essence, energies, experiences, and best practices that emerged through the collaborative efforts of our community of co-authors. Our mantra was and is,

> Be the change you want to see in the world.
>
> *Mahatma Gandhi*

We began our journey hoping to write a book and articulate what a sustainable enterprise is. Now that we have significantly achieved our original objectives, we see our role within an even larger community whose objective is nothing short of making the world sustainable for all who inhabit it today — and, more importantly, for those future generations we know we will never see but to whom we bequeath the stewardship of this precious planet.

▨ 'Business case' for a sustainable enterprise

Companies that want to succeed and thrive in the future are increasingly being encouraged to find ways to *simultaneously* meet both their own strategic needs and those of society (Porter & Kramer, 2006). More than ever before, companies are being asked to emphasize a broader and more balanced array of outcomes such as those characterized by the "triple bottom line" of people, planet, and profits (Savitz & Weber, 2006). In the 21st century, rather than focusing singularly or even primarily on the "financial bottom line" and the financial assets they possess, the most sustainable companies are looking at themselves and their future through the lens of the "five capitals model" of natural, human, social, manufactured, and financial capital (Costanza, 2001).

At the same time, evidence continues to mount that demonstrates that corporate social-environmental performance is strongly associated with financial and marketplace success (Cusack 2005; Innovest Strategic Value Advisors[1]). And we see more and more evidence on almost a daily basis that the professional investment community, corporate executives, and directors appear to be increasingly focused on the degree to which firms are managed sustainably (Dixon, 2003; Margolis & Walsh, 2001).

What is the most important ingredient in Coca-Cola's success? Water. The syrup is what gives the product its competitive advantage, but without water Coca-Cola could not supply the world with its products. When the company became aware of the global challenge facing potable water, it co-founded the Global Water Challenge to address the problem. Sustainability makes business sense.

So why do we need *The Sustainable Enterprise Fieldbook?* And why now? Although the desired *outcome* of sustainability is becoming increasingly clear, the *process* by which one can best *develop and implement* sustainability is considerably less so. Our book is designed to help address both the *what* (what is a sustainable strategy for a company or organization?) and the *how* of sustainable enterprise (how do we go about building a sustainable enterprise?).

Although we use the term *enterprise* throughout this book (a term that is usually associated with the for-profit business sector), we firmly believe that the disciplines, case studies, tools, and references presented throughout our *Fieldbook* are applicable to organizations within the government, education, nonprofit, and nongovernmental organization (NGO) sectors as well. Furthermore, wherever possible we intentionally include examples of successful public–private partnerships, collaborative initiatives operating across multiple stakeholders and institutions, and organizations working in the "in-between space" to build sustainable enterprises. We believe these cross-sector, collaborative partnerships may offer the greatest hope for solving many of the globe's most intractable problems.

1 www.innovestgroup.com (accessed May 12, 2007).

■ Purpose of *The Sustainable Enterprise Fieldbook*

The purpose of the *Fieldbook* is to help forge a path to a better world and a more sustainable future by supporting employees, managers, and leaders at every level and in every function, sector, and industry in three key ways:

- Increasing their understanding and awareness of the meaning of sustainability on a conceptual, practical, and personal level

- Energizing and expanding their commitment to building sustainable enterprises that can contribute to enhancing the sustainability of the world and its ecosystems for generations to come

- Providing readers with the tools and techniques needed to individually and collectively take appropriate actions that will improve their personal and enterprise sustainability performance in the short and long term

■ Missing ingredients and *The Sustainable Enterprise Fieldbook*

The Sustainable Enterprise Fieldbook is designed to align with an emergent framework of best-practice enterprise qualities. In it, we pay particular attention to those areas with identified gaps between current practices and risks and future practices and risks that were identified during a global sustainability survey of business leaders and managers (American Management Association [AMA], 2007).

We believe this *Fieldbook* is unique in at least six respects:

1. It is based on a stream of original research, both qualitative and quantitative, focused on the qualities of a sustainable enterprise and state-of-the-art best practices. This research is summarized later in this chapter and interspersed throughout the book with specific illustrative examples from businesses and other organizations

2. It offers concrete and practical ways to close the significant gaps that our recent worldwide study revealed in the role that managers in every function need to play to build a sustainable enterprise. For example, there are significant gaps between how important managers think a variety of sustainability-related issues are, and what they and their organizations are actually doing about them in their day-to-day practices

3. We focus on the critical role that human capital (i.e., people) needs to play in the transformational journey to sustainable enterprise. We believe that this is the missing ingredient in transforming rhetoric into action, and we are committed to helping pave the way for people to take the actions needed to, quite literally, save the world

4. We engage with you, our readers, by sharing the experiences some of our authors have had working with businesses, nonprofits, and educational institutions to design and implement elements of an organizational model founded on principles of sustainability, integrity, inclusivity, mutuality, and self-organizing leadership

5. By offering a complementary online *Living Fieldbook* (see below) we strive to model sustainable principles and practices. In fact, our hard-copy book was itself created on a collaborative worldwide sustainability knowledge network portal that we now invite all readers to join. Going forward, readers can contribute knowledge and insights and share their own stories, accomplishments, and challenges

6. We have taken action, and we seek to continuously learn and improve on all elements of our current understanding and the future iterative learning we will all experience during the global journey to sustainability

The Sustainable Enterprise Fieldbook and its innovative *Living Fieldbook* and online community support services offer a missing ingredient in the elements we think must come together to create a sustainable world.

How should a person be if he or she has values aligned with sustainability?

We acknowledge our own imperfections, weaknesses, and biased perspectives, and invite all readers to join and expand our learning community. We welcome all comments and suggestions, positive and negative, on what you like and how to improve on what we have created. We will continue to ask: What more needs to be done?

To support our efforts, the ESAT (Enterprise Sustainability Action Team) authors agreed to base our work on these principles:

- Holistic, emergent view
- Collaborative, sharing, inclusive, open approach
- Inquiry–action–inquiry . . .
- Act with integrity and help each other; be respectful
- Win–win–win
- Listen deeply — for understanding — and create the space for conversations
- Work in the in-between space and across boundaries
- Stay present to our intention, focus on improving the world
- Be attractors
- Be careful that we understand what we mean
- Seek to discover and serve mutual interests
- Walk in others' shoes
- Be committed and accountable
- Create room for the difficult conversations
- Live what we want to become; pay attention to our "way of being"
- Develop tangible actions and short-term successes

Following these principles yielded many positive outcomes for the ESAT. Among these are:

- Increased energy levels

- Humbled, fascinated, and intrigued

- Focused our attention on the power of individuals and the common threads that unite us

- Reinforced the power of sustainability

- Created the conditions to help people bring their aliveness to their roles

- Reinforced the importance of continuing to capture and share our passion for sustainability

Our hope is that these principles and the outcomes they generated ignite the passions and actions of readers worldwide as they did for our team.

■ Using *The Sustainable Enterprise Fieldbook*

The Sustainable Enterprise Fieldbook is designed so that the reader may quickly and easily reference any individual enterprise quality and find resources, case studies, tools, and related materials that can be used to help transform any enterprise from its current state to a more sustainable future state. Although all chapters cover distinctly different sustainable enterprise qualities, a consistent set of content categories are highlighted by icons throughout the *Fieldbook* to provide users with a quick visual guide and to enhance the *Fieldbook's* utility.

Activities for awareness and understanding (**A**)

Throughout the chapters we introduce a number of activities, frameworks, thought questions, and the like. All of these are intended to increase awareness and understanding and are denoted by an **A**. Wherever an **A** appears, we suggest that managers lead a simple activity, such as having their group read and discuss the associated text (essay, framework, and the like). In some cases, we supplement the **A** with an **L** for *Living Fieldbook* (see below). The **L** lets readers know they will find more detailed thought questions, discussion guides, and specific exercises aimed at further increasing awareness and understanding around that activity on the *Living Fieldbook*.

Case examples (**C**)

The Sustainable Enterprise Fieldbook uses case examples throughout the chapters as an effective way to make our messages more real to *Fieldbook* users. A **C** highlights case studies.

Tools (**T**)

The Sustainable Enterprise Fieldbook provides sample tools that lead to action. These were strategically selected by each chapter subteam as we discovered and used them during our work or learned about how others were using them by interviewing practitioners and identifying case examples. A **T** highlights tools.

Collectively we hope the Activities for awareness and understanding (**A**), Cases (**C**), and Tools (**T**) help inspire people to ACT.

Living Fieldbook collaborative workspace

The authors not only of this Introduction, but of *The Sustainable Enterprise Fieldbook* as a whole, recognize the constraints imposed by a physical book with hard page limits, deadlines, and production costs that make it impossible in one physical book to keep up with the rapid pace of learning and change related to sustainable enterprise practices. We hope to accommodate these limitations by supplementing the physical book content with an online *Sustainable Enterprise Living Fieldbook* workspace. The workspace is referred to throughout this book and can be freely accessed at www.TheSustainableEnterpriseFieldbook.net.

Since the beginning of our ESAT discussions, we determined that there was an abundance of highly valuable reference materials, tools, and case studies that individual team members were aware of and wanted to share. This shared knowledge became so expansive that we began to explore ways to introduce the best themes of these works within our book and offer readers an efficient way to identify and access our references and learn more deeply about any selected topic. We also recognized that, as standards and best practices rapidly evolve, our *Living Fieldbook* would provide a way to keep our insights current and even support open discussions and feedback forums where different opinions could be openly progressed, and completely unanticipated insights and solutions could naturally emerge.

This *Living Fieldbook* workspace is hosted within the Sustainability Knowledge Network platform introduced in Chapter 8. The business model to support the *Living Fieldbook* and similar more interactive and open content-sharing services are in their formative stages and are still evolving. All of the material on the *Living Fieldbook* that is referred to in this physical book (e.g., at the beginning of Chapter 1, we refer readers to the *Living Fieldbook* for an essay by Theresa McNichol) was purposefully made to be freely accessible.[2]

As we gained experience using our own collaborative workspace, we began to explore new social network technologies and communities. We recognized that we could be more effective by expanding our own collaborative community and purposefully connecting with selected networks with aligned and complementary values and objectives. We committed ourselves to sharing and leveraging our online workspace by connecting it with others in social network communities and participating in related, relevant groups. Our hope is that members of those related sustainability social network communities may choose to connect with and contribute their own unexpected innovations to our work. We are currently actively engaging with others through several strategic online networks such as Facebook[3] and Second Life.[4] We want to engage and collaborate with people within the online communities in which they are already actively par-

---

2 Interested readers are also invited to join a premium service portion of the *Living Fieldbook* for a fee in order to access selected additional resources and services including some premium tools, restricted copyright articles, webinar archives, and expert moderated forums.

3 Sustainability and Sustainable Enterprise Group at www.facebook.com/s.php?k=100000004&id =4698033510&gr=2.

4 ESAT in Second Life at slurl.com/secondlife/Cedar%20Island/159/209/33.

ticipating. We are also using the *Living Fieldbook* workspace to develop network maps, beginning with our core group of 29 ESAT members and strategically adding connections through an extensive group of collaborating partners. (See Chapter 8 for more on social networks.)

While these efforts are action learning experiences in themselves, we expect that they will bring more breadth and depth to our work and, most important, extend the reach and impact of our message as we strive to positively influence the path toward a more sustainable world.

■ Context: acknowledging current reality, best practices, and iterative learning

The vast majority of the more than 6.5 billion people living on the planet today are poor, hungry, disconnected from the rest of the world, and often afraid (Curtis, Bedell, & Christian, 2005). As we continue to better understand and appreciate how we are all connected, we trust that all efforts to improve ourselves and our affiliated enterprises as we collectively journey toward sustainability will positively impact everyone.

Our community of co-authors, along with a minority, but rapidly growing number, of enlightened people, has only recently become aware of our unsustainable personal practices. We have struggled to resolve our own confusion and paralysis to initiate actions, but, as we began to appreciate "reality," the true condition of our world today, we knew that we must change. Here are a few of our observations that motivated us to examine our personal actions as well as the actions of our enterprises.

Current reality

The ESAT team has used the work of hundreds of other people who were our teachers, mentors, and peers as we began to define what a sustainable enterprise might be like. The works of Peter Senge and his colleagues, including *The Fifth Discipline* (Senge, 1990), *The Fifth Discipline Fieldbook* (Senge, Kleiner, Roberts, Ross, & Smith, 1994), and his more recent book, *Presence* (Senge, Scharmer, Jaworski, & Flowers, 2004), provided a solid foundation for our team. That foundation included our use of systems thinking (the fifth discipline), thinking of the whole system as one holistically integrated, continually changing organism rather than a sum of discrete parts. Senge also describes how to see things more clearly from a higher perspective that allows us to acknowledge the reality of the whole system as opposed to only seeing reality through the narrower lens of one of its parts.

The following subsections provide several facts and observations that we offer as a way to quickly let our community of readers better appreciate our current global state of affairs. It represents real challenges to be addressed and, for our sustainable enterprises, opportunities to provide solutions.

Environmental sustainability[5]

- **Rainforests.** Between 20 and 40 years remaining at current deforestation rates

- **Atlantic cod.** Stocks collapsed and not recovering

- **Grain.** Harvest less than consumption globally for fourth year in a row

- **Freshwater.** Two-thirds of all people in severe shortage by 2025

- **Top soil.** Agricultural land area the size of China at "very high risk" of human-induced desertification

- **Polar ice cap.** 20% gone in the last 25 years

- **Ecological footprint.** A resource management tool that measures how much land and water area a human population requires to produce the resources it consumes and to absorb its wastes under prevailing technology. Today, humanity's ecological footprint is more than 23% larger than the planet's regeneration capacity.[6] In other words, it now takes more than one year and two months for the Earth to regenerate what we use in a single year[7]

Economics

- Every day more than 3 billion human beings live on less than $2 (Curtis et al., 2005)

- The three richest people in the world control more wealth than 600,000,000 people in the poorest countries on Earth (Curtis et al., 2005)

- Eighty of the world's poorest countries are poorer now than they were 20 years ago (Curtis et al., 2005)

- The cost estimate of ending starvation and malnutrition everywhere is US$19 billion per year (Symes, 2006)

- Globally, US$47 billion is spent every year on ice cream (Symes, 2006)

- Globally, more than US$1 trillion each year is spent on weapons (Symes, 2006)

- The 2005 Carbon Disclosure Project survey of CEOs and the climate change and carbon management practices of their companies were endorsed by more than US$30 trillion of investment capital (Morrow, 2006)

Social justice

- One in five of the world's children gets no schooling whatsoever (Symes, 2006)

- The United States spends more money every year on building prisons than it does on schools (Symes, 2006)

- There are currently more than 30 ongoing armed conflicts in the world and roughly one-third of the world's population is at war (Symes, 2006)

---

5 All the information in this section, except for that on the ecological footprint, is from *Your Planet Needs You* (Symes, 2006).

6 The ecological footprint is covered more extensively in Chapters 7 and 8.

7 Global Footprint Network homepage, www.footprintnetwork.org (accessed June, 2007).

● The United Nations reported that the global population has increased by 500 million people since 1999, to more than 6.5 billion people today (United Nations Population Division, 2006)

● The United Nations estimates that by 2050 the population will grow almost 50% again to approximately 9.1 billion with almost all of these increases occurring in developing countries (United Nations Population Division, 2006)

▓ Iterative learning: action research efforts evolve our understanding

Like most communities seeking to gain a better understanding of sustainability, we had read numerous books and attended numerous conferences that greatly informed our understanding of current reality and the many significant real-world challenges that cause us to act unsustainably today. Each of these efforts was valuable, but we knew so much more was needed. Although all the team members were forging ahead, engaged in enterprise-specific projects and teaching others about sustainability, the specific question about exactly what a sustainable enterprise is remained unanswered.

So in early 2006, several team members and other close associates at the Fairleigh Dickinson University Institute for Sustainable Enterprise (FDU-ISE) self-organized and initiated a research project specifically intended to learn the qualities of a sustainable enterprise. The results of that research and its associated **Sustainability Pyramid model** were a major step forward in our team's collaborative journey. Interim publications were written and several presentations given to share and obtain feedback on our insights. We were all gratified that we had learned much, but again asked ourselves, "What more needs to be done?"

Subsequently, we completed additional research work, including a recent worldwide sustainability survey (AMA, 2007), the highlights of which are shared below. We have also embarked on a number of other related independent projects and initiatives.[8] One of our most important findings so far has been about our iterative learning process itself. We all are deeply committed to the process of **action learning**. Through this process, we are intentional about creating value by taking small (and sometimes bigger) steps, capturing the essential learning points, applying them, and sharing this learning with others. We have embraced this iterative learning process as we prepare to take our next steps along the journey. We also see iterative learning as a large-scale transformative process that will cycle among individuals, enterprises, and large-scale global systems. As long as we remain open to learning more, we believe this collaborative approach will lead to self-fulfillment, sustainable enterprises, and global sustainability.

8 For more information about these ongoing initiatives, see www.fdu.edu/ise (accessed January 17, 2008).

The Sustainability Pyramid model

Our recent study of nine of the world's most sustainable companies (Wirtenberg, Harmon, Russell, & Fairfield 2007)[9] identified a "pyramid" of seven core qualities associated with successfully implementing sustainability strategies and achieving triple-bottom-line results. This model also illustrates the necessary contributions of human capital practices (see Fig. i.1).

Figure i.1 **The Sustainability Pyramid: qualities associated with highly successful sustainability strategies**

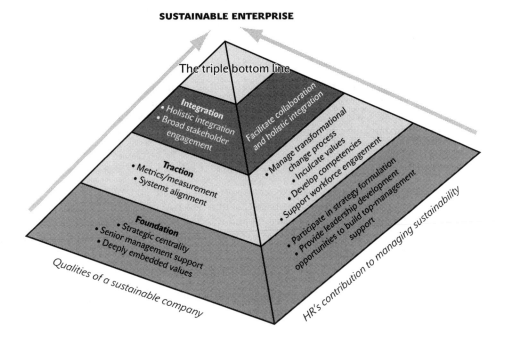

Source: Copyright 2006, Institute for Sustainable Enterprise.
Reproduced with permission.

Foundation layer

At the base of the pyramid and along the left face is the "Foundation." It contains deeply held corporate values consistent with sustainability, top management's visible support for sustainability, and its placement as central to overall corporate strategy.

9 The companies were Alcoa, Bank of America, BASF, The Coca-Cola Company, Eastman Kodak, Intel, Novartis AG, Royal Philips, and Unilever. All are listed in "The Global 100 Most Sustainable Corporations in the World," a project initiated by Corporate Knights, with Innovest Strategic Value Advisors. Details on its methodology and results can be found at www.global100.org (accessed January 17, 2008).

Traction layer

At the next level up is "Traction," which can be achieved by engaging employees, developing sustainability metrics ("we manage what we measure"), and aligning formal and informal organization systems around sustainability.

Integration layer

Toward the top of the pyramid is "Integration," which occurs via broad stakeholder engagement and holistic integration. At this level, many facets and functional domains of sustainability are coordinated in an integrative fashion. Even the nine highly rated firms studied seemed to be struggling with reaching this cross-boundary, multistakeholder, integrative pinnacle. Wirtenberg and her colleagues (Wirtenberg et al., 2007) conjectured that deeply infusing sustainability-oriented values and creating holistic integration are the highest-level challenges associated with implementing sustainability strategies.

The three sustainable enterprise pyramid layers and subsequent enterprise qualities are used to provide an overall framework for *The Sustainable Enterprise Fieldbook*. More detailed case studies, learning, and stories obtained from our research with some of the world's most sustainable companies are included in several *Fieldbook* chapters.

Worldwide sustainability survey results

While our team was extremely pleased to have developed an initial framework for defining a sustainable enterprise, we appreciated that our view was limited by the small number of companies included in this research and that the people included in the study represented only senior managers. We asked ourselves, "What more needs to be done?" And we continued to identify actions we could take to learn more. Precisely such a learning opportunity became available when our team leader, Jeana Wirtenberg, was approached by the Human Resource Institute to support the AMA in conducting a worldwide sustainability survey (AMA, 2007). Wirtenberg immediately engaged her colleagues at the FDU-ISE (AMA, 2007).[10]

Consistent with earlier research by Wirtenberg et al. (2007), the AMA (2007) study found that respondents rated every element in the Sustainability Pyramid as *very important* for building a sustainable enterprise (from about 3.9 to 4.4 out of 5). But we also found sizable gaps between the perceived importance of these qualities and the degree to which the average responding organization actually demonstrated these qualities (from 2.8 to 3.3; see Table i.1).

These gaps may be closed over time as more companies adopt sustainability qualities to a greater extent. Throughout the book, we provide some examples of exemplary sustainability companies and their specific practices from which organizations might learn. It is important to note, however, that we do not hold up any single organization as the best example of all sustainability practices. Even organizations with exemplary practices in one area may act in "unsustainable" and sometimes even irresponsible ways in other parts of their organizations. Further, sustainability should be considered an "end state" that will be redefining itself each day as we move forward on the journey to sus-

---

10 *Creating a Sustainable Future* was written under the auspices of the AMA, and in conjunction with the Human Resource Institute (HRI), by M. Vickers, J. Wirtenberg, J. Harmon, A. Lindberg, J. M. Lee, and D. J. Dennis. Contributors were K. D. Fairfield, S. Nickbarg, and W. G. Russell.

Table i.1 **Degree to which companies have the qualities of sustainable enterprises** (mean responses on a 5-point scale, where 1 = not at all and 5 = to a very great extent)

Qualities of a sustainable enterprise	Extent company has these qualities	Importance to building a sustainable enterprise
Top-management support. The CEO, the chairman of the board and senior management teams show public and unwavering support for sustainability	3.33	4.36
Centrality to business strategy. Sustainability is central to the company's competitive strategy	3.23	4.07
Values. Key values related to sustainability are deeply ingrained in the company	3.10	4.15
Metrics. The company deploys an array of rigorous sustainability measures	2.91	3.89
Stakeholder engagement. The company reaches out to and involves a broad array of external and internal stakeholders around sustainability issues, including customers, suppliers, governmental and non-governmental organizations (NGOs)	2.90	3.87
Systems alignment. The company's structure, systems, processes, and culture are aligned around sustainability	2.88	3.98
Organizational integration. Various aspects of sustainability are viewed holistically and integrated across the functions that have responsibility for them	2.82	3.88

Source: American Management Association. (2007). *Creating a sustainable future: A global study of current trends and possibilities 2007–2017*. New York: AMA, p. 30. Copyright 2007, American Management Association. Reproduced with permission.

tainability. With these caveats noted, the following is a list of some of the companies that are considered "current sustainability leaders" by the AMA (2007, p. 28) across a variety of industries.

- **Energy.** BP, Conoco-Philips, Florida Power and Light, Royal Dutch Shell, PG&E

- **Manufacturing.** Alcoa, Alcan, BASF, Dell, DuPont, Eastman Kodak, Electrolux, Epson, GE, Herman Miller, Honda, HP, IKEA, Intel, Interface, Johnson Controls, Nike, Philips NV, SC Johnson, Toyota, Volkswagen

- **Food.** Bon Appetit, The Coca-Cola Co., Frito Lay, Heinz, Stonyfield Farm, Unilever, Starbucks

- **Pharmaceuticals/Healthcare.** Johnson & Johnson, Novartis

- **Services.** Bank of America, Continental Airlines, Goldman Sachs, Kaiser Permanente, Swiss Re

Sustainability practices

In addition to validating the Sustainability Pyramid, the sustainability survey also looked at a number of other factors related to sustainability. How much do managers care about sustainability issues? How much do they think their companies care about these issues? How much are managers actually implementing sustainability practices?

Below is a quick review of the some of the key findings[11] from the worldwide AMA sustainability survey (AMA, 2007) of 1,365 managers around the world; these essentially form the business case and the burning platform for the *Fieldbook.* They helped to reaffirm our desire to write a book to assist managers understand the issues of sustainability management and advance their own organizations in this direction.

Respondents personally care more about sustainability issues than they think their organizations do, especially when it comes to social and environmental issues. Major gaps exist between the importance of a variety of sustainability issues from people's personal perspectives and their perceptions of the importance of these same issues from their organizations' perspectives. For example, people care much more about such issues as safe and reliable food sources, worker job security, climate change, well-being of employees, and poverty and homelessness, than they think their organizations or companies care about these issues.

Sustainability-related initiatives are not yet deeply ingrained in most organizations:

- About a tenth of respondents think their organizations are implementing a sustainability strategy to a very great extent, and another 25% think their organizations are doing so to an above-average extent

- Twenty-eight per cent said they see measurable benefits from sustainability initiatives to a very great or above-average extent

- Twenty-four per cent said their organizations supply and/or review information that is used to develop sustainability-related metrics to a very great or above-average extent

But **organizations that use sustainability strategies to a greater degree are also more likely to be high performers in terms of reported progress in the marketplace**. Although correlation is not causation, this suggests that sustainability might provide competitive advantages to organizations. Compared with lower-performing organizations, higher-performing organizations are more likely to:

- Engage in sustainability practices to a greater extent

- Attach greater importance to qualities associated with sustainability

- Have all sustainability qualities, as defined in the survey, to at least a moderate degree

---

11 For complete findings and a copy of the report, see the *Living Fieldbook* (**L**) or visit www. whenitallcomestogether.com (accessed January 17, 2008), www.fdu.edu/ise, or www.amanet. org/research.

It is important to note that **reducing or managing the risks of climate change was not highly rated in terms of its ability to drive key business issues, either today or in ten years**. In fact, it was ranked 24th out of 25 sustainability-related issues today, and only 23rd when respondents were asked to look ten years into the future. However, the study noted that "effectively addressing regulatory restrictions" was viewed as a key factor driving business issues, and the authors suggested that future regulations could drive up the importance of greenhouse gas emissions.

There is a correlation between the degree to which firms implement sustainability strategies and the degree to which they see measurable benefits from sustainability initiatives. That is, the more firms implement such strategies, the greater the extent to which they see measurable benefits.

What are the most important qualities that an organization needs to successfully implement a sustainability strategy? According to respondents, as we noted above, the top three are:

● Top management's visible support for sustainability

● Deeply held corporate values consistent with sustainability

● Sustainability's placement as central to overall corporate strategy

There are major gaps between the extent to which certain qualities are important for building a sustainable enterprise and the extent to which companies have these qualities, suggesting that companies have made only moderate progress toward sustainability, with definite room for improvement.

Out of 17 sustainability-related practices, the most widely used were:

1. Ensuring the health and safety of employees

2. Ensuring accountability for ethics at all levels

3. Engaging collaboratively with community and nongovernmental groups

4. Supporting employees in balancing work and life activities (see Table i.2)

There are no particularly strong barriers to making organizations more sustainable. None of the barriers asked about is seen as very strong. Those with the highest rating are a lack of demand from consumers and customers, a lack of demand from managers and employees, a lack of awareness and understanding, and a lack of standardized metrics or performance benchmarks.

Barriers to sustainability can come from outside or within organizations. Managers who are trained to believe that profit is the primary purpose of business may find it hard to believe that the financial bottom line can improve through social responsibility and environmental initiatives. Table i.3 shows the rank order of potential barriers and the mean values based on the responses to the worldwide sustainability survey.

Some of these issues are reflected in the results of the *2007 AMA Sustainability Survey.* The "lack of demand from consumers and customers" and the "lack of demand from managers and employees" were seen as the most powerful factors hindering companies from moving further in the direction of sustainability. Close behind were the third- and fourth-ranked reasons: "lack of awareness and understanding" and "lack of standardized metrics or performance benchmarks." But it should also be noted that none of these barriers received ratings that were above the moderate level. In other words, none was seen as a particularly strong barrier to sustainability.

Table i.2 **Top 12 most commonly used sustainability-related practices** (mean responses on a 5-point scale, where 1 = not at all and 5 = to a very great extent)

To what extent does your company have practices in place to do the following?	Mean responses
Ensure the health and safety of employees	4.02
Ensure accountability for ethics at all levels	3.95
Engage collaboratively with community and nongovernmental groups	3.47
Support employees in balancing work and life activities	3.35
Encourage employee volunteerism	3.29
Involve employees in decisions that affect them	3.28
Provide employee training and development related to sustainability	3.26
Reduce waste materials	3.14
Highlight our commitment to sustainability in our brand	3.12
Improve energy efficiency	3.06
Work with suppliers to strengthen sustainability practices	2.95
Get groups across organization that are working on sustainability-related initiatives to work more closely together	2.85

Source: American Management Association. (2007). *Creating a sustainable future: A global study of current trends and possibilities 2007–2017*. New York: AMA, p. 32. Copyright 2007, American Management Association. Reproduced with permission.

Clearly, if there is a lack of awareness and understanding, then few from the inside or outside of organizations would make a push to develop sustainable practices. Likewise, if companies possess no easy way to measure the success or profitability of such practices, they are less likely to undertake the effort and perceived expense of such a campaign. The findings do suggest that a lack of awareness, understanding, and demand are key factors. These are cultural issues that can be changed over time, and later in this book we suggest processes and methods to do just that.

The state-of-the-art sustainable enterprise

For enterprises to operate in a way that actively fosters sustainability, we believe[12] those organizations need to help restore — or at least not undermine — the capacity of the natural environment to provide resources and services. To earn the sustainability moniker, organizations must also actively contribute to stability in the communities and economies in which they operate.

12 These perspectives are entirely consistent with and covered more extensively in the AMA 2007 report as noted above.

Table i.3 **Factors that can hinder the movement toward sustainability practices, based on mean responses** (mean responses on a 5-point scale, where 1 = not at all and 5 = to a very great extent)

Potential barriers to sustainability	Rank	Mean
Lack of demand from consumers and customers	1	3.13
Lack of demand from managers and employees	2	3.13
Lack of awareness and understanding	3	3.11
Lack of standardized metrics or performance benchmarks	4	3.10
Lack of specific ideas on what to do and when to do it	5	3.08
Lack of demand from shareholders and investors	6	3.04
Lack of demand from suppliers	7	2.99
Unclear or weak business case	8	2.97
Lack of demand from the community	9	2.93
Lack of support from senior leaders	10	2.92
General risk aversion	11	2.80
Fear of competitor's taking advantage of us	12	2.38

Source: American Management Association. (2007). *Creating a sustainable future: A global study of current trends and possibilities 2007–2017*. New York: AMA, p. 21. Copyright 2007, American Management Association. Reproduced with permission.

We define a "state-of-the art" sustainable enterprise as one that adopts a long-term, collaborative, "holistic" or systems-oriented mindset. It integrates sustainable development into its core business strategy, and its activities result in the generation or regeneration of the planet's capital stocks: that is, natural, social, financial, human, and manufactured capital. A state-of-the-art sustainable enterprise implements ethics-based business principles and sound corporate governance practices that consider the rights and interests of all relevant stakeholders, not only the immediate interests of company shareholders.

A sustainable enterprise is likely to pursue a triple-bottom-line strategy that is tied to three broad domains of stakeholder needs: social, environmental, and economic. A sustainable enterprise is committed to transparency and accountability. Such an organization gives stakeholders opportunities to participate in all relevant decisions that affect them. A sustainable organization uses its influence to promote meaningful systemic change among its peers, within its neighboring communities, and throughout its supply chain. This is because it recognizes that, for sustainability to be achieved, it is not enough simply to change one's own organization; enterprises should also be a vehicle for encouraging the improved performance of others (Prince of Wales's Business and the Environment Programme, 2003).

Most importantly, the AMA 2007 sustainability study found that the degree to which sustainability practices and strategies were being implemented — and the extent to which those strategies reportedly produce benefits — was significantly stronger among the higher-performing organizations. Such performance was based on self-reported

Table i.4 **Implementing sustainability strategies and seeing measurable benefits, based on mean responses** (mean responses on a 5-point scale, where 1 = not at all and 5 = to a very great extent)

To what extent . . .	Lowest performers	Highest performers	All respondents
. . . do you believe that your organization is implementing a sustainability strategy?	2.65	3.33	2.99
. . . is your organization seeing measurable benefits from sustainability initiatives?	2.56	3.19	2.88

Source: American Management Association. (2007). *Creating a sustainable future: A global study of current trends and possibilities 2007–2017*. New York: AMA, p. 25. Copyright 2007, American Management Association. Reproduced with permission.

progress over a five-year period in terms of revenue growth, market share, profitability, and customer satisfaction (see Table i.4).

This last point supports our premise that sustainable development is associated with superior marketplace and financial performance. As mentioned above, these findings suggest that sustainability might provide competitive advantages to organizations. In addition, anecdotally, many organizations have made that assertion (Wirtenberg et al., 2007).

▓ Overview of this book

The Sustainable Enterprise Fieldbook is organized into five parts and nine chapters. Each part and the subsequent chapters in this book follow the framework of our pyramid model and provide activities, case studies, tools, and techniques to forge a successful path toward creating a sustainable enterprise.

Our goal in this book is to forge a path to a better world and a more sustainable future by supporting employees, managers, and leaders at every level, function, sector, and industry by educating, energizing, and sharing best practices.

Part I. Understanding reality: our context for *The Sustainable Enterprise Fieldbook*

Introduction and overview

This Introduction attempts to provide you with an appreciation of the formation of our team, the ESAT, a summary of our understanding of the current state of our environment, economic, and social systems, and the action research efforts we initiated in response to our ongoing question: What more is needed? We present our commitment to iterative learning and the research that focused our understanding and shaped the *Fieldbook's* framework. The Introduction also provides the background and rationale for focusing on the people factor, the missing ingredient, in the field of sustainability and the importance of providing practical tools and approaches to drive positive sustainable action. We will use key principles and models to show how each of the book chapters contributes a key ingredient to the challenge of building a sustainable enterprise.

The *Sustainable Enterprise Living Fieldbook* is introduced as a means to capture and share best practices in collaboration technology, knowledge management, and social networks for sustainability.

Part II. Preparing the foundation for a sustainable enterprise

Part II presents the qualities of a sustainable enterprise that provide a foundation from which enterprise sustainability can be advanced:

- Lead a sustainable enterprise (Chapter 1)
- Think about a sustainable enterprise (Chapter 2)
- Develop a sustainable enterprise strategy (Chapter 3)

Chapter 1. Leadership for a sustainable enterprise

Chapter 1 focuses on the way leaders see themselves and choose to be in relation to each other, employees, customers, communities, the larger society, the environment, and other stakeholders. Leaders in sustainable enterprise choose to purposefully engage with the people inside the organization as if it were a living system, while recognizing that they are simultaneously operating in the larger ecosystem of the world.

The processes of transformation and change begin with the leaders who then engage with the people in the organization; they all make it happen together. The aim of this chapter is to provide leaders with insights and examples of how this can be achieved in ways that produce superior results. To accomplish this, a **Leadership Diamond model** was developed, and essays that breathe life into the model are shared. The Leadership Diamond model integrates the roles of leaders in relating and influencing through the power of the enterprise intent and the embedded governing principles. It emphasizes the *way of being* that is so critical to sustainability. These essays focus on both theory and practical business examples (such as Microsoft, DuPont, and Toyota). The essays significantly expand traditional ideas regarding leadership.

Chapter 2. Mental models for sustainability

Chapter 2 focuses on the all-pervasive nature of the prevailing patterns of thought and shows the importance of becoming aware of the currently dominant models that reinforce wasteful and unsustainable behavior. The chapter recognizes that, for sustainable initiatives to succeed, organizations, their leaders, managers, and staff need to co-create more versatile, inclusive, and conscious thinking patterns. In this chapter, both theory and practices for making desired substantive changes in mental models are offered. ESAT member John Adams draws on his many years of research and consulting to lay out a structure with six dimensions for assessing and working with mental models. To illustrate the difference that mental models make regarding the challenges and opportunities corporations encounter along the journey toward sustainability, examples are presented from two companies – one in the energy industry and one chemical company – that have transformed their thoughts and actions in response to the communities in which they are situated. Three case studies follow that provide tools and exercises for effecting mental model changes and cultivating personal and group operating systems that support a high-quality, sustainable future.

Chapter 3. Developing a sustainability strategy

Chapter 3 helps leaders, managers, and change agents better understand how to craft and implement a sustainability strategy for their enterprise. For most organizations, this will involve reshaping the nature and goals of their existing strategy as well as changing the way they go about developing and executing it. The chapter focuses on the content and process of developing a sustainability strategy, by first briefly examining the core elements of *any* good strategic management process and then discussing what is different about a good *sustainability* strategy. Examples are provided of the myriad ways that actual organizations in diverse situations are using sustainability initiatives to improve their performance. The strategic formulation process is presented to integrate elements particularly critical to developing and implementing sustainability strategies. Finally the rich case example of Nike is presented. Many key elements noted in this and other chapters are evidenced in this case: systems thinking, mutuality, collaboration, leadership/champions, employee engagement, decentralized yet integrated internal and external social networks, and aligned performance management systems and metrics.

Part III. Embracing and managing change sustainably

Part III includes specific sustainable enterprise qualities that infuse innovation and personal and group commitment as well as the performance measurement information that allows all enterprise stakeholders to appreciate their progress along the journey to enterprise sustainability:

- Manage the change to a sustainable enterprise (Chapter 4)
- Engage employees in the sustainability journey (Chapter 5)
- Measure and manage your movement (Chapter 6)

Chapter 4. Managing the change to a sustainable enterprise

Chapter 4 presents the primary challenges to building an enterprise culture that embraces sustainable development values. The authors advocate application of an integrated change management approach blending elements of transformational change, project management, participative change management, and adult learning principles to cultivate sustainable enterprise cultures.

The chapter is built around an enterprise transformation methodology that has had demonstrated success in generating sustainable culture change. In particular, the authors advocate an iterative transformation of organizational "DNA" using the "FAIR" methodology:

- **Framing** enterprise mindsets to develop fresh mental models of what we are and what we can become
- **Aligning** economic models, physical infrastructure, and workplace processes to achieve a competitive level of performance
- **Igniting** growth and innovation through market focus, new business models, and technologies changing industry rules of competition
- **Refreshing** enterprise information metabolism to foster creativity, generate energy, and reinvigorate *esprit de corps* required for continuous enterprise regeneration

Chapter 5. Employee engagement for a sustainable enterprise

Chapter 5 looks at the importance of engaging employees at all levels in co-creating the enterprise's future, a crucial accomplishment if even the most enlightened leaders are to get beyond their own best intentions. What approaches are recognized as necessary to involve employees in any major organizational change? What is unique about involving them in sustainability management?

This chapter suggests some of the psychological dynamics that contribute to achieving employees' sense of ownership and commitment to taking on sustainability. It describes the power resulting from people experiencing autonomy and interdependence, and belonging to a community of kindred spirits. It describes how authentic leadership can resonate with people at all levels of an organization, as positive energy and resolve become contagious.

Five in-depth case studies illustrate distinctive approaches to employee engagement. One describes how senior management set up conditions for self-organizing at a previously underperforming plant at DuPont. Another case study elaborates on a multiyear effort to bridge labor and management differences to radically improve safety; yet another infused safety concerns through the constant drumbeat of companywide activities. Eileen Fisher lives out the keen social consciousness of its founder. Employee engagement even spreads across company lines when Eileen Fisher enlists management at overseas suppliers to improve working conditions for low-paid employees. Similarly, a grassroots effort in India paid dividends with social and environmental benefits for a whole community. Each situation exemplifies sound management concepts for unleashing the power, creativity, and insights made possible only by engaging a broad swath of the workforce.

Chapter 6. Sustainable enterprise metrics and measurement systems

How do you measure sustainability? Sustainability is an ever-changing end state; "one knows that one doesn't know" what that end state will be. Acknowledging and accepting that we do not know is an important part of designing and implementing sustainability metrics and measurement systems. The chapter supports developing an integrated framework of ecosystems, social systems, and economic system metrics and management systems that allow people to co-develop the collective awareness and understanding needed to energize and enable global, enterprise, and personal action.

This chapter provides overviews of the enormous progress being made on sustainable development indicators, measurement frameworks, and systems at the global, national, and enterprise levels. As with any science, measures over time get more refined. The outcomes of those systems, including the realization of how much is not known about them, have enabled the appreciation of the current condition of the world. Measures are provided for each of the relevant chapters in this book. This section is intended to help leaders and managers more clearly understand how they can apply measures to more qualitative sustainability attributes in order that they be measured and managed within a holistic sustainability metric and management program.

Part IV. Connecting, integrating, and aligning toward the future

Part IV offers critical insights about how people relate to each other within their sustainable enterprise, its extended stakeholders, their communities, and the world. The two chapters in this section cover best and leading-edge practices regarding how to:

- Operate in a global context (Chapter 7)
- Create alliances and social networks to fuel the sustainability journey (Chapter 8)

Chapter 7. Sustainable globalization: the challenge and the opportunity

Chapter 7 represents a breakthrough and a fundamental transformation in how we approach doing business in a global world in the 21st century. The authors use **six lenses of sustainable globalization** to provide fresh perspectives on global issues:

- Economic/financial
- Technology
- Poverty and inequity
- Limits to growth
- Movement of talent
- Geopolitical

An emphasis on multidisciplinary approaches is encouraged because of the complex and interconnected nature of the challenges facing the world today. Opportunities for sustainable globalization are introduced in case studies. The six lenses sustainable globalization tool provides readers with a means to assess the degree to which their organization is addressing each of the six lenses.

Chapter 8. Transorganizational collaboration and sustainability networks

Chapter 8 approaches the enterprise as a living system operating in a dynamic environment. Topics of collaboration, stakeholder engagement, and social networks are presented with application tools and processes.

The authors make the case for using second-generation Web — Web 2.0 — applications such as social networking, wikis, and virtual environments to purposefully engage individuals and their larger networks in co-creating sustainable enterprises. Issues of trust, control, competition, and network communities are explored.

Part V. When it all comes together

Consistent with the major conclusions from previous research, our concept of sustainability has evolved from mostly separate streams of parallel conversations into a holistic notion that rejects the premise that social, environmental, and economic issues are competing interests. This integrative perspective contends that social, environmental, and economic performance can and *must* be optimized simultaneously for both short- and long-term success.

Chapter 9. A new beginning: when it all comes together

Chapter 9 offers reflections on the journey we and our readers have traveled together. We have learned that the term *conclusion* may not be the best way to describe the ending of this physical book on sustainability. Each thing we collectively learn and share in our team makes us see even more clearly how much more information there is to learn and how many more insights and perspectives there are to explore if we are to have a lasting deep impact on the future of sustainability. In this chapter, we share what we have learned to this point and lay the foundation for a path forward that will provide for continued learning and sharing with the larger social network of sustainability we have chosen to contribute to. And, as members of this network, we hope to continue to contribute, engaging with others on the collective global journey to a sustainable world.

References

American Management Association (AMA). (2007). *Creating a sustainable future: A global study of current trends and possibilities 2007–2017.* New York: American Management Association.

Costanza, R. (2001, June). Visions, values, valuation, and the need for an ecological economics. *Bioscience, 51*(6), 459-468.

Curtis, R., Bedell, G., & Christian, A. (2005). *Make poverty history: How you can help defeat world poverty in seven easy steps.* London: Penguin.

Cusack, J. L. (2005). The interaction of the United Nations and the financial industry on sustainability. Research sponsored by UNEP Finance Initiative; a symposium sponsored by the International Business Group at Iona College School of Business and the Center for International Business Education and Research (CIBER) at the University of Connecticut, April 26, 2005.

Dixon, F. (2003, December). Total corporate responsibility: Achieving sustainability and real prosperity. *Ethical Corporation Magazine.* Retrieved February 5, 2008, from www.iccr.org/news/press_releases/dixonspeachb092304.PDF.

Margolis, J. D., & Walsh, J. P. (2001). *People and profits? The search for a link between a company's social and financial performance.* Mahwah, NJ: Lawrence Erlbaum Associates.

Morrow, D. (2006) *November 8th carbon call: A review of the Carbon Disclosure Project and the 2006 CDP4 Survey findings.* New York: Center for Environmental and Economic Partnerships.

Porter, M., & Kramer, M. (2006, December). Strategy and society: The link between competitive advantage and corporate social responsibility. *Harvard Business Review,* 78-92.

Prince of Wales's Business and the Environment Programme (2003). *The reference compendium on business and sustainability.* Cambridge, UK: University of Cambridge Programme for Industry.

Savitz, A. W. (with Weber, K.). (2006). *The triple bottom line.* San Francisco: Jossey Bass.

Senge, P. M. (1990). *The fifth discipline: The art and practice of the learning organization.* New York: Doubleday.

Senge, P. M., Kleiner, A., Roberts, C., Ross, R., & Smith, B. (1994). *The fifth discipline fieldbook: Strategies and tools for building a learning organization.* New York: Doubleday.

Senge, P. M., Scharmer, C.O., Jaworski, J., & Flowers, B. S. (2004). *Presence: An exploration of profound change in people, organizations and society.* New York: Random House.

Symes, J. (2006). *Your planet needs you: A handbook for creating the world that we want.* Chester, UK: Your Planet Needs You.

United Nations Population Division. (2006). *World population prospects: The 2006 revision population database.* Retrieved January 22, 2008, from esa.un.org/unpp/index.asp?panel=1.

Wirtenberg, J., Harmon, J., Russell, W. G., & Fairfield, K. D. (2007). HR's role in building a sustainable enterprise: Insights from some of the world's best companies. *Human Resource Planning, 30*(1), 10-20.

World Commission on Environment and Development (WCED). (1987). *Our common future.* Oxford, UK: Oxford University Press.

PART II
Preparing the foundation for a sustainable enterprise

1

Leadership for a sustainable enterprise[1]

Richard N. Knowles, Daniel F. Twomey,
Karen J. Davis, and Shakira Abdul-Ali

▓ Introduction

Richard N. Knowles

This chapter on leadership raises awareness about a new state of being and explores the personal development and transformation necessary for the leader if she or he is to help bring about the change to sustainability. Authenticity, strategies, mental models, ways of engagement, collaboration, and construction of social networks are all ideas that depend on the leader's seeing the organization in a new way. This requires a shift in paradigm, from seeing organizations as if they were machines to seeing them as if they were living systems, and this new perspective opens up vast possibilities for organizations, society, and the world.

Companies that are carrying out sustainability strategies are often the best financial performers, as the *2007 AMA Sustainability Survey* in *Creating a Sustainable Future* (American Management Association [AMA], 2007) clearly reveals.[2] The survey shows that, in companies that have successfully implemented sustainability strategies, top management strongly and visibly supports these practices and has deeply embedded the core values on which sustainability is based.

---

1 The authors gratefully acknowledge additional contributions to this chapter from Theresa McNichol and Douglas Cohen. For a case study on leadership in sustainable enterprise by Theresa McNichol, see "A call for a new American idea of leadership," in the *Sustainable Enterprise Living Fieldbook* (www.TheSustainableEnterpriseFieldbook.net) (▙).

2 See footnote 10 on page 12.

The most commonly used sustainability-related practices, according to the survey (AMA, 2007), focus on such issues as employee health & safety, accountability for ethical behavior, and a better balance between employee work and life issues. The data suggest that the most difficult to accomplish is advancing sustainability by reaching out to form collaborations[3] not only inside the firm but outside, with stakeholders, other organizations, and the community at large.

Top management needs to become more visible and to invite employees into conversations about how to make their companies more sustainable and cost-effective. Many employees and managers, according to the AMA sustainability survey (AMA, 2007), are already concerned about sustainability issues and believe their interest is stronger than that of company leadership. Thus, there is a clear opportunity for senior management to align its sustainability strategies with the values of middle- and lower-level employees.

This chapter provides insights into the importance of developing and implementing a successful sustainability strategy and offers tools to help leaders create an environment that encourages the successful implementation of such a strategy. For a detailed discussion of the process of crafting and carrying out a sustainability strategy, see Chapter 3.

Several characteristics mark sustainability. One is the **zero footprint**, which entails preserving the environment through the use, for example, of renewable rather than nonrenewable resources. Another is employing methods that restore both the environment and the spirit of the people in organizations and communities.

The command-and-control approach of the machine paradigm requires a constant flow of power and energy from the top. People are seen as interchangeable parts; many do as little as possible, and their creative contributions are relatively low. This way of leading has its usefulness. However, if employed over the longer run, it is wasteful, ineffective, and inefficient; the organization becomes less sustainable.

A sustainable enterprise behaves as if it were a healthy, living whole. The organization's values and mission are connected with those of its people who in turn are fulfilling a greater purpose in service to the organization and the larger society. People find meaning and come alive; energy and creativity flow. Together, people co-create their collective future. As a result of this, resistance to change almost disappears, and healthy, more sustainable organizations are created.

Leaders for sustainable enterprise purposefully engage the natural tendency of self-organization. Leaders help create the conditions that inspire people to seek a higher purpose — openness, honesty, and transparency — and then invite people to come together to co-create their shared future. They co-create the organization's "Bowl,"[4] which consists of their values, vision, goals, standards of performance, and expectations.

Leadership for sustainable enterprise makes up the foundation level of the Sustainability Pyramid discussed in the Introduction (pages 11-12). This way of leading requires the total commitment and active support of the people at the top of the organization as well as those in middle-management positions if it is to become fully internalized in the making of decisions and central to the business strategy. The organization becomes **leaderful**: people from anywhere in the organization who see a need, may step forward, take the lead, and make things happen as long as they are working within the Bowl.

---

3 This is the third level in the Sustainability Pyramid (see the Introduction, pages 11-12).
4 The idea of the "Bowl" is developed in the essay "Engaging the natural tendency of self-organization," by Richard N. Knowles, later in this chapter (pages 47ff.).

In this leadership mode, everyone can work at the high end of his or her skills moving purposefully toward the future together. The effectiveness of the organization rises by 30 to 40% when compared with the more common command-and-control organizations (Knowles, 2002).

This chapter consists of a series of holographic essays based on the **Leadership Diamond**, a figure developed by Daniel F. Twomey. The diamond provides a visual picture of aspects of leadership that are critical for a sustainable enterprise revealing a new **way of being** that focuses on **integrity, mutuality,** and **sustainability.**

The essays reflect the contributors' own insights; no attempt has been made to blend them or force them into a uniform voice or set of ideas. Each will speak to different readers in different ways, providing a variety of insights about this way of leading. All are connected, however, at a deep level.

In the first essay, Twomey explores integrity, mutuality, and sustainability. He discusses domains of leadership that are critical for leaders to understand, to operate in, and to use. He identifies many of the processes, practices, and principles that will enable leaders to be more conscious of what they are doing and how they engage the world around them.

Karen Davis's essay holds up a vision of a "global wisdom society." Global wisdom embodies a system perspective and has a deep respect for natural systems, human needs, and future generations. It requires that people trust the dynamics of self-organization, learn from the new sciences, and serve society ethically. In this essay, Davis calls for a new *way of being* and invites the reader to listen deeply to rediscover the ancient lessons of indigenous traditions and Earth wisdom.

Shakira Abdul-Ali's essay emphasizes that leaders must listen to the voice of the community if they are to lead in a more sustainable way. The problems faced in the movement toward sustainability are too big and broad for any one individual or organization to go it alone. Leaders for sustainable enterprise must recognize the need to consent — rather than concede — to share power; this comes from an environment of authentic, trusting relationships. Abdul-Ali calls for co-creating and self-organizing shared values and processes.

Richard N. Knowles's essay brings focus to a fundamental pattern of self-organization as an omnipresent, subtle, and powerful force that can be purposefully engaged by anyone who is willing to work in the ways described in this chapter. This idea runs through all the essays here, which recognize this force as a basic feature of the human way of being. Purposeful engagement results in a sense of urgency, clarity, resoluteness, and hope, and opens everyone to growth and new potential. Possibilities emerge that people can consider, develop, and embrace.

This essay introduces ways to help leaders engage and experience this force presenting a novel, powerful, validated model of how to hold and preserve the difficult conversations that help people co-create their future and at the same time — using a model called the **Process Enneagram**[5] — develop a strategic map for their journey ahead.

---

5 An introduction to this model is developed later in this chapter, in the essay "Engaging the natural tendency of self-organization," by Richard N. Knowles (pages 47ff.).

■ The Leadership Diamond: zero footprint and a life-giving workplace

The **Leadership Diamond** (see Fig. 1.1), created by Daniel F. Twomey, illustrates key ideas about a more sustainable way of leading.

Figure 1.1 **Leadership Diamond.** Sustainable enterprise: zero footprint and a life-giving workspace

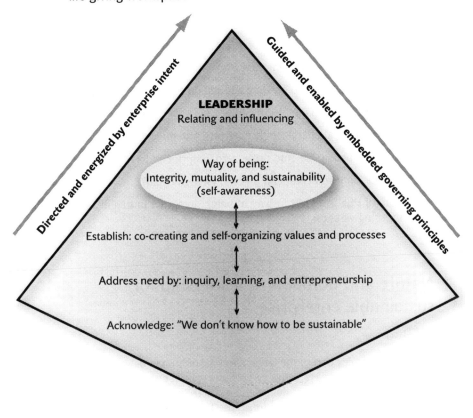

Source: Copyright 2007, D. F. Twomey. Used with permission.

The most important role of top management is enabling the self-organizing creativity and energy of the enterprise. This is largely accomplished by articulating a clear, compelling, and sustainable enterprise intent and embedding the principles that will govern behavioral relationships and routines. The enterprise intent and governing principles inform strategy formulation. Within this framework, everyone becomes a leader: she or he establishes positive and productive relationships and influences others within the unit as well as in the greater relevant network.

The leadership process starts with not-knowing and proceeds with an inquiry, learning–action cycle as individuals and units co-create innovative approaches to a sustainable enterprise. **Way of being** takes on much of the aligning, controlling, and disciplining functions of the traditional organization. It includes the following: **integrity** –

claims and behaviors are consistent; **mutuality** — genuinely connecting with others; and **sustainability** — development toward higher levels of awareness and commitment to society.

Our current situation is:

- Faulty (nonsustainable) assumptions

- Faulty (nonsustainable) processes and structures

- Lack of integrity, mutuality, and sustainability (way of being)

The elements of the diamond are:

- We need to acknowledge, "We don't know how to be sustainable"

- We need to address this by inquiry, learning, and entrepreneurship

- And, together, establish co-creating and self-organizing values and processes

- Which are guided and enabled by embedded governing principles

- This is directed and energized by enterprise intent

- And leads to sustainable enterprise: zero footprint and a life-giving workplace

- With an absolute and compelling vision (shared by all)

- The core of this is a shift in way of being: integrity, mutuality, and sustainability (self-awareness)

■ Nature and domains of leadership for sustainable enterprise

Daniel F. Twomey

Leadership is a complex part of the larger dynamic of human behavior that varies based on contextual factors. The 21st century presents special challenges, with its context of high connectivity and interdependency and its increasingly overstressed resources and unstable political and economic relationships. The question addressed here is: "What kind of leadership is needed to create thriving sustainable enterprises that will reverse the negative trends and help restore the environment and society?"

Leadership

As a society, we are facing a new and enormous challenge in a rapidly changing world. We need to release the creativity, initiative, and goodwill of all people inside and outside the enterprise. Within the enterprise, top management can no longer be the sole source of innovation and influence; these must emanate from all levels. Foundational theories of conventional management systems, accepted as valid, must be challenged. Ghoshal (2005) shows how the pretense of knowledge, unfounded negative assumptions about people, and other "bad theories" have made a substantial contribution to failed conventional practices, such as those employed by Enron.

The sustainable enterprise is focused, but not by top-down plans and controls or "aggrandized" leaders. Rather, a shared, noble, and compelling purpose; the principles that govern behaviors and routines provide the energy and integrity of the enterprise, self-organizing and self-disciplining at all levels. As enterprise moves to distributed leadership and self-organizing processes, the way of being of all employees becomes increasingly important, especially integrity, mutuality, and sustainability (Torbert & Associates, 2004).

These leadership qualities are the cornerstone of the leadership of a sustainable enterprise:

- **Integrity.** What we say or claim is consistent with our behaviors

- **Mutuality.** Genuinely connecting with others to collaboratively create intent and actions

- **Sustainability.** Capable of continuous learning and development toward higher levels of societal benefit for future as well as present generations

The Leadership Diamond provides the context for leadership that both builds relationships and influences and is influenced by others, a radical change from conventional leadership. To appreciate this radical change, this essay examines the underlying dynamics, asking, "Is a fundamental change necessary?" Ways of being are used as lenses to explore this question.

We need to examine and change the language of leadership including the strongly entrenched words and concepts that assume a top-down articulated hierarchy of influence. Here I use **domain** to replace the top-down paradigm with one that enables self-organizing behaviors. The *American Heritage Dictionary* (1992) defines *domain* as "a sphere of activity, concern, or function." Domains are not defined by size, importance, title, or pay, which are associated with top-down hierarchy. Rather, domains are primarily determined by the spheres of activity within an organization. Someone in "top management" may have a small, not very important domain, and someone lower in the hierarchy may have a large and important domain. Furthermore, persons may operate in more than one domain.

Like the conventional organization, a sustainable enterprise needs to differentiate roles and responsibilities. Rather than distinguishing leadership roles by levels of unilateral power based on a top-down hierarchy, a sustainable enterprise determines them by the needs of the sphere of activity (domain) in which the individual operates. When people see the organization as a blended set of domains in which everyone exercises leadership within his or her sphere, it can become a life-giving workplace characterized by integrity, mutuality, and sustainability. Yet this aspect of sustainability is often neglected; leadership is viewed as a top-management or HR responsibility.

Leadership approaches and characteristics

The leadership model for sustainable enterprise is founded on the assumption that the best vehicle for providing goods and services to society is a free-market economy based on the innovation and productivity of profit-making businesses. Although leadership and the role and practices of business are different issues, they are linked. Mental models and values of fairness, equity, and mutuality underpin both leadership behaviors and business practices. For example, when top executives exploit employees by establishing disproportional salaries — such as CEOs who make 500 to 1,000 times the average employee's salary — one might expect the firm to also exploit its suppliers from small, emerging-market countries.

A radical approach: integrity

The underlying issue of whether one should advocate for radical leadership change is one of integrity — being truthful about the situation as one sees it. Do the vision and strategies that drive the actions needed for sustainability represent a paradigm shift from conventional practices? Is there a need for transformation, a fundamental change at the root level? It seems clear if we look at the theories-in-practice, rather than the espoused theories, of a few thought leaders, that Western leadership still operates within the top-down, charismatic decision-maker model in which the focus is on maximizing winning for the leader. This appears to be the case especially at the top of large corporations in which salary and privilege exemplify the belief that most of the intelligence and creativity belongs to the CEO, CFO, and other C-level executives and that the role of leaders is to drive their values and decisions down through the organization. A common "truth" throughout these organizations is that any initiative must have top management's approval and support. This belief seals a self-reinforcing dynamic that dis-enables bottom-up creativity and initiative.

A co-creative approach: mutuality

A fundamental difference in a new leadership model is the recognition of mutuality and interdependence. We are all part of the contemporary leadership model, and only by working together will we achieve the transformational change many of us seek. We who are writing this book and advocating change don't have the answers. Many of the answers must come from those, such as corporate executives, who have responsibility for action. We need to find ways to learn together to create the transformation. The people who populate the lower levels of organizations are as important to the change in leadership as those at the top, and they have as much right and responsibility to initiate and support change. Also, customers and others served by the enterprise, as well as those in the next generation who will populate these enterprises, are voices that need to be heard; they also can share in the leadership of sustainable enterprise.

A learning approach: sustainability

There is no particular leadership model that will carry us successfully into the future; rather, leadership will change as people and organizations learn and evolve. The ideas and distinctions made here about leadership provide signposts for inquiry, action, and learning, but they are not the immutable truth. As the values, beliefs, and salaries of top-down leadership topple, and as more people participate in the continuous process of leadership transformation, emerging forces will define a true sustainable leadership model. Argyris and Schön (1996) and Senge et al. (1994) have contributed greatly to an understanding of the learning organization, yet those ideas still have only spotty application.

The question about radical change versus incremental change is, "Will a gradual modification of the existing leadership model meet the needs of sustainability?" I believe it will not for the following reasons: the world has a relatively short time to make fundamental corrections; the contemporary model, in its most fundamental values, beliefs, and behaviors, is diametrically opposed to what seems to be needed; and, despite growing public awareness and calls for change, the leadership structure and systems of major corporations seem unable to change significantly. Therefore, the best hope for sustainable enterprise is a new paradigm for a transformed leadership model.

Domains of leadership[6]

Leadership belongs to everyone in the sustainable enterprise. Leadership is the enabling of others to be powerful and innovative in support of the organization's governing principles and enterprise intent. Although all leadership for sustainable enterprise has the common characteristics of awareness, not-knowing, inquiry, and learning from actions, different domains require specific perspectives and skills. Typically the organization designates each employee's role, activities, and responsibilities, which in turn determines his or her domain (sphere of activity) and, in part, the leadership capabilities needed in that position. I specify three possible domains to illustrate different spheres of activity. The activities in these domains call for particular leadership capabilities as well as the core leadership qualities: integrity, mutuality, and sustainability. Hence, domain C — macro-systems leadership — is different from, but not necessarily more important than, domain A — action-learning level. Not all domain C leaders are at the top of the organization, and not all domain A leaders are at the bottom of the organization.

In domain A, leaders create positive relationships and influence actions by fostering a culture of collaboration at the individual and group levels, thereby increasing value to the unit and to its output. In domain B — a systems-aligning sphere — the leader has an awareness of the larger system and the patterns and factors that affect the unit and its output, as well as the ability to collaboratively influence leverage points in ways that create systemic benefits. In domain C the leader has both an awareness of enterprise-level dynamics and the ability to co-design the enterprise intent and governing principles that will enable positive emergent dynamics and self-organizing leadership throughout the enterprise. Richard Knowles (2006), and in the essay "Engaging the natural tendency of self-organization" in this chapter (pages 47ff.), asserts that self-organizing is a natural human behavior that is an omnipresent, subtle, and powerful force that can be purposely engaged.

A leader can shape and expand his or her domain, and leaders may operate in more than one domain. For example, an entry-level employee in a domain A role may be especially good at seeing patterns (domain B) before they become part of the internal system. A good self-organizing system would embrace this new perspective, which typically is ignored in conventional organizations. The idea is to create a more fluid and integrated structure, one that encourages the emergence of leadership within every domain.

Jim Collins (2001) describes qualities in sustainable leadership that would apply to any of the domains. He identifies five types of leader in successful firms. Of these, level 5 leaders are best at creating sustainable enterprises. The level 5 leader is modest, relies principally on inspired standards, demonstrates unwavering resolve, apportions credit to others, and is a catalyst for transition from good to great. She or he frequently uses advocacy to challenge assumptions and the status quo, or changes the context of inquiry. The integrity, mutuality, and sustainability evident in level 5 CEOs are also needed for the individual, group, unit, systems, and each of the domains in the enterprise.

Domain A: relationships and local action

In the self-organizing enterprise, everyone has both the opportunity and the responsibility to create productive relationships and positively influence decisions and actions

6 See also Table 6.7: "Leadership quality indicators" (page 191), a tool whose indicators are derived from these domains and Shakira Abdul-Ali's "listening-into-being" leadership model (page 45).

within his or her network. Each person and every conversation has the potential to have an impact on the nature and outcome of interactions with other people. Much of the culture and many routines of the enterprise are created and/or modified in individual-to-individual and informal group interactions. When these relationships and the culture are positive and aligned with the vision of the enterprise, opportunities for improvement are present, whether they are to better serve the customers, to make the workplace safer, or to create a new product. Leadership in domain A creates the mutuality and intent that supports high performance of the unit and the co-creation of improvement within that job, task, or unit. Integrity, mutuality, and sustainability may be centered at the group-peer level, but they extend to the entire enterprise, so that self-initiating and self-organizing behaviors are aligned across the enterprise. Without fully enabled leadership in this domain, the greatest resource of talent, energy, and potential in the enterprise is wasted. Yet contemporary enterprises do little to enable this leadership domain, and they do much to discourage it.

Domain A leadership is not only found in enterprises, but is frequently seen in communities where individuals create the relationships and provide the influence that enable the community to become a force for positive change.

Domain B: patterns and leverage

The domain B leader, in addition to being aware of and influencing events, sees, understands, and influences trends. This leader identifies routines, patterns of behaviors, and sequences of events in ways that reveal leverage points. Such an appreciation of historical and systemic patterns and forces enables the leader to shift the unit's relationships and expand the synergistic influences that are occurring at the local or event level.

Domain B leadership is strategic as well as synergistic at the unit level as well as across units. It involves bringing together the right people, creating the conditions, and sometimes reframing the conversation for self-organizing at the unit level and across unit levels. Integrity at this level is evident in the unit strategies. Mutuality and sustainability are seen in and across units, as well as aligned with the enterprise. As leaders take on more complex domains of leadership, there is an increased need for knowledge creation. Knowledge creation becomes a more deliberate and intensive process that uses experience and tacit knowledge from diverse sources to conceptualize understanding and actions (Nonaka, Toyama, & Noboru, 2000).

Domain C: purpose, design, and emergence

In domain C, the leader, while appreciating events and patterns, is closely attuned to the purpose of the firm and its role in society. She or he recognizes the global dynamics and trends presently threatening the survival of our civilization and understands that releasing the creativity and energies of the organization in service of a noble purpose is the best way to rise to this world challenge and ensure that the enterprise will thrive. To achieve this goal, the leader infuses the enterprise with a clear and compelling intent, as well as with values and principles about how people within the enterprise self-organize. This may include embracing paradoxes and shifting the paradigm. Domain C leaders design the factors that enable the emergent organization's structure, processes, and behaviors (Twomey, 2006). Design is a co-creation process that brings together diverse views in a context of knowledge creation that enables the experience and tacit knowledge of the group to synergistically emerge as actionable knowledge. Through this process, the leader demonstrates and embeds integrity, mutuality, and sustainability in the fabric of the enterprise in ways that encourage and support other enterprises to do the same for the benefit of the entire world.

Life-giving workplace

Many of the leadership practices that enable enterprises to make substantial gains in their quest toward a zero footprint — preserving the physical environment — also serve the enterprise intent of a life-giving workplace. While there is a synergistic relationship between achieving zero footprint and achieving a life-giving workplace, the life-giving workplace calls for some unique, and often overlooked, leadership traits. The trend line for many of the requirements is down.

A truly life-giving workplace would attract, develop, and retain the best, brightest, and most committed talent for all leadership domains and levels within the enterprise. It would provide a safe and secure environment in which all of a person's creative and productive capabilities are welcomed and nurtured, even when the individual has major life disruptions. It would be a place in which:

- Equity and diversity are a part of all relationships
- Organizations, departments, and individuals with particular responsibility for people, such as human resources and organizational development, are empowered to be advocates and problem solvers
- Leadership encourages an environment that enables people to balance all aspects of their lives, family, community, work, and more
- These life-giving values and practices are promulgated in all people in the enterprise and its network and supply chain

Processes and practices for sustainable enterprise

Table 1.1 shows some distinctions that leaders and their teams may use for reflection and inquiry into the enterprise's leadership and its journey to sustainability. These dichotomies, principles, and practices are to be used to trigger deeper inquiry into current behaviors or future possibilities, and not as benchmarks to judge progress. Users are encouraged to add to these lists or create their own using personal experiences and the diverse perspectives in this leadership chapter.

Sustainable principles and practices at all levels

- Reflections (e.g., at beginning and end of meetings)
- Nonauthoritarian action language: requests, offers, and the like
- Nonjudgmental questions and inquiry
- Structuring and welcoming diversity of ideas
- Self-awareness: noticing one's own behavior
- In all relationships, first establish mutuality
- Systems thinking: ask why, assume interdependence

Table 1.1 **The enterprise's journey to sustainability**

Issue	From	To
Goals	Fixed	Multiple, evolving
Paradoxes	Simplify/deny	Embrace
Focus	On self	On benefit to others
Decisions	Advocate/enforce	Shared inquiry, action
Solutions	Knowing, inflexible	Informed, committed
Design base	Past experiences	Emerging future
Value	Tangible/countable	Social/intangibles
Differences	Difficulties, barriers	Opportunities, enrichment
Perspective	Narrow, single	Wide, multiple
Business	Combative job	Noble profession
Status quo	Supports	Challenges
Facing threats	Fearful, reactive	Confident, proactive
Communications	Demanding/positioning	Inquiry to enable action
Competition	Dominating/exploiting	Level playing field
Competitors	Diminish	Collaborate with
Sharing	Never enough	Plenty

Principles and practices for fostering a self-initiating culture

- Don't blame (Southwest Airlines avoids blaming to create high-performance, aircraft-turnaround-team effectiveness)

- Reduce win–lose dynamic of all reward systems

- Create equity

- Expect and enable self-resourcing: most individuals or groups can start initiatives without getting funding from the enterprise, if the enterprise doesn't discourage or prevent them from doing so

- Fully share information

- Create clear, compelling, and actionable vision (Fairleigh Dickinson University has a vision of being "The Leader in Global Education." It provides a clear and compelling direction, and almost every employee may take action at one or more of the leadership levels)

- Management "walks the talk" (integrity): top management truly and fully behaves in ways that are consistent with the vision

● Map self-initiated and self-organized activities and projects. This shows the kind of initiation and organizing that is possible at each level of the enterprise. The ratio of top-down compared with bottom-up initiatives, as well as the degree of self-organizing, informs the continuous redesign

■ Reflections on leadership from ancient traditions and Earth wisdom

Karen J. Davis

> The distorted dream of an industrial technological paradise is being replaced by the more viable dream of a mutually enhancing human presence within an ever-renewing organic-based Earth community.
>
> *Thomas Berry*

> Whatever befalls the earth befalls the sons and daughters of the earth. Mankind did not weave the web of life; we are but one strand in it. Whatever we do to the web, we do to ourselves . . . All things are bound together.
>
> *Chief Seattle*

Learning other cultures' stories and exploring their ways of knowing, being, and acting may compel us toward a sustainable society in which everyone is a leader. So where do we begin?

● What questions do we need to ask ourselves, each other, our organizations, and our world?

● What new stories are necessary to replace the currently engrained ones that only reinforce the dominant culture's ways of being and doing?

● What types of leadership are essential for people to co-create stories of sustainability?

● What and how can we learn from Mother Earth and all her creatures — and from Father Sky?

● How can multiple ways of knowing enhance the journey toward sustainability?

● How is what we are doing now affecting the lives of people seven generations in the future?

These are only a few of the questions that we might hold as we rediscover the values-based ways of being and knowing, individually and collectively, that are rooted in ancient and indigenous cultures and traditions, and in the wisdom of Earth.

Global wisdom organizations and leadership

From the information knowledge era (with its focus on the human mind and intellectual capital), we are approaching an era of spirit (with focus on consciousness and wisdom) in which community is the model.

A global wisdom society with global wisdom organizations values all cultures and traditions and skillfully utilizes multiple ways of knowing for the greater benefit of all life.[7] Institute of Noetic Sciences research suggests that a global wisdom society will be marked by the following:

- A profound recognition of universal interconnectedness among all peoples and all life

- A commitment to right action for the benefit of all, guided by the mysterious intelligence of the whole

- Valuing learning and openness above certainty and closure, and embracing multiple ways of knowing

- Living in ecological balance

- Perhaps most important, acknowledging that humans exist in a universe alive with consciousness and spirit

A global wisdom organization (Davis, 2003) embraces the following:

- Holding a systemic perspective and always looking at the wholeness, interrelatedness, and harmony and balance of living systems and the universe

- Operating from a deep understanding of and respect for natural systems and cycles, human needs, and future generations (WindEagle & RainbowHawk, 2003)

- Trusting the dynamics of self-organizing and collective consciousness (Owen, 2004) as well as co-intelligence; that is, having the capacity to evoke creative responses and initiatives that integrate each person's diverse gifts for the benefit of all (Atlee, 2003)

- Learning from the new sciences

- Ethically serving society and Earth in life-affirming, sustainable ways, including those that are in harmony with natural ecological and global environmental systems; being in stewardship of the whole

In a global wisdom culture, everyone is both leader and follower. The essence of leadership is co-creating and holding the space for people to talk and act with each other about what is important to them, their organization, their community, and the world. Rather than physical space, this is *energy* space for reflection and deep inquiry whereby a deeper source of meaning can arise. One function of a leader is to help people discover the expertise and wisdom in themselves and in others.

Other elements, which are not usually a focus of leadership, are important and worthy of consideration:

- **Asking and holding the right questions.** Native American wisdom is that the First People had questions, and they were free; the Second People had answers, and they became enslaved (WindEagle & RainbowHawk, 2003). Questioning taps wisdom. Knowing the answer limits possibilities

7 Institute of Noetic Sciences, www.noetic.org (accessed July 9, 2002).

- **Storytelling.** For indigenous peoples who have an oral tradition, storytelling is a way of life (Anguita, Baker, Davis, & McLean, 2005, p. 487):

  > Through stories we can remember who we are and share experiences using past histories and accumulated wisdom, beliefs, and values . . . Stories tie us to our humanness, and they link the past, present and future by teaching us to anticipate the possible consequences of our actions.

- **Trusting oneself.** Trusting oneself precedes trusting someone else. Healthy trust implies the presence of honesty, integrity, and transparency

- **Learning and relearning together.** Deep learning is seeing other world perspectives and leaving aside one's own judgments and stereotypes. Understanding one's own mental models strengthens economic, social, and environmental competencies. (For more on mental models, see Chapter 2.) Systemic thinking is fundamental to awareness of interdependence and the impact of one's actions (Anguita et al., 2005)

- Being comfortable with ambiguity, uncertainty, and paradoxes

- Being one (in harmony and balance) with the universe

- **Trusting multiple ways of knowing.** Being open to modes of consciousness that are beyond rationality. Insight into ways of knowing is gained by exploring intuition, the subconscious, and dreams. The continuum of knowing ranges from a feeling, sense, or "the little voice inside" to technology

In their profile of the fourth-wave biopolitical leader, Maynard and Mehrtens (1993) highlighted the importance of being aware of one's own unconscious programming and inner character, integrating feminine and masculine aspects of self, avoiding domination and passivity, having a positive frame of mind, living intentionally and intuitively, addressing moral, cultural, and economic questions, perceiving realities of global conditions, and dealing effectively with issues of ecology and technology.

Leaders in global wisdom organizations may attain these aspects of leadership, and more, through high levels of consciousness, intention, and responsibility.

Stories from nature

Through the years, I have found lessons and stories from nature to be powerful teachings and constant reminders of ways of knowing and being.

The stories and ways of being of some creatures in nature are lessons of leadership. How can individuals and groups reflect some of these leadership qualities?

- As hummingbirds, which fly right, left, up, down, backwards, even upside down

- As geese, which fly in V formation, rotating and sharing leadership, encouraging one another through honking, and taking care of each other

- As eagles, which soar the heights, thus having a broad perspective of the world. The eagle is sacred to some indigenous cultures and represents divine power and enlightenment. The eagle teaches us the importance of seeing the whole pattern or big picture. The eagle gently reminds us of connecting with our higher power

● As monarch butterflies, whose lifecycle includes metamorphosis, and which migrate each year thousands of miles from Canada to Mexico and back involving three or more generations

These are but a few of Earth's creatures and collectives from which leaders might learn. Over millennia of human life, people have continuously engaged in rediscovering and learning from the natural world and its complex living systems. There is little that is new; rather, knowledge is being rediscovered time and time again. By listening deeply to the universe and the collective consciousness, all people can receive this wisdom.

Lessons from indigenous cultures

There are endless possibilities for leaders in sustainable enterprise to learn from indigenous cultures whose people live as one with nature and Earth. Indigenous peoples do not see the environment as something apart from them; they see themselves as co-stewards of the land with other creatures (and, in some cases, with spirits).

It can be useful for a leader to reflect on some of the indigenous ways of partnering with complexity from the work of anthropologist Hugh Brody (Pollard, 2006):

● Generosity (both with knowledge and material possessions) and egalitarianism are essential elements of these cultures, and produce an environment of reciprocity and trust

● Much of the activity enables the building of self-confidence and high self-esteem, freedom from anxiety (fear of the unknown), freedom from depression, the acquired respect and trust of others, and a culture of collaboration and consultation

● Telling stories is the way of giving advice and instruction and of answering questions. The process is consultative rather than hierarchical. Elders, chiefs, and shamans are respected, but do not have or seek power or authority over others. Children learn about leadership from stories and example

● People in these cultures not only depend on the conscious mind to process information, they appreciate how the subconscious, dreams, and instincts enrich their understanding and decision-making process

● There is a profound respect for individual decisions; after sharing of knowledge, if there is no consensus on action, each individual is trusted to do what he or she thinks is right and responsible, and there are no recriminations for not conforming to what others think is appropriate

● Authority is more horizontal than vertical — a result of the necessity of reaching unanimity on a decision before any action is taken (Harris, Moran, & Moran, 2004)

● Children are not asked what they want to be when they grow up (as in the dominant culture that lives mostly for the future). Children already *are*; they are children and they do not have to wait *to be* (Harris et al., 2004)

And finally a note on *time*, for which there is no word in many indigenous cultures (Pritchard, 1997). In the mainstream culture, time is to be used, saved, and spent; people are paid for their time. Indigenous cultures generally view time as a continuum that is related to the rising and setting of the sun and to the changes of the seasons.

Ancient wisdom council

Bringing Earth wisdom and indigenous traditions into the workplace and individual lives is a focus of the Ehama Institute (WindEagle & RainbowHawk, 2003). One powerful and holistic way is through the ancient wisdom council. This is an integral part of many tribal cultures for clarity and decision-making; it accesses wisdom for addressing an issue or solving deep conflict, allowing the community to put their agreement and energy behind new solutions.

The ancient wisdom council is based on universal intelligences that are held and expressed through the lens of a sequence of perspectives (Kinney-Linton, WindEagle & RainbowHawk, 2007, p. 197):

> Creation Intelligence: freedom and creativity
>
> Perceptual Intelligence: present condition and appreciation
>
> Emotional Intelligence: power and danger
>
> Pathfinding Intelligence: purpose and direction
>
> Sustaining Intelligence: maintenance and balance
>
> Predictive Intelligence: interrelatedness and timing
>
> Decisive Intelligence: clarity and action
>
> Energia Intelligence: integrity and vitality

A leader embraces all perspectives while holding a safe space for people to bring forth universal intelligences.

The possibility of everyone's "leading" through a blending of Earth wisdom and high technology is a powerful way of being and making a difference in organizations and the world.

Knowing that every beginning is an ending and that every ending is a beginning, I invite us to again ask the "right" questions of ourselves and each other, including, "What do we need to be asking at this time for future generations?"

■ New frameworks for leading sustainable enterprise

Shakira Abdul-Ali

Leading an enterprise that follows the path of natural production — the path that leaves no footprint and facilitates life-giving workplaces — cannot possibly rely on the genius of the individual imagination. It is implausible, even unfair, to expect that individual insight and vision, regardless of the depth of inspiration, will be up to the task of gauging critical process factors that ensure waste-free production, while valuing people and maximizing profits — the process recognized as the triple bottom line. Leaders must acknowledge that an authentic birth of this kind of workplace comes from the tension that radiates from the merging of multiple sources of intelligence. Some believe that this will require new values and new paradigms. In fact, it may only require expanding the reign of knowledge and intelligence that is currently perceived as being "of value."

Lessons from nature

Elisabet Sahtouris, a noted evolutionary biologist, has often referred senior business leaders to lessons the natural world offers. Sahtouris is widely known for describing ways in which human communities can imitate and learn from the mature societies that live in the plant and animal worlds. Consider how she applies the lessons from the caterpillar to our economy (Sahtouris, 2003):

> The best metaphor I've found . . . comes from the biological world . . . It's the metamorphosis of a caterpillar into a butterfly [that is] bloating itself until it just can't function anymore, and then going to sleep with its skin hardening into a chrysalis.
>
> What happens in its body is that little imaginal disks (as they're called by biologists) begin to appear in the body of the caterpillar and its immune system attacks them. But they keep coming up stronger and they start to link with each other . . . until the immune system of the caterpillar just can't function any more. At that point the body of the caterpillar melts into a nutritive soup that can feed the butterfly.
>
> I love this metaphor because it shows us [that] . . . the caterpillar is unsustainable so it's going to die. What we have to focus on is, "can we build a viable butterfly?" . . . because that's not guaranteed.

Consider those imaginal disks as being representative of the outlying sources of intelligence that are focusing on questions whose exploration will promote sustainable practices, eliminating waste and maximizing energy.[8]

Organization culture

How can leaders infuse those imaginal cells to which Sahtouris (2003) refers into the cultural milieu of their organizations? What might it look like when they transform their culture in order to achieve accountability within a framework of a triple bottom line? In fact, two prominent corporate leaders may demonstrate what it looks like when those imaginal cells are cut loose in an organization and empowered to thrive. One is Microsoft and the other is Toyota.

Note the informal online commentary of one Microsoft employee:[9]

> Everyone at Microsoft "gets" software — the managers, the administrative assistants, the vice presidents . . . Even many of the "blue collar" workers (cooks, janitors, bus drivers) know something about software — it's not normal! . . . Elevating the common denominator in this way makes Microsoft a wonderful workplace for people who love making software . . . Microsoft gives software developers a lot of personal freedom over both the work and the work environment . . .

---

8 Sahtouris's reference to imaginal disks might be likened to the emergence within organizations of "green teams" that are tasked with alerting stakeholders at all levels of the organization to look for opportunities to conserve energy, minimize waste, and maximize quality-of-life practices for employees.

9 Michael Brundage's home page, "Working at Microsoft," www.qbrundage.com/michaelb/pubs/ essays/working_at_microsoft.html (accessed January 7, 2007).

> For the most part, I determine what I work on and when I will get it done. There are exceptions — tasks others ask you to do for them, external deadlines or dependencies — but these goals are set cooperatively with your management and coworkers, taking into account your interests and abilities . . .
>
> Very few projects at Microsoft have "small" impact . . . You have the opportunity to earn, save, or cost the company millions of dollars through your work. It's an awesome responsibility, but an awesome chance to create widely influential software.

While it might seem like a risky venture to allow these imaginal cells of employees to go off on their own, who can argue with the genius of Bill Gates's leadership, his empowering of employees in this way? Yet perhaps a more widely practiced and better-known model for the creative use of teams may be found in an ostensibly more "regimented" organization than Microsoft. Toyota follows ISO 9000 procedures and has recently emerged as the world's leading automaker. Do Toyota employees — dedicated practitioners of "the Toyota Way" — operate as imaginal cells? Maybe, since any single employee:

> can pull a cord to stop the production line at any time . . . The plant is decorated with photos of company sports teams. Upbeat slogans (written by employees) hang from the ceiling. Each production team has its own cheery melody that rings out when a member needs to catch management's attention. Combined with perky beeps and electronic signals that mark important events, the plant sounds like a gigantic pinball machine. (Christian & Hideko, 2006)

Clearly, there is something uniquely generative about the cultures that prevail in these companies — something that spurs their employees to behave independently for the greater good of the corporation, while pursuing their own personal objectives.

Two organizations that emerge from the African American experience may offer a methodology and models for achieving the kind of employee empowerment found in Toyota and Microsoft. These two organizations were created to transform the reality of the African American community and experience by way of supporting African Americans in their self-image and way of being. The method and models implemented in these organizations may offer a pathway for all institutions — private, public, and government, among others — to achieve sustainability through a way of communicating that enables a reassessment of what is really important.

Listening into transformation and being-ness

The International Black Summit and the Black African Heritage Leadership Development Caucus present a unique notion: "Listening" people and communities into transformation and being-ness.

The International Black Summit (IBS) was organized in 1991. It grew out of a conversation between two women who each had completed a course in personal empowerment run by the Landmark Education Corporation (LEC). The LEC is itself an offspring of Werner Erhardt's iteration of the "human potential movement" of the 1960s: "est" (Erhardt Seminar Training).

IBS's mission, known as the Declaration, was crafted during the first summit weekend in October 1991. This Declaration has been the driving force behind all subsequent

IBS summits and initiatives since its founding.[10] The Declaration is a brief series of assertions that includes the following statement:

> WE STAND for the expression of our spirituality; ending the murders of our men, women and children; building economies responsible for funding our community; maintaining wellness of being in our bodies; providing human services; establishing nurturing relationships; altering the conversation of who we are in the media; empowering our youth.

Curiously, the Black African Heritage Leadership Development Caucus (BAH) was also born in October 1991. The BAH was established by people of black African heritage who were trainers and members of the National Coalition Building Institute (NCBI). NCBI is a diversity-training organization founded by Cheri Brown for the purpose of building relationships between black and Jewish students on US college campuses. According to BAH director Joyce B. Johnson Shabazz,[11] The Black African Heritage Leadership Development Caucus emerged as a leadership development resource team of the NCBI. The participating trainers of black African descent needed to explore a methodology to interrupt the limited perspectives on racism held by many well-meaning allies. To that end, during the course of an annual three-day intensive, BAH participants pursue a conversation that reconstructs the mindset of victimization based on the historical application of racial oppression.

What distinguishes each of these organizations from nearly all others in the African American community is that both organizations were created solely for the purpose of *transforming the behavior* of their members. To that end, they may offer a pathway toward organizational transformation, toward sustainability and the attainment of the triple bottom line.

Since their formation, both the IBS and the BAH have ushered thousands of individuals of African descent from around the globe (East, West, and southern Africa, Canada, the Caribbean, and Brazil, as well as the United States) through a conversation that has enabled participants to experience fundamental shifts in their attitudes about themselves and the lives that they lead. Many BAH participants say they have experienced, often for the first time, total liberation from the constrictions of internalized oppression.

The conversations generated by each group support the participants in arriving at a common understanding; yet, remarkably, each participant is informed by the conversation in a manner that suits his or her own unique life framework and way of being.[12]

In other words, while the participants move together, in the same direction — rafting in the same stream — each person in the communally oriented conversation is given the opportunity to hear and receive a message that is crafted through that conversation for her or his own personal transformation and guidance. This offers compelling lessons for leaders who seek to transform the behavior of employees toward sustainable, triple-bottom-line–oriented behavior that is self-generated and self-correcting.

Echoing the way Sahtouris describes nature's richly diverse ecosystem, one of the primary elements of the leadership model practiced within IBS and BAH is a near-reverence for diversity. Both organizations welcome, embrace, and appreciate individuals from all

---

10 IBS home page, www.blacksummit.org/x_declaration.asp (accessed April 28, 2007).

11 Personal communication with J. B. Johnson Shabazz, telephone conversation, January 8, 2007.

12 Way of being, in this context, generally refers to an unconscious set of patterns and habits that an individual implements in order to conduct both the ordinary and the extraordinary day-to-day business of life.

Table 1.2 'Listening-into-being' leadership qualities and characteristics

Leadership model: qualities and characteristics	International Black Summit	Black African Heritage Leadership Development Caucus
Organizing principles	● Commitment to the Summit Declaration ● Authentic listening ● Acknowledgment of *distinctions* as means of processing information within the context of life's conversation ● Everyone's voice counts ("No insignificant person has ever been born" [N. D. Simmons]) ● There's no "out there"; everything is a projection from that which lies within ● There is already an answer to every question, at the moment it is asked ● "Trigger – the "rub" or charge that results in a new or deeper assessment of an issue or situation, relative to its impact (on an individual) ● Ongoing self-actualization ● We're all in it together ● Operates simultaneously in the linear and nonlinear domains ● Trust the process; it is as valuable/vital as the outcome	● Spiritual attunement ● Authentic listening ● A transformational continuum of an ongoing conversation given by life ● Every voice is necessary; every voice must be heard ● Open and full disclosure of issues/concerns (abuse occurs in secrecy and seclusion) ● Complete significance in the black race social identity ● Reclamation of personal power ● Political and economic consciousness ● Self-love and valuation of the black community ● Acknowledgment and respect for ancestors ● Being in relationship with our history ● Cooperative economics
Decision-making process	● Alignment – a sacrosanct process through which the entire Summit Body (down to the last voice) acknowledges "the answer" (what's "so;" what "already is") ● Alignment is *not*: majority rule; voting; cajoling; manipulating; not even consensus	● Contributory process; reliance on synergy ● There is an expectation and a requirement for accountability to an outcome
Response to conflict/resistance	● Embracing it/welcoming it/"going for the gold" in it ● Acknowledging that any conflict is generally within an individual; usually points to something in the person that is unresolved ● When conflict shows up, it offers direction; there is completion in conflict; it helps to move obstacles out of the way ● Everything that happens needs to happen	● Seen as a necessary part of evolution; it is welcomed ● Inviting it/exploring it/finding the direction in it ● Anticipate it with open arms, acknowledging it as "a part of everything" ● Living under a racist system requires that we make peace with conflict in order to sustain a quality of life

Sources: Personal communication with IBS leaders: P. Parks, Jr (California), J. K. Young (Delaware), K. Copper (Georgia), S. Shelton (California), telephone interview, January 4, 2007; and IBS leaders R. Blake (New York), N. D. Simmons (New York), O. Sanders (North Carolina), telephone interview, January 6, 2007. Personal communication with BAH director J. B. Johnson Shabazz, telephone interview, January 8, 2007.

socioeconomic, political, and religious backgrounds and strive for total class integration. Further, within both organizations, leadership is not always vested in the people who have "the right" credentials — that is, the right education, work experience, or social pedigree. Instead, leadership is vested in the person who most effectively and convincingly "shows up" inside the task at hand. The IBS community describes this as:[13]

> looking for who the person [leader] is Being, in relationship to the task, and how well that person communicates intentionality and integrity in pursuit of that task. A leader is someone who can stay with the Conversation [and], the Alignment process until the last person in the room can see the Alignment, all the while staying detached enough to recognize when Alignment is not present.

The challenge that this type of deep diversity brings along with it is an ongoing presence of tension and confrontation — sometimes experienced as conflict. The quality of this conflict is rarely angry or mean-spirited. It is not the kind of conflict based on competition, where one idea *beats* another. Rather, it has the quality of birth — a high-energy struggle to deliver authentic, precious, and meaningful data.

Table 1.2 describes the qualities and characteristics of the "listening-into-being" leadership model practiced within these groups.

Conclusion

Many of the characteristics of the IBS/BAH leadership practices are reflected in elements that are presented in the works of Sahtouris (1998, 2003). Such elements include self-creation, in which each participant must confront his or her own barriers to transformation within the context of the relevant inquiry; complexity (diversity of parts), whereby each participant is enriched by the views of people who are different from him or her; empowerment/employment of all component parts; and communications among all parts.

These models offer an atypical framework for exploring the challenge of achieving sustainable production. Natural lifecycles and organization culture are just two viable reference points for guidance in leading the sustainable enterprise. Other reference points will likely include perspectives from which the focus is on *integration* as opposed to *domination*. The message here is for leaders to be willing to acknowledge the value of information, practices, and leverage points that emanate from sources to which they are unaccustomed.

The IBS and BAH models have tapped into a conversation technology that empowers each participant to achieve alignment on his or her respective agendas. Participants arrive at a common ground, regardless of differences in status, professional achievement, public acclaim, national origin, or religious affiliation. Leaders of sustainable enterprise might wisely choose to explore the power of this process. It is hoped that, through this text, leaders throughout the organization will, together, create the tools, ideas, and strategies to help them on the journey toward this crucial goal.

---

13 Personal communication with R. Blake, telephone interview, January 6, 2007.

■ Engaging the natural tendency of self-organization

Richard N. Knowles

When a typical manager walks around the facility, he or she often spots people talking together in small, informal groups. They are talking about something that is important and interests them. Perhaps it is a sports event or a political situation or family problem; maybe they are just getting caught up with each other; often they are talking about their work. Managers routinely interpret this as a waste of time, so they push the people to get back to work. Push, push, push takes a lot of energy, creates friction, and demoralizes everyone; it wears them out. It is a huge waste of time and energy, and thus an unsustainable way to lead.

What is happening when people gather to talk? What is going on here? Why? What can managers learn from this? Is it just a waste, or is there something deeper here that could be a key to opening up the energy and creativity of the organization? What would an organization be like if everyone were working to his or her best, applying herself to doing what it takes for the business to succeed? What would it be like if each person were working on an opportunity such as improving workplace safety while lowering costs and simultaneously improving productivity, quality, and customer service?

When leaders choose to purposefully engage with this way in which people come together, it can open up the effectiveness, efficiency, and productivity of the organization by 30 to 40% (Knowles, 2002).

This phenomenon is called self-organization, which sounds like chaos, anarchy, and potential failure. When I first heard of this, about 15 years ago, I almost fell out of my chair. After all, I was the plant manager and was supposed to keep things organized and tight. But over the years, in learning how to engage with this natural tendency of self-organization, I found that persistently talking with and listening to all the employees about important issues such as safety, quality, costs, sustainability, the enterprise's impact on the community, and the quality of work life, significantly improves the organization's performance. Injuries dropped by 98%, productivity rose 45%, emissions dropped 88%, and earnings rose 300%. Together we confronted and struggled with the issues and developed clarity about what we were trying to do and why this was important to all of us. This was done with openness, honesty, and hard work.

Engaging the natural tendency of self-organization

All living systems naturally "self-organize." This tendency can be seen throughout nature at all levels, from tiny bacteria to large ecosystems. In this essay, a system is loosely defined as a collection of similar things, a group or an organization. There is a shared identity that defines a sort of boundary around this collection of things.

This self-organization is so pervasive and subtle it's usually not even noticed. Yet it is occurring all the time.

This natural tendency is powerful, yet subtle; it is like the current in a flowing river. Often people join the flow and engage purposefully in their conversations, in informal gatherings such as family reunions, or in high-performance work teams. Many of us who have been managers have, however, worked against this by trying to impose our wills on people, using a command-and-control approach, when we have had a specific task to do or a goal to reach. This is nonpurposeful engagement with the natural tendency of self-organization. Using the command-and-control approach is like trying to take the twists and turns out of a river and make it flow the way we want. But, in purposeful engagement, leaders join the river and draw great energy and focus from it.

Much of the vast literature on management and leadership is directed at ways that one's will can be imposed on the people in the organization to accomplish the tasks at hand. Most managers crave stability, reliability, predictability, and control in their organizations. While imposing conditions such as these is necessary for a machine such as an airplane, this approach suppresses the vitality, energy, and creativity of people. When this command-and-control mode of managing and leading is used in an enterprise, people self-organize in ways that are seen by the organization as nonpurposeful, becoming lethargic, unresponsive, and resistant to change. Such organizations behave as if they are mechanical things that must be pushed and shoved by their leaders. They are like unhealthy living systems: torpid and passive. There is a growing frustration with this way of leading because of the less-than-hoped-for results, the effort required to keep things moving, the lack of sustainability, and the negative self-organizing behavior that it generates in people.

Our leadership choice

As leaders and managers, we always have a *choice* to make about the way we engage the natural tendency for people to self-organize. There are times when the situation is such that one of these choices may be more appropriate than the other. However, if we can purposefully engage, we will be in the most sustainable position. This is not about "good" or "bad," but rather about choosing the most effective way to lead in a particular situation, at a particular time. Leadership is a temporal process in which the leader must be conscious of what is happening and must choose the most appropriate leadership engagement process for the situation; this is the "leadership dance."

Most managers have learned how to use command-and-control management processes, but only a few have learned how to use management and leadership processes that purposefully engage the natural tendency to self-organize. Often, these few are the intuitive leaders who know that the command-and-control processes aren't very effective over the long term.

Increasingly, a language and models that are useful in working in this area are surfacing (see Chapters 2, 3, 4, and 5; and Knowles, 2002). Combining powerful models and explicit terminology with intuitive insights provides an effective way to purposefully engage the tendency to self-organize. I call leadership processes that purposefully engage this natural tendency "self-organizing leadership." With purposeful engagement, vitality, energy, and creativity increase, and the organization behaves as if it were a healthy, living system. The fundamental idea speaks to the nature of relationships as they are developed and expressed in conversations. Stacey (2001) is leading explorations into the importance of conversations and the exchange of gestures in organizations in his work on complex responsive processes (CRP).

The theoretical foundations of self-organization are critical to building a solid groundwork for this important work for leaders. CRP looks at the conversations among the people in the organization as temporal events. Leaders have direct engagement with people and are not separated from what is currently taking place in the organization. On the other hand, the theory of complex adaptive systems (CAS) looks at systems and organizations as things to be acted on. With the CAS approach, the engagement is with the people in the organization as if they were different from the leader, as if they were objects. Both CRP and CAS approaches are useful in helping develop deeper insights into what is happening in organizations, providing that the distinction between the two methods is understood and made explicit.

All leaders need to do to purposefully engage the natural tendency of self-organization is to begin to have the important, often intense, sometimes difficult conversations about the critical issues facing us and invite others to join in the exploration. Three areas provide important conversational pathways. These are the fundamental pathways for self-organizing leadership:

1. Abundantly sharing important, relevant information, such as aspects of how the organization is performing — the competitive situation, the cost of what the people in the organization are doing, earnings, and the potential impact of all this on the organization's future

2. Building interdependent relationships and trust by spending time with people on their turf, listening and sharing ideas, keeping one's word, taking public responsibility for mistakes, and talking together about how to correct the situation

3. Helping people discover how they and their work fit into the whole picture, helping them to see the positive impact of their work — discovering meaning in the work

Authentic conversations, one person at a time, begin to open up the connections that are the medium of successful self-organization.

These authentic conversations must be about the questions and issues that are truly important and critical to the success of the organization's work and its goals. The conversations may be difficult, so it requires courage, concern, commitment, and care to stay in the "heat" and find new ground on which to build. Leaders and employees have to be open, honest, and transparent. *If transformation is to occur, everyone in the organization needs to be engaged in the processes of the organization* and *must not act on the organization as if it were an external thing.*

There are a number of ways to open up these conversations. Leaders and employees together build trust and meaning as they talk and work together. They can ask questions about what they see or sense and ask why. Storytelling is a way for people to find meaning in what is happening. Margaret J. Wheatley (1992) was one of the early thinkers to reveal and publicize this way of leading. Leaders can use the "open space technology" of Harrison Owen (1991) to explore people's interests in a particular subject. The "future search" approach of Marvin R. Weisbord and Sandra Janoff (1995) helps find out what is important to people and identify those in the organization who care enough to carry it forward. David Cooperrider's "Appreciative Inquiry" approach (Cooperrider, Whitney, & Stavros, 2005) is also an effective way to open up the conversation. Sometimes it is necessary to have the hard conversations that Susan Scott talks about in *Fierce Conversations* (2004). Sometimes using Glenda Eoyang's approach (Eoyang, Olsen, Beckhand, & Vail, 2001) to explore the difference makes the difference. The challenge is to keep the conversations open, flowing, and authentic over time.

As new ideas are shared, exciting possibilities are discovered, and opportunities may open up for significant improvement. It's important to document the conversation, to keep the conversational space open, to keep the conversation alive, and to carry it forward to engage others.

Mapping conversations: the Process Enneagram

One way to effectively address and document the critical questions and issues is through a cyclical progression of discussions that develop successively deeper, clearer, more coherent insights. In my experience in working in organizations, I have found that almost all the information an organization needs to accomplish its work is already scattered among the various individuals within the organization. This open, honest progression of conversations provides a way to develop a shared awareness and understanding of all we know.

This cyclical progression of conversations can be easily mapped onto a **Process Enneagram**[14] map (Knowles, 2002; see Fig. 1.2) through a series of Process Enneagram workshops, to capture the ideas, to keep open the space for future conversations, and to develop a living strategic plan. The Process Enneagram is a fundamental archetypal pattern for the deep processes of self-organizing leadership. It can be transferred and used in any organization. A. G. E. Blake (1996) has written extensively about the Process Enneagram.

Figure 1.2 **Process Enneagram: the core process with the full participation of the people in the organization**

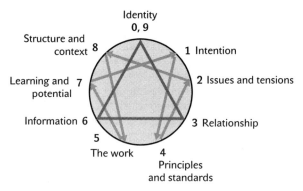

Source: Copyright 2002, R. N. Knowles. Reproduced with permission.

The progression begins with a conversation designed to collectively define a clear, compelling question or challenge. The group moves on to a focused conversation about who its members are, about its identity. The participants then define the group's intention, so they can develop a shared, co-created picture of exactly what they want to accomplish. This leads into conversations about the issues and tensions facing them and the dynamics of how their co-created principles and standards of behavior will enable everyone to work together more effectively. Co-created principles and standards profoundly affect relationships and impact many of the issues already identified. Next the group looks at how to best structure and organize itself to accomplish the issues that need to be addressed. The specific tasks and work it will do are the next focus. This moves to how members will continue to share meaningful information and learn and grow and discover the future together. As this is carried forward into more and more cycles and the conversation widens, other insights will emerge that can be added to the map the group is creating. In this cyclical process, participants move up a spiral of learn-

14 An enneagram is a nine-pointed geometrical figure.

ing and growth. This cyclical progression of conversations enables the development of a very high level of coherence, purposefulness, sustainability, and will for action.

Control shifts from management edicts and pronouncements to the co-creation during the Process Enneagram workshops of what I term the "Bowl" (**A**) (Knowles, 2002, p. 99), which consists of the organization's mission, vision, expectations, principles, and standards of performance. All who are involved, at all levels, in the question being addressed by the Process Enneagram workshops co-create this when developing the Process Enneagram map. Once established, the *Bowl* provides order and focus for the organization, and within the *Bowl* people work with a high level of freedom to accomplish the tasks before them.

The advisory board of the Institute for Sustainable Enterprise of the Fairleigh Dickinson University Silberman College of Business is using the Process Enneagram as a planning and guidance tool to help leaders be clear about their work (Fig. 1.3). It provides a map of the whole with details about the specific parts so that, when deep in the weeds, one never loses sight of the whole and the interconnections of its parts.

When people engage in this way, energy and creativity flow and the effectiveness of the organization improves significantly. Resistance to change almost disappears.

Some thoughts on emergence

I describe behaviors emerging from three different leading processes in *The Leadership Dance: Pathways to Extraordinary Organizational Effectiveness* (2002, pp. 169-176). These leading processes — each of which consists of three interdependent ideas — are embedded in the Process Enneagram (Knowles, 2002, p. 30). In actual practice, all of these are running all the time, but it useful for this analysis to look at them as if they were separate.[15]

The most basic and important leadership process is the self-organizing leadership process of **identity**, **relationship**, and **information**. There are two other leadership processes embedded in the Process Enneagram: **operational leadership** is focused on the issues (problems), structure, and assigning the work; **strategic leadership** is focused on the intention (the new thing that needs to be done), principles and standards (the new behaviors that the new thing that needs to be done requires), and learning (how to do and sustain this new thing).

Self-organizing leadership connects the Process Enneagram points 0, 3, and 6. Operational leadership connects points 2, 8, and 5, and strategic leadership connects points 1, 4, and 7. All three of these leadership processes are embedded within the Process Enneagram. Moving among these forms of leadership as the immediate situation requires is called the **leadership dance**.

Emergence in the self-organizing leadership process

Identity, relationship, and information emerge as everyone in the organization engages in dialogue about questions and issues that are very important to them. Through this dialogue, leaders are engaging the natural tendency of self-organization in purposeful ways. Reflecting on the importance of these conditions for self-organization, people can look at them from the perspective of their threefold relationship. They are forces that are interacting all the time. Through the interaction of the parts of this triad, new behaviors emerge releasing energy and creativity (Fig. 1.4):

15 For more on operational leadership and strategic leadership, see an expanded version of this essay in the *Sustainable Enterprise Living Fieldbook* (www.TheSustainableEnterpriseFieldbook.net). See the Introduction (pages 7-8) for information on the *Living Fieldbook* (**L**).

Figure 1.3 **Process Enneagram: Institute for Sustainable Enterprise workshop held on March 30, 2006**

Structure
- Structure and committees established curriculum, research and service
- Gerard, Jeana, Joel, Dan; leading
- Build on CHRMS and move beyond it
- Multidisciplinary and diverse
- Connecting with companies, UN, universities: e.g., Interface, Philips North America, Ricoh, UN Global Compact, NJ HEPS

Context
- FDU Silberman College of Business: formal recognition
- First movers: Case Western Reserve, MIT Society of Organizational Learning, INCAE, UNC Center
- Competency/network base: e.g., AOM Practitioner Series
- Around 20 business schools have sustainability programs
- Current world situation: we can destroy everything
- Major differences across countries and cultures

- Vision: "Creating Collaborative Opportunities and Processes for Organizations to Enhance their Sustainability from a People, Environmental, Societal, and Financial Perspective"
- ISE
- We are an advisory board
- Jeana Wirtenberg, Dan Twomey, Joel Harmon, Gerard Farias
- About 31 others from academia, business, government, consultants, nonprofits; years of personal activity experience; cross-section of skills/functional experience
- Strong business case for the Center
- FDU Silberman College base
- There is an underpinning of deep purposefulness for being together in this work; passion for change and transformation
- Some in the group have strong relatedness
- Globally connected
- Authenticity; connecting to our higher selves and purpose
- Learn from others

- Experiential curriculum
- Case studies, stories, publicity
- Action research studies; *Fieldbook* project
- Gatherings; Advisory Board dialogue
- Reach out and learn from others; learn from our mistakes
- Can be huge impact: collaboration can shift the world
- 2007 Forum
- SKN Portal

- Share all information
- Sustainability literature
- Papers and reports generated by ISE
- Networks and SKN Portal
- Each other; dialogue

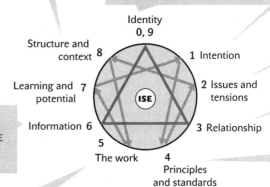

Identity
0, 9

Structure and context 8

1 Intention

Learning and 7
potential

2 Issues and tensions

ISE

Information 6

3 Relationship

5

The work   4

Principles and standards

- Connect with other sustainability efforts
- North–South dialogue: Costa Rica project
- *Sustainable Enterprise Fieldbook* project
- SKN Worldwide Web and database, Bill Russell
- Continue development of:
  - Research, thinking and programs
  - Curriculum
    - Ex. MBA program
  - Services
    - Corporate partners

- "Managing Sustainability" workshop
- Fundraising
- Collaboration and alliances with UN, universities, developing nations
- Support campus projects
- Define success factors
- Build alliances
- Develop an economic model
- Compile concrete examples

- Mission: Educate current and future leaders of business, government, nonprofit, and educational institutions on managing sustainably by focusing on products, processes, and services that add value to the organizations and are beneficial to people and the planet
- Create a sustainable and collaborative institute
- Change organizations; create life-giving workplace
- Curriculum development: transform business education
- World-class/renowned center of excellence: standard of quality and influence
- Global, whole-system, multifaceted perspective; safe space for conversations: engage people
- A catalyst for links, conversations, learning, and action, linking economics, the social, and environmental; balance theory and practice
- Inquire into more effective collaboration and models; collaborative mindset; between-space models
- Identify, communicate, and embed new ways of thinking to garner widespread support and participation
- Applied research; concrete examples; measure what we're doing
- Use appropriate timeframes (longer) for evaluation and solutions
- Be unstoppable; entrepreneurial
- Services; spread the work; knowledge transfer; be public

- Focus locally or broadly, or both?
- Who is "us"? Right people in room? More younger generation
- How to speak as change agents without alienating?
- Managing the complexity/diversity?
- Integration of what we're doing; focus
- Efforts in "between spaces," where it all comes together?
- Change is an inside job; individual commitment?
- How much secondary education to take on?
- Resources vs. desires, focus; balance among constituents
- Need money: selling, marketing, publishing, grants
- Balance personal time and energy
- Balance operating and action principles
- Differing expectations and levels of commitment
- Talking vs. the rubber hitting the road

- Open, honest, respectful
- Enthusiastic; collaborative, and synergistic
- Mutuality and reciprocity
- Trust; increasing integrity

- Holistic view
- Build on the values of CHRMS
- Use collaborative, co-creation, cyclic processes; open to synergy
- Open to and welcome emergence
- Inquiry–action–inquiry . . .
- Want to improve the world
- Inclusiveness; hear all voices
- Experimental
- Create the space for conversations
- Share all information
- Be open about potential conflicts of interest
- Act with integrity and help each other; be respectful
- Win–win–win

- Listen deeply, for understanding
- Work in the inbetween spaces and across boundaries
- Stay present to our intention
- Be attractors
- Be careful that we understand what we mean
- Walk in others' shoes
- Seek to discover and serve mutual interests
- Be committed and accountable
- Create room for the difficult conversations
- Live what we want to become; pay attention to our "way of being"
- Develop tangible actions and short-term successes

AOM = Academy of Management
CHRMS = Center for Human Resource Management Studies
FDU = Fairleigh Dickinson University
ISE = Institute for Sustainable Enterprise
MIT = Massachusetts Institute of Technology
NJ HEPS = New Jersey Higher Education Partnership for Sustainability
SKN = Sustainability Knowledge Network
UNC = University of North Carolina

Figure 1.4 **Emergence in the self-organizing leadership process**

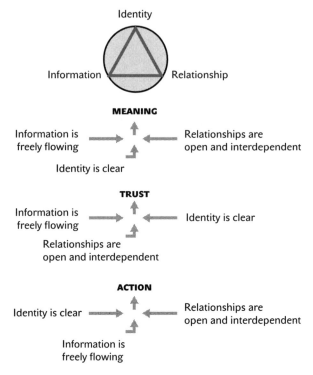

Source: R. N. Knowles. (2002). *The leadership dance: Pathways to extraordinary organizational effectiveness* (p. 130). Niagara Falls, NY: Center for Self-organizing Leadership. Reproduced with permission.

- When everyone has an interdependent relationship and an abundance of information, as people become clearer about their identity **meaning** emerges

- When everyone has a clear sense of identity and an abundance of information, as people's relationships become more interdependent **trust** emerges

- When everyone in the organization together has a clear sense of identity and an interdependent relationship, as new information becomes available people can move into **action**

These new behaviors emerge depending on the ways leaders choose to engage the people in the organization. These choices lead to vastly different outcomes. Purposeful engagement leads to a sense of urgency, clarity of purpose, resoluteness, hope, new potential, and new possibilities. Nonpurposeful engagement leads to fear, anxiety, confusion, struggle, cynicism, frustration, and resistance to change. These ideas are developed further in Knowles (2002).

The leader's choice in engaging the natural tendency of self-organization may lead to vastly different outcomes.

The choice of the mode of engagement is simple, but the execution can be difficult.

Some examples

An example from when I was plant manager at the DuPont plant in Belle, West
Virginia, will help illustrate these ideas further. When we began a construction project
to convert from pneumatic to electronic process control systems at Belle, we involved
the engineers, operators, mechanics, and all supervision deeply in the communications
and planning processes. Our goal was to convert to the new chemical process control
systems without maintaining parallel systems for transition and backup. This was a
high-risk approach, so we knew that everyone needed to be involved in the weekly project status reviews, planning sessions, design meetings, and the like; many of the operators, mechanics, and engineers were sent to the Honeywell School for computer training. All the information was shared on a continuous basis, and interdependent
relationships were developed. There was a lot of give-and-take in these meetings as
everyone tried his or her best to make the project a success. At the end of the project,
the unit was started up without incident, making quality product in record time. This
approach cut the costs and time in half, from the original estimate of US$6 million in
investment and two years to implement. Then 15 more projects were successfully put
into place in record time and at lower-than-forecast investment without running any
parallel processes, clearly showing the success of self-organizing leadership processes.

In another example using engagement processes such as these, the City of Niagara
Falls, New York, Leadership Team worked together with the mayor in a way that
resulted in cutting out US$15 million from a US$62 million budget over a four-year
period. This was the first time in the city's history that the Leadership Team worked
together this way, and saved so much money. Sharing information, building interdependent relationships, and getting very clear about the mission to make the city as
strong as possible were keys to this success. A lot of the savings resulted from people
talking about what was going on, so, for example, we knew to put the new sewers into
place before paving the streets.

Surely, most of you reading this book can think of examples in which well-intended
projects with high expectations were started from the top of the organization with little
employee involvement. The people resisted the changes, slowing things down to the
point that the organization lost energy and interest, finally giving up altogether. Many
of the quality improvement efforts over the last 20 or more years have ended like this.
However, this is not because of the poor quality of the technology, but rather the lack
of deep involvement of all the people.

Application across cultures

The self-organizing leadership processes described in this essay have been used across
many cultures for more than ten years. For example, Tim Dalmau[16] has used these
processes in companies and communities in Australia, New Zealand, South Africa,
Namibia, Thailand, United States, Mexico, Malaysia, Germany, Indonesia, China, and
Singapore. Steve Zuieback[17] has used them extensively in the state of California school
system. I have used them extensively in Australia, New Zealand, United States, Canada,
and the United Kingdom in organizations ranging from heavy industry — such as steel,
coal, and chemicals — to school districts, accounting firms, the United Way of Niagara
Falls, city government, and various community projects such as the Niagara County

16 www.dalmau.com (accessed January 22, 2008).
17 www.stevezuieback.com (accessed January 22, 2008).

Study on Services for the Aging. Claire Knowles[18] uses this approach very effectively in her work with women in transition.

This approach is not limited to any particular sort of work, culture, or organization. It applies to situations ranging from individuals to very large groups; it is fractal in nature in that it works at multiple levels of scale.

There seems to be an archetypal nature to this work that makes it useful and transferable. Although the specific situations differ in each instance and are not transferable, the deeper patterns and processes of the Process Enneagram are highly consistent and transferable.

Conclusion

As leaders, we have a choice to make about how we engage the natural tendency to self-organize. Historically leaders and managers have tried to impose their wills — there will still be occasions when leaders need to do this — but we are finding that purposefully engaging the natural tendency to self-organize produces vital, coherent, energetic, creative, highly effective, and more sustainable organizations. Self-organizing leadership provides pathways for leaders to effectively and purposefully engage the natural tendency of self-organization.

These are the core processes of the Leadership Diamond, discussed earlier in this chapter.

This work requires a high level of openness, integrity, courage, and commitment. For an organization to arrive at a point where people are listening deeply, asking the tough, deeper questions, and respecting and truly valuing each other requires the leader to be working from a deep sense of self, purpose, and integrity. This sustainable way of leading is more about *being* than about having a set of skills, as important as they are.

▓ Conclusion

The essays in this holographic ensemble bring together many of the key features of leadership for sustainable enterprise. One of these essays may make more sense to you than the others. If so, concentrate on the approach it offers; study it to develop your own thinking and leadership skills. There are many approaches, but no final answers. This offers all of us the opportunity to create our own approaches to building more sustainability and value into our own enterprises. Let's build a better world together.

▓ References

American Heritage Dictionary of the English Language. (1992). *The American Heritage Dictionary of the English Language* (3rd ed.). Boston, MA: Houghton Mifflin.

American Management Association (AMA). (2007). *Creating a sustainable future: A global study of current trends and possibilities 2007–2017.* New York: American Management Association.

Anguita, J., Baker, M. N., Davis, K. J., & McLean, G. N. (2005). Global Organization Development. In W. J. Rothwell and R. Sullivan (Eds.), *Practicing organization development* (2nd ed.) (pp. 287-289). San Francisco: John Wiley.

18 www.lightsonworkshop.com (accessed January 22, 2008).

Argyris, C., & Schön, D. A. (1996). *Organization learning II: Theory, method, and practice.* Reading, MA: Addison-Wesley.

Atlee, T. (2003). Co-intelligence: A vision for social activism. *IONS Noetic Sciences Review, 62*, 22.

Blake, A. G. E. (1996). *The intelligent enneagram.* Boston, MA/London: Shambhala.

Christian, C., & Hideko, T. (2006) Corporate culture: The J factor. *Newsweek Magazine,* May 9, 2006. Retrieved February 16, 2007, from findarticles.com/p/articles/mi_hb3335/is_200505/ai_18039410.

Collins, J. (2001). *Good to great: Why some companies make the leap and others don't.* New York: HarperCollins.

Cooperrider, D. L., Whitney, D., & Stavros, J. M. (2005). *Appreciative Inquiry handbook.* San Francisco: Berrett-Koehler.

Davis, K. J. (2003). Global practice of OD. In M. Wheatley, R. Tannenbaum, P. Griffin, K. Quade, & National Organization Development Network (Eds.), *Organization development at work: Conversations on the values, applications, and future of OD* (pp. 103-105). San Francisco: John Wiley.

Eoyang, G. H., Olsen, E. E., Beckhand, R., & Vail, P. (2001). *Facilitating organizational change: Lessons from complexity science.* New York: Jossey-Bass/Pfeiffer.

Ghoshal, S. (2005). Bad management theories are destroying good management practices. *Academy of Management Learning & Education, 4*(1), 75-91.

Harris, P., Moran, R., & Moran, S. (2004). *Managing cultural differences: Global leadership strategies for the 21st century.* Amsterdam: Elsevier.

Kinney-Linton, WindEagle, & RainbowHawk. (2007). Ancient wisdom council. In P. Holman, T. Devane, & S. Cady (Eds.), *The change handbook* (2nd ed.) (pp. 195-200). San Francisco: Berrett-Koehler.

Knowles, R. N. (2002). *The leadership dance: Pathways to extraordinary organizational effectiveness.* Niagara Falls, NY: Center for Self-Organizing Leadership.

Knowles, R. N. (2006). Engaging the natural tendency of self-organization: Transformation. Retrieved April 29, 2007, from www.worldbusiness.org.

Maynard, H. B., & Mehrtens, S. E. (1993). *The fourth wave: Business in the 21st century.* San Francisco: Berrett-Koehler.

Nonaka, I., Toyama, R., & Noboru, K. (2000). SECI, Ba and leadership: A unified model of dynamic knowledge creation. *Long Range Planning, 33*, 5-34.

Owen, H. (1991). *Open space technology: A user's guide.* San Francisco: Berrett-Koehler.

Owen, H. (2004). *The practice of peace* (2nd ed.). Circle Pines, MN: Human Systems Dynamics Institute and Open Space Institutes.

Pollard, D. (2006). Let-self-change: Learning about approaches to complexity from gatherer-hunter. Retrieved August 21, 2006, from blogs.salon.com/0002007/2006/08/06.html#a1606.

Pritchard, E. (1997). *No word for time: The way of the Algonquin people.* Tulsa, OK: Council Oak Books.

Sahtouris, E. (1998). The biology of globalization. Retrieved March 13, 2007, from www.ratical.org/LifeWeb/Articles/globalize.html#p8.

Sahtouris, E. (2003). After Darwin. Lecture delivered at Wasan Island, Canada, August 30, 2003. Retrieved March 17, 2007, from www.ratical.org/LifeWeb/Articles/AfterDarwin.pdf.

Scott, S. (2004). *Fierce conversations: Achieving success at work and in life, one conversation at a time.* New York: The Berkeley Publishing Group.

Senge, P. M., Kleiner, A., Roberts, C., Ross, R., & Smith, B. (1994). *The fifth discipline fieldbook: Strategies and tools for building a learning organization.* New York: Doubleday.

Stacey, R. D. (2001). *Complex responsive processes in organizations.* London/New York: Routledge.

Torbert, B., & Associates (2004). *Action inquiry: The secret of timely and transforming leadership.* San Francisco: Berrett-Koehler.

Twomey, D. (2006). Designed emergence as a path to enterprise sustainability. *E:CO Emergence: Complexity & Organization, 8*(3), 12-23.

Weisbord, M. R., & Janoff, S. (1995). *Future search.* San Francisco: Berrett-Koehler.

Wheatley, M. J. (1992). *Leadership and the new science: Learning about organization from an orderly universe.* San Francisco: Berrett-Koehler.

WindEagle & RainbowHawk (2003). *Heart seeds: A message from the ancestors.* Edina, MN: EHAMA Press/Beaver Pond Press.

2

Mental models for sustainability[1]

John D. Adams, Linda M. Kelley,
Beth Applegate, and Theresa McNichol

Mental models are the constructs we bring to any situation that we are attempting to impact. They include what we know — what we value — what we believe — what we assume — out of which emerges a context for action or inaction.

John D. Adams

■ Introduction

Linda M. Kelley

Mental models for sustainability are operating systems or paradigms that value and generate respect for one's self, respect for other people, respect for peoples, and respect for our Earth. Respect is also a keystone for leaderfulness[2] throughout any organization. Operationally, mental models are intrinsically both personal and social.

In this chapter, we offer both theory and practices designed to help people make substantive changes in their mental models. Defining mental models as he does above, John

1 The authors gratefully acknowledge contributions from Thomas Drucker and Thomas Stewart to this chapter.
2 An organization is leaderful when the information flow is open, relationships are healthy, employees are involved in decision-making, and initiative is encouraged. If an employee in the organization, regardless of level, sees something that needs to be done, she or he steps forward to meet the need and is supported in that effort by upper management.

VALUES: A COMPASS THAT GUIDES

The *2007 AMA Sustainability Survey* (American Management Association [AMA], 2007) shows how important values are to the creation of sustainable enterprises.[3] The survey's 1,365 respondents, from global, multinational, and national organizations, rated values second only to the support of top management in qualities necessary to build a sustainable enterprise. These two factors are closely related as leadership tends to set the tone in terms of corporate value systems, according to *Creating a Sustainable Future* (AMA, 2007), AMA's report based on the results of the survey.

Values related to sustainability are deeply ingrained in the "DNA" of companies well on their way toward sustainability, found Wirtenberg and her colleagues (Wirtenberg, Harmon, Russell, & Fairfield, 2007) in a study of nine companies across the globe. These values are typically embedded by organizational founders and are especially evident among the European-based companies in their sample. One executive said,

> You can't talk to anyone [in our company] without them speaking about doing things that make a difference for people. So there is this interaction between the vision, the mission, and the culture, that is all wrapped up in a history of paying attention to this kind of stuff. (Wirtenberg et al., 2007, p. 14)

Another said, "People here don't get promoted if they don't have the values . . . a sustainable mindset. If someone is immune, they don't make it; they don't have the followership" (Wirtenberg et al., 2007, p. 17).

Although several of the companies in this study (Wirtenberg et al., 2007) had been through major changes, including downsizings, the unwavering commitment to their sustainability values was seen as the compass that guided them through those changes.

Adams draws on his many years of research and consulting in the chapter's pivotal essay, "Six dimensions of mental models," in which he lays out a structure comprising six dimensions of consciousness: time orientation, focus of response, scope of attention, prevailing logic, problem consideration, and life orientation.

The three case studies that follow use these dimensions as a framework to show practices and exercises for making desired changes in how the people in the profiled organizations view and operate in the world.

In the first case study, "Cultivating mental models that support sustainability in a technically oriented organization," Linda Kelley demonstrates how people can make lasting fundamental changes. The objective of this program is to cultivate a broad base of leaders who understand both the details of the individual projects and the way in which these projects fit into the organization's overall purpose and goals. The exercises and practices Kelley presents integrate current scientific research and world-wisdom traditions, and expand systems thinking to include the whole thinking-feeling-acting person.

3 See note 10 on page 12.

In "Mental models in civil society," Beth Applegate shows the importance of mental models to the development of a culturally competent[4] strategic plan. The organization featured is a progressive nonprofit agency whose staff and members had to change their mental models to bring their actions in line with what they said they valued. The clients are led through exercises designed to make important changes in one or more of Adams's six dimensions of mental models.

Finally, in "Appreciative Inquiry case study: executive MBA candidates," Theresa McNichol introduces readers to the framework of Appreciative Inquiry (AI) and shows how it can provide tools for transforming one's concepts and mental models from either/or to those that recognize interdependence and are inclusive, both–and systems. McNichol points out that it takes more than goodwill and a person's best thinking to effect this conversion. In addition, she emphasizes the importance of leveling the playing field so that the process is both collective and collaborative.

Each of the case studies presents work that brings about changes in ways that are respectful of people, their organizations, and the world in which they operate. The processes they highlight are complementary, and the exercises[5] reinforce each other.

▓ Six dimensions of mental models

John D. Adams

Perhaps the best way to understand the relationship between mental models and sustainable initiatives is to start with a few quotes about the all-pervasive influence mental models have on all of our efforts and, consequently, how they determine our successes or failures.

> The range of what we think and do is limited by what we fail to notice. And because we fail to notice that we fail to notice, there is little we can do to change, until we notice how failing to notice shapes our thoughts and deeds.
>
> *Ronald D. Laing* (quoted in Zweig & Abrams, 1991, p. xix)

> If we continue to believe as we have always believed, we will continue to act as we have always acted. If we continue to act as we have always acted, we will continue to get what we have always gotten.
>
> *Marilyn Ferguson*[6]

> It ain't what you don't know that gets you into trouble. It's what you know for sure that just ain't so.
>
> *Mark Twain* (quoted in Gore, 2006, pp. 20-21)

> So do you not feel that, buried deep within each and every one of us, there is an instinctive, heartfelt awareness that provides — if we will allow it to —

---

4 **Cultural competency** is the ongoing and ever-deepening practice of building genuine relationships that lead to just outcomes and accountability without dominance.

5 For more on the exercises and tools in this chapter, and for supplemental cases, exercises, and tools, see the *Sustainable Enterprise Living Fieldbook* (**L**) online (see pages 7-8 for information).

6 Personal communication with M. Ferguson, Rhinebeck, New York, March 1983.

the most reliable guide as to whether or not our actions are really in the long-term interests of our planet and all the life it supports? This awareness, this wisdom of the heart, may be no more than a faint memory of a distant harmony rustling like a breeze through the leaves, yet sufficient to remind us that the earth is unique and that we have a duty to care for it.

HRH Prince of Wales (2000)

Once upon a time, there were four people. Their names were: Everybody, Somebody, Nobody, and Anybody. Whenever there was an important job to be done, Everybody was sure that Somebody would do it. Anybody could have done it; but in the end Nobody did it. When Nobody did it, Everybody got angry because it was Somebody's job. Everybody thought that Somebody would do it; but Nobody realized that Nobody would do it. So consequently, Everybody blamed Somebody when Nobody did what Anybody could have done in the first place.

anon. (quoted in Adams, 2000b, p. 101)

These comments remind us that our thought patterns determine our behaviors, and strongly influence the success or failure of our efforts to change. As Laing (Zweig and Abrams, 1991) points out, most of the time most people operate from a default mode of thinking that operates out of their conscious awareness; that is, the assumption that one holds an accurate and relevant view of reality is most of the time unquestioned and taken for granted. Those who disagree, by default, are considered to be wrong or misguided.

The mental models that prevail at the beginning of the 21st century are so far working to preserve the status quo and hindering the sustainable initiatives that most people now *know* are necessary to preserve a choice-rich human presence on the planet. For example, one of the most compelling mass mental models that has been instilled in the US public is that of consumerism — (**A**)(**L**) the concept that it is important for us to continually buy "things" in order to keep the economy healthy. We are told constantly that we will be happier if we buy the latest version of product X. It is so widespread that we generally don't think about it. For at least the last 50 years we have been inundated with "Buy now, before it's too late!" "Never again at this price!" and similar messages.

Vance Packard (1957) wrote about this in the late 1950s, with extensive explorations into how marketing experts influence our inner minds (i.e., mental models). In the late 1960s, Toffler (1970) made consumerism one of the primary dimensions of "future shock," calling it *overchoice*. But modern marketing has prevailed, and these voices from the past are largely ignored.

As a result, today 10% of Americans have rented personal storage space because, even though house size has doubled in the last 20 years, people can't afford houses big enough to store all their acquisitions (Vanderbilt, 2005; Torpy, 2007). In addition, the average household credit card indebtedness, for households that have credit cards, is approximately US$10,000 (CNNMoney.com, 2007). Furthermore, in the aftermath of 9/11, the president of the United States encouraged us to go shopping — not to have compassion, not to care about the world, not to understand the underlying reasons for the attacks, not to get closer to our families, but to go out and buy things.

Lester Brown (2006) builds a compelling case that, with business as usual, the trends we see unfolding now may ultimately lead to the failure of our civilization itself. He argues that, if we continue on the course we are now on, more and more nation states will fail until civilization itself begins to unravel.

The take–make–waste linear consumption model that prevails today is very nicely portrayed in an animated video called *The Story of Stuff*. (**A**)(**L**) The video develops an alternative circular consumption model that will be necessary for a high-quality sustainable future.

To illustrate how prevailing default mental models most often reinforce the status quo, making successful change difficult or impossible, I present a framework (Adams, 2000a, b, 2004, 2006) consisting of six dimensions of thinking: time orientation, focus of response, scope of attention, prevailing logic, problem consideration, and life orientation. Preliminary surveys I've conducted of perceived mental models in five countries in North America, Europe, and South Asia suggest there is some degree of global universality of these ways of thinking.

Table 2.1 describes the primary drivers behind contemporary institutional strategy. Maximize profits now; defer losses and big costs to the future. However, the future is always "in the future," so the "big costs" of environmental degradation, depletion of non-renewable resources, and overconsumption of renewables are deferred as long as possible. Equally irresponsibly, in order to maintain present-day economic "growth," governments are running up huge deficits that will have to be rectified by future generations.

Table 2.1 **Self-centered choices of modern organizations**

	Sure, here and now	Unsure, far and later
Gains	Favored	Disfavored
Losses	Disfavored	Favored

Source: L. Zsolnai. (2002). Green business or community economy? *International Journal of Social Economics, 29*(8), p. 656. Copyright 2002, *International Journal of Social Economics*. Reproduced with permission.

Many years ago, I began asking groups of managers to use adjectives to describe "how people think around here." (**A**) As time went on and the number of adjectives grew, it became clear that there were consistent themes: time orientation (urgency and short-term focus predominated); response focus (quick reaction to external stimuli); scope of attention (local or parochial — us versus them); prevailing logic (reductionistic and either/or thinking predominated); how problems get considered (finding fault and placing blame); and life orientation (life in the workplace most often focused on activity, workload, and materialism).

As categories emerged, I decided to set up each theme as one pole on a continuum, and then collect frequency data related to where along the continuum most people "did their thinking" most of the time. The following six dimensions were taken forward:

- **Time orientation:** short term to long term

- **Focus of response:** reactive to creative

- **Scope of attention:** local to global

- **Prevailing logic:** either/or to both–and

- **Problem consideration:** accountability-and-blame to learning

- **Life orientation:** doing-and-having to being

The results were quite revealing, as can be seen in Table 2.2, which contains a summary of how 158 managers and consultants from the United States, Canada, the United King-

Table 2.2 **Mental models and sustainability: summary of responses (n = 158). Assessments by executives, managers, and organizational development (OD) professionals of prevailing mental models in their organizational environments**

	Left ⅓	Middle ⅓	Right ⅓	
Short term: Focus on deadlines, immediate priorities, sense of urgency	93	48	17	**Long term:** Vision and strategies, potentials, opportunities
		Time orientation		
Reactive: External drives, prevailing rules and procedures	98	36	24	**Creative:** Taking initiative, new approaches, internal drives
		Focus of responsiveness		
Local: Focus on self or immediate group, competition	87	32	39	**Global:** Whole organization, inclusive, ecumenical, larger community
		Focus of attention		
Separation: Either/or, specialization	78	45	35	**Systems:** Both–and, holistic, interrelationships
		Prevailing logic		
Accountability/blame: Clear assignments, self-protection, it's not my fault (don't get caught)	71	50	37	**Learning:** Understanding, building on all types of experience
		Problem consideration		
Doing/having: Materialism, greed, cost-effectiveness, financial performance, quantitative growth	81	40	37	**Being:** Having enough, self-realization, "greater good," intangibles valued, qualitative growth
		Life orientation		

Source: Copyright 2006, J. D. Adams. Used with permission.

dom, the Netherlands, and India experienced the predominant modes of thinking in their organizations and primary client systems. A high percentage of the responses cluster near the left-hand side of each category — short term, reactive, parochial, either/or, blame placing, and doing-and-having. Tables 2.3 and 2.4 provide more details on the left- and right-side focuses of the six dimensions.

If these are the predominant styles of thinking (collective mental models) in contemporary "successful" organizations, then what sort of long-term sustainability can we expect to achieve? Because a person's mental models drive his or her focus and actions, if these mental models are maintained, Lester Brown's (2006) projection about China's rapid economic development and the attendant growth in its citizens' standard of living will not be able to be realized.[7] Instead, organizations will continue to operate with a high degree of urgency and activity, short deadlines, and priority on immediate results

7 Lester Brown's disquieting projection of China's economic growth and the need for natural resources that growth will generate is discussed in Chapter 7 (pages 207-208).

Table 2.3 **Working with the left-side focuses**

Focus	Messages that reinforce this focus	Questions to bring focus here	Positive value of focusing here	Result of overuse of this focus
Short term	• Don't fix it if it ain't broke • Just do it	• What needs attention now? • What are your immediate priorities?	• Establishing priorities • Acting with efficiency	• Lose the big picture • Overlook long-term consequences • Put bandages on symptoms
Reactive	• Do as you're told • If it feels good, do it • Life's a bitch and then you die	• What is the established policy, procedure, or practice? • What has been done before in this kind of situation?	• Consistency • Responsiveness • Loyalty	• Stuck in a rut • Unable to flow with change
Local	• Look out for "number one" • You've got to expect that from a ___!	• What makes you different or unique? • What is special about this situation?	• Survival • Protection • Maintaining position	• Loss of perspective • Ethnocentrism • Loss of diversity
Separation	• The best way to understand it is to take it apart • A place for everything, and everything in its place	• What are the relevant facts in this situation? • What do you get when you "crunch the numbers"?	• Convergence • Specialization • Rationality	• Fragmentation • Low synergy • Get lost in minutiae
Blaming	• It's not my fault! • All right, who's to blame here?	• What are your reasons for your actions? • What's wrong with this picture?	• Judgment, law, and rule enforcement	• Win–lose polarization • Risk aversion
Doing-and-having	• What's in it for me? • Faster, cheaper, better!	• What is the most cost-effective thing to do? • What's the bottom line?	• Financial performance and material comforts	• Attachment to possessions • Loss of human sensitivity • Burnout

Source: J. D. Adams. (2004). Mental models @ work: Implications for teaching sustainability. In: C. Galea (Ed.), *Teaching business sustainability: From theory to practice* (pp. 18-30). Sheffield, UK: Greenleaf Publishing, pp. 25-26.

Table 2.4 **Working with the right-side focuses**

Focus	Messages that reinforce this focus	Questions to bring focus here	The positive value of focusing here	The result of overuse of this focus
Long term	● Create a vision ● Plan ahead	● What do you anticipate? ● Where are we headed? ● Where do we want to go?	● Anticipation ● Prediction ● Possibilities ● Contingencies	● Lose timely responsiveness ● Ignore pressing realities
Creative	● Take responsibility for yourself ● You can be anything you want to be	● Is there a different or better approach? ● What would you do about this situation if you had a magic wand?	● Innovation ● New ideas ● New directions	● Overlook proven processes ● Reinvent the wheel
Global	● Look at the big picture ● Let's think about the consequences of this decision	● What's best for the organization as a whole? ● How can you make a difference in the world?	● Comprehensive view ● Inclusiveness ● Value of diversity	● Idealism ● Loss of initiative or drive ● Inattention to detail
Systems	● Solving one problem almost always creates others ● "The whole is more than the sum of its parts"	● Who are the key stakeholders? ● If we take this action, what consequences can we predict?	● Divergent ● Holistic ● Finding key interrelation-ships	● Equate models to reality ● Get lost in the clouds of complexity or theory
Learning	● "Let one who is without sin cast the first stone" ● Here's another learning and growth opportunity	● What can you learn from this experience? ● How might you benefit from letting go of that grudge?	● Ease of exploration ● Seeking growth and learning	● May be taken advantage of ● Self-sacrificing ● Loss of discipline
Being	● You'll never walk alone ● Trust the process ● As ye sow, so shall ye reap	● What really matters in your life? ● What does your "higher self" say about this?	● Self-realization ● "Greater good" point of view	● Become ungrounded ● Lose touch with "mainstream"

Source: J. D. Adams. (2004). Mental models @ work: Implications for teaching sustainability. In: C. Galea (Ed.), *Teaching business sustainability: From theory to practice* (pp. 18-30). Sheffield, UK: Greenleaf Publishing, pp. 27-28.

and routing the competition at all costs, while blaming someone for the inevitable short-falls and living the insupportable myth that working hard and earning ever more money will lead to fulfillment and happiness in life.

Building versatility to ensure a sustainable future

A key concept is **degree of versatility**: What is the normal range of collective thinking across each of the dimensions? What is the comfort zone within the company? Subjec-tively at least, each of the groups that contributed to the data in Table 2.2 agreed that the versatility or comfort zones are narrow most of the time in most places.

We will see versatility in action later in this essay when we look at the sustainability efforts of two large corporations in the chemical and energy industries. The remaining material here was provided by Thomas Stewart,[8] a consultant to these two companies.

Corporate mental models: chances and challenges

Corporations provide simultaneously both the hope for and the challenge of developing a sustainable future. Corporations, by their nature, tend to be conservative in their actions, reacting slowly or even negatively to change, and avoiding new endeavors except within predefined parameters for growth and development. At the same time, they have highly effective channels for production and distribution, keen marketing and communication vehicles for promotion and sales, and powerful lobbying capabilities to protect their interests and ensure their continuation. Unfortunately, endeavors that fit within the current corporate context of growth and development probably don't often contribute to or support sustainable endeavors.

For example, changing the perspectives of business executives regarding planned obsolescence, what constitutes an acceptable rate of return on investment, or incorpo-rating externalities into the price of goods or services may not fit within a corporate strategic model. Nonetheless, these actions, conscious or unconscious, intended or unin-tended, may affect the quality of people's lives or the environment in a negative way. Creating awareness within corporations is a continuing and uphill struggle. Yet signifi-cant opportunity exists for corporations to create sustainable endeavors — in no small measure because of their pervasive influence and control of capital, resources, and peo-ple. In the modern context of proliferating multinational corporations, and the resultant global enterprises, this multiplies and expands to include the very real potential to impact the planet for good or ill, for benefit or degradation, perhaps even for life itself as we know it. The opportunities and consequences are staggering.

One reason why mission and vision statements, and their related goals and objectives (or strategies and tactics), are so important within a corporate context is that these con-structs define what an organization believes it is in business to do, what success looks like, and the steps that are necessary to get there.

As with any model for any system, there are inputs and outputs that define what that system or model can accomplish, as well as its limitations. Relating these mental mod-els to major corporations and sustainable endeavors, we find that each organization has its own unique character, or "culture," that defines what the organization is ultimately capable of doing and the extent to which it is capable of acting or reacting as conditions change. If sustainability is a high priority, then moving toward practices that ensure that what we have today will exist, for ourselves and for future generations, is critical.

---

8 Personal communication with T. Stewart, San Francisco, December 18, 2007.

Within a "green" enterprise, such as a recycling operation or a buyback center, underlying assumptions might look like "the more we return to productive use, the better our bottom line in terms of sales of recycled materials." However, this presumes that return on investment is a priority. If that's not the case, then the volume of recyclables recovered and reintroduced into productive use might be the guiding priority and the yardstick against which our performance should be evaluated. Change the criterion for success and the target changes as well.

Alternatively, if a major corporation, say an industrial operation, incorporates into its mental models "valuing a clean environment," and, at the same time, doesn't wish to create negative impacts associated with the manufacturing processes, then it might opt to decrease the use of hazardous or toxic chemicals in those processes, or choose to invest in solar panels to offset the cost of electricity and reduce its carbon footprint. At the same time, to maintain competitiveness and still do what is environmentally responsible, citizens might cooperate with lawmakers to mandate the application of "green" regulations across an industrial sector, say oil extraction and refining. That action could have the effect of both creating a more sustainable environment and, at the same time, restricting competition to those corporations able to afford the cost of those regulations. Doing good can also mean doing well.

Yet the current pressure to expand without limits, which many have seen as a driving force behind globalization and the proliferation of multinational corporations, can be both a blessing and a curse. As a blessing, it exists within a corporation as the potential to apply best business practices to assure diversity and reduce discrimination, or it may be the use of best available control technology to reduce the magnitude and frequency of industrial incidents. However, it may also lead to one country's exploiting another's resources — including human resources — to fill its own needs because regulations are less rigorously enforced in one area and labor is cheaper and less organized.

The emerging global economy is also a global community in which globalization exists for the benefit of people who, in the past, might have been cut off from one another and exploited.

Chemical companies case overview: a community awakens

A chemical manufacturing plant and a petrochemical refinery, both San Francisco Bay Area facilities of multinational corporations, change in response to communities, both local and national.

Background

No one knows who the first person was to utter the phrase "knowledge is power." Few would dispute that what we are able to conceive can open up or, alternatively, limit what we are able to do subsequently. In the years since the first Earth Day (April, 1970), as people have witnessed such notable industrial incidents as Union Carbide's killing thousands and injuring many more in a chemical release (1984) in Bhopal, India, and the *Exxon Valdez* despoiling the waters of Prince William Sound off the coast of Alaska (1989), people have come to view industrial operations with suspicion and distrust, at a minimum, and often with outright fear.

Changing conditions: new conditions erode old mental models

Two companies operating chemical and refinery facilities in the San Francisco Bay Area initially opposed but subsequently embraced the realities of such conditions as global warming, species extinction, and climate change and recognized them as factors to be addressed now in their operations. These changes have not been easy to launch, and their magnitude and pervasiveness evolved over time, as new mental models emerged.

Before the first Earth Day, industrial operations and related activities in these two companies existed as a sort of preemptive right to operate, without consideration for the communities or the environment in which these industrial facilities existed. In those days, the companies allowed their facility managers to operate essentially without oversight at the corporate level. "Profits at any cost" may not have been explicitly espoused, but it was certainly the norm.

This mental model began to erode as incidents multiplied, both globally and locally, impacting communities and resulting in damage claims against these corporations to the tune of hundreds of millions of dollars. The "hands-off" approach clearly was having unwanted effects. These claims eventually got the attention of shareholders and of management at the highest levels. They recognized that something needed to change. At the national and international levels, major incidents drew the attention of the media and both the courts of public opinion and of jurisprudence began to swing decidedly away from corporations and in favor of people and the environment.

Industrial corporations in the Bay Area began to be viewed as an evil: blighting their communities, they were seen as villains and interlopers. A post-Bhopal survey conducted by the then Chemical Manufacturing Association (CMA) showed that people did not distinguish between chemicals: sodium chloride (table salt) was judged to be just as harmful as sulfuric acid. Juries, regulators, and elected officials throughout the area became increasingly unsympathetic to the frequency and impact of industrial incidents.

Grassroots organizations proliferated in the region in which these companies were operating and were able to litigate on behalf of communities, further contributing to a change in mental models that had existed since the industrial revolution. More significant still, the acceptance of the implied right of these facilities to continue to operate in these communities began to erode. People called for them to shut down.

Industry responds

Industry responded nationally and locally. At the national level, CMA instituted its Responsible Care initiative which included best practices review, risk assessment, the use of best available technology, emergency preparedness and response, and community interaction, among other initiatives. At the local level, county government introduced the first of its kind Industrial Safety Ordinance (ISO) which tied land use, a power vested at the local level, to enhanced safety reviews prior to any change in processing or facility expansion.

All these factors contributed to transforming the previous mental models from an unassailable, and ultimately unsustainable, prescriptive right to operate into a new and revolutionary concept first articulated by management in the county where the two companies operated. The facility managers and staff began to accept the fact that their companies only operate within the ongoing authority and approval granted by the communities in which they existed, an authority that, unlike a right, could be taken away depending on performance and, more recently, on the communities' perception of their value.

New mental models arise

These changes were fed up the corporate ladder and became manifest as changes in the corporate mental models of what constitutes a safe and sustainable relationship between a community and the industry that operates within it, with frequency and magnitude of incidents being the determining factors.

While not fully recognized at the time, other changes were occurring in the mental models. Specifically, because of the public's unwillingness or inability to distinguish a "good" (incident-free) facility from a "bad" (incident-ridden) facility, all were presumed guilty until proven innocent. The demonstration of innocence emerged as industries became more visible within their host communities, contrasted with the previous priority on invisibility and lack of interaction.

Expectations regarding the roles of the plant managers began to shift as well; no longer would they simply be responsible for the operations of the facility, they would also serve as the primary focus and representative of the corporation within that community. A new skill set was demanded of managers, most of whom were chemical engineers. These expectations became codified in the mission and vision statements, both locally and at the corporate level, and individual and collective bonuses became tied to safe and incident-free operation.

Change persists, in the community and in the corporations

This level of engagement has expanded over the years to the extent that a host community is regularly informed of its host industry's safety performance through public reports and ongoing engagement by means of community advisory panels (CAPs) or councils. Corporations and industrial facilities throughout the Bay Area regularly and routinely communicate with, and seek input from, their host communities regarding how that industry can contribute to that community's sustainability.

Key learnings

What has caused this "sea change" in perspective and in the mental models that support it, which one also sees emerging in corporations?

Corporations are people too. Industry is not unaware or unconcerned about the growing inability of the planet to sustain life as we know it. Corporations, like individuals, wish to survive and, if possible, prosper. Those same perspectives appear within corporations in areas such as supporting diversity, respect for others, sensitivity to the environment, increasing emphasis on renewable sources of energy and products, and so on.

When communities self-empower, miracles can happen. The San Francisco Bay Area communities that are host to the two chemical corporations discussed here took ownership of their neighborhoods, with lasting, far-reaching results. Within communities, because of the Internet and the pervasive accessibility of knowledge, a violation in one community can be challenged in another to prevent the same thing from occurring in that community.

Authentic dialogue leads to accepted solutions. The overarching objective must be to establish effective, meaningful, and ongoing vehicles for authentic dialogue that leads to mutually beneficial and generally supported solutions. In the aftermath of 9/11, the county community warning system, paid for by industry to communicate with residents in the event of an industrial incident, has been evaluated as an "all hazard" system capable of notifying large numbers of people following a fire, earthquake, abduction, or other perceived threat. Through ongoing dialogue and interaction, the needs and priorities of communities can be addressed; and the mental models of what constitutes sustainability within those communities constructed and implemented.

Effective resolutions involve all. Solutions that incorporate *everyone* who has a stake in the issue and its resolution, to the extent that such is feasible, make everyone an *owner* of the success of the undertaking.

Lasting outcomes

One of the outcomes observed at the local level is community members standing up and opposing those they see as merely self-serving or as self-aggrandizing interlopers. Another outcome is the growth of trust through communication, which has resulted in a more connected and informed industry, better able to direct its community philanthropy. Believed to be a necessary cost of doing business, directing funds within a community where it will do the most good — after input from community members — leads to more sustainable communities.

Industries have become major advocates for an increased focus on vocational careers, recognizing that not everyone is going to go to a university and that existing highly paid employees in industry need to be replaced with local residents as the workforce ages. These local residents will, in turn, advocate for what they believe to be in the best interest of their communities and, this too, directly impacts the sustainability of these communities.

Conclusion

If one looks for problems, problems seem to abound. Likewise, if one looks for enemies, they will appear at every turn. Alternatively, if one looks for friends and solutions to the challenges faced by communities, in areas such as education, the environment, even in industry, these will likewise be found. Be it global or local, sustainability benefits from models that incorporate rather than isolate and that promote involvement, not exclusion. We are a social species, and are most content when we act in concert with others, most satisfied when we are helping others, and any model of a sustainable endeavor must incorporate these components.

■ Cultivating mental models that support sustainability in a technically oriented organization

Linda M. Kelley

This case study is about a program that prepares systems engineers to be leaders. To be the versatile leaders this organization requires, these engineers need to have mental models that are inclusive, global, creative, and promote learning. Technically oriented individuals who were assessed to have considerable potential were invited to participate in a special mentoring program. The sponsoring government agency recognized that it needed future leaders whose vision transcended the boundary of any specific project. My partners and I crafted a program to develop leaders who would understand the details — technical and nontechnical — of a variety of projects, see how those fit into the overall picture, and communicate effectively. The goal was to make these changes rapidly with lasting results.

This agency's mission is to pioneer the future and expand knowledge about the Earth, its solar system, and the universe. Its scientists and engineers pursue basic research and innovative technological development, much of which is transferred to the public domain. Work done by this agency has made possible significant advances in the fields of health and medicine, transportation, computer technology, and environmental management, and has greatly increased scientists' understanding of greenhouse effects on the Earth.

Background

Mental models constitute a personal operating system, complete with boundaries of perceptions, which structures the way a person thinks, feels, and acts. They persist because a person exercises supporting neural pathways and muscular tensions again and again. These habit patterns confine people to predictable ways of thinking and acting. In order to shift a mental model, it is necessary to change the related habit patterns.

Might the difficulties people encounter while trying to change be due primarily to the approaches they are using to make those changes?

For the most part, people approach major changes by talking about the problems and possible fixes. As important as they are, words are seldom enough to effect major changes in how a person operates.

Words symbolically re-present mental images from past experiences. According to the neuroscientist Antonio Damasio (1999, p. 318), these images are mental patterns constructed using our sensory modalities: "visual, auditory, olfactory, gustatory and somatosensory." These mental images revive associated neural networks from dormant states. When the desired change has similarities to a person's previous experiences, he or she may draw on these correspondences. When the changes are outside the realm of past experiences, there are no associated ways of thinking, feeling, and moving to revive. The person has to develop new networks of supporting neural pathways. No wonder substantive change seems so hard to achieve.

What could a person do differently to make intentional change both achievable and enduring? Richard Feynman, talking with Freeman Dyson about Einstein's process of genius, provides some insights (Gleick, 1992, p. 244):

> Feynman said to Dyson . . . that Einstein's great work had sprung from physical intuition and when Einstein stopped creating it was because "he stopped thinking in concrete physical images and became a manipulator of equations." Intuition was not just visual but also auditory and kinesthetic. Those who watched Feynman in moments of intense concentration came away with a strong, even disturbing sense of the physicality of the process, as though his brain did not stop at the gray matter but extended through every muscle in his body.

When asked to describe his thinking processes, Einstein said they included elements that were visual and muscular, without words (Gleick, 1992). He described his thoughts as image entities that could be voluntarily reproduced and combined so he could play with them. For Einstein, according to Gleick, these thoughts-before-thoughts were visual and muscular in nature. Conventional words or signs weren't present until he arrived at a second stage of thinking, and even then he found it difficult to create logical constructs in conventional words to communicate his thoughts.

The process of communication appears to be consistent with what Einstein reported about his mode of thinking. According to research, less than 10% of what we convey comes from the words we say; 90% comes through our vocal and nonverbal presentation (Mehrabian, 1971). It is not surprising then that attempting change by verbal approaches alone leaves a gap between knowing *what* to do and actually being able to do it. Including the nonverbal dimensions dramatically increases the likelihood that a person will *be* the change he or she wants.

This leadership mentoring program integrates thinking, feeling, and moving — both verbal and nonverbal aspects — to produce change.

> Rather than something packed inside a solitary skull, [the mind] is a dynamic entity defined by its transactions with the rest of the world . . . Just as gold's value derives not from its composition but from public agreement, the essence of thought is not its isolated neural basis, but its social use. (Brothers, 1997, p. 146)

Leadership mentoring program case study

> You are the first organization you must master.
>
> *Stuart Heller*[9]

A core part of this program was to help to change the meaning and the mental model of "systems engineer" from "someone who is an expert at everything" to someone who gains the respect of the project teams and adds value by asking good and sometimes difficult questions that further the agency's overall purpose. Through effective communication including voicing the needs and concerns of many projects, the engineer-leaders are able to clarify agency-wide issues, develop a common understanding, and work out meaningful solutions to critical problems. A key to the success of this program was that the engineer-leaders develop the confidence to take leadership roles without having project authority. Many projects in this government agency span years, so engineers typically stay teamed for a long time. During this program, the participants were removed from their regular project groups and assigned to other groups for six months at a time.

At the end of each rotation, the participants presented the program advisory board with what they learned and shared their ideas about how projects could work differently and more effectively.

The cases shared here are examples of work with individual engineers in cross-functional, mid-level leadership positions. We held an initial three-day intensive workshop to lay out the basic principles and provide the program participants with strategies, models, and core practices they can use to produce rapid and real self-retooling. During the following six months, monthly group sessions were held in which participants learned to use their new tools effectively in real-time simulations. Additionally, each participant had private workouts addressing personal goals.

The technology we used, illustrated in *Retooling on the Run: Real Change for Leaders with No Time* (Heller & Surrenda, 1994), is designed to produce rapid and real acquisition of essential leadership qualities and competencies by facilitating *extraordinary learning* in ordinary states.

Leadership mentoring program: cases

Case 1. Scope of attention: local vs. global — a long shot comes in first

Assessment
This lead mechanical engineer had already proven she had the technical skills to be a top-rated systems engineer, but she was not perceived as decisive. Being relationship-oriented, it was easy for her to see expanding fields of overlapping details. Her challenge was to pull details together into a single, contained focus.

---

9 Personal communication with S. Heller, Boston, January 1990.

Goal

She wanted to be seen as calm, solid, decisive, and authoritative, and be able to hold a vision of the big picture.

Prescriptive practices (T)(L)

We coached this engineer helping her to better balance the details and the greater whole, to strengthen her ability to make decisions, and to make these changes an integral part of who she is. Her combination of exercises dramatically changed how she felt and was perceived by others. Since she was a doodler, this woman was shown that she could focus by intentionally drawing a square, then a second, then a third, placing each over the previous one. At the same time, she was to consciously keep her feet on the ground — legs uncrossed — and sit slightly forward in her chair.

Results

Although less qualified on paper, this engineer applied for a senior systems engineering position with high visibility. The way she presented herself and handled the difficult "human systems" questions during her interview was a key factor in the decision to hire her. She impressed all the interviewers with her poise, knowledge, and leadership qualities. The panelists who knew her before she entered the mentorship program said they were impressed by how dramatically she had matured in such a short time.

Case 2. Focus of response: reactive vs. creative — from intimidation to effective communication

Assessment

This tall, male systems engineer and technical administrator is passionate about his work. He is also a hockey player, competitive and willing to go to the edge to accomplish his goals. Typically, he stood with his feet firmly planted on floor, leaning slightly forward and looked intimidating. Colleagues found him threatening and felt he invaded their space, physically and intellectually.

Goal

He wanted to be able to recognize when he was scaring someone. Once aware that his manner was not working, he wanted to be able to shift his attitude, style, and stance so he would be more effective and successful.

Prescriptive practices

The coaching exercises helped him recognize when he was entering a high-intensity state. He practiced shifting his position and personal center of gravity, moderating his presence without burying his passion.

Results

Now each time he finds people are no longer listening to what he is saying, he can shift, and then shift again, demonstrating versatility and inviting other people to be included, yet doing it in such a way that he isn't letting go of his intention to achieve his goals. He became a project manager. An ongoing exercise for him is "winning without fighting," in which he lets people's reactions move him, and then drops into an appropriate stance, as he does in hockey, but does not hold any position beyond its time.

Case 3. Prevailing logic: either/or vs. both–and — more effective power and real control

Assessment
This experienced systems engineer joined the program both to become more effective and to better control himself when confronting conflict. He had a habit of holding himself back, especially in situations of impending conflict. He maintained a wall between "being nice" and "being powerful," and he had no stops between "in control" and "going berserk."

Goal
He wanted to be well considered, perceived as gentle yet powerful and in control during conflict.

Prescriptive practices
This man was coached through conflict simulations using Filipino martial arts Escrima practice sticks. At first he shredded the padded covers with his forceful attack and the strength of his hits. But with practice, he found states between "being nice" and "going berserk" in which versatility of response can emerge.

Results
He learned to express himself calmly and clearly with power and control. To accomplish his goal, he learned to reframe his negative characterization of "slow." Drawing on an analogy from fluid mechanics — when a tube is wide, the liquid moves slower, and when the tube narrows, that same liquid moves faster — he was able to use the familiar language of physics to help him make changes in his personal operating system. He no longer judges fast responses to be "better" or slow responses to be "worse." Now, he can employ the response that best fits any situation. He is now a mentor for the next group of participants.

More than two years into this coaching program, the careers of all participants have advanced more quickly than had been expected, and faster than they had done in the past.

Cultivating versatility and the capacity for change: key points for mental models of sustainability

- There is no real separation between the technical and the human. The unifier is the indivisible body–mind whole

- The way a person moves through life can be seen in the way he or she moves through space. By working with how he or she moves through space, a person can change how he or she moves through life

What a person is able to do depends on *where* the person is, *who* the person is at the time, and *where* he or she wants to go. Through the use of the language of movement, achieving lasting change is wholly consistent with the strategies of nature. Nature is inherently versatile. By paying attention to how nature works, and working with habits rather than fighting against them, people can make changes that endure.

Human nature is not a machine to be built after a model, and set to do exactly the work prescribed for it, but a tree, which requires to grow and develop itself on all sides, according to the tendency of the inward forces which make it a living thing.

John Stuart Mill (1859/1997, Chapter III, Section 4)

The heart of the technical leadership mentoring challenge

. . . for the first time ever, our enemies are no longer outside us. We're quite well suited to battles with foreign powers, evil corporations or heartless states. But now we face many challenges where the enemy is us — our desires and our myopias may be what stand in the way of survival.

Geoff Mulgan (2006, p. 34)

Sustainability requires the ability to harmonize situational leadership with principled leadership. Leadership is learned in action. New mental models are built in action. Fostering respect and trust among people, and engaging them to work toward a common goal, happens in action.

A mental model includes both internal focus and external vision. Well before acting, a person focuses attention either outward toward the external situation — people and events — or inward toward principles and values.

Additionally, people rarely have access to their best thinking when they need it. The way of thinking required to build a spacecraft recognizes that change is a process that involves coordinated interactions among many different functions and organizations. However, when it comes to making personal changes, this process is often ignored. Albert Einstein (Gleick, 1992) said that one's job is to make things as simple as possible — but no simpler. In shifting mental models, there are important differences between the simple and the simplistic approaches.

Typical model for change[10]

$$I \longrightarrow R$$

The simplistic equation, **Intention** drives **Results**, is the way most people try to effect change. Because it leaves out the *process* of change and accomplishment, this approach lends itself to swings between excitement and the depression that dashed expectations generates.

Including the change factors

The successful application of situational leadership depends on the leader's ability to see, listen, and adapt to what is actually going on. Therefore, it is necessary to add **Responsiveness** shapes **Results**.

When designing a spacecraft or technical instrument system, engineers build in feedback mechanisms to connect the control systems with the sensor systems. The next factor to add is: **Intention** and **Responsiveness** influence each other.

The final factor, and the one that makes the greatest difference, is: **Habits** bias everything. Habits link together thoughts and actions so one can

---

10   All figures on pages 75-76 copyright 2007, Stuart Heller and Linda M. Kelley. Used with permission.

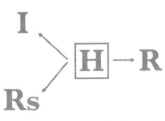

accomplish often-repeated tasks without thinking. Unrecognized habits, however, are the enemy of change because by nature they maintain the status quo. "All of the learning that led to one kind of success becomes implicitly coded and works against your ability to unlearn. The challenge then becomes how to uncover those deeply ingrained assumptions" (John Seely Brown [1999, p. 85]).

To change is to go through a process of keeping what is important, letting go of what is no longer needed, and adding what is now required. Although this may seem obvious, people often skip the step of letting go of what is no longer needed.

Holding on to habits beyond their time sabotages change initiatives and pulls people back into old behaviors — even when they have the best of intentions. Results suffer without alignment between intention and habit.

1. Intention drives results

2. Responsiveness shapes results

3. Intention and responsiveness influence each other

4. Habits bias everything

5. The interactions between these factors — intention, responsiveness, and habits — generate results

Change process: results model

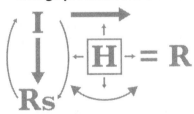

From a systems view, the optimal solution for any particular situation is also optimal for the system as a whole. "Think globally, act locally" is more than a slogan.[11] It must be the operational framework for acting as well as thinking. This attitude encourages breadth along with the depth essential for sustainability.

Models of sustainability are inclusive, holistic systems in which each aspect influences and is influenced by every other aspect (Fig. 2.1). As Bruce Mau (2004, p. 129) said when defining integrated systems, "When everything is connected to everything else, for better or for worse, everything matters."

Versatility, essential to long-term success and sustainability, is a both–and mindset that includes being able to hold a vision of the big picture that transcends specific projects or circumstances *and* the detailed view required to drill down through the particulars by asking pointed questions. These abilities, required of systems engineers, are also essential to leadership for sustainable enterprises.

Human beings are integrated, complex, living systems. At their best, people are incredible learning systems who have the ability to purposefully shift styles, modes, and

11 This phrase was coined by David Brower when he founded Friends of the Earth in 1969.

Figure 2.1 **Versatility within a sustainable whole**

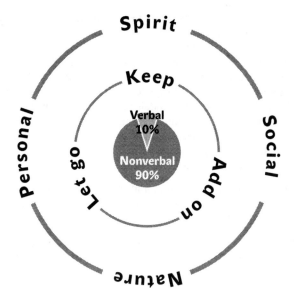

methods as appropriate to cultivate the versatility, strength, resilience, perception, and inspiration required for sustainability even when situations are unknown and unknowable in advance. People who grasp this can adjust their own mental models and help others to adapt, invent, and succeed under changed and changing circumstances.

These stories give a small taste of what is possible when mental models are shifted, by letting go of what is no longer important and including new possibilities for thinking, feeling, and moving. Sustainability is a process of release, growth, and nurture. With much at stake for individuals, enterprises, and the viability of the planet, people need inclusive, bold, generative mental models that support sustainability.

■ Mental models in civil society

Beth Applegate

On the path to sustainability, enterprise leaders and staff will encounter situations in which formerly successful ways just don't work. If the leaders take a good look they will usually find that employees on all levels have numerous transferable skills and competencies that the organization may have missed. Often, important qualities are dismissed — discouraging talented people from taking on tasks outside their job descriptions — because the dominant mental models in the organization precluded them. When mental models of inclusion and respect predominate, however, people are seen as skilled and versatile, and they offer to help. They step up to challenges because they believe that who they are, what they know, and what they can do matters — and that their help will be appreciated. The journey to sustainability accelerates when people at all levels of an organization participate.

This is a case study about changing fundamental mental models in order to develop and implement a "culturally competent" strategic plan — that is, a strategic plan for building relationships, without dominance, that lead to just outcomes and accountability. The leadership of a progressive, advocacy-model-based civil rights organization proposed a new mental model to bring the organization into alignment with its mission.

The transformation in thinking that propelled this change was based on a framework for assessing and working with mental models presented by John Adams earlier in this chapter. Adams identifies six dimensions that reinforce the status quo, forestalling the journey toward cultural respect, inclusive community, and sustainability.

The board and staff leadership explicitly chose to engage in a culturally competent strategic planning process that required them to:

- Reexamine their core values, vision, and mission, and develop new five-year goals viewed through a systemic lens of power, privilege, and oppression by the full board and staff

- Own, analyze, and share openly, knowledgeably, and compassionately both thoughts and feelings about the intersection of systemic privilege, power, and oppression in the organization as well as the different and overlapping individual cultural biases

- Strive to build a community of inclusion

Mental models: the personal is political

Worldviews and personal belief systems are shaped by mental models that filter information and limit a person's capacity to understand the workings of the world. Like values, these models have many sources, including religion, race, age, gender expression, sexual orientation, class, and culture. All people subconsciously carry a repertoire of mental models that determine what they see, the interpretations they make, and the conclusions they draw about everything (Senge, Kleiner, Roberts, Ross, & Smith, 1994).

These mental models shape and give meaning to reality. Most of them function outside people's awareness, and researchers and practitioners have only begun to realize the importance of learning how to bring mental models to consciousness and then to make intentional choices about whether to believe their meanings (Klein, 2001).

Just as mental models frame an individual's personal worldview, organizational mental models frame the way an institution values its core competencies. Even within an organization, people can use the same words to describe their objectives, but, if they hold conflicting mental models, it is difficult to reach common understanding. For the organization to succeed with a culturally competent strategic planning process, each board and staff member needed to reflect on and perhaps change her or his mental model of what an organization that advocates for equality and justice is. Each had to take a new look at the organization's policies, practices, and programs, and future strategic goals.

To help the board and staff bring to the surface their mental models of privilege and oppression, exposing hierarchical relationships as well as hidden advantages and penalties embedded in the system, tools based in systems theory and action research were introduced. Participants were also coached to reveal and shift mental models of white domination visited on people of color and indigenous peoples.

One goal throughout the process was to raise consciousness about operative mental models that impede the movement to sustainability. Another goal was to help participants reflect on and discuss mental models that shaped their current worldview regarding equality and justice. Together we helped them test whether those mental models were congruent with the programs, policies, actions, and behavior of the organization as a whole.

Revealing and changing mental models

The group used a variety of exercises to reveal prevailing mental models. Adams's six dimensions model presented earlier in this chapter helped us explore the versatility of the mental models of the organization and its stakeholders, better understand the organization's comfort zone, and identify which mental models needed to be reframed. This process resulted in demonstrable changes in the participants' personal and organizational mental models.

Aligning mental models with organizational mission: cases

Case 1. Timeframe: short-term vs. long-term

Assessment
The organization's day-to-day activities had increased significantly over the past few years and staffing levels had increased, but infrastructure planning lagged behind. The organization was operating without approved strategic or operational plans. Because longer-term strategic aspirations had not been established, nor had medium-term plans been developed or the required resources identified, staff were constantly struggling to meet existing fundraising, program, and policy commitments — and were not able to engage in the long-term thinking and acting necessary to create a sustainable organization.

Change goal
From the beginning of the process, the goal we developed with the leaders was to close the gap between the organization's focus on the implementation of its short-term mandate and the need to engage in a strategic planning process for the long term.

Tools and exercises
"Fixes that backfire" is an exercise from *The Fifth Discipline Fieldbook* (Senge et al., 1994, pp. 125-129). We shared the story below (Senge et al., 1994, pp. 125-129) and then adopted a series of questions to raise awareness of and to reveal the prevailing mental models about time.

> How many times have you heard the saying, "The squeaky wheel gets the oil?" Whoever or whatever makes the most "noise" will often grab our attention. Now imagine someone who knows nothing at all about mechanics — and who, told hastily to grab oil, mistakenly picks up a can of water and splashes it on the wheel. With great relief, she'll hear the squeaking stop. But after a brief time, it will return more loudly as the air and water join forces to rust the joint. Once again, before doing anything else, she rushes to "fix" the problem — reaching for the can of water again, because it worked the last time.

Often, although people are aware of the longer-term negative consequences of applying a quick fix, the desire to immediately alleviate pain is more powerful than consideration of delayed negative effects. But the relief is temporary, and the symptom returns, often worse than before; unintended consequences snowball over a period of time, continuing to accumulate as the expedient solution is repeatedly applied.

Reflection questions:

- How does the "fixes" story help you understand the unintended consequences of focusing only on what begs for immediate attention?

- How does the story help you identify the real problems that the organization faces regarding the focus on time?

- How can you minimize the undesirable or unintended consequences created by attending primarily to short-term priorities or problems?

Outcome

Together, the board, staff, and constituent planning committee that led the 22-month internal process increased awareness of the unintended consequences of short-term fixes and made the commitment to address the real problem. According to the theory, every fix that backfires is driven by an implicit goal. By working through the questions, the group identified the root time-orientation problem the organization needed to address to move on to a strategic plan.

Case 2. Focus and response: reactive vs. creative

Assessment

This organization was hierarchical in structure, and did not allow for constructive questioning; nor did it create an environment that fostered responsibility, learning or innovation.

Change goal

We coached the leadership team members to help them understand their individual cultural biases in the context of the larger system of power, privilege, and oppression so that they could establish organizational norms that would support them in the journey toward establishing a more inclusive, respectful learning organization.

Tools and exercises

We developed an exercise, "creating common agreements," to reexamine the mental models underlying both a hierarchical structure based on positional power — the "do as you're told" culture — and the lack of individual and collective responsibility within the organization. We built on previous exercises to help the leadership team better understand their individual cultural biases within the larger societal and organizational system of power, privilege, and oppression.

Outcome

The common agreement exercise helped bring to the surface the organization's operative mental models and created a space for the leadership team members to express their values and desires. The common agreements that resulted reflected a set of culturally competent norms for the leadership team and the organization and established a foundation for creating innovative norms for the organization's future work.

Case study conclusion

Using Adam's six dimension framework to examine their mental models, the leadership team, staff, and board members became aware of the individual and collective mental models by which they were filtering information and inhibiting their understanding of how the world works, especially in relation to power, privilege, and oppression. Through the strategic planning process, the stakeholders in this nonprofit, progressive, advocacy-model-based organization acquired the awareness, confidence, and skills necessary to raise questions about decisions faced by the organization. Moreover, they became more conscious of their process of making choices, and of the importance of choosing whether to continue to believe their operative mental models or develop new ones, thus bringing their own mental models more into alignment with the values espoused by the organization.

▓ Appreciative Inquiry case study: executive MBA candidates

Theresa McNichol

Mental models, as John Adams points out earlier in this chapter, have not kept up with the increasing focus on worldwide sustainability. Nor have science, applied research, and other disciplines come close to creating the global tipping point needed for building sustainability practices into the social and business terrain of our flattened world. However, there are signs that alternatives to the deficit approach to organizational design and development are pushing their way into the mainstream.

Consider this scenario: In a strategic planning session, two facilitators take radically different approaches with their respective groups. One facilitator asks the proverbial question, "What burning problem keeps you awake at night?" The other facilitator comes at the process from a completely different direction asking, "What has been a high point for you in the life of this company, a time when you were a member of the team that not only achieved maximum results but also had a positive impact on the community in which it operated?"

In Jim Lord's recent book, *What Kind of World Do You Want? Here's How We Can Get It* (2007), from which the above questions are adapted, the author reports on the profound impact of the second question. Often people become overwhelmed in response to the first question: there are so many problems, missed opportunities, and the like. What happens in the process, however, if the focus is taken off what is defective, and instead placed on what works — and, even more important, on what makes the entire enterprise soar?

Think back to a time when an idea generated excitement and energy, a time when no one minded pulling an all-nighter and everyone was energized by the process and the camaraderie. A way to engage this sense of excitement is through **Appreciative Inquiry**, a dynamic approach being used with positive and, more often than not, transformative results. Developed in the early 1980s, Appreciative Inquiry (AI) has provided an alternative to the deficit model by focusing on assets, resulting in the uncovering of a wealth of latent talent and creativity that was just waiting to be tapped. Using AI, individuals in systems start to work beyond mere function and co-create an entity that excels.

The Appreciative Inquiry process, framework, and tools

Appreciative Inquiry, which was developed by David Cooperrider when he was a graduate student at Case Western University, Cleveland, Ohio, delves deep into the life-giving forces of a system. Instead of focusing on problems, it focuses on discovery, dream, design, and destiny (deliver). Appreciative Inquiry, as well as being a practical philosophy for aligning a person's inner and outer worlds on a day-to-day basis, is a highly adaptable process for engaging people in building the kinds of organization and world they want to live in. AI involves a collaborative process of uncovering what gives a system life when it is at its peak on the human, economic, and ecological levels. It creates new knowledge that ultimately contributes to the fluidity and expansiveness of organizational lifecycles.

The tools

The 4D cycle of AI comprises the tools used in this case study:

- **Discovery:** appreciating and valuing the best of "what is"

- **Dream:** envisioning "what might be"

- **Design:** dialoguing "what should be"

- **Destiny (deliver):** creating "what will be"

The framework

The framework of Appreciative Inquiry provides tools to move our concepts to the far right of the continuum in Table 2.2, in John Adams's essay "Six dimensions of mental models" presented earlier in this chapter (page 63). As Adams explains, this is the optimum zone, but a person's best thinking does not get him or her there. Instead, people get stuck in their default zone, repeating the same action over and over but expecting different outcomes. To effect change in an organization, two things need to take place:

- The field must be leveled so that information does not move only hierarchically from the top down but rather throughout the organization in all directions – circular, horizontally, vertically, and diagonally. Unlike in the "expert" model, everyone participates, so the process is both collective and collaborative

- Knowing the facts is seldom enough to move people to the right side of the continuum, so AI is used to tap the uncultivated part of thinking where insight, imagination, and innovation reside

Executive MBA candidates: case

In this case, we work with executive MBA candidates, a "cohort" of ten students and three coaches who are preparing for their third integrated course as a unit. They have been focusing on stretch goal breakthroughs in their organizations and assessing their own personal effectiveness. Here, using Appreciative Inquiry, we coach them through a long-term look at their leadership capabilities, identifying past core strengths as a way of illuminating possibilities for the future.

Discovery process

Interview is one process of discovery. Participants work together in pairs for about 30 minutes — 15 minutes to interview and 15 minutes to be interviewed. Rather than being analytical during the process, participants are to focus on emotion — what animates the speaker — and note that aspect of the story.

Participants begin by surfacing glimpses from personal experience that may inform future possibilities. To help articulate what's possible, they consciously focus on those situations that have enlivened and animated them, as it is from one's best experiences that the inspiration and confidence to aspire and act with boldness and conviction arise.

- Participants are asked to think back to a time in their careers when they experienced a peak moment, a glimpse into themselves as a level 5 leader (Collins 2001),[12] which energized them and made them feel sure this was exactly what they wanted to be doing now and forever. What about that situation made them feel that way? Who was involved and what was going on?

- In considering what each participant values most deeply, he or she is asked, "What is the most important thing your company has contributed to your life? To the lives of others? Without being humble, what do you value as your most important contribution to your work?"

Each interviewer prompts: "Tell me more . . . ," "How did that affect you?" "Why was that important to you?"

After this, the interviewers debrief, one-on-one.

Dream

Thirty minutes is allowed for participants to work on the dream section. In this part of the exercise, the original pairs come together and self-organize into two groups, still remaining in pairs. They imagine it is the year 2012 and company XYZ or ABC (depending on the group) has been featured in *Harvard Business Review* because it had just received the Geraldine R. Dodge Foundation's prestigious "Most Livable World Award."

HANDOUTS GIVEN TO MBA EXECUTIVE GROUP #1
AND MBA EXECUTIVE GROUP #2

ABC Corporation's mission is to focus leadership's and staff's unique energy, technology, manufacturing, and infrastructure capabilities to develop tomorrow's solutions, such as solar energy, hybrid locomotives, fuel cells, lower-emission aircraft engines, lighter and stronger materials, efficient lighting, and water purification technology.

XYZ Corporation, an architectural firm, specializes in four categories: residential, community design, commercial, and institutional. With its staff of architects, planners, and leaders in sustainable design, the firm helps clients worldwide craft designs for buildings and communities that embody new and enduring standards of economic, ecological, and social effectiveness.

---

12 For more on Collins's level 5 leader, see page 33 in "Nature and domains of leadership for sustainable enterprise" by Daniel F. Twomey in Chapter 1 (pages 30ff.).

A facilitator asks each participant questions that had been crafted prior to the event by the facilitators in conjunction with the sponsoring organization, such as, "What is all the excitement about?" "What type of guidance and advice are other company leaders looking to you to give them?"

Design

Each group is instructed to give form to the dream so they can articulate it to the other group. Props are provided, so the groups can describe their version of "a most livable world" in 2D, as a chart, drawing, or map; in 3D as a small-scale model; or on stage, as a collaboratively conceived performance or skit.

Destiny (Deliver)

It is not enough to have a dream or a vision if it is not paired with a plan for delivery. The fourth stage of the Appreciative Inquiry framework stimulates action so that participants leave firmly intending to take the first step toward making the dream become a reality. One approach is "constructing the provocative proposition" (see Figs. 2.2 and 2.3), coined and described by David Cooperrider (2002) in *Tips for Crafting Provocative Propositions*.

Provocative proposition
The participants crafted a provocative proposition (**A**)(**T**) designed to encapsulate themes that each group identified from their interviews. Group #1 (ABC Corporation) identified a pattern of words that began with the letter C: *Communities, Connectiveness, Contagious courage,* and *Continuous learning.* Group #2 (XYZ Corporation) recognized three themes that surfaced in their interviews: the vision to see beyond the task at hand; the passion that an individual of integrity brings to his or her work; and the empowering engendered by a safe creative workspace imbued with vision and passion.

The provocative proposition reads:

> ABC and XYZ corporations will collaborate so that together they can create the kind of world they want to see in the future. By combining human capital locally and globally, they will enhance the intellectual and economic vitality of their enterprises. In addition, they will contribute to a new economic framework based on the vision of a more equitable distribution of goods worldwide.

Case conclusion

The participants reflected on the right-side focuses of Adams's six dimensions of mental models (see Table 2.4 on page 65), particularly those in column 4, "The positive value of focusing here." They agreed that the AI component had imbued them with a sense of anticipation rich with possibilities, but that to bring these possibilities into reality they had to adhere to their conscious commitment to collaboration — and to Adams's "right-side focuses," long term instead of short term, global rather than local, systems over separation, and the like. Information sharing, a keystone to their vision of the future, presents a risk, but they determined it is worth taking given the likelihood it will lead to innovation and new ideas.

With a blueprint for the future, the members of the cohort determined that, when they returned to their organizations, in addition to following time-honored leadership traditions, they would strive to realize their vision of a more livable world of the future.

Figure 2.2 **Criteria for good propositions**

→ Is it **provocative** . . . does it stretch, challenge, or interrupt?

→ Is it **grounded** . . . are there examples that illustrate the ideal as real possibility?

→ Is it **desired** . . . if it could be fully actualized would the organization want it? Do you want it as a preferred future?

→ Is it stated in **affirmative** and bold terms?

→ Does it follow a social architecture approach (e.g., 7-S model, etc.)?

→ Does it expand the zone of "proximal development?"
   • Use of third party (outside appreciative eye)
   • Complemented with benchmarking data

→ Is it a high involvement process?

→ Is it used to stimulate intergenerational organizational learning?

→ Is there balanced management of: continuity, novelty, and transition?

Source: D. Cooperrider. (2002, February). Tips for crafting provocative propositions. Cleveland Heights, OH: Weatherhead School of Management, Case Western Reserve University. Retrieved July 18, 2007, from connection.cwru.edu/ai/uploads/Crafting%20prov%20propos2-02.doc. Copyright 2002, David Cooperrider. Reproduced with permission.

Figure 2.3 **Constructing provocative propositions**

A provocative proposition is a statement that bridges the best of "what is" with your own speculation or intuition of "what might be." It is provocative to the extent to which it stretches the realm of the status quo, challenges common assumptions or routines, and helps suggest real possibilities that represent desired possibilities for the organization and its people.

In many ways, constructing provocative propositions is like architecture. Your task is to create a set of propositions about the ideal organization: what would our organization look like if it were designed in every way, to maximize and preserve the topics we've chosen to study. Organizational elements or factors you may wish to include:

STRATEGY	STRUCTURES	SYSTEMS
STYLE	SHARED VALUES	SKILLS
STAKEHOLDER RELATIONS	SOCIETAL PURPOSES	STAFF

Source: D. Cooperrider. (2002, February). Tips for crafting provocative propositions. Cleveland Heights, OH: Weatherhead School of Management, Case Western Reserve University. Retrieved July 18, 2007, from connection.cwru.edu/ai/uploads/Crafting%20prov%20propos2-02.doc. Copyright 2002, David Cooperrider. Reproduced with permission.

▓ Conclusion

For all the people in these case studies, power issues surfaced: inequalities of power, overbearing power, and, especially, the fear of having less power. Transforming our ideal of leadership from that of powerful, solitary hero to that of leader who engages people to work with one another to create the values, vision and practical innovations necessary for sustainability is one of the biggest challenges enterprises face today.

Enterprises in the developed world operate primarily from mental models where prevailing logic = either/or and time orientation = short term. In combination, these position sustainability in opposition to competitive advantage and profitability. What changes would come about if the overarching mental model became both–and?

Switching from the individual level to the global or societal level, in his recent book *Capitalism at the Crossroads*, Stuart Hart (2007, pp. xxxix-xl) says:

> Global capitalism now stands at a crossroads: Without a significant change of course, the future . . . appears increasingly bleak . . . Failure to address the challenges we face — from global-scale environmental change, to mass poverty, to international terrorism — could produce catastrophe on an even grander scale than that experienced in the first half of the twentieth century: Constructively engaging these challenges thus holds the key to ensuring that capitalism continues to thrive in the coming century — to everyone's benefit . . . By creating a new more inclusive brand of capitalism, one that incorporates previously excluded voices, concerns, and interests, the corporate sector could become the catalyst for a truly sustainable form of global development — and prosper in the process. To succeed, however, corporations must learn how to open up to the world: Strategies need to take into account the entire human community of 6.5 billion, as well as the host of other species with which we share the planet.

Do your mental models, and your organization's, keep you blind to the opportunities sustainability presents? Do they maintain illusions of security while buttressing obsolete technologies, reinforcing dysfunctional attitudes, and inhibiting innovation? Or, do they enable the values, understanding, creativity, and strategies essential to adapt, invent, and lead for a sustainable future?

The late American fiction writer Philip K. Dick (1978) gave us a useful touchstone for determining what is real and what is not. He said, "Reality is that which, when you stop believing in it, doesn't go away."

Human beings are truly wondrous. As a species, humans have engaged with life in ways that have changed the world, some for better and some for worse. We have learned many skills, made our own technologies, and gone through many transformations in the process. We have not yet, however, become sustainable — nor have we established sustainable communities. This is our new frontier.

Sustainability of our world will only come about if each of us does his or her part, individually and collectively. Getting there is an iterative process in which every present step is a new beginning, informed by the past and anticipating the future. As we move ourselves and our enterprises toward sustainability, our concepts of success, rewards, satisfaction, and even what is true and real will change with us.

■ References

Adams, J. D. (2000a). Six dimensions of a sustainable consciousness. *Perspectives on Business and Global Change, 14*(2), 41-51.

Adams, J. D. (2000b). *Thinking today as if tomorrow mattered: The rise of a sustainable consciousness.* San Francisco: Eartheart Enterprises.

Adams, J. D. (2004). Mental models @ work: Implications for teaching sustainability. In C. Galea (Ed.), *Teaching business sustainability: From theory to practice* (pp. 18-30). Sheffield, UK: Greenleaf Publishing.

Adams, J. D. (2006). Building a sustainable world: A challenging OD opportunity. In B. Jones & M. Brazzel (Eds.), *Understanding organization development: Foundations and practices* (pp. 335-352). San Francisco: Pfeiffer/John Wiley.

American Management Association (AMA). (2007). *Creating a sustainable future: A global study of current trends and possibilities 2007–2017.* New York: American Management Association.

Brothers, L. (1997). *Friday's footprints: How society shapes the human mind.* New York: Oxford University Press.

Brown, L. R. (2006). *Plan B 2.0: Rescuing a planet under stress and a civilization in trouble.* New York: W. W. Norton & Company.

CNNMoney.com (2007). Money 101: Top things to know. Retrieved December 20, 2007, from money. cnn.com/magazines/moneymag/money101/lesson9.

Collins, J. (2001). *Good to great: Why some companies make the leap and others don't.* New York: HarperCollins.

Cooperrider, D. (2002). Tips for crafting provocative propositions. Cleveland Heights, OH: Weatherhead School of Management, Case Western Reserve University. Retrieved July 18, 2007, from connection.cwru.edu/ai/practice/toolsPropositionsDetail.cfm?coid=1170.

Damasio, A. (1999). *The feeling of what happens: Body and emotion in the making of consciousness.* New York: Harcourt.

Dick, P. K. (1978). How to build a universe that doesn't fall apart two days later. Retrieved November 29, 2007, from deoxy.org/pkd_how2build.htm.

Gleick, J. (1992). *Genius: The life and science of Richard Feynman.* New York: Pantheon.

Gore, A. (2006). *An inconvenient truth.* Emmaus, PA: Rodale.

Hart, S. L. (2007). *Capitalism at the crossroads: Aligning business, Earth, and humanity* (2nd ed.). Upper Saddle River, NJ: Wharton School Publishing.

Heller, S., & Surrenda, D. S. (1994). *Retooling on the run: Real change for leaders with no time.* Berkeley, CA: Frog.

HRH Prince of Wales. (2000, May). Sacredness and sustainability: A reflection on the 2000 century. BBC Reith Lectures. Retrieved August 10, 2007, from www.garynull.com/Documents/LAPIS/Sacredness.htm.

Klein, D. (with Morrow, K.). (2001). *New vision, new reality: A guide to unleashing energy, joy, and creativity in your life.* Center City, MN: Hazelden.

Lord, J. (with McAllister, P.). (2007). *What kind of world do you want? Here's how we can get it* (Prepublication honorary gift edition). Retrieved January 22, 2008, from whatkindofworld.com/ordering-the-pre-publication-honorary-gift-edition.

Mau, B. (2004). *Massive change.* London: Phaidon Press.

Mehrabian, A. (1971). *Silent messages.* Belmont, CA: Wadsworth.

Mill, J. S. (1997). *On liberty* (original work published 1859). Retrieved June 21, 2007, from www.serendipity.li/jsmill/on_liberty_chapter_3.htm.

Mulgan, G. (2006, September/October). The enemy within. *Resurgence, 238,* 34.

Packard, V. O. (1957). *The hidden persuaders.* New York: The David McKay Company.

Seely Brown, J. (1999). The art of smart. *Fast Company, 26,* 85. Retrieved July 23, 2007, from www.fastcompany.com/magazine/26/one.htm.

Senge, P. M., Kleiner, A., Roberts, C., Ross, R. B., & Smith, B. J. (1994). *The fifth discipline fieldbook: Strategies and tools for building a learning organization.* New York: Doubleday.

Toffler, A. (1970). *Future shock.* New York: Random House.

Torpy, B. (2007, December 5). Lots of stories in storage, and business is booming. *Dallas Fort Worth Star-Telegram.* Retrieved December 20, 2007, from www.star-telegram.com/business/story/337563.html.

Vanderbilt, T. (2005). Self-storage nation. *Slate Magazine.* Retrieved December 20, 2007, from www.slate.com/id/2122832.

Wirtenberg, J., Harmon, J., Russell, W. G., & Fairfield, K. D. (2007). HR's role in building a sustainable enterprise: Insights from some of the world's best companies. *Human Resource Planning, 30*(1), 10-20.

Zweig, C., & Abrams, J. (1991). *Meeting the shadow.* Los Angeles: Jeremy P. Tarcher.

3

Developing a sustainability strategy

Joel Harmon, Flynn Bucy, Susan Nickbarg,
Govi Rao, and Jeana Wirtenberg

> The roots of the problem — explosive population growth and rapid eco-
> nomic development in the emerging economies — are political and social
> issues that exceed the mandate and the capabilities of any corporation. At
> the same time, corporations are the only organizations with the resources,
> the technology, the global reach, and, ultimately, the motivation to achieve
> sustainability.
>
> *Stuart Hart* (1997, p. 250)

Earlier chapters have defined sustainability, introduced some of the forces driving it, and discussed the types of mindset and leadership critical to achieving it. Clearly, sustainability is not reached in a single great leap but rather is best viewed as a never-ending journey. Recall from the introductory chapter that *making sustainability central to an organization's overall strategy* appears to be a foundational quality for creating a sustainable enterprise (Wirtenberg, Harmon, Russell, & Fairfield, 2007; American Management Association [AMA], 2007). A coherent strategic framework for sustainability is like a compass for the journey, providing direction and serving to coordinate all the organization's activities that must contribute to its overall sustainability. An executive from a company rated very highly for its sustainability said, "For us sustainability *is* business. This is business stuff; it's not something that sits outside" (Wirtenberg et al., 2007, p. 14). Even though the company recently went through severe profit challenges and laid off a significant number of senior people, the executive reported, "I never had even the most hard-edged analyst ask me, 'Oh, by the way, when are you guys going to stop monkeying around with the sustainability stuff and pay attention to your margins?' "

However, AMA (2007) survey respondents rated the *importance* of strategic centrality to building a sustainable enterprise significantly higher (mean of 4.1 out of 5) than they did the *extent* to which they believed sustainability was in fact central to their own organization's strategy (a mean of only 3.2 out of 5). Thus, there is considerable room for improvement in closing the gap between perceived importance and actual practice when it comes to integrating sustainability into a company's core strategies.

The purpose of this chapter is to help leaders and change agents better understand *how to craft and implement a sustainability strategy for their enterprise.* For most organizations this will involve reshaping the nature and goals of their existing strategy as well as changing the way they go about developing and executing it. But exactly what is a good sustainability strategy for any particular organization; what are the key elements it should contain? And what is the best way to execute a sustainability strategy in a particular unit or throughout the organization; are there unique or especially difficult implementation challenges that need to be managed carefully?

The majority of the chapter focuses on the content and process of developing a sustainability strategy. We begin by briefly examining the core elements of *any* good strategic management process and move to the question of what is different about a good *sustainability* strategy. We then review some of the evidence linking corporate sustainability to performance and provide some examples of the myriad ways that actual organizations in diverse situations are using sustainability initiatives to improve their standing. Finally, as a framework for binding together the chapters that precede and follow, we lay out a **strategy formulation process model** that integrates elements particularly critical to developing and implementing sustainability strategies such as leadership, employee engagement, broad stakeholder involvement, transorganizational collaboration, resources, and metrics

The nature of strategic management

Viewed through a *strategic management lens*, a good strategy for sustainability must first and foremost be a fundamentally sound strategy for achieving relative advantages over other organizations, lest the enterprise not survive (Porter & Kramer, 2006). This applies to any type of organization, whether a corporation that strives for market share and profitability or a NGO (nongovernmental organization) that strives for clients and funding support. Thus, from this perspective, a good sustainability strategy essentially represents an enhancement of a solid basic strategic management process.

The strategic management process

Figure 3.1 visualizes the essential elements of the strategic management process. In essence, a successful strategy is one that positions the organization so as to create an alignment or "fit" between its inside and outside worlds at any point in time. One aspect involves taking an "outside-in" perspective, analyzing the general and industry-specific forces in the organization's external environment to discern opportunities and threats.[1] Another aspect involves taking an "inside-out" perspective, analyzing the organization's value chain, resources, and capabilities to discern its own "core competencies": what can it do to create value that is relatively rare among its rivals and hard for them to imi-

---

1 Students of strategy will recognize this perspective as grounded in neo-Darwinian theories of population ecology and industrial ecosystems; see, for example, Aldrich (1979).

Figure 3.1 **Strategic management: alignment of organization–strategy–environment**

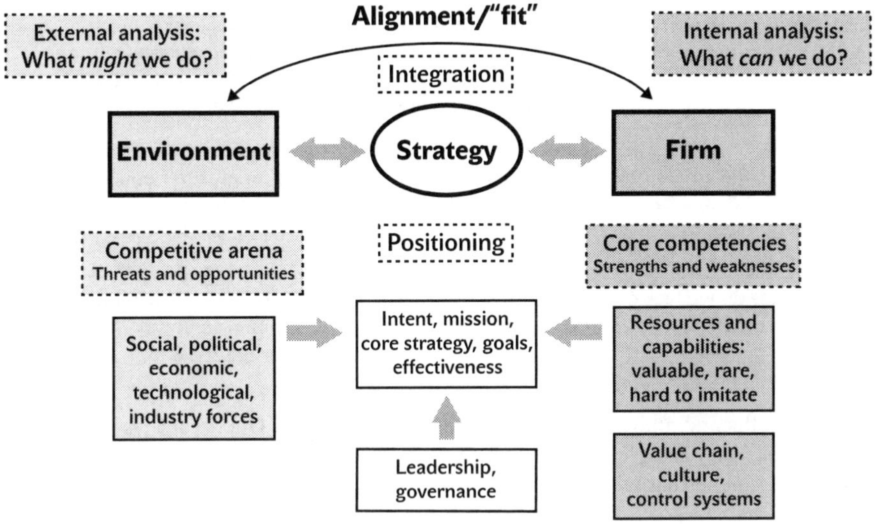

Source: Copyright 2008, J. Harmon. Used with permission.

tate easily?[2] A wise strategy adopts a mission and goals that continually position the organization favorably in the outside world and that guide the creation and re-creation of the competencies necessary to succeed there in a sustainable manner.

It is useful at this point to distinguish two interrelated sets of strategic management activities. The first set, which initially is our main focus here, involves *formulating* (or developing) the direction and content of a strategy: mission and goals. The second set involves *executing* a strategy: the numerous activities that an organization needs to engage in to implement its strategy, which we will focus on later in the chapter. It is important to recognize the back-and-forth and emergent nature of the strategy formulation–execution process (Mintzberg, 1978). Although implementation plans initially derive from strategic intent/content/direction, the strategy itself is informed and shaped by the challenges and results of implementation. Put simply, an organization tries to adopt approaches to the world that it believes will create success but adjusts its intentions according to realities encountered along the way. That is why top executives are not the only ones who have a critical leadership role to play in developing strategies for the complex, rapidly changing, 21st-century global economy. People at all levels, especially those who work at the organization's boundaries with customers, suppliers, regulators, and community groups, often can make powerful contributions to shaping and modifying their organization's strategy.

Finally, for *strategic action-planning* purposes, it is useful to introduce the notion of a "SWOT" analysis as shown in Table 3.1. Strategic management is often pragmatically defined as the pattern of management actions to accomplish mission and goals by lever-

2 Students of strategy will recognize this perspective as grounded in resource-based theories of the firm; see, for example, Barney (1991) and Prahalad and Hamel (1990).

Table 3.1 **A generic SWOT framework for strategic analysis and action planning**

	Opportunities What conditions in the outside world could we really take advantage of?	**Threats/risks** What conditions in the outside world might really hurt us?
Strengths What things do we do really well or possess that have great value?	How can we leverage our strengths to exploit these opportunities?	How can we leverage these strengths to neutralize or minimize these threats/risks?
Weaknesses What things do we lack or do very poorly?	How can we address these weaknesses to exploit these opportunities?	How can we address these weaknesses to neutralize or minimize these threats/risks?

aging **S**trengths and addressing **W**eaknesses to capitalize on **O**pportunities and counter **T**hreats (see, for example, any good basic strategic management text, such as Hill & Jones, 2007). Note that when done well a SWOT analysis requires an organization to:

- Scan and make sense of both the broad and the industry-specific dynamics that to some extent drive its behaviors and results

- Assess the organization both for valuable resources and capabilities and for areas of relative weakness

Distilling this analysis (which would go into the gray cells of Table 3.1) provides the strategic framework for formulating actions (the white cells of Table 3.1).

▓ The nature of sustainability strategies

Viewed through a *sustainability lens*, a sound, well-aligned organizational strategy for the 21st century, interdependent, global economy must be green and socially responsible if it is to succeed in the moderate to long term. Sustainability is in its simplest terms about how to do well now without destroying the ability to do well in the future (i.e., it is bifocal in being able to see both close-up *and* further away).[3] It's also about taking a well-rounded approach to making personal, governmental, and business decisions that put environmental awareness and social responsibility on a par with sound economics. This is also referred to as the **triple bottom line**. One can see these multiple elements in a business-oriented definition of sustainability as: "a company's ability to achieve its business goals and increase long-term shareholder value by integrating economic, environmental and social opportunities into its business strategies" (*Profiles in leadership*, 2001, slide 1). Similarly, according to the Dow Jones Sustainability Index:[4]

---

3 Note that this short- and long-term time-orientation is discussed in depth in Chapter 2, and in particular is incorporated into the framework described in John Adams's essay (pages 60ff.).

4 Personal communication with C. Wais at Dow Jones Sustainability Index, telephone interview, May 9, 2008.

Corporate Sustainability is a business approach that creates long-term shareholder value by embracing opportunities and managing risks deriving from economic, environmental and social developments. Corporate sustainability leaders achieve long-term shareholder value by gearing their strategies and management to harness the market's potential for sustainability products and services while at the same time successfully reducing and avoiding sustainability costs and risks.

Note in this definition the articulation of sustainability into essentially a SWOT framework, accounting for the opportunities and risks arising from business–society interdependences.[5]

The three interrelated domains that together comprise sustainability – economic/financial, social/governance, and environmental stewardship – are depicted in Figure 3.2. Within each of these domains are a number of areas in which the policies and practices of an organization across its entire value chain can have both short-term and longer-term impacts for the organization and society.

Figure 3.2 **Total sustainability management model**

Source: Copyright 2008, J. F. Bucy. Adapted with permission.

5 In his comprehensive guide to sustainability, Blackburn (2007, p. 201) presents a sample SWOT analysis specifically focused on a broad range of sustainability-related issues.

■ A shifting strategic context for sustainability

An online search showed that, in 2006 and 2007 alone, thousands of books and articles appeared on various aspects of societal and corporate sustainability. Special issues were devoted to the topic by such respected mainstream publications as *The Economist, Business Week, Fast Company*, and *Fortune*. What is driving this attention to sustainability? Perhaps it is that:

● One can't turn on the television or pick up a newspaper or magazine without hearing about climate change, human rights abuses, health epidemics, starvation, government corruption, and terrorism

● It has become hard to ignore the possibility that we are doing irreversible harm to our natural environment which threatens to extinguish many species of both plants and animals; to shift where and how well we live, how we get our water and grow our food; and to disrupt the critical resource supply chains of many industries

● We see that wasteful use of energy from fossil fuels not only degrades our environment but increases our dependence on sources of energy from the most unstable areas of the world

● We realize that, in an interconnected, 21st-century, global economy, social problems that arise from almost anywhere threaten the ability of people and businesses everywhere to flourish: no person, business or country is immune

But why are governmental and nongovernmental agencies looking to the business community to drive solutions to sustainability dilemmas and, perhaps more interestingly, why are they responding? Georg Kell, who heads the UN Global Compact, a world consortium of several thousand businesses and NGOs, has stressed that global agencies need to speak the language of business if they hope to enroll businesses in the sustainability journey. He appeals to business leaders by saying, "In an increasingly interconnected world, social, environmental and governance issues are no longer just 'soft' business concerns but are increasingly becoming material for long-term viability . . . because helping to build social and environment pillars makes the global marketplace stronger" (Wirtenberg & Harmon, 2006, p. 1). Ray Anderson, the sustainability pioneer who heads Interface Inc. and was the surprise hero of the movie *The Corporation*, maintains that it is only through the power of business that the world can make significant progress toward sustainability. He said,

> Business and industry, together the largest, wealthiest, most powerful, most pervasive institution on Earth, and the one doing the most damage, must take the lead in directing Earth away from the route it is on toward the abyss of man-made collapse. (Anderson, 1998, p. 43)

■ The strategic logic or business case for the sustainable enterprise

It appears that many businesses are responding to the call for them to develop sustainability strategies as much because of the "business case" as because of their sense of citizenship. Sustainability is now "right at the top of the agendas" of more US CEOs, especially young ones, says McKinsey Global Institute Chairman Lenny Mendonca (Engardio, 2007, p. 52). Leading firms are seeing that an integrated "triple bottom line" (i.e., people, planet, profits) that balances attention to employees, society, and the environment with financial outcomes is critical not only to the world's sustainability, but also to their own long-term viability in the global marketplace.

An editorial in *The Economist* (June 2006, p. 2) argued that:

> the criticism that climate change has no more place in corporate board-rooms than do discussions of other partisan political issues is surely wrong . . . Most of the corporate converts say they are acting not out of some vague sense of social responsibility but because climate change creates real business risks and opportunities. And although these concerns vary hugely from one company to the next, few firms can be sure of remaining unaffected.

Sunny Misser, PricewaterhouseCoopers' global leader of sustainable business solutions, said,

> Sustainability has moved from the fringes of the business world to the top of the agenda for shareholders, employees, regulators, and customers . . . Any miscalculation of issues related to sustainability can have serious repercussions on how the world judges a company and values its shares. (Harmon, 2006, slide 5)

According to Patrick Cescau, group CEO of Unilever, there is an "increasing awareness within business itself that many of the big social and environmental challenges of our age, once seen as obstacles to progress, have become opportunities for innovation and business development." He went on to note that:

> developing and emerging markets will be the main source of growth for many multinational companies in the years to come, [it already counts for 40% of Unilever's sales and most of its growth] and those that make a positive contribution to economic development and poverty reduction in these countries will be better placed to grow than those that do not. (Engardio, 2007, p. 52)

Drawing from the works of numerous authors who have written about various aspects of the triple bottom line (see, for example, Adams & Zutshi, 2004; Prahalad & Hart, 2002; Esty & Winston, 2006; Hitchcock & Willard, 2006; Savitz, 2006), the potential organizational benefits of sustainability can be summarized as:

- Greater employee engagement
- Better recruitment and retention of talent
- Increased employee productivity
- Reduced operating expenses
- Reduced risk/easier financing
- Increased innovation (in both processes and new products)
- Increased revenue/market share (in existing and particularly in new markets)
- Increased social/reputational capital

■ Doing well by doing good: the sustainability advantage

As noted in the Introduction, evidence is accumulating that corporate social-environmental performance may be linked to financial and marketplace success, and corporate directors and the investment community are getting tuned in to the degree to which firms are managed sustainably. As they do, serious money is lining up behind the sustainability agenda. Assets of mutual funds that are designed to invest in companies meeting social responsibility criteria have swelled and institutions with trillions in assets, including charitable trusts and government pension funds in Europe and states such as California, pledge to weigh sustainability factors in investment decisions. Jean Frijns, Chief Investment Officer of ABP Netherlands (the largest pension fund in the world) said,

> There is a growing body of evidence that companies which manage environmental, social, and governance risks most effectively tend to deliver better risk-adjusted financial performance than their industry peers. Moreover, all three of these sets of issues are likely to have an even greater impact on companies' competitiveness and financial performance in the future. (Eggink, 2006, p. 24)

Rising investor demand for information on sustainability has spurred a flood of new research, both in the academic community and in the major brokerages that have formed dedicated teams assessing how companies are affected by everything from climate change and social pressures in emerging markets to governance records. Innovest, Dow Jones Sustainability Index, Smith Barney, and others have designed new sets of metrics to quantify the quality of a company's strategy and management and its performance in dealing with opportunities and risks deriving from economic, environmental, and social developments, and they are using these metrics to identify and select leading companies for investment purposes (see Chapter 6 for more details on these metrics).

An example of the findings from Innovest is shown in Figure 3.3.[6] The chart compares the market performance from 1996 to 2005 of firms in the automotive sector that scored in the top and bottom halves, respectively, on one of its sustainability indices. As can be seen, firms in the top half outperformed those in the bottom half by 50% over this period. Innovest has reported similar patterns for a variety of other sectors, including utilities, telecommunications, and pharmaceuticals.

Another example shown in Figure 3.4 compares the market performance of firms that are members of the Dow Jones Sustainability Index (DJSI) (which requires firms to meet certain sustainability standards) with that of the general market from 1993 to 2005.[7] As can be seen, DJSI firms outperformed the market by about 30% over that period.

A report released by Goldman Sachs (Goldman Sachs Group, 2007) showed that those energy, mining, steel, food, beverages, and media companies considered as leaders in implementing environmental, social, and governance policies outperformed both the general stock market and their peers since August 2005.

---

6 Innovest rating methods include nontraditional drivers of risk and shareholder value such as companies' performance on social, environmental, and strategic governance issues. Further information can be found at www.innovestgroup.com (accessed January 24, 2008).

7 www.sustainability-indexes.com.

Figure 3.3 **Automotive sector correlation to share price performance (Innovest EcoValue Index)**

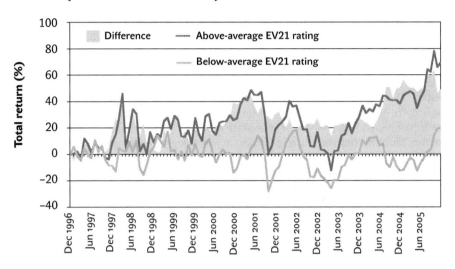

Source: Copyright 2007, Innovest Strategic Value Advisors. Reproduced with permission.

Figure 3.4 **Market performance of Dow Jones Sustainability Index firms vs. general market (US$, total return index)**

Note: The MSCI is a stock market index used in Europe, equivalent to the S&P.

Source: Copyright 2006, Dow Jones Sustainability Index. Reproduced with permission.

Although results such as those noted above are beginning to convince CEOs and boards that profitability and sustainability can go hand in hand, some words of caution are warranted. Quantifying sustainability performance is a tricky business and the indices of Dow Jones, Goldman Sachs, Innovest, and others are still works in progress. In addition, neither the DJSI nor GS sustainability opportunity reviews/analyst recommendations are proactive; both are specifically designed to assist investors to "pick" the few stocks with the best sustainability-driven return on investment. They make no attempt at raising capital markets overall to a level where all companies are efficient and sustainable. Further, although one academic study looking across much of the emerging empirical research affirmed the linkage between corporate social-environmental performance and financial and marketplace success (Orlitsky, Schmidt, & Rynes, 2003), another failed to confirm this relationship across a slightly different set of studies (Margolis & Walsh, 2003).

Nevertheless, it is worth noting that the statistics linking sustainability to performance were achieved even though the current market does not explicitly recognize external costs and benefits related to an enterprise's more sustainable performance. As resources become more scarce (and expensive) and external ecosystem-service values (i.e., climate change) become more internalized or at least appreciated by shareholders, the stock performance gaps between good and bad sustainability performers may well widen even further.

■ The progression toward integrated sustainability strategies

The journey to corporate sustainability can be viewed as a progression of stages (**A**)(**L**) and steps toward meeting societal expectations (Willard, 2005, pp. 26-27; Hitchcock & Willard, 2006). The earliest stages are compliance-driven, with a focus on reputable business practices (e.g., laws, regulations, contracts). In midpoint stages, organizations move beyond mere compliance to concerns for customer expectations (e.g., quality) and employee needs (e.g., health, safety, quality of work life). Advanced stages are characterized by a more integrated strategic approach infused with purpose and passion and marked by environmental stewardship and deep concerns for community needs. Some early adopters of advanced-stage sustainability qualities were founded on social-environmental ethical principles and have it in their "DNA." It is simply how they operate: what they do and have always done (see Unilever sidebar on page 102, and Eileen Fisher case in Chapter 5, pages 152ff.). Others reaching this stage have experienced a transformational breakthrough (see Interface sidebar on page 101) or have progressed more gradually (for example, see Nike sidebar on pages 112ff.).

Results from the AMA 2007 survey suggest that most organizations are well below the more advanced stages of the sustainability journey. Respondents were asked what sustainability-related factors appeared to be driving their organization's decisions (**A**)(**L**). As shown in Table 3.2, the only items that were rated above 3.5 (on a 5-point scale) were those relating to marketplace (customer), workforce (employee), and stakeholder (shareholder/investor/regulator) issues. Issues relating to environmental stewardship, human rights and migration, and collaborating with a broad range of other stakeholders (e.g., suppliers, communities) appeared to be receiving more modest attention.

Porter and Kramer argue in their award-winning 2006 *Harvard Business Review* article that a strategy of *"corporate social integration"* (2006, p. 92) — the most advanced

Table 3.2 **Sustainability-related factors driving organizations' decisions**

On a scale of 1–5, to what extent does each of the following items drive key business decisions for your company today?

Types of issues	Today	
	Rank	*Mean*
Workforce issues		
Ensuring our workers' health and safety wherever we operate	1	4.2
Increasing workforce productivity	2	4.1
Attracting and retaining diverse top talent	3	4.0
Improving employee morale, engagement, and commitment	4	3.9
Addressing challenges of healthcare systems and reducing healthcare costs	5	3.8
Environmental and operational issues		
Increasing security for our employees, customers, and the communities in which we operate	1	3.6
Enhancing operational efficiency through energy and waste reduction	2	3.5
Marketplace issues		
Effectively addressing regulatory restrictions wherever we operate	1	4.0
Enhancing innovation for competitive advantage	2	4.0
Providing products and services that are good for the world	3	3.8
Enhancing current customer satisfaction and loyalty through sustainability initiatives	4	3.6
Attracting new customers and developing new markets through sustainability initiatives	5	3.6
Stakeholder issues		
Improving our reputation/brand image with shareholders and the public	1	4.1
Meeting expectations of investors and lenders	2	4.0

Note: Mean responses on a 5-point scale, where 1 = not at all and 5 = to a very great extent.

Source: American Management Association (AMA). (2007). *Creating a sustainable future: A global study of current trends and possibilities 2007-2017.*. New York: AMA, p. 65. Copyright 2007, American Management Association. Adapted with permission.

stage of the sustainability journey — will become increasingly important to competitive success. Applying to sustainability strategy the inside-out and outside-in aspects of strategic alignment that were introduced earlier in the chapter, they note that the interdependence between business and society takes two forms: "inside-out linkages" in which company operations impact society, and "outside-in linkages" in which external societal forces impact companies (2006, p. 84). Looking outside-in requires a company to understand the social-environmental influences in its competitive context that affect its ability to improve productivity and execute strategy. Looking inside-out requires a firm to map the social-environmental impact of its value chain. Because no business can solve all of society's problems, each company must prioritize issues that intersect the most with its particular business, because that will provide the greatest opportunity to leverage the firm's resources — and benefit society. In short, they assert that the strongest mutual business–societal impact comes from applying corporate strategic thinking to both leverage positive social and environmental benefits and mitigate negative social and environmental impacts in ways that enhance competitive advantage (Baue, 2007).

Reflecting this view, Gene Kahn, vice president of sustainable development at General Mills, told SocialFunds.com:

> We can make a larger societal contribution through activities that are intimately tied to our business activities. I believe that the integration of CSR into business strategy is the only approach that will result in achieving true social and environmental sustainability. (Baue, 2007, p. 1)

■ The unique and varied nature of sustainability strategies

There is no one-size-fits-all approach to sustainability. Rather, as Porter and Kramer (2006) noted, sustainability strategies need to take many different shapes and forms, depending on the unique interrelationship between a specific organization and society, and the unique social, environmental, and economic opportunities that result from that interrelationship. Thus it should not be surprising that organizations are introducing green and socially responsible practices in a wide variety of ways according to the unique strategic opportunities and risks that confront them.

According to the Dow Jones Sustainability Index,[6] leading sustainability companies display high levels of competency in addressing global and industry challenges in a variety of areas:

- **Strategy.** Integrating long-term economic, environmental, and social aspects in their business strategies while maintaining global competitiveness and brand reputation

- **Financial.** Meeting shareholders' demands for sound financial returns, long-term economic growth, open communication, and transparent financial accounting

8 Personal communication with C. Wais at Dow Jones Sustainability Index, telephone interview, May 9, 2008.

● **Customer and product.** Fostering loyalty by investing in customer relationship management and product and service innovation that focuses on technologies and systems, which use financial, natural, and social resources in an efficient, effective, and economic manner over the long term

● **Governance and stakeholder.** Setting the highest standards of corporate governance and stakeholder engagement, including corporate codes of conduct and public reporting

● **Human.** Managing human resources to maintain workforce capabilities and employee satisfaction through best-in-class organizational learning and knowledge management practices, and remuneration and benefit programs

These strategic competencies, the notions of inside-out- and outside-in-driven strategy, and the SWOT principles of leveraging strengths and addressing weaknesses to capitalize on opportunities and counter threats can all be seen in the examples shown in the sidebars on the following pages (101-114).

Interface (**C**) (see sidebar below) is perhaps one of the best examples of a company with a deeply embedded inside-out-driven, highly integrated sustainability strategy. In his book *Mid-Course Correction* (Anderson, 1998), chairman Ray Anderson describes how, while researching for a speech to some of his employees on sustainability (a subject he knew virtually nothing about at the time), he came to have an epiphany: *he was*

INTERFACE INC.

Interface Inc. is a pioneer in the area of corporate sustainability and has situated sustainability at the center of the company's corporate strategy. One of the largest carpet and interior furnishings businesses, Interface has become a showcase for sustainability and triple-bottom-line practices, according to the AMA sustainability survey (2007). It has saved more than US$300 million since 1994, and founder, chairman, and CEO Ray Anderson is determined that Interface will save US$80 million per year when the company reaches its goal of zero waste. "Our goal is to take nothing from the earth by 2020," said Anderson (quoted in Newman, 2006).

One of the innovative ways in which Anderson tries to transform the corporate world is by reaching out to other business leaders. Clearly, his company's savings are an attractor to others who have been leery about moving in this direction.

Among the numerous initiatives Interface has established to move it closer to its future goal of zero waste, benign emissions, and renewable energy, are programs for cutting waste, emissions, and energy use now. In its journey, the company's practices span all aspects of the business: people (customers, employees, suppliers, community, management); product (design, packaging, manufacturing, marketing, purchasing); and place (facility and operations).

Interface has halved its total carbon dioxide emissions within a decade through a number of "cool" initiatives. Customers can choose to offset all emissions, from the extraction of raw materials to manufacture, transport, and use of their carpet, through tree planting and renewable energy projects in Canada, New Zealand, and the United States.

UNILEVER

Unilever's group CEO, Patrick Cescau, is a strong advocate of assisting developing nations, and he embraces the notion that this is tied to the company's strength in the marketplace and fiscal well-being. According to Engardio (2007, p. 52), Cescau sees the importance of "helping such nations wrestle with poverty, water scarcity, and the effects of climate change as vital to staying competitive in the coming decades."

The company promotes its soap and detergent in an impoverished area of São Paolo, Brazil, by running a free community laundry. In that same country, Unilever supports tomato growers' efforts to adopt environmentally friendly irrigation systems by contributing financially to the program. In addition, at a toothpaste factory, it focuses on recycling waste.

In Ghana, Unilever brings potable water to communities in need and teaches people how to reuse waste.

So that poor women in Bangladesh can buy soap and water, and to help ensure their future, Unilever helps them start micro-businesses. It also sponsors a floating hospital in that country.

In response to green activists, the company discloses how much hazardous waste and carbon dioxide its factories release worldwide. As environmental regulations grow tighter around the world, Unilever believes it must invest in green technologies or its leadership in packaged foods, soaps, and other goods could be imperiled.

Unilever's efforts in these areas have profited not only the people in developing nations but the company itself. About 40% of the company's revenue now comes from developing countries, as does much of its growth.

---

plundering the Earth. Since then, he has become a relentless, passionate, and eloquent champion for sustainability values and practices, both in his own firm and throughout industry. As described in the sidebar, Interface has been at the vanguard of sustainability among US firms, literally transforming its value chain activities and capabilities through a variety of process and product innovations (turning weaknesses into strengths) to realize efficiencies and minimize negative environmental externalities. These efforts have translated into enormous cost savings, goodwill, and market and profit growth; Interface is now number one in its industry.

Unilever (C) (see sidebar above) is a good example of a company in whose strategy both the inside-out and outside-in dynamics appear to be at work. A leading, global, consumer goods firm, Unilever was founded on values consistent with sustainability — deep inside-out concerns for the communities in which it operates, such as addressing endemic poverty. Confronted also with the outside-in threat of market saturation in its established markets, it is striving to position itself for new growth opportunities in emerging markets. As it does so, the company appears to be rethinking its product development processes and strengthening its capabilities to engage local communities in capacity and market-building activities.

Philips Electronics (C) (see sidebar opposite) is another fine example of a company that appears to have an advanced-stage sustainability strategy that integrates inside-out and outside-in considerations to build a strong corporate strategy around global mega-

PHILIPS ELECTRONICS

Responding to trends predicting that, by 2050, 85% of people will live in developing nations with acute shortages of healthcare, Philips Electronics is developing special medical vans that will allow urban doctors to reach remote villages to diagnose and treat patients via satellite. It has also developed low-cost water-purification technology and a smokeless wood-burning stove that could reduce the 1.6 million deaths annually worldwide from pulmonary diseases linked to cooking smoke. In perhaps its most striking move, Philips recently announced that it will abandon its leading incandescent lighting business in favor of more energy-efficient compact fluorescent, and eventually LED lighting (Engardio, 2007).

trends. Social and environmental responsibility has been in the firm's DNA since its founding over a hundred years ago. "For us, sustainability is a business imperative," says Philips Chief Procurement Officer Barbara Kux, who chairs a sustainability board that includes managers from all business units (Engardio, 2007, p. 64).

In the services sector, HSBC can also be noted for its integrated sustainability strategy. It was the world's first bank to become carbon-neutral in September 2005. The bank has begun working with customers to help them reduce emissions as well.

Some firms with a generally good but mixed track record of corporate citizenship behaviors may be accelerating their sustainability strategies more from an outside-in perspective, stimulated predominantly by opportunities and threats from the external environment. For example, Sony, responding to opportunities, is an industry leader in developing energy-efficient appliances. It also now has a whole corporate infrastructure for controlling its vast supplier network, helping it avert or quickly fix problems. However, this attention to the supplier network may have arisen due to external threats. Sony has had problems with its "famously dysfunctional home electronics arm" (Engardio, 2007, p. 58): it was embarrassed by exploding laptop batteries and long delays in bringing its Playstation 3 game console to market, both problems partly caused by suppliers, and it experienced a fiasco in 2001 when its Playstation was banned in Europe just before the Christmas rush buying period because some of the wiring purchased from suppliers contained illegal cadmium (banned under pre-RoHS Dutch regulations).

It's not very surprising that companies with fairly long-standing commitments to corporate citizenship, such as Alcoa, Citigroup, Coca-Cola, Dow, Goldman Sachs, HSBC, HP, Intel, Johnson & Johnson, Kodak, Philips, Sony, and Unilever, should be given top ratings for their sustainability initiatives by independent rating agencies such as Dow Jones, Innovest, and the Global Reporting Initiative (see Chapter 6 on metrics for more detail on these indices). But when huge and profoundly influential organizations such as General Electric and Wal-Mart (**A**)(**L**) — never reputed for their citizenship behaviors — make major strategic commitments to social/environmental sustainability, many skeptics start to take notice.

General Electric (**C**) (see sidebar overleaf) can be viewed as an example of a company whose approach appears to be consistent with a mid-stage, outside-in-driven sustainability strategy primarily seeking to maximize profit and market share. GE is a market leader in a variety of sectors partly based on a core competency in technology development. Carrying the reputational damage caused by past environmental transgressions, and anticipating a changing landscape of environmental regulations (e.g., it

---

GENERAL ELECTRIC

GE has taken the lead and embarked on a number of new initiatives to provide solutions to the world's environmental ills, such as through its Ecomagination initiative.[9] This initiative brings together products from GE's different businesses that are either intrinsically green, such as wind turbines, or have been certified as being more competitive and producing fewer emissions than equivalent products on the market.

GE's plans include significantly reducing its greenhouse gas emissions while stepping up its sales of equipment in renewable energy, efficient power generation, water purification, and so forth. GE has doubled its investment in R&D for environmental technologies to US$1.5 billion, doubled its expected sales of environmental products from US$10 billion to US$20 billion in five years, and more.[10]

GE has introduced a credit card that allows cardholders to forgo a 1% cash rebate on purchases and earmark that amount for projects that reduce greenhouse gases. Each Earth Day GE will use the total collected to buy offsets of greenhouse gas emissions. GE believes that its Ecomagination initiatives have increased sales revenue by several percentage points (*The Economist*, 2005; Kranhold, 2007).

---

is advocating for governmental regulations on carbon emissions to create opportunities it can exploit) and changing customer demand, it has embarked on a campaign — Ecomagination — opportunistically positioning itself as first mover in providing state-of-the art environmental technologies. GE is betting billions to position itself as a leading innovator in everything from wind power to hybrid engines, and has pledged to cut its greenhouse gas emissions by 2012 to 1% of 2004 levels (*The Economist*, 2005; Kranhold, 2007).

However, although *The Economist*'s 2005 special report "The Greening of General Electric" suggested that GE's newfound embrace of "greenery" is genuine (as opposed to a "greenwashing" PR ploy), it also noted two potential obstacles. First, the environmental markets GE is counting on may not materialize and, even if they do, they may not generate the kinds of profitability that GE's shareholders are used to. Second, GE's culture may not be well suited to creating the innovations and new businesses that the green strategy requires. Kranhold (2007) notes friction among some key GE executives over "customer grumbling" and concerns that Ecomagination may well slow profit growth, and that CEO Jeffrey Immelt seems willing to push GE only so far. Lacking a long tradition of inside-out sustainability values, it is unclear whether GE will stay the course if profits begin to lag.

Wal-Mart (℃) (see sidebar opposite), it seems from all available information, can also be viewed as an example of a company that has a mid-stage sustainability strategy driven mostly by outside-in considerations of external effects on its corporate strategy. Wal-Mart has mastered a cost leadership strategy based on competencies for superior operating efficiencies. Seeking to further strengthen efficiencies as well as possibly repair reputational damage from its past labor practices and impacts on communities, it has announced a series of initiatives to "green" its entire value chain. Assessing Wal-Mart's strategy in terms of the SWOT framework, the company's embracing of environ-

---

9   "Ecomagination," ge.ecomagination.com/site/index.html#press (accessed May 9, 2008).
10 This paragraph is adapted with permission from AMA (2007), p. 31.

Wal-Mart, harshly criticized for its labor and global sourcing practices, and insensitivity to its impacts on local communities, has made a series of high-profile promises to: slash energy use overall, from its stores to its vast trucking fleets (including use of energy-efficient equipment and hybrid vehicles); vastly reduce waste and harmful materials in its entire supply chain; and purchase more electricity derived from renewable sources. It has even hired renowned environmentalist Amory Lovins to be one of its top strategic advisors, and endowed a Sustainable Enterprise Foundation at the University of Arkansas. (See Chapter 5, page 145, for another example of Wal-Mart's sustainability efforts.)

mental efficiencies is building on and enhancing its low-cost strength. It also serves to mitigate its reputational risk associated with labor and community relationship weaknesses. However, as with GE, Wal-Mart may not continue to address those weaknesses to the extent that profit or market share growth is slowed.

Stronger interventions by governments, NGOs, and consumers are likely to be needed to pull these large, high-impact companies toward strategies that will enable the achievement of global sustainability.

■ The process of formulating and implementing sustainability strategy

There is little doubt that infusing green and socially responsible objectives into an organization's strategy can be a daunting task, particularly if it represents a major shift in direction. Although the particular challenges can vary widely, the process of developing a sustainability strategy appears to have several distinguishing and particularly challenging elements:

- It takes into consideration in the strategic planning process a *broad range* of short- and long-term issues

- It views these issues holistically and manages them in an integrated way

- It engages a broad array of stakeholders in the process in an *inclusive, collaborative* manner

Most fundamental will be the adoption of the kinds of mental model (discussed in Chapter 2) that embrace mutuality and systems thinking. A key mindset shift is from a focus only on the short-term, financial bottom line to one that is committed to a joined economic, social, and environmental triple bottom line. In addition, global mindsets that fully appreciate the issues of globalization discussed in Chapter 7 will be needed, especially for organizations with international operations. Leadership will be another essential aspect: not only the presence of top-level leadership most often associated with advanced sustainability strategies but also the kind of widespread, self-organizing leadership and shared control/accountability discussed in Chapter 1. Given the scope of constituencies affected by sustainability strategies, architecting participation in a spirit of trust and collaboration will be vital as well — processes that are detailed in some depth in the chapters on managing change (Chapter 4), employee engagement (Chapter 5), and building social and transorganizational networks (Chapter 8).

Clearly, any strategic sustainability initiative, whether large or small, will benefit from a sound project management structure. In that spirit, we offer a process model below as a general structure that can be adapted to any organization. However, given the fundamental nature of sustainability issues and strategies, the process is highly unlikely to be as top-down or linear as it may appear. It is essential to infuse the entire process with the qualities described above. Further, ample opportunities should be built in for interim moments of reflection that will allow for emergence and discovery along the way, and milestones should be intentionally inserted to plan for the inevitable adaptation of target state outcomes during the journey. Following the process model, we offer an integrative case study on Nike, which ties many elements of this chapter together.

Application of a universal strategy formulation process model

As identified above, there are many dimensions to sustainability as it relates to the environment, society, and economics. The seven-step universal strategy formulation process model shown in Figure 3.5 is intended to serve as a tool to address any one or all of these dimensions and identifies the basic process elements for developing and implementing any sustainability strategy.

The strategy formulation process model consists of seven elements. Each of these seven elements is designed to increase understanding of an essential aspect of the sus-

Figure 3.5 **Universal strategy formulation model**

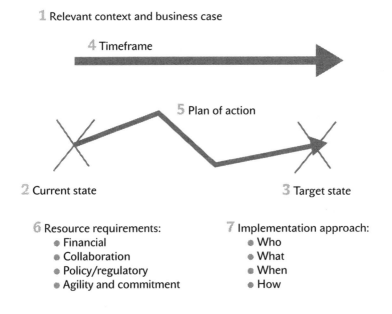

1 Relevant context and business case

4 Timeframe

5 Plan of action

2 Current state

3 Target state

6 Resource requirements:
- Financial
- Collaboration
- Policy/regulatory
- Agility and commitment

7 Implementation approach:
- Who
- What
- When
- How

Source: Copyright 2007, J. F. Bucy. Used with permission.

tainability journey and to help organize the transformation to sustainability under a variety of circumstances.

1. Relevant context and business case

Every strategy takes place within a specific *context* and set of circumstances which need to be taken into consideration. The first step in developing a strategy is to determine the relevant scope and thinking behind it. A much broader set of factors will need to be considered when trying to develop a comprehensive strategy for a global corporation (see Chapter 7) than for a single, domestically focused business unit or just one department. Similarly, the scope will be different for developing a new sustainability product, from that of developing a community engagement plan.

It is critical to understand and clearly articulate the scope of the initiative being planned. The following questions will help refine the strategy.

- What is the type of initiative being planned?
- What is the scope of the initiative?
- What are the drivers for the change?
- What are the factors that need to be considered? (Refer to the earlier SWOT discussion in this chapter)
- How will various interrelated parts of the organization system be affected?
- What are the impacts of the initiative?
- Who are the decision-makers who will need to endorse the plan?
- What is the "business case" — the benefit, or pay-off for the organization?

2. Current state

The "current state," represented by the first large X on the model (see Fig. 3.5), refers to all the facts and factors in the present situation. Effectively acknowledging the essential features of the current circumstances is a critical step in defining a strategy. This will require both an inside-out and an outside-in analysis. One of the most common mistakes made in developing any strategy is not learning enough about the current state. A full understanding of the present situation, although often difficult and time-consuming, is critical to understanding what changes need to be made to reach the desired objectives. Again, depending on the scope of your initiative, the set of factors that need to be taken into consideration can vary widely. Gathering not only the facts, but also information about organizational politics is critical.

Moreover, we note that, as of 2007, many companies are still choosing to ignore current-state realities associated with resource depletion, population increase trends, external environmental and financial costs, and so on. Ignoring these current-state facts ultimately leads to larger future costs and long-term threats to the organization's very survival.

The following questions are intended to help identify and clarify the essential features of the current situation:

- What is the current situation and system you are trying to change?
- What are the metrics that help you define the current state?

- Whose perception of the current state do you need to take into consideration?
- What are the factors outside the organization that need to be brought into focus?
- What are the impediments to making changes?

3. Target state

The other large X in the model (Fig. 3.5) represents the "target state." Just as it is often difficult to describe all the relevant issues in the current state, it is often difficult to describe exactly how things are expected to work in the desired target state. However, clarity regarding the vision, objectives, and expected outcome(s) of any strategic initiative is essential. This should include an examination in the context of the underlying mental models (see Chapter 2) as well as the metrics by which the target state will be measured (see Chapter 6). The more completely the changes required and the potential benefits derived can be described, the more likely it will be to get buy-in and support. Some specific guiding questions are:

- How will the target state of your initiative be defined?
- What would be different from the situation that exists today?
- What are the specific objectives to be accomplished?
- What benefits would accrue to the organization?

4. Setting the timeframe

Establishing a reasonable timeframe in which to make the intended changes is critical. Estimating how much calendar time will be required to move from the current state to the desired situation is difficult. You are often caught on the horns of a dilemma between how much time you want or think you need and how much time you have because of external pressures. Most strategies involve a lot of people and moving parts, so how long something will take is often not easy to control. Nevertheless, plotting the timeframe is a fundamental element of creating a strategy. An initiative usually cannot be accomplished overnight, but it is useful to consider whether it will take, say, a week, a year, three years? You want to move as quickly as possible, but need to be realistic in terms of the time it will take to make the changes planned. Some guiding questions are:

- How long do you think it will take to complete the initiative?
- What are the factors that could slow your progress?
- How quickly has your organization made similar changes in the past?
- What are the negatives to giving your initiative more time to unfold?
- What types of resource are needed and how long will it take to get them?
- How long do you have to make the changes (may be driven by governmental regulations, environmental, or market factors)?

Incorporating a sense of urgency
It is important to note that certain SWOT elements may require a greater sense of urgency and more aggressive timeline to position the company on a trajectory to a more

sustainable target state. In such cases, more weighting toward an *outside-in* SWOT prioritization may be required, especially for companies that have been less engaged in the sustainability journey.

5. Plan of action: charting a path

Like identifying all the elements of a complete strategy, charting a path is more complex than it may first appear. Laying out a solid plan requires thinking through each of a series of decisions and steps for making changes.

The model in Figure 3.5 shows a jagged line connecting the current state and the target state. This represents the set of steps, or "path," involved in making the desired change. Understanding and communicating the sequential activities that eventually lead to the anticipated outcomes requires a solid work plan and schedule, ideally using any of a number of available project management methods and software, such as PERT or Gannt charts. This involves identifying what needs to happen in a sequential fashion. Developing a solid work plan is important to getting the participation from the people who need to support the initiative.

- What are the major elements that need to be changed?

- What are the steps that each of these elements must go through if those leading/guiding the process are to accomplish the change from the current state to the target state?

- What are the key benchmarks or outcomes for each step of the process?

- How do the different elements affect each other?

6. Identifying resource requirements

An extremely wide array of things must come together to implement an action plan. The types of resource listed in Figure 3.5 include the following:

- **Financial.** Acquiring the money needed to implement the plan is always an issue, but often not the most critical one

- **Collaboration.** Getting cooperation and support from the many groups and individuals who will be affected by the proposed changes may be a primary challenge to effectively implementing a sustainability strategy. (See Chapters 4 and 8 for more extensive coverage of the processes and tactics for addressing these issues with internal and external stakeholders)

- **Policy/regulatory.** Understanding how the organizational and political landscape accelerates and empowers or impedes and slows down an initiative is imperative

- **Agility and commitment.** Key resources are human resilience, flexibility in problem solving, and the capacity of individuals to adapt and persevere in the ever-changing landscape of the journey

Independent of available external resources, the success of a sustainability venture will be largely dependent on the capacity of individuals to self-organize around issues that excite and energize them (as discussed in detail in Chapters 1, 4, and 5). Their enthusiasm is self-perpetuating; radiating outward, it will encourage others to share in the journey. The inner resources of the key champions, torchbearers, and frontline workers (see "Generating sustainability champions" opposite) can be the secret to successful strategy development; as their energy expands, others are invited to bring their ideas, abilities, and talent to the table.

The types of question to consider when identifying the needed resources for the initiative include the following:

- What specific resources are needed to execute the plan of action?
- From where will the required resources come?
- What will it take to secure those resources?

7. Implementation approach

The implementation approach is the final step in organizing your initiative and assigning responsibilities, deadlines, deliverables, and evaluation processes. It is often the failure to bring a plan down to the executable level — to map out the tasks and review processes that make up the journey — that yields an unsuccessful strategy. Although envisioning a future state is a must, creating a solid implementation approach is just as important, including specifics as to who will be expected to do what by when.

- How will you organize your initiative?
- How will your approach be communicated to the set of people that need to participate?
- What are the critical hurdles that need to be overcome to successfully complete the initiative?

Additional key elements for successful implementation worth elaborating are:

- Making sustainability part of the leadership agenda
- Investing in education: project- and classroom-based
- Investing in communications: internal and external
- Generating sustainability champions

Making sustainability part of the leadership agenda

As with any significant change effort, the impetus and drive often start at the top. In a research survey conducted by SVN Marketing comprising 50 *Fortune* 500 companies, all representatives from each of the industry sectors — financial, pharmaceutical, financial, manufacturing, and retail — agreed, unanimously and independently, that, for sustainability to succeed in their organization, it had to be endorsed by the CEO and included in the mission statement (Nickbarg, 2005). As discussed in Chapter 1, there is much research to support the notion that a company's direction depends largely on the leader's vision and the values espoused by the company.

Investing in education: project- and classroom-based

Education is an integral part of any change management process. On the journey toward sustainability, education is critical. Developing new mental models require un-learning for some and re-learning for others, an area that companies have just begun to uncover as a key to changing their "DNA." Further, managers and leaders in organizations need to acquire specific sets of new tools for the sustainability journey. It is wise to leverage project-based education that is relevant to the stakeholder/employee's role and job. Supplementing this with classroom seminars will reinforce the journey while providing people with the necessary tools.

Investing in communication: internal and external

Communication is integral to understanding, team building, perception, and accountability through the entire value chain of an organization. Managers and leaders need to have a sustainability communications approach embedded into their strategy so employees, shareholders, and all outside stakeholders (vendors, suppliers, NGOs, communities, and the like) are being connected with the same understandings and can give and receive input into goals, metrics, and processes.

Generating sustainability champions

In order to internalize a sustainability strategy, the organization must often explicitly charge specific individuals with developing, overseeing, and coordinating the sustainability or corporate social responsibility (CSR, sometimes shortened to CR) function more formally so that it ties to the core organizational or business strategy. It is becoming increasingly necessary to set up a sustainability staff whose function is to more directly embed the sustainability initiatives into, and align them with, the operating strategy to ensure the long-term sustainability of the enterprise (see Nike case below).

Establishing a tiered approach that involves structuring a champion, a torchbearer, and frontline worker at each level of the organization usually makes for the best chance of integrating sustainability practices successfully. Embarking on a mission to push the business into heightened sustainability strategies, processes, and outcomes takes a coordinated effort.

For a company to sign up for sustainability often means a change in trajectory, which includes increasing receptivity and establishing a form of engagement in which all stakeholders interact with the organization (see Chapters 4 and 5). It means recognizing sustainability as a formal organizational function as well as an outcome — one that must be incorporated into every facet of the business if the company is going to do more than pay lip-service and actually achieve results (see Nike case below).

The ideal case is a champion at the board of directors and C-suite level (vice presidents and above), a torchbearer who is a titled chief responsibility or sustainability officer, and frontline workers and managers in each organizational unit, with positions such as sustainability environmental officer or sustainability communications manager, among others, depending on the type and size of the organization. A sustainability structure can be centralized, decentralized, or a hybrid model that is at once both centralized and decentralized.

Other chapters in this *Fieldbook* contribute a rich set of frameworks and examples regarding such key implementation aspects as leadership, mindsets, managing change, employee engagement, metrics, and transorganizational collaboration.

Integrative case: Nike

Nike seeks to differentiate itself through capabilities for high-performance athletic products and brand image. It had become a magnet for criticism over widespread child labor abuses in low-cost foreign production sites. As can be seen in the sidebar overleaf, Nike evidences progression toward the most advanced stages of sustainability strategy: a passion-driven, highly integrated approach. Building on its earlier CSR initiatives, it has formally adopted the triple-bottom-line scorecard in its core business strategy and has

NIKE

Nike is building a new approach to corporate responsibility (CR) that considers how it can harness the power of its business to influence social and environmental change and the power of that change to help its business grow. Nike is made up of many smaller business units as well as functions, regions, distinct profit and loss centers, and the like. As of 2006, its overarching goal was to see each and every business unit incorporating CR goals into its growth strategies, business scorecards, and team accountabilities. It will measure success by the extent to which businesses meet their milestones for corporate responsibility as well as business growth.

The company stated:

> CR must evolve from being seen as an unwanted cost to being recognized as an intrinsic part of a healthy business model, an investment that creates competitive advantage and helps a company achieve profitable, sustainable growth. For that to happen, we saw we needed to transition our corporate responsibility efforts beyond the standard risk and reputation management approach usually taken, beyond the work of an isolated function within the business model. We realized that effective strategies are ones that embrace the whole enterprise. Responsibly competitive outcomes result from holistic approaches and business processes that extend from factory workers to consumers, from sources of raw materials to communities where we can influence social and environmental change, from our workplace to the world we all share.
>
> An environmentally friendly product made under poor labor conditions is a hollow success. A product made under good conditions but that is bad for our planet is a missed opportunity. We don't believe in trade-offs. We do believe — passionately so — in innovating to create new and better solutions.

In 2004, Nike began an intensive, large-scale review of its strategies and long-range goals, based on four essential premises:

1. Leverage market forces and open-source approaches to problem solving recognizing that we are all part of a complex interwoven ecosystem in which no single organization can achieve systemic change alone. Partnership, collaboration, and open-source approaches that lead to sustainable market-based solutions can generate system change

2. Create the business case with a deep understanding of business growth and innovation strategies and ways to integrate corporate responsibility into those strategies

3. Seek root causes, then prototype new models rather than bandaging the symptoms. Build systemic change by looking at the overall system to identify root causes that are often buried far from where a problem surfaces

4. Listen, partner, and embrace transparency as the first step toward open-source approaches to problem solving with external stakeholders. Nike expects multistakeholder partnerships to increase in importance as it learns to work together in unusual alliances and partnerships that couple nongovernmental organizations with new industry partners, leveraging the core competencies of each

(continued opposite)

In FY05, Nike set new priorities, goals, and programs. In FY06, it implemented a redesigned, more fully integrated approach, as follows:

- Deepened business integration of responsible practice into business and decision-making processes. Nike leveraged its matrix organization structure and reorganized the various corporate responsibility functions to be managed jointly by its formal CR team and leaders across the business – from strategic planning to product creation and manufacturing through to marketing

- Ensured a leadership voice through a more formalized approach to governance and accountability in which the CR team reports into Nike's CEO and the vice president of CR sits at Nike's senior leadership table to influence the company's strategic direction

- Ensured holistic approaches by breaking down walls that existed even within the CR team – between compliance, community, and environment

- Delivered innovation-driven solutions by aligning its corporate responsibility goals to Nike's innovation and growth agenda. Nike is looking for levers in different places in the company: delivering sustainably designed product to market; testing new approaches to community investment programming that move beyond philanthropy and more into sustainable ventures; focusing less on compliance violations and more on supply chain efficiency by designing out root causes of systemic issues in the business pipeline

- Began to measure qualitative impact by taking a systematic approach to answering such difficult questions as: How would it know if a worker's experience on the contract factory floor had improved, or if its community investments helped improve a young person's life? The company is grappling, as are many others, with the challenges of assessing real, qualitative social impact. Nike was working in FY06/07 with key stakeholders to develop a simple set of agreed-upon baseline indicators and then to measure changes in sample areas around the world

- Increased understanding of its global footprint by identifying areas where it has the greatest environmental and social impact. The company sees this as essential for building a robust business case for CR and prioritizing its efforts

- Looking to the future to identify and understand the broader environmental and social trends that have potential for long-term impact on its business and where its business may have a long-term impact on the issue

- Deliver a return on investment (ROI) by embracing ROI thinking to build the business case for CR and measure the broader impact of its work. Nike has developed a unique financial formula called "ROI-squared" to measure the exponential return from integrating CR into its business as a source of growth and innovation

(continued over)

Nike realizes that these goals are ambitious. It said,

> They're challenges we've set for ourselves to take us beyond our current performance and into the way we see CR of the future: focused on root causes and requiring a unified approach deeply embedded in every part of the business.[11]

formalized an organizational structure that embeds environmental and social responsibility into operations at every level of the organization. Many key elements noted in this and other chapters of this book are evidenced in this case study, such as systems thinking, mutuality, collaboration, leadership/champions, employee engagement, decentralized yet integrated internal and external social networks, and aligned performance management systems and metrics.

Conclusion

> . . . the future is difficult to achieve, but let us take courage from the fact that the present is impossible to continue.
>
> *A. K. N. Reddy*[12]

This chapter has defined the unique qualities of sustainability strategies (above those of any good organization strategy), laid out the business case for corporate sustainability, provided examples of customized ways in which firms are pursuing a sustainability advantage, and described a seven-step model for structuring the sustainability strategy formulation and implementation process (with links to other chapters in this *Fieldbook*). Sustainability must become central to corporate strategy. Any good strategy creates a strong alignment or fit between an organization's inside and outside worlds. Dramatic, ongoing challenges of an interdependent 21st-century economy — climate change, resource depletion, energy scarcity, governmental instability, healthcare crises, poverty — are compelling organizations to adopt sustainability strategies that *integrate social, environmental, and economic issues for long- and short-term success.* The evidence linking sustainability strategies with corporate performance has been strong enough to constitute a persuasive "business case" and demand the attention of CEOs, boards, and the investment community. The fact that corporate sustainability performance has become an investable concept is crucial in driving interest and investments in sustainability to the mutual benefit of companies and investors. As this benefit circle strengthens, it will have a positive effect on the societies and economies of both the developed and developing world.

Every sustainability strategy will be unique; no one size will fit all. Each organization needs to consider outside-in linkages — the ways that social-environmental issues impact its effectiveness — and inside-out linkages — how its value-chain activities impact society. Win–win scenarios result when the unique sets of social investment that an organization makes both strengthen its particular strategy and benefit society. Our total sustainability management model (Fig. 3.2, page 93) listed key areas in which the poli-

---

11   Information and quotes in this sidebar are from Nike (2007).
12   Presentation to Rockefeller Foundation Trustees, September 14, 1992.

cies and practices of an organization across its entire value chain can have both short-term and longer-term impacts for the organization and society.

We have shown how organizations (such as Nike, Interface, Unilever, Philips, Sony, HSBC, Wal-Mart, and GE) are at various stages in the sustainability journey (ranging from early, compliance-oriented to advanced, highly integrated and passion-driven stages), and have illustrated through SWOT analysis how sustainability strategies are allowing them to leverage strengths and address weaknesses to capitalize on opportunities and neutralize threats. Further interventions by governments, NGOs, and customers appear necessary to create conditions that will accelerate progression to sustainability by the world's high-impact global corporations.

The process of developing and executing sustainability strategies is particularly challenging because of the holistic and integrated way that a very broad range of short- and long-term issues need to be considered, and the broad array of stakeholders that must be engaged in an inclusive, collaborative manner. We offered a universal model for structuring the sustainability strategy formulation and implementation process that can be custom-fit to the particular needs of any organization, and have outlined some of the approaches to maximize success, most of which are discussed further in some depth in other chapters of this *Fieldbook*. Organizations need to embrace an adaptive and emergent yet also workable and practical process to ensure that sustainability is tightly connected to and deeply embedded in the organization's vision, mission, and overall objectives. Strategic and tactical efforts must span every aspect of the organization. Keys are the commitment and stewardship of organization leaders and managers to the environment and the community, and collaborative engagement with the broadest range of internal and external stakeholders.

Sustainability is a long-term, ongoing process of evolution that can continue to enhance the strength and viability of companies, and the world, for years to come; which is after all what sustainability is all about. As Unilever's group CEO Patrick Cescau said in an interview with *Business Week* (Engardio, 2007, p. 52):

> You can't ignore the impact your company has on the community and the environment. CEOs used to frame thoughts like these in the context of moral responsibility, but now, it's also about growth and innovation. In the future, it will be the only way we do business.

▨ References

Adams, C., & Zutshi, A. (2004, November). Corporate social responsibility: Why business should act responsibly and be accountable. *Australian Accounting Review.* Retrieved June 23, 2007, from www.mei.monash.edu.au.

Aldrich, H. (1979). *Organizations and environments.* Englewood Cliffs, NJ: Prentice Hall.

American Management Association (AMA). (2007). *Creating a sustainable future: A global study of current trends and possibilities 2007–2017.* New York: American Management Association.

Anderson, R. (1998). *Mid-course correction.* White River Junction, VT: Chelsea Green.

Barney, J. B. (1991). Company resources and sustained competitive advantage. *Journal of Management, 17,* 99-120.

Baue, B. (2007, April 10). Porter and Kramer Framework melding CSR with business strategy wins Harvard award. *Sustainability Investment News.* Retrieved April 15, 2008, from www.socialfunds.com/news/article.cgi/2268.html.

Blackburn, W. R. (2007). *The sustainability handbook.* Washington, DC: Environmental Law Institute.

The Economist. (2005, December 10). Special report: The greening of General Electric. *The Economist.* Retrieved February 7, 2008, from www.economist.com/displaystory.cfm?story_id=5278338.

The Economist. (2006, June 10). Can business be cool? Companies and climate change. *The Economist, 379*(8481). Retrieved February 7, 2008, from www.economist.com/business/displaystory.cfm?story_id=7037026.

Eggink, J. (2006). *Managing energy costs.* Lilburn, GA: Fairmont Press.

Engardio, P. (2007, January 29). Beyond the green corporation. *Business Week*, pp. 50-64.

Esty, D. C., & Winston, A. S. (2006). *Green to gold.* New Haven, CT: Yale University Press.

Goldman Sachs Group Inc. (2007, June 22). *GS Sustain.* New York: The Goldman Sachs Group.

Harmon, J. (2006, November). Corporate sustainability: Social and environmental responsibility for sustained economic/financial prosperity. PowerPoint presentation to ISE Advisory Board, Madison, NJ.

Hart, S. (1997). From global citizenship to sustainable development. In N. M. Tichy, A. R. McGill, & L. St. Clair (Eds.), *Corporate global citizenship: Doing business in the public eye* (pp. 249-259). San Francisco: The New Lexington Press.

Hill, C. W., & Jones, G. R. (2007). *Strategic management* (7th ed.). Boston, MA: Houghton Mifflin.

Hitchcock, D., & Willard, M. (2006). *The business guide to sustainability: Practical strategies and tools for organizations.* London: Earthscan.

Kranhold, K. (2007, September 14). GE's environment push hits business realities. *Wall Street Journal*, pp. A1-A6.

Margolis, J. D., & Walsh, J. P. (2003). Misery loves companies: Rethinking social initiatives by business. *Administrative Science Quarterly, 48*, 268-305.

Mintzberg, H. (1978). Patterns in strategy formulation. *Management Science, 24*, 934-948.

Newman, R. (2006, September 16). Industrialist sees no need to kill the planet: Environmentally minded businessman speaks at FDU. *The Record*, p. A13.

Nickbarg, S. (2005). Mainstreaming corporate social responsibility survey. Unpublished report.

Nike. (2007). *Global corporate responsibility strategy report.* Retrieved January 10, 2008, from www.nikeresponsibility.com/pdfs/color/2_Nike_CRR_Strategy_C.pdf.

Orlitsky, M., Schmidt, F., & Rynes, S. (2003). Corporate social and financial performance: A meta-analysis. *Organization Studies, 24*, 403-441.

Porter, M., & Kramer, M. (2006, December). Strategy and society: The link between competitive advantage and corporate social responsibility. *Harvard Business Review*, 78-92.

Prahalad, C. K., & Hamel, G. (1990). The core competencies of the corporation. *Harvard Business Review, 68*(3), 79-93.

Prahalad, C. K., & Hart, S. (2002, 1st quarter). The fortune at the bottom of the pyramid. *Strategy + Business, 26*, 54-67. Retrieved February 3, 2008, from www.cs.berkeley.edu/~brewer/ict4b/Fortune-BoP.pdf.

Profiles in leadership. (2001, October). PowerPoint presentation given at *Symposium on Sustainability*, New York.

Savitz, A. (with Weber, K.). (2006). *The triple bottom line.* San Francisco: Jossey Bass.

Willard, B. (2005). *The next sustainability wave: Building boardroom buy-in.* Gabriola Island, BC, Canada: New Society Publishers.

Wirtenberg, J., & Harmon, J. (2006, Winter). UN Global Compact comes to Institute for Sustainable Enterprise (ISE). *ISE/CHRMS Newsletter.* Retrieved February 3, 2008, from view.fdu.edu/files/newsletwint0506.pdf.

Wirtenberg, J., Harmon, J., Russell, W. G., & Fairfield, K. D. (2007). HR's role in building a sustainable enterprise: Insights from some of the world's best companies. *Human Resource Planning, 30*(1), 10-20.

PART III

Embracing and managing change sustainably

4

Managing the change to a sustainable enterprise

Gregory S. Andriate and Alexis A. Fink

▨ Achieving sustainable enterprise in the 21st century

Just being profitable, just delivering excellent service, or just fulfilling your mission as an organization isn't enough anymore. Government, business, and social enterprises have recognized that approaching *success* as a single dimension (such as profit, or clients served) is insufficient in the new century. Sustainable organizations appreciate the value of operating in ways that ensure their capability to achieve enterprise goals and simultaneously *increase long-term shareholder value* by integrating economic, environmental, and social opportunities into their strategies (Saling & Kicherer, 2002; United Nations Industrial Development Organization, 2002). Moreover, business enterprises have discovered that competitive advantages may be captured by measuring success in terms of the triple bottom line (TBL): social equity, ecological integrity, and financial profitability.

Effecting the transformation to ecological, social, and financial sustainability requires more than adding a collection of sustainability practices and change tools to an organization. The Brundtland Commission (World Commission on Environment and Development [WCED], 1987), in a report that many consider the beginning of the global dialogue on sustainability, challenged every organization to meet the needs of the present generation in ways that are economically viable, environmentally sound, and socially equitable, and to ensure that future generations will have the resources to do the same. They recognize sustainable development as "a process of change in which the exploita-

tion of resources, the direction of investments, the orientation of technological development, and institutional change are made consistent with future as well as present
needs" (WCED, 1987, p. 25). Simply stated, sustainable development is about *meeting
today's needs without hampering future generations.*

Managing the change to sustainable enterprise

As evidenced in the results of a worldwide sustainability study conducted by a number
of authors of this book (American Management Association [AMA], 2007, pp. 24-25),[1]
many high-performing enterprises have already embraced the challenge of creating and
nurturing sustainable enterprise business practices. Not surprisingly, most organizations recognized by leading sustainability indices (such as Dow Jones Sustainability
Index, Innovest's Global 100, Domini 400 Social Index, and FTSE4Good Index Series)
have a well-established business culture that values and balances elements of economic
viability, environmental responsibility, and social equity (Assis & Elstrodt, 2007; Benson, 2007; McGraw-Hill, 2007). These enterprises have learned to deliberately and consistently pursue environmentally and socially responsible goals, balancing immediate
needs of investors and consumers without sacrificing the long-term viability of our
planet or its inhabitants (Spivey 2006). (See the sidebar "Sustainability is a good investment," overleaf.)

For such organizations, the future challenge involves emphasizing, extending, and
reinforcing core organization values to perpetuate sustainable enterprise practices. For
other organizations, the future challenge will be far greater, potentially requiring the
creation and installation of new values throughout the enterprise. In the words of one
senior executive, creating a business culture that embraces sustainable development
values may well require "fundamental changes in organizational DNA" on a global basis.

Taken together, accountability for social equity, ecological integrity, and financial
profitability form a triple bottom line measuring sustainable development practices. Our
approach to managing the change to sustainable enterprise in the 21st century is based
on six assumptions:

1. Achieving sustainable enterprise requires a fundamental shift in managing and
   measuring enterprise success via TBL metrics

2. Achieving successful performance on TBL metrics requires fundamental
   changes in traditional approaches to markets, customers, stakeholders, and
   stockholders

3. Changing traditional approaches to markets, customers, stakeholders, and
   stockholders requires driving TBL concepts into key enterprise processes and
   daily business practices and decisions

4. Driving TBL concepts into daily business decisions requires new sustainable
   enterprise values that are readily understood and embraced by decision-makers at multiple levels of the organization

5. Installing sustainable enterprise values (people, planet, and profit) often
   requires cultural transformation at all levels of the organization

---

1 See footnote 10 on page 12.

SUSTAINABILITY IS A GOOD INVESTMENT

Innovest Strategic Value Advisors, an internationally recognized investment research and advisory firm specializing in analyzing companies' performance on environmental, social, and strategic governance issues, develops sustainability-aligned investment ratings to assist financial analysts and fund managers in making better investment decisions. Its in-house system assesses the impact of nonfinancial aspects of institutional performance on competitiveness, profitability, and share price performance. Its system presumes companies embracing sustainability can help avert costly setbacks from environmental disasters, political protests, and human rights or workplace abuses. Innovest reviews environmental, social, and governance (ESG) issues that could impact long-term profitability, and documents institutional ESG strengths and weaknesses at every level of a corporate structure. Its recent review of stock performance for 263 of the world's largest banks and financial institutions reports that major banks incorporating environmental assessments as a fundamental component of the lending process consistently outperform competitors who weigh environmental concerns as only a secondary risk (Engardio, 2007).

SUSTAINABILITY-RELATED FACTORS DRIVING KEY BUSINESS DECISIONS IN THE NEXT DECADE

A recent global survey (AMA 2007) reports several findings relevant to managing the change to sustainable enterprise (see Table 4.1). First, respondents (N = 1,365) believe that sustainable enterprise values are more important to them personally than they are to the company for which they work. This suggests that increasing alignment between individual and company values would capture the minds and hearts of those working to add value to all TBL constituencies. This will, in turn, help harness the discretionary effort essential for installing a sustainable enterprise culture and successfully propelling the entire organization into the future.

A second, and perhaps more important, finding reveals that respondents expect a shift in the top three sustainability-related factors driving key business decisions over the next ten years.

This shift in the importance of "sustainability-related key business drivers" suggests that enterprises nurturing capabilities to "improve image, enhance innovation, and secure diverse top talent" are more likely to reap the benefits of sustainable enterprise than those simply installing and practicing basic TBL policies. Consequently, cultivating an enterprise culture that embraces and promotes sustainable development values is likely to create positive advantages essential for achieving and sustaining success in the 21st century. (See the Introduction for additional discussion and implications of AMA global survey for achieving sustainable enterprise in the 21st century.)

Table 4.1 **Rankings (out of 25 factors investigated) of sustainable enterprise factors driving key business decisions**

Sustainability factor	Today	10 yrs
Ensuring workers' health and safety	1	4
Increasing workforce productivity	2	5
Improving image with shareholders and public	3	1
Effectively addressing regulatory restrictions	4	6
Enhancing innovation	5	2
Meeting expectations of investors and lenders	6	7
Attracting and retaining diverse top talent	7	3
Improving employee morale and engagement	8	8
Addressing challenges of the healthcare system	9	9
Providing goods and services that are good for the world	10	11

Source: Sustainability: An evolving business paradigm. Slide show by the American Management Association (AMA) (2007), slide 8. Slides available from view.fdu.edu/files/amawebcastppt.pdf (accessed January 25, 2008); webcast available from www.amanet.org/editorial/webcast/2007/sustainability.htm (accessed January 25, 2008). Copyright 2007, American Management Association. Reproduced with permission.

6. Creating sustainable enterprise business cultures may require behavior change from every person at every level of the organization

Creating cultures that embrace sustainable business practices, and are based on seeing the organization as if it were a living system, grows progressively more important to long-term success in all types of organization. Increasing economic globalization necessitates ever more frequent reviews and adjustments to enterprise portfolios, creating significant turnover and fluidity in workforce members. New workforce entrants from diverse backgrounds are likely to increase as we continue to move toward **flattened workscapes** and virtual employee populations (Friedman, 2005). These new entrants must all learn ways of doing business that ensure perpetuation of sustainable enterprise values, even in those organizations presently demonstrating best-in-class sustainable development practices. Thus, cultivating enterprise cultures that embrace sustainable development values will remain a core capability essential to achieving and sustaining success in the 21st century. (See the sidebar "Sustainability-related factors driving key business decisions in the next decade," on page 120.)

Challenges in changing enterprise culture

Creating significant cultural change at every level of the organization is far easier said than done. Even a casual review of contemporary management literature suggests that most companies dramatically underestimate the challenge faced in creating and imple-

SUCCESS VS. FAILURE IN ENTERPRISE-WIDE CHANGE

It is no secret that most change initiatives fall short. Findings across multiple studies suggest that 50–80% of corporate change efforts fail to achieve desired results. Even worse, this is especially true for attempts to change corporate culture. In his 1996 book *Leading Change*, John P. Kotter reports that 85% of companies fail to achieve their change objectives. Paul Strebel (2000), in his *Harvard Business Review OnPoint* article, reports that 50–80% of change efforts in *Fortune* 1000 companies fail. A *Wall Street Journal* (Lancaster, 1995) review of 1,005 reengineered companies reports that only 50% met cost targets; only 22% achieved projected productivity increases; about 80% ended up rehiring some laid-off employees; less than 33% achieved profit expectations; and only 21% achieved satisfactory return on investment.

Capra (2007) provides insights as to why so many change efforts fail:

> Although we hear about many successful attempts to transform organizations, the overall track record is very poor. In recent surveys, CEOs reported again and again that their organizational change efforts did not yield the promised results. Instead of managing new organizations, they ended up managing the unwanted side effects of their efforts . . . When observ[ing] our natural environment, we see continuous change, adaptation, and creativity; yet our business organizations seem to be incapable of dealing with change.

Indeed, the same business culture can provide both an advantage and liability, depending on prevalent business conditions. Studies of DEC (Digital Equipment Corporation) reveal that the same culture contributing to the once-mighty company's success also prevented it from adapting to a changing context — even though the need for change was recognized (Schein & Kampas, 2003). This cultural rigidity ultimately cost DEC its existence as an independent company. Choices made by entire societies about their cultural values, and the ultimate outcomes that those choices have on sustainability, have been similarly investigated (Diamond, 2005).

---

menting significant organizational change (Adams, 2003). Experts report (see the sidebar "Success vs. failure in enterprise-wide change" above) that:

- Only 20–50% of strategic change initiatives fully realize expected benefits
- Less than 50% of planned change efforts successfully overcome employee inertia
- Failure to fully implement strategic change undermines realization of business results and jeopardizes achievement of competitive advantage

Most cultural change initiatives fail because they are driven by the need to cut costs in the short term. All too often, this involves reductions in force that decimate organizational expertise and severely reduce capability to reach enterprise goals. As such, cost-driven transformation efforts are nonsustainable.

Factors essential for successful change

The good news is that we know what differentiates success from failure in creating sustainable change. Successful enterprise-wide change efforts are visibly championed by senior management, and are typically characterized by:

- Committed leadership willing to make essential investments (information technology [IT], capital, and the like)

- Shared mindset and co-created values: agreement on what's needed and how to get there; shared priorities; willingness to take risks; aligned incentives; and reward systems

- Disciplined change management using integrated project structures, clear roles and responsibilities, recognition and management of resistance, and willingness to provide resources (time and budget) required to implement changes

- Effective communication and stakeholder management generating critical mass of stakeholder support by providing access to information, focusing on desired outcomes, and frequently reporting progress

- Organization culture characterized by high degrees of trust between management and workforce, typically embracing collaboration, teamwork, empowerment of individuals to act without permission within the scope of their own role, and commitment to staff development

Committed change leadership, manifested across diverse activities and practiced by change leaders operating across multiple levels, is an absolute necessity for driving successful organizational change. Sterman (2001) reported six shared characteristics of 23 "successful" change efforts: clear vision of future; specific goals for change; use of IT; leadership involved and committed; clear milestones and measurements; and training of participants in process analysis and teamwork. *Harvard Business Review OnPoint* (2000) reports a slightly different set of six key levers in successful change efforts: structure, skills, information systems, roles, incentives, and shared values. Both these studies emphasize the importance of attending to the entire system in driving change efforts. It is insufficient to attend simply to the "hard" elements such as IT investments, or exclusively to the "soft" elements, such as aligned values. Transformational change occurs only when the entire system moves in a coherent fashion.

Indeed, successful transformational change may involve looking at the organization in a new way, which embraces the messy complexities of the natural world. Capra (2007) argues: "Once we have that understanding, we can design processes of organizational change accordingly, and create human organizations that mirror life's adaptability, diversity, and creativity." Thus, an understanding of natural change processes is a prerequisite to establishing lasting change in the organization.

▦ Transforming enterprise culture

Enterprise transformation approaches provide valuable insights for generating successful change. Proven approaches typically rely on creating organizations that accept and embrace deliberate renewal of workforce talent; responsible use of environmental resources; and alleviation of major societal ailments (Gouillart & Kelly, 1995). In particular, we advocate the orchestrated redesign of **organizational "DNA"** using four transformational elements: **Framing, Aligning, Igniting,** and **Refreshing (FAIR)**:[2]

- **Framing.** Shifting corporate mindsets to develop fresh mental models[3] of *what we are* and *what we can become*; expanding corporate identity to infuse new visions, aspirations, and new resolve

- **Aligning.** Adjusting economic models, aligning physical infrastructure and redesigning workplace processes and procedures to achieve a competitive level of performance. This is more than simply restructuring organization charts to cut heads and reap fast financial payoffs; reinvention requires comprehension and apprehension of fresh capabilities needed to sustain enterprise advantage

- **Igniting.** Kindling growth by achieving market focus, inventing new businesses, and using technology to change the industry rules of competition; promoting organic growth and stimulating new competitive capability most clearly differentiate organization transformation from mere downsizing

- **Refreshing.** Adjusting enterprise information metabolism to foster creativity, generate energy, and restore *esprit de corps*; investing individuals with new skills and purposes, thus permitting the organization to regenerate itself; revitalizing enterprise *sense of community* is the most challenging, yet potentially most potent, transformation tool available to organization leaders

The **FAIR** model represents the fundamental life skills that any organization needs to survive and thrive in the sustainable development world of the 21st century.

▨ Participative change and sustainable enterprise cultures

Organizations can change only as quickly as the people in them change. Successful organization transformations require expansion of conversational space, thus enabling all employees to think and act differently. We know that people learn in many different ways, and good organizational change will leverage several of them, including social and individual learning experiences, as well as active versus passive (or observational) learning.

We have found an *immersion approach* to be most effective in helping people make these transformations. Change immersion relies heavily on the principle of modeling; with modeling, people learn not only through their own experience, but also by observing the experiences of others. Creating visible examples of the consequences of embracing or rejecting new behaviors fosters organization-wide learning, which can have a profound effect on employee decisions to embrace new behaviors.

Adult learning theory holds that people need time and reinforcement to adjust to the idea of new behaviors and learn associated skills. Employee understanding is itself only

---

2 The FAIR model and its description are copyright 2008, Organization Innovation LLC. Used with permission.
3 For more on transforming mental models to bring them in synch with sustainable enterprise, see Chapter 2.

a first step in driving successful enterprise transformations. Beyond ensuring that workforce members have the time to help co-create, understand, and embrace the purpose of the changes (at least enough to give it a try), we must also address three additional factors. First, we must revamp reward and recognition systems to ensure new behaviors are adequately maintained over time; this typically involves significant adjustment to core human resources and management systems, and is seldom undertaken lightly. Second, we must deliberately recruit or create active, visible role models who practice the new enterprise behaviors; people are far more likely to try out (and continue engaging in) new behaviors if they see them modeled by others (especially those they respect and admire). Third, we must ensure that everyone is provided with the time and resources to learn new skills to do what is required of them in the future. For adults, this typically involves five steps: listening, co-creating, absorbing, using experimentally, and integrating into existing knowledge. Many organizations set themselves up for failure by "scrimping" on this vital component of successful transformations.

Thus, creating an environment of participative learning is essential to the success of any cultural transformation, and the chances of achieving sustainable change are far greater when all four of the above factors (co-creating a new understanding with the employees, revising reward systems, ensuring the presence of visible role models, and providing the means for employees to acquire new skills) are present.

Many change initiatives fail because they focus only on the tangible components of the business enterprise: its basic structures, technologies, systems, and work processes. The reality is that transformational change is fundamentally about changing the intangible components of the business enterprise: the way people perceive their roles, approach their jobs, and make choices on a daily basis. In our work, four elements have proved essential for successfully changing the way people work together: co-creating a compelling future state to which people can aspire; co-developing shared values and behaviors aligned with achieving the future vision; ensuring that everyone receives the knowledge and skills required to succeed in the future environment; and creating an environment in which people at all levels see visible, functional examples of the behaviors they've been asked to embrace.

Seasoned managers recognize that alterations in basic work routines often pose a daunting challenge. They have learned that any attempt to alter habitual work behaviors requires a *deliberate effort*, necessitating conscious examination of assumptions about *why and how* someone works. These questions inevitably lead to reexamination of personal and professional priorities, and can often entail fundamental reassessment of *employment value propositions*. Such excursions can be perilous, and are seldom lightly undertaken.

VALUE PROPOSITIONS FOR INTERNAL VS. EXTERNAL STAKEHOLDERS

The challenge of optimizing value propositions for internal versus external stakeholders increases as organizations grow in size and complexity. This is primarily because those directly accountable for delivering value to external stakeholders (such as shareholders, local community, government) are seldom directly responsible for delivering products or services to clients or customers on a daily basis. See Chapter 1 for insights addressing the alignment challenges senior executives face when they become further removed from those they rely on to deliver target results on a daily basis.

▪ Iterative transformational change methodology

An integrated approach for managing the change to sustainable development cultures can be created by merging the FAIR model, participative change management, and traditional project management methodologies. This method combines an understanding of how organizations change (FAIR), how people learn (participative learning theory), and four conditions essential for changing the way people behave at work. The intentional, tenacious application of integrated concepts, driven by action learning teams advocating sustainable development principles, produces organization-wide changes in how people think about their work: how work is structured, how success is measured, and how materials and information move through the organization. In our experience, this total approach consistently creates, develops, and installs sustainable enterprise cultures that balance people, planet, and profit goals in the development of sustainable value propositions essential for achieving triple-bottom-line success in the 21st century. A common misconception about transformational change interventions is the notion that they follow traditional "beginning–middle–end" sequences so ingrained in Western thinking. Perhaps, paradoxically, transformational change actually starts with an *ending*. Lewin (1951) conceived a three-stage change model ("unfreezing–moving–refreezing") suggesting that individuals must first "let go of" — literally stop — old behaviors before they can begin engaging in new behaviors. That is, rather than beginning with what the new will be, effective change actually requires letting go of the old before addressing the new directly. Although starting at the end is counterintuitive for many, it is absolutely essential for changing the way people think about their work.

Overlaying the FAIR model on to traditional change management stages provides a neat solution to this dilemma. This approach permits us to think about managing transformational change interventions in discrete stages, with each of the FAIR elements operating iteratively within sequential stages of the change process.

This **iterative transformational change methodology** (see Fig. 4.1) has proven particularly effective for creating and implementing sustainable enterprise values, while simultaneously providing powerful developmental experiences for emerging leaders; creating internal advocates for reinvented work processes and practices; and building

Figure 4.1 **Iterative transformational change methodology**

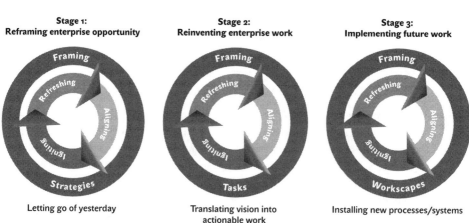

Source: Copyright 2008, Organization Innovation. Used with permission.

the foundation for an adaptive culture that continually strives to tackle future challenges in the struggle to achieve sustainable enterprise practices.

The recommended methodology ensures all elements essential for successful enterprise change are assessed, addressed, and monitored throughout the transformational change engagement. This systematic, systems-level approach to creating and managing change employs principles of modeling at multiple stages and multiple levels of an organization to systematically transform the way everyone thinks about and performs their work on a daily basis.

The key to transformational success involves creating cross-functional collaboration across a set of interdependent interventions managed as a single, integrated organizational intervention. (See Chapter 8 for more on collaboration, including mode and frameworks, tools, exercises, and best practices.) The primary driving mechanism is an empowered action learning team (the **core team**, Fig. 4.2) charged with managing stakeholder interests and coordinating intervention activities across multiple project stages or phases. As owners of the transformational change methodology, the core team must ensure application of the FAIR model with each new constituency encountered as the intervention iterates through multiple levels and functions within the larger enterprise. Our empowered action learning team approach ultimately involves chartering and launching multiple teams over sequential 100-day periods. The principle "7–70–700" refers to the number of workforce members engaged in three successive 100-day periods. In a typical transformational change project, each core team member in stage 1, "Reframing enterprise opportunity," becomes the leader of a natural work redesign team in stage 2, "Reinventing enterprise work." Similarly, one or more members of each

Figure 4.2 **Empowered team intervention structure**

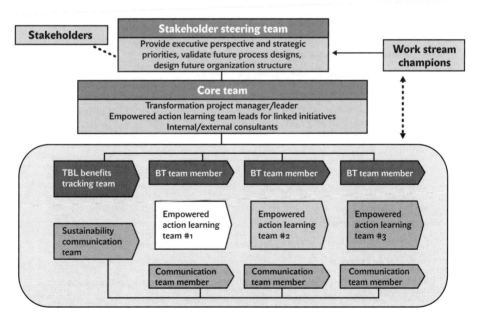

Note: Typical project structure for empowered action learning team interventions employed in iterative transformational change methodology stage 2: "Reinventing enterprise work."

Source: Copyright 2007, Organization Innovation. Used with permission.

redesign team in stage 2 will lead implementations teams in stage 3, "Implementing future work."

The empowered action learning team approach is equally appropriate for use in business enterprises, civic organizations, and social networks. Major elements include co-creating and identifying organizational performance opportunities, reinventing core work processes, aligning employee engagement and commitment, and mobilizing workforce resources to implement new ways of delivering value to all stakeholders (customers, employees, shareholders, local community, and the like). This approach has been successfully applied in a variety of industries, countries, and cultures, including Argentina, Brazil, Canada, the United Kingdom, Germany, Mexico, Spain, and the United States. This approach, having proven equally effective with workforce members in Europe, North America, and South America, is offered without hesitation to anyone seeking a robust methodology for creating and implementing new values within existing enterprise cultures.

ASSESS YOUR ORGANIZATIONAL READINESS TO MOVE TO SUSTAINABLE ENTERPRISE: CHANGE READINESS DIAGNOSTIC TOOL

This tool measures organizational readiness to meet major challenges encountered in the journey to sustainable enterprise: meeting today's needs without compromising the ability of future generations to meet their own needs. Best-practice enterprises define success in terms of an integrated triple bottom line: accountability for social equity, ecological integrity, and financial profitability. To assess your organization's readiness to move to sustainable enterprise, simply rate the following 12 statements on a scale from 1 to 5, where:

1 = not characteristic; this *never* happens here
2 = somewhat characteristic; this *seldom* happens here
3 = characteristic; this *sometimes* happens here
4 = very characteristic; this *frequently* happens here
5 = extremely characteristic; this *always* happens here without exception

1. ☐ Senior leaders visibly support and communicate benefits of sustainable enterprise business practices

2. ☐ People here appreciate how embracing sustainable enterprise values will impact our company, businesses, and jobs

3. ☐ People here agree about what does and does not need to change as we move toward sustainable enterprise

4. ☐ People here understand the scope and time requirements for becoming a sustainable enterprise

5. ☐ Managers typically recognize and address individual resistance to adopting sustainable enterprise business practices

6. ☐ Management recognizes and rewards those leading and supporting the change to sustainable enterprise

---

(continued opposite)

7. ☐ People here respect and value those working to create a sustainable enterprise culture

8. ☐ Employees get time and support for learning new skills essential for future success

9. ☐ Managers rebalance job responsibilities of people assigned to change projects

10. ☐ Goals of sustainable enterprise efforts are aligned across company departments

11. ☐ People here are willing to share information and ideas to achieve the best results

12. ☐ We have high levels of trust and cooperation between management and employees

Calculate your score: total the 12 numbers assigned to each statement. If your score equals:

55–60: Change master – primed and ready to handle major challenges

46–54: Change leader – likely to cope with challenges, with some bumps in the road

36–45: Change dilettante – proceed with caution; high risk of unrealized benefits

<36:   Change novice – seek guidance from organizational change masters

Note: This assessment provides a high-level overview of several more robust diagnostic tools, supplying a preliminary diagnosis of five major change dimensions impacting successful transformation to sustainable enterprise for the 21st century.

Source: Copyright 2005–2007, Organization Innovation LLC. Adapted with permission.

▨ Iterative guide to sustainable development workscapes

Stage 1. Reframing enterprise opportunity

Re-envisioning enterprise opportunity is the first step in the enterprise evolution. It's about moving beyond the confines of *who we are* and *what we do* to address *what we must become*. Changing enterprise identity strikes at the root of fundamental organizational DNA, involving adjustments to:

● Dominant approach to conducting business

● Standards for measuring performance

● Workforce motivation and engagement

● Freedom to innovate, experiment, and push the boundaries of acceptable practices for achieving the long-term mission

Thus, reframing the enterprise invariably requires mobilizing workforce engagement, re-creating a shared vision of the future, and building new metrics for determining individual and organization success in achieving enterprise goals. (See Chapters 5, 6, and 8 for additional insights into addressing these challenges.)

The core team functions as a primary engine and integrative force, and is specifically chartered to deliver results for all key activities addressed in stage 1. Typically, the team must be equipped to diagnose and address the following critical success factors: thorough understanding of current state; assessing gaps between current and best practice capabilities; and building a business case for enhancing organizational performance on TBL metrics (social equity, ecological integrity, and financial profitability). The ultimate goals of the "Reframing enterprise opportunity" stage are improving the value proposition for all stakeholders (employees, customers, local community, government, and shareholders), while simultaneously engaging the minds and hearts of the people working to deliver increased shareholder value.

EMPLOYEE ENGAGEMENT AND ORGANIZATIONAL RENEWAL

There's a chicken-and-egg aspect to the relationship between employee engagement and organizational renewal. Organizational renewal offers employees the opportunity to more fully leverage their potential. As seen in Chapter 5, engaged employees are proud of their organizations and offer discretionary effort.

Both of these topics are deep and rich — too much to cover here with any justice. Instead, we offer a thought: A key component of employee engagement is pride in the organization. To encourage engagement, especially in times of change, organizations can be pride-worthy. Taking a TBL perspective is a great start to being pride-worthy. Doing right by your employees, doing right by the community, and doing right financially all contribute to an organizational image that employees feel good about. (See Chapter 5 for a detailed discussion of this robust concept, especially pages 143-145 and 159-160.)

A typical core team includes members representing multiple levels and a cross-section of key functions within the current organization. In our experience, a fulltime team leader (100% time allocation), with team members assigned at 50% workload, has the greatest probability for meeting or exceeding targets defined in the team charter. Although there is no absolute core team member profile, those selected typically bring deep expertise in the following disciplines: project management (team leader), finance/accounting, manufacturing/engineering, logistics, maintenance, communication/change management, and organization structure and design. All members will be expected to function as change agents in their own areas, and must therefore be credible, respected, and viewed by colleagues as capable of representing the greater interests of the entire group. In keeping with principles regarding social equity, core teams should also reflect multiple aspects of diversity (e.g., gender, ethnicity/nationality, profession, age/seniority).

Once assembled, the core team will introduce and manage a portfolio of tools designed to mobilize and engage the entire workforce in identifying and quantifying potential opportunities for improving organizational efficiency and effectiveness; for

QUICK WINS: 'EARNEST MONEY' ON THE CHANGE

Often, as you begin to explore a problem space in earnest, you'll come across a golden opportunity to start the change. Something so easy, so obvious, so visible! Grab those low-hanging fruits with both hands and make a big show of it. These *quick wins* should be carefully positioned as little baby steps and not the end game, but there is tremendous power in demonstrating your commitment to change. Doing a small thing well — executing well and communicating well — increases others' trust in you. They begin to believe that maybe you'll be able to do a big thing well. It also puts a chink in the armor of denial; right out of the gate, with this project, things are different.

creating a more positive workplace; and for implementing a *quick hit/quick win* process, or workplace enhancement improvements on an accelerated schedule.

Typical opportunity identification activities include:

- **Creating transparency in value creation dynamics, metrics, and current performance.** This normally requires reviews of financial statements, strategic initiatives, capital investment plans, and the like. This work often forms the skeleton around which the rest of the opportunity identification activities are built

- **Assessing workforce readiness for transformational change** (see the sidebar "Assess your organizational readiness to move to sustainable enterprise" on pages 128-129). Formally assessing change readiness of the organization informs change management

- **Extensive interviews.** Although ostensibly for information gathering, these function more as a step in the change management effort. They are an opportunity to set expectations, allow people at multiple levels and in multiple functions of the organization to feel heard, and they begin to get people engaged. These interviews can also be a time to begin identifying potential team members for the next phase of the project

- **Process opportunity mapping.** Application of high-touch–low-tech methodology engaging key stakeholders in capturing optimization opportunities for key work processes and work flows

- **"Day in the life of" (DILO) assessments of people, process, equipment** (see the sidebar "Understand the problem you are solving," opposite)

Throughout all these activities, the team demonstrates new sustainable enterprise values, modeling a new approach to conducting business and introducing TBL standards for measuring performance. At the same time, they actively engage employees at all levels in actions demonstrating freedom to innovate, experiment, and push the boundaries of acceptable practice.

Leadership alignment and support are essential components of any transformational change effort. Typically conducted in workshop format, this work ensures senior managers understand how to use the empowered team process to simultaneously deliver improved organizational performance and develop essential business and team skills

UNDERSTAND THE PROBLEM YOU ARE SOLVING

Good, thorough research can yield surprising answers to mundane questions. The opportunity identification tools are designed to help understand not just the "obvious" solutions, but the root causes.

One important such identification tool is the **Day in the life of** (DILO) exercise. Here, team members meticulously follow a person, object, form, sample, order, or other unit of analysis all the way through the system.

A favorite example of a DILO is the "great forklift shortage." Operators in a particularly sprawling facility spent inordinate amounts of time — several hours of every shift — hunting around for available forklifts. The shortage of forklifts was a real problem. Just buying more posed a problem, because of the requirements for safe operation in this particular facility. The ones they needed were very, very expensive.

Enter the DILO, conducted by operators from the very same plant, people with a clear agenda to prove they needed more of the expensive forklifts. What did they find? It wasn't the *availability* of the forklifts that was the problem; it was the *location*. By following several forklifts around over the course of several days, they learned that each one was used for only a very small percentage of any given shift. The wasted time was all in hunting around, for 30 minutes or more at a time, to find one. Each person just left it parked wherever it had last been used.

The solution? A set of designated parking spots. In the end, rather than purchasing more forklifts, the plant was actually able to retire some, another step in its efforts to reduce its environmental footprint.

The magic of a DILO is its irrefutability. In the forklift example, how would such a solution have been received if had been dictated from on high? Instead, a group of peers set out to solve their own problem — and they did, though not in the way that they intended. When lunchroom grumbling about needing to put things away started up, the DILO researchers were there to set the record straight. Management was happy with the cost avoidance. Employees were happy with the reduced frustration that never being able to find the equipment they needed had engendered. Win–win was achieved!

---

throughout the organization. In the ideal situation, leadership workshops take place before teams are formally commissioned. In cases in which pre-positioning is unrealistic, workshops may be run in parallel with work redesign teams described above, or, if absolutely necessary, even scheduled as a direct lead-in to organization redesign work.

Leadership alignment workshops are essential to the smooth, sustainable operation of the empowered action learning team model, for both practical and political reasons. Empowered action learning team methodology is fundamentally bottom-up in nature, and requires that leaders await team recommendations before taking action. This runs counter to the normal management practices (and perhaps even instincts) of most leadership teams. Therefore, it's essential to help senior leaders resist the urge to impose order, accelerate actions, or otherwise disrupt the empowered team process.

Experience demonstrates patience is far easier when leaders are confident that empowered teams will return solutions aligned with company priorities and management time schedules. Consequently, it becomes incumbent on core team members to make sure that senior managers receive solutions they can live with, and successful projects most frequently require core team members to bridge any potential gaps between company priorities and team member/employee self-interests. Fortunately, this alignment is often a natural outcome of the frequent, candid discussions between the core team and the enterprise or organization's leaders or leadership team; in a typical project, the leader of the core team not only has a standing one-to-one briefing with the enterprise leader each week, he or she also typically becomes a full member of the enterprise's leadership team for the duration of the project.

The culmination of stage 1: "**Reframing** enterprise opportunity" is a recommended case for change. Although a case for change may take many forms, at minimum it should include a reinvention plan supported by a sustainable enterprise business case. (Note: a case for change is also the typical culmination of any change management intervention. This can contribute to confusion regarding our approach, in which some expect neat, linear steps in the change process.) A good business case for change will invariably include *three buckets* supporting recommended changes: quantitative/financial analyses ("real money") projections demonstrating benefits to shareholders; nonquantified/financial analyses (real money impacts expected from changes, with no specific or reliable data available for accurately estimating benefits); and nonquantifiable benefits (intangible but "real" benefits; these may be necessary enablers or preconditions for benefits in the first two categories) that may be expected to result from changes. It is important to note that nonquantified financial benefits are included intentionally. First, they hold the promise of an additional financial upside beyond those quantified in the first category (i.e., quantified financial). Further, identifying but not calculating benefits providing low return on investment of time and effort supports the credibility of the team and its work. Although some change efforts advertise suspicious numbers, based on several layers of assumptions, our methodology explicitly separates the "hard, take-it-to-the-bank" benefits of a project from the "expected, aggregated, increased value" sorts of return.

The *three bucket* approach permits integration of TBL metrics into the business case, and ensures change decisions are based on more than simple short-term profit motives. This balances the needs of external and internal stakeholders and recognizes that increases in shareholder value are inextricably tied to improving the employee value proposition. Therefore, the case for change reframes business priorities, optimizes returns for all constituencies, and clarifies the path for achieving environmentally and socially responsible goals balancing immediate needs of investors and consumers without sacrificing long-term viability of our planet or its inhabitants.

Stage 2. Reinventing enterprise work

The **reinventing** component of enterprise transformation entails redesigning key activities embedded in the processes, systems, and tools supporting achievement of organizational goals. This work focuses on creating new economic models for pursuing and measuring sustainable success, redesigning work architectures to achieve a competitive level of performance, and aligning physical infrastructure to ensure resource focus on areas providing optimal results for all constituencies.

Primary goals of the reinventing stage include: designing future work processes and systems; clarifying key organizational roles and responsibilities; defining future organization structures; improving morale and motivation by promoting trust, encouraging teamwork, and alleviating *fairness* concerns; and creating employee ownership and commitment to sustainable enterprise values.

During reinvention, the active engagement of workforce members is formally expanded beyond the original core team, which now assumes a project management–coordination function. This allows the knowledge and experience of those core team members to scale more broadly, as each core team member takes leadership of a specific workstream in the reinventing phase. As depicted in Figure 4.2 on page 127, people are assigned to multiple empowered action learning teams formally chartered to design the future processes essential to achieving sustainable enterprise. The number of teams generally depends on the key changes identified in the sustainable enterprise business case; 5 to 12 is a typical range. These generally take the form of natural work teams (redesigning future work processes), coordination teams (core, benefits/metrics), governance teams (leadership alignment, organization design, steering), and enabling teams (communication, workforce competence enhancement); the organic formation of these teams is congruous with the perception of the organization as a living system.

HOW TO LEVERAGE INTERNAL RESOURCES WITH LITTLE OR NO ADDED EXPENSE

The content or process expertise that a good consultant brings can be an essential component of effective change. However, the credibility brought by your current workforce — their expertise in your work processes, your culture, all the details that make your workplace unique, is beyond value. The sincere advocacy of one skeptical, informal leader in your organization may be the single greatest change tool you have. That sincere advocacy can't be bought, but it can be earned through the approaches outlined in this chapter.

Using our "7–70–700" rule, we now increase the total number of immersed employees by a factor of 10. This necessarily involves revisiting many of the same issues originally addressed by members of the core team during stage 1. Although this may seem like the process is slowing down, this is a critical step in achieving successful transformation; in this case, slowing down will help us go faster in the long run as it provides an opportunity for team members to be fully immersed and engaged. Permitting new participants to ask the same questions, address the same concerns, and discover the same answers is an absolutely essential element for increasing the critical mass of employees actively embracing the core elements of the new sustainable development culture.

Though this may seem inefficient, there is no substitute for permitting each team member to learn the *new company truths* at his or her own pace and in his or her own way. This issue may be particularly problematic for members of the senior management team, who are understandably anxious to capture benefits of new opportunities as quickly as possible. Successful change consultants have learned to leverage this leadership impatience by creating champion roles that give leaders an active role in shaping empowered team thinking. This satisfies the leaders' need to move forward while providing empowered teams with the space to explore and address the new sustainable development concepts at their own pace.

Frequently, an essential component of the reinvention stage is **igniting** the enterprise, or reinventing primary components of the business model. This may take the form of igniting growth by achieving market focus in existing markets, migrating to new geographic regions, inventing new businesses, or utilizing technology to change the industry rules of competition. Igniting provides an opportunity to breathe new life into an organization. In situations in which igniting opportunities have been identified in the business case for change, empowered action learning teams are tasked with designing and implementing work processes, systems, and tools required to bring each opportunity to fruition. It is interesting to note that the same workplace reinvention processes used to streamline operations and cut costs may also be applied to designing and implementing enterprise growth opportunities. We have run interventions in which some natural work teams focus on improving operational efficiency and effectiveness while others focus on creating the growth engines that will sustain the enterprise during changing business conditions. This combination is particularly effective, as it offers the opportunity to align the organization to capture both relatively immediate, or short-term (efficiency), and longer-term (growth) benefits, rather than setting up a conflict between the two.

Igniting and aligning the fundamental value propositions underpinning basic business models is often an essential component of moving to a sustainable enterprise. The people, planet, profit perspective inherent in a TBL approach frequently necessitates reexamination of fundamental operational assumptions, many of which were developed and conceived during periods when organizations were designed primarily around a single bottom line.

Igniting is the single greatest factor distinguishing organization transformation interventions from mere downsizing. (See the sidebar "Do you need to downsize?" overleaf) In our experience, the most successful and sustainable enterprise transformations are conducted in organizations on the verge of significant (or even exponential) growth. The willingness to optimize and transform organization cultures as they approach periods of significant capital investment often distinguishes sustainable enterprises from those companies merely struggling to remain afloat. Even in cases in which downsizing may be essential, it still makes sense to engage the line employees in redesigning their future. It is discouraging to read accounts of companies that involved workers as simply a ploy to pacify workforce members, and it is important to note that true transformation requires more than mere lip-service to employee participation in the change process.

It is impossible to overstate the importance of pilot testing during this phase. Smart pilot testing is an iterative process, which takes advantage of opportunities to refine improvements on a small scale. This approach has the advantage of fostering broader engagement with the ultimate solutions as well as allowing additional people to contribute to refinements.

Hallmarks of smart pilot testing:

- **Position it specifically as a pilot test.** Pilot tests nearly all have hiccups, glitches, and things you just didn't think about. Set the stage by declaring that this is a "beta" version!

- **Start in fertile ground.** Maximize your odds for success in the first pilot test. Ideally, the first pilot test will provide you with lots of feedback, including feedback to make corrections and improvements if needed

- **Integrate learnings.** All your work to build credibility may come down to this moment: your ability to accept that some things could be better and you might not have been completely right on a thing or two. Some find analyzing pilot

DO YOU NEED TO DOWNSIZE?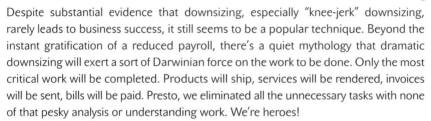

Despite substantial evidence that downsizing, especially "knee-jerk" downsizing, rarely leads to business success, it still seems to be a popular technique. Beyond the instant gratification of a reduced payroll, there's a quiet mythology that dramatic downsizing will exert a sort of Darwinian force on the work to be done. Only the most critical work will be completed. Products will ship, services will be rendered, invoices will be sent, bills will be paid. Presto, we eliminated all the unnecessary tasks with none of that pesky analysis or understanding work. We're heroes!

The above unkind characterization is not to suggest that downsizing is never necessary, or that, when necessary, it cannot be done with intelligence and integrity (Cascio, 2002).

Armed with a thorough understanding of the work to be done and the staffing required to do it, one can make intelligent staffing-level decisions. In the ideal case, changes can be absorbed in the natural ebb and flow of the organization over the change period. In other instances, wise use of vendors and contractors is indicated.

When staffing legitimately needs to be reduced, it is still possible to approach the situation with a TBL perspective. These people that you let go — they go somewhere. They accept positions with your suppliers, with your customers, with your competition, as your competition, on your city council, and on your kids' school board. In this world of mergers and acquisitions, they frequently end up back on your payroll. When planning a downsizing, be sure to consider not only the financial bottom line of the process, but also the human and community outcomes as well.

Best practices for downsizing well:

- **Transparency and high integrity.** Be clear and honest about why the steps you are taking are necessary, perhaps including alterative scenarios, or multiple options. Don't ask any questions or offer any options unless you are willing to live with the answers. Make clear the criteria for who is staying and who is going, and state any exceptions upfront. Occasionally, employees can be retrained or dedicated to new tasks, or groups of employees can move to reduced work schedules; if these are options, the same guidance regarding transparency and high integrity applies

- **Allow sufficient, appropriate, and clearly defined timelines.** Depending on the circumstances, this may vary dramatically. We've shared examples here of planned transitions lasting over a year. Others will be much shorter

- **Provide some exit support.** Many organizations have severance policies that include pay and/or benefits continuation. Not all organizations can afford such exit support. Depending on circumstances, organizations can offer exit support in the form of a guest office for a limited time for job hunting purposes, and to offer a sense of normalcy to the former employees. Human resources or recruiting can offer guidance on résumé writing, can make connections with other recruiters, or take other steps to help former employees with their job searches such as offering outplacement assistance tests invigorating; others are crushed by small failures. A smart leader, firmly in the "invigorating" camp, recently said, "We had a successful pilot. We learned that our model doesn't work. Thank goodness we didn't go straight for the global launch!"

- **Pilot again.** This time, pilot in the most hostile conditions that your process will face. You've demonstrated that it *can* work at this point; now you are demonstrating that it *will* work, even under adverse circumstances

Essentially, through pilot testing, you are creating a *bulletproof* process, as well as creating a growing group of advocates.

Throughout the change, but especially in this phase, the role of leadership is to set direction and communicate priorities. Leadership alignment workshops focus management energy on clarifying enterprise mission, vision, values, and guiding principles that everyone will follow on the journey to sustainable enterprise. Many interventions include clarification of business drivers and/or anticipated obstacles the organization must overcome during its multiyear transformation process. Our interventions all include a **transformation map**, providing a powerful communication tool illustrating specific milestone goals, metrics, critical success factors, and high-level action plans to be achieved on a multiyear journey to sustainable enterprise. (See the sidebar "The case for mission statements," overleaf; see Richard Knowles's essay "Engaging the natural tendency of self-organization," in Chapter 1 (pages 47ff.) for additional insights into co-creating organizational or project Bowls capturing employee imagination.)

Stage 3. Implementing future work

Implementing sustainable development work routines involves three distinct components:

- Co-creating integrated implementation plans
- Refreshing workforce capabilities
- Mobilizing workforce resources

Refreshing the enterprise entails refreshing the *esprit de corps* of the people investing their lives in the success of the organization. Refreshing is all about investing individuals with new skills and purposes, thus permitting the organization to regenerate itself. Renewal is an integral component of the empowered action learning team approach, and every aspect of creating, developing, and sustaining positive team dynamics must be modeled and practiced at every stage of the transformational intervention.

The nature of this work results in changes that truly are *better*: not simply more profitable, but solutions and approaches that eliminate persistent frustrations. The use of iterative pilot studies offers the opportunity to tangibly engage a growing portion of the organization. Combined with effective communications, and an intentionally inclusive project approach, tools such as pilot studies help these projects take advantage of natural tipping points to convert skepticism and resistance into enthusiasm.

Throughout this process, there is a gradual transfer of ownership for the change. In its initial phases, the change is driven very much by a small set of experts. However, as a project progresses, that small set of experts programmatically fades into the background. The job of this elite group is more to stretch the others with whom they work than it is to deliver results single-handedly. Though they may initially take a very directive role, by the end of a project they are entirely in the background. The crucible of an

THE CASE FOR MISSION STATEMENTS

Most mission statements are useless, forgotten documents, full of meaningless clichés. Energy is poured into endless wordsmithing, and the final product is unveiled with much fanfare, only to be forgotten by the end of the quarter. Take a look at your organization's mission statement: is there anything in that paragraph that is unique to your organization? Mission statements are commonly mundane and indistinct. And that's a pity.

Useful mission statements function in two ways. First, crafting a meaningful, common understanding of the purpose of an organization is an important exercise. Here, leadership teams can come to agreement on fundamental points of their business model — points that might otherwise have created discord, and suboptimal results.

In one dramatic, and painful, example, a struggling leadership team battled over whether their job was to maximize profits for their division, or maximize profits for the business as a whole, through driving the value chain of the larger organizational *big bet*. This situation of dual, unarticulated priorities had existed for years and drained money and energy from the business. Only by confronting it head-on, as a leadership team, were they able to come to a unified strategy. As a result of the mission conversation, behavior changed. Thinking changed. And the business turned around.

The second way a good mission statement is useful is as a decision aid for the organization as a whole. A good mission is specific enough to help employees decide, should I do A or B? It will add transparency and accountability to the priorities set by leadership.

Even the best mission statement, however, is only as good as the leadership team backing it up. Actions do speak louder than words. A mission cannot drive sustainability in a system where all the reward systems are calculated on quarterly results.

---

intense change project often hones capability in a dramatic way. The gradual transfer of ownership through the three phases — **reframing**, **reinventing**, and **implementing** — of this work and the intentional scaling by an order of magnitude at each step means that progress is less likely to halt when or if the core group is transitioned to new work. Rather, ownership and engagement are sufficiently diffused that the change will continue even after the original architects of the change have moved on.

■ Conclusion

Achieving sustainable enterprise in the 21st century requires fundamental changes in the ways organizations manage enterprise processes and approach markets, customers, stakeholders, and stockholders. This chapter has discussed approaches to making that transition.

The concepts and ideas discussed in this chapter are really just the next step in a natural evolution. Both organization development and change management employ a systems approach advocating a multidimensional perspective of a complex whole. The evolution to embracing triple-bottom-line perspectives simply applies this same sophistication to sustainable development outcomes that we already recognize in inputs and throughputs in any organizational system.

Transformational change typically requires everyone to adopt new ways of thinking and behaving. The bottom line is that any enterprise will only perform differently when its people adopt new work behaviors supported by realigned systems, tools, and talent management processes. Simply stated, this means co-creating and embracing new priorities and assuming new work routines in the daily course of adding value to the overall enterprise.

The secret to successful transformation to sustainable enterprise lies in the application of TBL perspectives on an organization-wide basis. This requires the willingness to expand traditional definitions of external stakeholder interests, while simultaneously engaging the minds and hearts of employees working to deliver increased value to all stakeholders. Sustainable enterprises embrace win–win–win strategies optimizing the needs of customers, employees, shareholders, communities, and governments, while avoiding attempts to maximize returns for any one group (such as shareholders) at the expense of others. They recognize that increases in shareholder value are inextricably connected to improved value propositions for all constituencies, and deliberately balance the needs of external and internal stakeholders. This multidimensional balance must be sustained through co-created conversations, at all levels, addressing issues critical to all enterprise stakeholders.

■ References

Adams, J. D. (2003). Successful change: Paying attention to the intangibles. *OD Practitioner, 35*(4), 3-7.

American Management Association (AMA). (2007). *Creating a sustainable future: A global study of current trends and possibilities 2007–2017.* New York: American Management Association.

Assis, V., & Elstrodt, H.-P. (2007). Positioning Brazil for bio-fuels success. *The McKinsey Quarterly, Special Edition: Shaping a New Agenda for Latin America, 2,* 1-6.

Benson, J. (2007). DEP — Use sustainability as a standard: Commissioner delivers keynote speech at UConn Natural Resources Forum. *The Day.* Retrieved March 10, 2007, from www.theday.com.

Capra, F. (2007). Life and leadership: A systems approach (Executive summary). Retrieved December 21, 2007, from www.fritjofcapra.net/management.html.

Cascio, W. F. (2002). *Responsible restructuring: Creative and profitable alternatives to layoffs.* San Francisco: Berrett-Koehler.

Diamond, J. (2005). *Collapse: How societies choose to fail or survive.* New York: Viking-Penguin.

Engardio, P. (2007, January 29). Beyond the green corporation. *Business Week,* pp. 50-64.

Friedman, T. L. (2005). *The world is flat: A brief history of the 21st century.* New York: Farrar, Strauss, & Giroux.

Gouillart, F. J., & Kelly, J. N. (1995). *Transforming the organization.* New York: McGraw-Hill.

Harvard Business Review OnPoint Collection (2000). *Creating followers: Framing change initiatives to maximize employee participation.* Boston, MA: Harvard Business School Publishing.

Kotter, J. P. (1996). *Leading change.* Boston, MA: Harvard Business School Press.

Lancaster, H. (1995, January 17). Reengineering authors reconsider reengineering. *Wall Street Journal,* p. 81.

Lewin, K. D. (1951). *Field theory in social science: Selected theoretical papers.* New York: Harper & Row.

McGraw-Hill (2007). *Greening of corporate America* (McGraw-Hill SmartMarket Report: Design & Construction Intelligence Series). New York: McGraw-Hill Construction.

Saling, P., & Kicherer, A. (2002). Eco-efficiency analysis by BASF: The method. *International Journal of Life Cycle Assessment, 7*(4), 203-218.

Schein, E. H., & Kampas, P. J. (2003). *DEC is dead, long live DEC.* San Francisco: Berrett-Koehler.

Spivey, A. (2006, Fall). A golden rule for business: How sustainable enterprise serves the triple bottom line. *UNC Business,* pp. 7-11.

Sterman, J. D. (2001). System dynamics modeling: Tools for leading in a complex world. *California Management Review, 43*(4), 8-25.

Strebel, P. (2000). Why do employees resist change? In *Harvard Business Review* OnPoint Collection, *Creating followers: Framing change initiatives to maximize employee participation* (pp. 23-36). Boston, MA: Harvard Business School Publishing.

United Nations Industrial Development Organization (UNIDO). (2002). *Eco-efficiency for SMEs in the Moroccan dyeing industry. Phase I: A sustainable approach to industrial development* (UNIDO Project Report). Vienna: United Nations Industrial Development Organization.

World Commission on Environment and Development (WCED) (1987) *Our common future.* Oxford, UK: Oxford University Press.

5

Employee engagement for a sustainable enterprise[1]

Kent D. Fairfield, Richard N. Knowles, William G. Russell, Jeana Wirtenberg, Sangeeta Mahurkar-Rao, and Orrin D. Judd

As described in earlier chapters, developing the sustainable enterprise depends on leaders who demonstrate commitment, inspiring vision, and operating savvy based on mental models of sustainability. At the heart of managing such change, however, is the engagement of employees at all levels to unleash their energies to co-create the enterprise's future. This chapter lays out some fundamental principles of employee engagement in the context of sustainability management, provides illustrative case studies of five exemplary organizations, and offers some conclusions about how today's managers can use this knowledge in their own organizations.

Considerable evidence exists that employees welcome the chance to exercise autonomy and creativity when given the opportunity (Goleman, Boyatzis, & McKee, 2002). By this thinking, managers need to lay out the direction, provide resources and guidance, and then move to a supportive role. Studies also have shown that employees want to be involved with sustainability initiatives. The participants in one survey reported overwhelmingly that they would rather be employed by a company that practices sustainability; 96% said they would like to work at "a successful company that also aspires to be good" (Willard, 2002).

1 The authors gratefully acknowledge contributions from Thomas K. Robinson to the PSE&G case.

The importance of employee concerns is underscored in the *2007 AMA Sustainability Survey* in *Creating a Sustainable Future* (American Management Association [AMA], 2007).[2] When managers were asked which of 26 factors relating to sustainability were the most important drivers of business decisions today, their first and second choices were ensuring workers' health and safety and increasing workforce productivity. Attracting and retaining diverse top talent ranked seventh most important, but it rose to third when respondents looked ten years ahead. The need to improve employee morale, engagement, and commitment was seen as the eighth most important driver of business decisions now and in the future. When the survey asked respondents what they consider to be potentially the most important factors hindering sustainable practices, lack of demand from managers and employees ranked second. This reinforces the notion that employee engagement is a crucial factor for the successful management of sustainability.

Involving employees in managing an enterprise begins with recruiting and hiring people who show the interest, drive, and dedication to achieve company goals. This will continue to challenge employers in the future, as the availability of talent gets more restricted with the retirement of baby boomers (Human Resource Institute, 2000; Dychtwald, Erickson, & Morison, 2006). In addition, some observers argue that future employees now in their teens and 20s will place more importance than their predecessors did on jobs that offer meaning and balance, and will not be content to just follow the dictates of a boss (Kaye & Jordan-Evans, 2005). Such tendencies will make it all the more imperative that managers involve employees at a deeper level than is traditional.

■ What employee engagement looks like

In their well-known book *The Leadership Challenge*, Kouzes and Posner (2007) say that employee engagement has to build on a foundation of creating a climate of trust, listening in depth, and sharing information and resources. They urge leaders to build a sense of interdependence, which, they say, stems from cooperative goals and roles, norms of reciprocity, and face-to-face interactions. They stress the importance of employees' feeling powerful and in control of their lives. Skillful leaders engender this sense of self-determination, which breeds ownership and motivation. One young manager was thrilled when his boss asked his opinion and gave him the leeway to make an important decision about how to carry out a demanding task. "He backed me up completely . . . and I subsequently did everything I could to ensure our success. There was no way I was going to let us not be successful" (Kouzes & Posner, 2007, p. 254).

This manager exemplifies the natural dynamic in which more power and authority lead to a greater sense of accountability. As people doing collaborative projects begin to trust that their colleagues will perform their tasks, everyone feels responsible for carrying out his or her own job. Thus, more power and autonomy interact with more accountability and more ownership, which increases the chance for success. Kouzes and Posner (2007) also hold that developing competence and confidence are foundational to employee involvement. As people develop their competence and confidence, they feel effective in what they do. Research shows that such self-efficacy contributes greatly to taking initiative, persisting under duress, and even enjoying better heath (Bandura, 1997; Saks, 1995).

2 See footnote 10 on page 12.

Another approach engages employees by building on what is seen as the natural tendency to self-organize. Practitioner and consultant Richard Knowles argues that people will organize themselves around anything that is important to them, whether management intends it or not (Knowles, 2002, 2006; see also pages 47ff.). If unprompted, they may work out problems together, gossip together, or work counter to corporate intentions: self-organizing will continue no matter what, and, depending on whether leadership encourages it, the self-organization will be productive or non- or counterproductive. The challenge of management, he says, is to set up conditions for employees to enthusiastically address the key issues for success – productively self-organizing. He recommends a series of conversations in which leadership shares important information with workers. These conversations build interdependent relationships and trust and help people discover how they and their work fit into the work at large – thereby encouraging employees to find meaning in their work (▲).

People's natural energy fuels such an approach, as opposed to a command-and-control mode, which "is like trying to remove the twists and turns from a river and forcing it to flow the way we want" (Knowles, 2006, p. 2). Instead, management's real role is to help clarify the foundation principles co-created by leadership and employees, such as vision, mission, and standards of performance – a "Bowl" in which everyone operates – and then step back allowing the workers to self-organize into teams for the work ahead. At the DuPont plant in Belle, West Virginia, according to Knowles (see the DuPont case in this chapter, pages 146ff.) workers self-organized into scores of teams and management moved out of the way, thus encouraging the productive self-organizing tendencies of the workers to come to the fore.

A third perspective that focuses on mobilizing energy comes from Linda Gratton (2007), who asserts that the most outstanding performance arises from "hot spots," work units characterized by cooperation, energy, innovation, productivity, and excitement. Organizations that create such hot spots elicit people's potential around what they find most meaningful. Gratton argues that hot spots arise from a cooperative mindset, spanning of boundaries, and an igniting purpose, in concert with productive capacity.

▨ Employee engagement in sustainability management

The value generally derived from employee engagement can be further amplified in organizations that aspire to sustainability management. Most executives in such organizations will articulate the vision of an enterprise that is prospering economically, contributing to social values in-house and in the world, and encouraging environmental stewardship, or, taken together, the triple bottom line. Employees tend to relate these goals to their own values. One HR executive at a multinational firm commented (Wirtenberg, Harmon, Russell, & Fairfield, 2007, p. 16) on how employee engagement and sustainability work together for corporate success:

> A big advantage to sustainability is getting employees engaged because they want to make a difference in the world. I work with a lot of committed people whose lives are about making a difference and choose to do it here at [our company] . . . Everyone agrees that's what is going to help make us one of the greatest companies in the world.

The AMA sustainability survey (AMA, 2007) asked how important 18 different sustainability-related issues — such as a safe work environment, clean water, fighting corruption, affordable clean energy, and global climate change — are to the respondents. They rated 80% of them as highly important, averaging 4.3 on a scale of 1.0 to 5.0, ranging from 3.8 to 4.8. Interestingly, the respondents also said they believed their organizations viewed every one of these issues as being appreciably less important than they did. Presumably they would find it more satisfying if their organizations pursued such sustainability factors more vigorously. If their leaders issued the invitation, the people would follow.

In fact, organizations engaged in sustainability management are at an advantage in hiring top talent. In a recent study (Wirtenberg et al., 2007, p. 16) of the most highly regarded sustainability management companies, one HR executive said,

> The better [our firm] is branded as a company that's sustainable and doing the right thing, the better I'm going to be able to attract talent, because the talent wants to work with the best companies, and the best companies are those that not only get results, but do it in a way that creates a sustainable environment.

Recent psychological research helps explain how people working for what they regard as a good cause feel better physically and are galvanized to exert exceptional effort toward related goals. Martin Seligman (Seligman & Csikszentmihalyi, 2000) has done seminal research in this area and founded a school of thought called "positive psychology." His research shows how people engaging in acts of altruism, generosity, and the like exhibit beneficial physical symptoms and higher levels of happiness. More recently, organizational researchers have established a new field — "positive organizational scholarship" — that embraces the impact of positive actions in the context of an enterprise or community (Cameron, Dutton, & Quinn, 2003). To the extent that employees feel deeply about the aims of sustainability — and they can see the connection between their job and those aims — they can regard their work as holding special meaning. Studies have shown that people perform at a higher level when their work is not "just a job" but is more of a calling (Wrzesniewski, 2003), and "those with callings often feel that their work makes the world a better place" (Wrzesniewski, 2002, p. 232). Some have described this dynamic, in which employees feel part of something greater than themselves and realize personal aspirations and potential, as achieving "transcendence" (Ashforth & Pratt, 2002).

Goleman and his colleagues (Goleman et al., 2002) explain how neuroscience helps to elucidate the biochemical reasons for these reactions. They argue that excellent leaders exhibit high levels of emotional intelligence, founded on keen self-awareness of their own emotions, the ability to regulate their emotions, and a high degree of empathy for the emotions of others. As a result, such leaders are skilled at managing relationships with others, including building rapport, leading teams, solving conflicts gracefully, and inspiring others to action. Such *resonant leaders* are transparent in what they do. They are genuinely authentic in that their actions and language are fully congruent with their values, which is essential to the move toward sustainability management.

More recently, Boyatzis and McKee (2007) have reported their research that resonant leaders are mindful, or fully conscious, of themselves, others, nature, and the larger world. They deal with the world with hope and an optimistic, confident vision of achieving their dreams. In addition, resonant leaders exhibit compassion toward their co-workers and those whom they serve. Neuropsychological research has provided evidence for why such emotions are literally contagious insofar as others react positively at a subconscious level. This dynamic can produce powerful collective action.

Some companies have taken concrete steps to engage their employees in highly personal ways in the cause of sustainability (**A**)(**T**). For example, the multinational mining and metals company Alcoa has invited employees' children to do drawings of what a sustainable world would be like. This naturally prompts family discussions that can help employees see the subject through youthful eyes — and through a lens of their legacy for future generations.

While many people associate Wal-Mart with its well-known efforts to provide low prices through rigorous cost controls, outsourcing, and low wages, the company has taken major strides to place environmental sustainability at the center of its strategic focus (Scott, 2005). One far-reaching program of employee engagement arranges for thousands of Wal-Mart employees at all levels to attend workshops about sustainability. They return to their stores and offices and invite their co-workers to design a "personal sustainability project." These projects may be as simple as replacing light bulbs with low-energy alternatives at home or riding a bike more. Discussions about the projects take place at work, and headquarters tracks their progress (Sacks, 2007). Such a program clearly attempts to encourage employees to feel a new affinity for the environment and to begin to align their own values with those of the company — deriving meaning from being a part of something bigger. While each project may be small, the potential impact on the thinking of some portion of the company's 1.9 million employees and the cumulative effect on the world could be considerable.

▓ Case studies

Five case studies illustrate some of the above approaches to employee engagement and provide a basis for developing other strategies and tactics for outstanding management.

1. **A story from the DuPont Plant in Belle, West Virginia.** The author describes his own experience dealing with a potentially hazardous manufacturing plant by enabling self-organizing practices that lead to dramatic improvements in safety, operating results, and morale

2. **Energizing people to create a safer, healthier workforce at PSE&G.** A multi-stage effort brings union members and management together with new initiatives reducing accidents and stimulating creative solutions

3. **Engaging employees in social consciousness at Eileen Fisher.** An apparel manufacturer founded on principles of simplicity, joy, and human connection achieves consistent profitability while remaining devoted to improving the lot of women and the environment

4. **Environmental, health, & safety issues at Alcoa Howmet.** One man conducts a long-standing campaign to ensure that safety concerns are infused into every activity and person in a high-precision metals fabricator

5. **Employee engagement at T-Systems: sustaining the organization and beyond.** A grassroots employee effort to deal with intolerable traffic conditions becomes an organization-wide change project that spreads over the whole community, with clear human and environmental benefits

This section starts with a first-person account of a broad-based management effort in a DuPont manufacturing plant.

Case 1. A story from the DuPont Plant in Belle, West Virginia

Richard N. Knowles

When I was appointed plant manager at the Belle, West Virginia, plant, I found its overall performance was dreadful, especially in safety. Although people were trying to do a good job, they had been performing so poorly for so long that it seemed acceptable. The main task of the 1,300 workers was to safely handle highly hazardous materials to make chemical intermediates and products. The plant dealt with large quantities of these materials. For example, from time to time, there would be 10 to 15 tank cars of hydrogen cyanide and up to 10,000 tons of anhydrous ammonia awaiting use as raw materials.

Actions

At the corporate level, DuPont had long singled out safety as a critical value, and the Belle Plant was nearly the poorest performer in the company. As I met everyone over the first three weeks, I was very clear that we had to get safety under control. My core belief was, "I don't have a right to make my living at a place where it is okay for you to get hurt." Most of the operators, mechanics, truck drivers, and railroad operators were intrigued by this, since they were the ones who were sustaining the injuries.

My safety focus began with the plant staff; this was serious, and the staff needed to establish new standards. I used a tough, top-down approach and had to terminate a few people because of safety performance problems. I walked the plant four to five hours a day, talking about this. There were many heated arguments about sticking to necessary procedures. Twice a week, I had one-hour business meetings in an operating area, shop, office, or the lab. After reviewing our safety and environmental situation, I invited questions and answered every one. I promptly distributed meeting minutes to everyone. After many acrimonious sessions in which people vented their frustrations, the meetings became more purposeful. Together we talked about the plant's challenges and how we should go forward. I placed responsibility for safety clearly on the shoulders of line supervisors rather than on staff safety specialists, who were to function in a support role. During these times, people told me they began to see me as focused, honest, determined, and fair.

Within about 18 months, the plant's safety performance improved to about average for DuPont. However, people were still getting hurt, so this was not good enough. The top-down process was moving us in the right direction, but the results were only mediocre. Furthermore, the arguments over safety had become tiresome and insufficient. The top-down approach was clearly unsustainable.

As new leadership staff came on board, we decided to use a plant-wide team approach that we thought could be much more effective if we did it right. The staff began with the development of the "Belle Treatment of People Principles." These were simple statements about how we on the management staff wanted to work with everyone. They included such principles as the importance of interesting, challenging work with the potential for learning and growth, personal accountability, involvement in decision-making, and the need for fair and consistent management. The management staff posted these principles around the plant, asking for people to hold staff accountable for living up to them. The workers' first reaction was to laugh at us. "You SOBs won't do this." But when they saw the managers were trying, they held us to it and really castigated us if we messed up. In fact, after about nine months of this rough-and-tumble approach, most of the people were adopting these as *their own* values — a fundamental shift.

Having established a clear mission and values and clarified the issues facing us, we introduced a team approach. The management staff spent about six months talking with everyone about teams and training people to be team leaders and facilitators. Everyone in the entire plant then moved, over one weekend, to form about 125 self-organizing teams, markedly transforming how we worked together. The transition was a bit ragged as everyone gradually became accustomed to the new system, but our total performance, including safety, did not drop during this time. Nearly all the self-organizing teams were coming up with better ways to improve performance and lower costs; valuable new bottom-up change initiatives went from a trickle to three or four a month. The work that started on safety issues had spread to all aspects of the plant. In safety, our plant became the third best in all of DuPont, even though the plant had to make reductions in the workforce.

All through this work, the leadership approach had to be flexible and responsive to the business- and people-related situations that came up. Our preferred approach was centered on engaging purposefully with the force of people's self-organization tendencies by actively sharing information, increasing trust, and building interdependence. In our conversations together, I helped everyone see how they fit into the larger picture and were helping to make a difference. Still, there were times when the standards dropped, and I had to take decisive action to reestablish them. Shortly before I moved on to another assignment, a supervisor committed what everyone acknowledged was a gross safety violation, and I had to fire him.

I regard this way of leading as a "dance" that requires leaders to pay attention to patterns and processes and constantly adjust to the demands of the present moment. I am proud to say that during these seven and a half years, the patterns and processes of sustainability became so deeply embedded within the people at the Belle plant that even a decade later their safety performance has continued to improve. For several years, the Belle plant actually posted the best safety record in DuPont.

Critical results

Over a period of less than eight years, the injury rate dropped 98%, plant emissions dropped 87%, productivity rose 45%, and earnings rose 300%. This persuasively exemplifies the triple-bottom-line benefit of sustainability management. It could not have happened unless everyone was pulling together. No one person could have brought this about. This employee-involvement effort was one in which I invited everyone to come together to help make the plant the best it could be. My role evolved from slave-driver to cheerleader, which was a lot more fun and satisfying.

Key learnings

Achieving this kind of transformation with vigorous employee engagement and high levels of performance requires leaders who:

- Can see the patterns and processes of behavior involved in how work really gets done
- Understand that different situations require different leadership approaches

- Are willing to share information freely with employees and be as transparent as possible, maintaining conversations across all levels

- Can build trust and interdependence between workers and managers

- Help people create a vision and mission that is credible and important for everyone, allowing them to see how they fit into the larger picture

- Have the courage, caring, and commitment to stay in the process and help make it happen

The cornerstone of this employee engagement rested on management's genuine desire to enlist the best ideas and effort from employees while standing firm for standards that were nonnegotiable. Leadership had to be authentic, open, and honest. When we made mistakes, we apologized and moved on. Eventually employees sensed a calling to take responsibility for success and could see every day how their behavior contributed to it.

Key ideas and tools illustrated here

- Taking a stand for high standards and humane practices

- Seeing the limitations of top-down management and transitioning to more employee-driven methods

- Inviting all levels of an organization into dialogue and acting on resulting ideas

- Building engagement around self-organizing teams

The next case study concerns another industrial challenge, but here the challenge is faced by PSE&G, a company with hundreds of different sites.

Case 2. Energizing people to create a safer, healthier workforce at PSE&G

Thomas K. Robinson and Jeana Wirtenberg

Public Service Electric & Gas, New Jersey's largest energy company, reacted to several workforce fatalities by commissioning a team in 1997 to benchmark other companies to determine the critical elements of their success in health & safety. This led to a multi-faceted safety system, a Commitment Statement endorsed by management and union leaders, and a grassroots-led council structure.

Although consistently improving over the five years after the team was commissioned, the safety record seemed to plateau by 2003 at around the 2.5 OSHA (Occupational Safety & Health Administration) incident rate, meaning that approximately 150 people were injured annually. While this represented a significant improvement over previous years, the new president of PSE&G challenged a small team of safety and organizational effectiveness people to devise an approach that would enable the company to reduce the rate even more. This effort took place during a period of uncertainty caused by a highly publicized pending merger and resulting staff reductions.

Actions

In formulating its plan, PSE&G could build on strong working relationships between company and union leadership that were forged during earlier total quality management initiatives. Together they built a new effort on this foundation, using well-established change management principles, including a clear, compelling vision, leadership support, employee engagement, regular reporting, recognition and celebration of short-term wins, and reinvigoration with new projects and people.

Creation of vision

Leaders conducted a series of facilitated visioning sessions in mid-2003 with approximately 150 grassroots employees representing many locations. Participants identified four major components of the desired culture of the future: pride, caring, trust, and "health & safety is good business." They also envisioned a variety of desired values and practices that represented a significant departure from the early days' sometimes-distant labor–management relations (see Fig. 5.1).

Figure 5.1 **Health & safety culture transition**

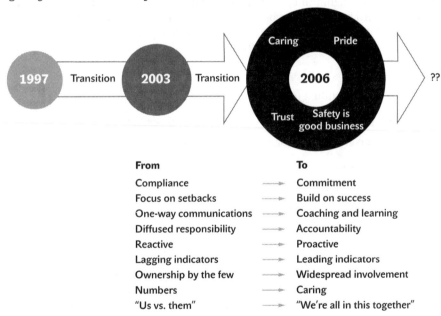

From		To
Compliance	→	Commitment
Focus on setbacks	→	Build on success
One-way communications	→	Coaching and learning
Diffused responsibility	→	Accountability
Reactive	→	Proactive
Lagging indicators	→	Leading indicators
Ownership by the few	→	Widespread involvement
Numbers	→	Caring
"Us vs. them"	→	"We're all in this together"

Source: Copyright 2008, PSE&G. Reproduced with permission.

Leadership commitment and employee participation

Armed with the new vision, the consulting team formed the Health & Safety Culture Transition Team, comprising about 70 people. The team's initial objectives were to:

- Develop alternative measures for safety and benchmarking where applicable

- Create a strategy where union and management trust each other and work well together

- Design and develop a robust, interactive approach to safety communications

- Originate a method to build a learning organization

- Construct a plan to develop and nurture an expanded cadre of safety leaders

All participants volunteered for a particular subteam, each of which was championed by a member of the PSE&G senior leadership team and supported by a subject matter expert, such as internal communications or health and wellness. The leadership also appointed a core team, consisting of the subteam leaders and champions, union safety leaders, and subject matter experts. The core team was to monitor progress and approve initiatives as they were developed by the subteams. Approved initiatives became part of the agenda for the full team at subsequent quarterly update meetings.

Reinvigoration with new projects

Based on the successful outcomes of the first two years and input obtained by the benchmarking subteam, project leadership created in 2006 two additional subteams, driving safety and ergonomics. Patterned after the original subteams, both of these groups have made significant contributions to ongoing results. In fact, the driving safety team's efforts led to the creation of a new safety system component. Such evolving contributions reinforce the important principle of emergence to continually reinvigorate an initiative and remain open to new learnings.

Critical results

The health & safety culture transition team's major accomplishments include:

- A safety and wellness intranet site providing access to resources

- Annual health & safety plans for each location

- The safety leading-indicator measurement system

- Knowledge-sharing sessions with external best-practice organizations

- Pilot ergonomic efforts to decrease the incidence and severity of musculo-skeletal injuries

The OSHA recordable accident rate has steadily declined; the 2006 results were almost half those of the previous five years. Also the injuries that have occurred have been less serious, as shown in the lost time incident and severity rate charts (Figs. 5.2 and 5.3). Employees at many locations have worked for extended periods without a personal injury. These results were especially noteworthy considering the reduced staffing levels in anticipation of a pending merger and related uncertainty about employees' future.

Learnings

This case illustrates that sustainability is a journey that must start from a solid foundation of focus, commitment, and participation. It also highlights how application of solid change management principles can enable the creation of a safer and healthier work environment, ultimately contributing to improved performance. It clearly shows that creative, focused efforts by a group of dedicated people can achieve extraordinary results, even during periods of exceptional uncertainty and distraction. These efforts have laid the foundation for continued improvement into the future.

Figure 5.2 **PSE&G OSHA lost time incident rate**

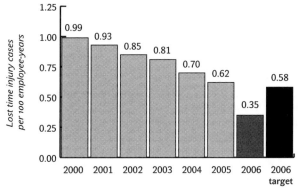

Source: Copyright 2008, PSE&G. Reproduced with permission.

Figure 5.3 **PSE&G OSHA lost time severity rate**

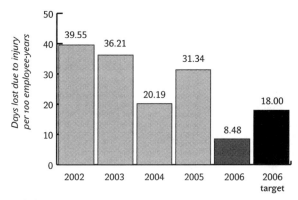

Source: Copyright 2008, PSE&G. Reproduced with permission.

Key ideas and tools illustrated here

● Building on strong working relationships between management and union leadership

● Visible senior leadership support as a critical lever

● Use of total quality management tools in supporting health & safety initiatives

● Importance of having a clear and compelling vision that everyone creates and supports

Other companies approach sustainability with a focus on social justice and human welfare. Eileen Fisher founded her company around such principles, as described in this case study.

Case 3. Engaging employees in social consciousness at Eileen Fisher

William G. Russell

Eileen Fisher invested her US$350 in savings in 1984 to purchase materials and have a seamstress make up four pieces of clothing that she herself wanted to wear, products that would simplify life and delight the spirit. She promptly caught the eye of retailers at an industry show, and an enterprise was born. As of 2007 this still privately held company boasted US$225 million in sales, 39 of its own retail stores, and 1,000 department store outlets. Some 700 employees, 80% female, work for the firm, augmented by an extended labor force in suppliers' factories located in the United States, China, India, Western Europe, and South America.

Actions

Fisher built her company on a foundation that stressed social consciousness, particularly for enriching the lives of women. These principles are evident in the company's leadership, employee policies, and relationships with suppliers.

Leadership

Employee engagement for Eileen Fisher begins with its leadership and the enterprise's values, vision, and performance standards. The enterprise is highly decentralized, but operations are still simple and encourage connection among people and groups. The Social Consciousness Team bears direct responsibility for shepherding the firm's employee engagement.

The corporate mission statement demonstrates how central employee engagement is to the company's foundation principles. The mission is "to inspire simplicity, creativity, and delight through connection and great design" and specifies four core practices: individual growth and well-being, collaboration and teamwork, joyful atmosphere, and social consciousness (Hall, 2006).

Employee policies

Eileen Fisher infuses its values and social consciousness messages across all stages of an employee's experience, beginning even before hiring (Hall, 2006). A potential employee finds the company's vision, values, and commitment to social consciousness throughout its website. During the interview process, recruits experience the office's scenic views, eco-friendly products, and energy-efficient lighting. They hear about the firm's concern for global standards for workplace conditions and employment practices and are asked about their own interests regarding social issues.

New hires receive more than standard training programs. Each is paired with a peer partner who personally reinforces the company's values and social consciousness programs, which appear in strikingly handsome print and electronic materials. The company's values and social programs are the focus of periodic brown-bag lunch sessions and further reinforced in newsletters, which also highlight charity events the company gets involved in. Employees can take advantage of on-site wellness programs and savor organic and locally produced catered food. Everyone receives an annual US$1,000 allowance to spend on her choice of outside wellness activities. All communications encourage employees to express company values in both their work and personal lives. In addition, the company affords employees numerous opportunities to grow professionally by joining one or more socially conscious committees, participating in in-store and community service events, and obtaining additional learning and leadership development training.

Supplier workforce practices

More than a decade ago, Eileen Fisher executives came to realize that their concern for their own employees needed to be expanded to embrace those people working for their suppliers. Like the company itself, these contractor partners hire predominantly women. They came to view suppliers as not just sources for clothes but also extensions of their own values and workforce. This realization drove the company to engage with suppliers to improve local working conditions. The UN SA8000 standards, governing the treatment of employees, child labor, and health & safety, became the working benchmark.

Eileen Fisher successfully persuaded many suppliers that certain humane practices produce short- and long-term financial benefits. Most of these companies were run by tough businessmen who reflected their national cultures, which were often characterized by rote learning and discouraged creativity. The company sometimes ran into resistance and distrust, with such responses as, "We have always done it this way."

Eileen Fisher has conducted its own training programs for suppliers' workers in some parts of the world. In China, for instance, where the typical wage earner has only a middle-school education, and may not have learned about feminine hygiene, sexual topics, or workplace rights, Eileen Fisher has instituted programs that address these subjects. Likewise, the company may teach workers techniques for, say, gracefully speaking up to a manager. The company has convinced some contractors to consider less punitive approaches toward employees and to move to more positive reinforcement and rewards. Many contractors have been delighted that these can really motivate employees, and they often report new levels of employee morale and loyalty. These suppliers are themselves becoming more creative, and some neighboring companies are starting to emulate them. Similarly, deeper partnerships between Eileen Fisher and suppliers are focusing more on environmental considerations, including lighting, air quality, and water quality.

Critical results

Eileen Fisher's 18-member leadership team is committed to balancing "Business, Product, and People and Culture," considering all of them equally. For example, it encouraged the company to integrate social consciousness and sustainability into product design decisions, which led to a line of garments made from organic cotton. Over the years, the vice president of people and culture and the social consciousness head have attempted to align their compensation practices with their values, by introducing, for instance, flat rate increases in salary. People are rewarded with growth opportunities, making it more of a place for growth and discovery, although not everyone has accepted this.

The company has been profitable since its founding. Refraining from becoming a broadly held public company, it set up an employee stock ownership plan (ESOP) in 2006. By 2012 employees will own 33% of the shares. Although the company does not, at the time of this writing, quantitatively measure the benefit of its social consciousness program, in the past it was primarily guided by what feels right. It is striving to better quantify the payoff from these investments and it is experiencing visible change in workforce practices. For instance, turnover has averaged just 15%, compared with an industry norm of 30 to 40%. The company's reputation attracted a dazzling 6,000 résumés in one year to fill 75 positions, one-quarter of which were filled internally (Hall, 2006). Eileen Fisher is highly rated by the Great Places to Work Institute, ranking no. 7 out of the top 25 companies identified. Management aspires to be no. 1.

Eileen Fisher clearly exemplifies the positive outlook of its founder. As Amy Hall, the director of social consciousness, reported, "We celebrate successes — individuals and teams, anniversaries, anything!"[3] The company listens to all the voices. In the spirit of collaboration, it doesn't dwell on mistakes; instead, it aims to make them a learning experience. Such openness can present a challenge (Hall, 2006, p. 51):

> Our staff has so much energy and so many ideas that it is often difficult to rein in people's well-intentioned enthusiasm . . . Helping staff see the big picture, and not focus just on their own sphere of influence, is time-consuming.

Heightening the challenge is the company's insistence on extending most initiatives to its far-flung supplier network, which requires such special efforts as translating key materials into Chinese and Spanish.

Unlike companies that have slowly come to incorporate social consciousness and sustainability management into long-standing practices, Eileen Fisher has built these into its corporate "DNA" from the beginning. While this offers the advantage of not having to retrofit new ideas onto old habits, it presents new challenges of how to find one's way. Through the continuing influence of its founder, the company has boldly broken much new ground and achieved remarkable results.

Key ideas and tools illustrated here

- Creating a culture that is aligned with the enterprise's distinctive values, vision, and performance standards, including consistent messages through peer partners, lunch-time discussions, newsletters, and community service events

- Engaging employees by emphasizing social consciousness, which incorporates individual growth and well-being, collaboration and teamwork, and a joyful atmosphere

- Integrating sustainability concerns into fundamental human resource practices, product design, and corporate facilities

- Extending the company's social consciousness agenda by working actively with its network of suppliers

Another industrial case study illustrates how Alcoa Howmet deals with critical safety management through comprehensive employee engagement.

---

3 Personal communication with A. Hall, telephone interview, September 20, 2007.

Case 4. Environmental, health, & safety issues at Alcoa Howmet

Kent D. Fairfield

> The key differentiator for success is not how we use Six Sigma, lean manufacturing and that sort of thing; it's *engaging people* into observing, identifying, and solving problems.
>
> *Jim Johnson*

Alcoa Howmet, a major business of Alcoa Inc., is a global leader in airfoil and structural castings, serving the aerospace and industrial markets. Such products result from a dirty and potentially dangerous production process. The division's 28 plants constitute what was formerly Howmet Corp., whose management has traditionally devoted considerable attention to safety and environmental concerns.

When Alcoa purchased the company in 2001, however, Alcoa management introduced extensive new strategies and more demanding standards for environment, health, & safety (EHS). Jim Johnson has seen the protocols for handling EHS evolve over more than 30 years. Starting on the shop floor at Howmet in 1978, Johnson became a first-line supervisor, later the plant manager, and eventually vice president of manufacturing for the whole division. He reports that, when he was plant manager, safety was just one of many issues he concerned himself with until its importance came home to him in brutal terms. "I thought hitting my numbers was the most important thing," he told one interviewer, until one day a mold broke "and I had a guy pour molten metal down his boot. It was a life-changing experience for me" (Kowalski, 2005).

Since this accident, Johnson has championed safety as the most important goal in all his plants. The assistance he gets from the Alcoa corporate office has reinforced his shift in priorities, including formalizing a robust EHS management system. For one thing, Alcoa ties incentive compensation to EHS results. When operations people meet, Johnson says, they ask each other, "Have you gotten anybody hurt? What did you do about it?" Naturally, industrial facilities have had basic safety measures in place for decades — the Occupational Safety & Health Administration (OSHA) requires detailed reporting — and Johnson says[4] it is possible to achieve basic safety benchmarks, "the low hanging fruit," by simply demanding it of employees. He had done that in one of his earlier management jobs, but he discovered people slipped back into more unsafe behavior after he left that location for a new assignment.

Johnson says that driving down accident rates further for more enduring results depends on engaging employees in more direct ways. One way Alcoa Howmet does this is by training all managers not only to execute safety procedures themselves but to train all their people in EHS. Although the company sometimes relies on outside consultants to design its training, it insists that all plant managers and others deliver the training themselves.

One exercise teaches participants to observe an operation with an eye toward potential breaches of safe practices. In the "Red Flag" program, all employees visit another department and place a red flag by any piece of equipment or action

---

4 Personal communication with J. Johnson, Dover, New Jersey, October 5, 2007. All information and quotes in this case study are from this interview unless otherwise indicated.

that appears to be a risk. Johnson reported that this program helps raise employees' consciousness of safety, not only in other people's work areas but also in their own.

Management pushes hard to get people to scrutinize working conditions from the EHS perspective and continually urges employees to feel free to speak up about any unsafe situation. Johnson quotes his boss challenging people: "Would you bring your kids in here and let them work where you work?" In an environment of molten metal and high-speed grinding and cutting machines, this sets a high bar for acceptable work practices.

One way the company ensures that managers focus on their training obligations is to require a detailed work plan. Managers have to draw up their own **leader standard work** — patterned after the standard work associated with line workers — in which EHS training activities may constitute as much as 40% of their time. A smart investment in training people about safety and sound environmental practices translates into less time dealing with emergencies and quick fixes. In fact, the company's most promising future plant managers devote most of their time to learning how to do the necessary EHS teaching and coaching. Even an invitation to a senior manufacturing manager to help in a sales presentation for customers does not preempt a planned safety activity. In addition, the company dispatches its best managers to other Alcoa Howmet facilities to conduct peer audits. Seeing outside executives scrutinize their facility helps employees recognize the importance of the right kinds of behavior.

Critical results

The various safety initiatives put in place since the Alcoa acquisition have paid off. The lost work day rate of 1.00 in 2001 was cut to only 0.034 in 2006. Average total OSHA recordable injury rate dropped over the same time from 7.06 to 1.90. The company could not maintain such a low rate in 2007, though, and the lost work day rate increased to 0.13, still a sizable improvement on the past. The company determined that 48% of recent accidents involve employees who have worked there less than one year, suggesting the need for better training and coaching of newer employees. Senior management also wants to instill in these workers the ability and confidence to speak up without fear of reprisal whenever uncertain or concerned about a safety issue.

Key learnings

Alcoa Howmet's record of improvement in safety exemplifies the progress that can occur when a company places high priority on the issue. Its executives clearly model the importance of safety; they do not just mouth vapid clichés about its desirability. Employees seem to get the message. This also illustrates the notion that setting goals and executing strategies in the name of sustainability coincides with improved business results. Fewer accidents represent the humane outcome and avoid the expense, regulatory entanglements, and bad publicity of an unsafe work history. Johnson's devotion to employee engagement is obvious when he insists, "Everybody has to understand the role that they play in assuring that all of our workers go home safe every night." And how does he justify all the attention to safety? If not, "I couldn't live with myself," he says (Kowalski, 2005).

Key ideas and tools illustrated here

● Going beyond demanding safe work practices and engendering employee-driven improvements

● Training the managers to train others in safe and proper practices

- Conducting peer safety audits between departments and across facilities to identify potentially dangerous conditions and practices and raise awareness for all

- Living out a passion for safety to achieve humane goals as well as pragmatic corporate objectives

The final case study here concerns employee engagement that originated at the grass roots and had repercussions for an entire community. It all started at the Indian offices of a major German information technology firm, T-Systems.

Case 5. Employee engagement at T-Systems: sustaining the organization and beyond

Sangeeta Mahurkar-Rao

The employees in the Pune, India, office of T-Systems were having tremendous difficulty reaching their office on time in June 2006. The traffic signal intersection at the corner by the office caused intense congestion, and irate commuters took to aggressive, undisciplined driving. The resulting gridlock meant that crossing the junction sometimes took as long as 40 minutes, affecting all T-Systems employees. Employee productivity was down and stress was up. In addition, the long wait exposed many employees on motorbikes and scooters to high pollution levels from the idling vehicles. This bottleneck was a consequence of enormous growth in the city. Many new office buildings and shopping areas had recently mushroomed along this road, straining an already stretched law enforcement capability and civic infrastructure.

Employees voiced their distress at a staff open-house meeting, along with their concern about the larger social issue it posed: the congestion affected countless people beyond their company. Employees decided to step forward and try to resolve the problem. They formed a task force including senior management, functional heads, and team members in June 2006 and took on the task of developing a suitable plan.

Actions

The task force brainstormed various possibilities and finally decided to try to facilitate the traffic flow themselves during peak hours. The initiative had the full support of senior management, which was vital, as it involved considerable investment of the employees' normal work time. The management believed it was part of their commitment to social responsibility.

The task force contacted the local traffic police and discussed its proposed initiative. The traffic police officers welcomed their suggestions, as their force was stretched too thin to tackle such localized problems. They also promised to support the effort however they could.

After gaining approvals and support from the management and local agencies, the task force developed the following plan:

1. Each morning from 8:30 to 10:30, employee volunteers would assume the role of traffic wardens and be physically present on the road to direct traffic

2. To enforce more disciplined movement, the wardens would use physical barriers to prevent vehicles from jumping signals

3. Other employee volunteers would hold placards that held messages for saving fuel and controlling pollution

4. Another group would hold placards that would reinforce the importance of following traffic rules, augmenting similar messages to be posted on nearby billboards

5. The employees would arrange to have tree branches cut to avoid obscuring important traffic signs

6. The task force would inform the local traffic police of its specific plan and seek any support required

This initiative had the active participation of the entire senior management team, which greatly encouraged broad employee involvement, and more than 100 of a staff of 500 employees volunteered their time.

Critical results

A key accomplishment is that having participated in achieving a sustainable social benefit, employees felt deeply satisfied. The initiative had a positive effect on all commuters at the signal. After a couple of unpleasant instances when commuters questioned the authority of the volunteers, people soon accepted the new arrangements. T-Systems employees were delighted to be able to reach the office on time. The previous waiting period of 35 to 40 minutes to cross the junction dropped to just 3 to 5 minutes, a vast improvement. The traffic police have taken note and helped ensure that during peak hours traffic wardens are posted for signal monitoring. Many residents expressed their appreciation, including parents of schoolchildren in the area. There was a visible improvement in the disciplined driving of local commuters as they began observing the traffic signals, contributing to the smoother flow.

The unique initiative received considerable coverage in local media, which helped inform the community of the project's underlying spirit and the reasons for the effort. The obvious improvements and the media attention motivated many other organizations located on the same road to offer their own volunteers. A rally was organized on Independence Day, August 15, during which responsibility was handed over to a larger contingent made up of volunteers from companies, social service organizations, government retirees, and youth, along with some traffic police. T-Systems employees took pride in having initiated and served as catalysts for this triumph of civic improvement.

Key learnings

This case is a powerful illustration that improving the sustainability of a single organization can have a positive impact that extends beyond the organization's boundaries. It reinforces the systems thinking view that what affects the organization necessarily affects the rest of the system of which it is a part, including other organizations and the community at large. The outcome benefited T-Systems employees, the company's productivity, neighboring commuters and organizations, pollution levels, and overall civic welfare.

Engagement of employees can result in powerful outcomes if the employees are suitably empowered and supported by management. It can also engender a strong sense of accomplishment, itself a critical factor for nurturing a sustainable organization.

Key ideas and tools illustrated here

- Listening to the serious concerns of employees about their welfare
- Endorsing grassroots efforts by providing management participation and support
- Sparking increased self-reliance and self-efficacy through projects outside people's job description
- Aiding employees with the practical concerns of getting to work and contributing to broader community welfare as well

▓ Conclusion

The five case studies illustrate how certain well-established psychological dynamics form a foundation for vigorous engagement by employees. The cases share a number of strategies and tactics that managers can use to bring about sustainability management with highly desirable outcomes.

Psychological dynamics

The work of Kouzes and Posner (2007) and Gratton (2007) stresses the psychological sense of ownership of a company's mission, particularly when employees experience their work as pertaining to the meaning in their life. Employees at Eileen Fisher and DuPont experience autonomy and self-determination, thanks to management values and practices that give them considerable leeway. Employees feel very much a part of a community of kindred spirits. In addition, they all tend to work in a system founded on interdependence, which Kouzes and Posner identified as critical to collective performance. Their positive attitudes are contagious, as Boyatzis and McKee (2007) would have predicted.

Strategy and tactics

While the cases describe a range of settings, from the industrial to white collar to manufacturing, considerable similarity exists in their strategy and tactics. Executives in all cases lay out certain understandings, standards, and guidelines for employee behavior. They also grant considerable freedom for employees to execute their plans and actions. As Knowles (2002, 2006) recommends, they often conduct conversations in the form of town hall meetings, or training sessions. Interestingly, leaders at both DuPont and Alcoa concede that a command-and-control approach[5] achieved middling improvements for safety and employee cooperation, and both found they had to genuinely involve their employees to achieve higher-level, long-lasting results.

One common strategy is to break down traditional barriers imposed by people's positions in an organization. PSE&G built its safety initiative on cross-level task forces. Alcoa placed frontline workers in the role of safety detectives. Another successful organization we came across promoted egalitarian communication through informal, outdoor

---

5 For more on the **command-and-control approach** in the journey toward sustainable enterprise, see Chapter 1, pages 27 and 47-48.

dialogues and a simple "rule": when you are within six feet of someone, whether a porter or top executive, say "hello." In a further attempt to dissolve the obstructions that organizational hierarchy can generate, the CEO of this same organization made a simple, authentic gesture; she moved her office from the top floor executive suite to a small office on the first floor near the cafeteria. Now when she leaves her office, she is in immediate contact with both clients and people from all levels of the organization, and spontaneous conversations arise daily.

A related strategy is to allow employees a clear line of sight to the outcomes stemming from their efforts. T-Systems' management nurtured a grassroots initiative so that staff experienced firsthand the improvement in traffic flow. The self-organizing initiative at DuPont allowed employees to see how their behavior improved the plant's safety record, increased its productivity, and contributed to a 300% escalation in earnings.

Outcomes

Employee engagement in each case study contributed to exceptional outcomes. Operating results improved markedly in all cases. The improvements were, for the people, both a cause and a consequence of this improvement. Employees felt called to new levels of self-reliance and autonomy, and they responded with energy, drive, and creativity. They exhibited new levels of ownership and accountability for unprecedented results. The all-too-typical resistance to change was minimal. A computer programmer acquires a new sense of self-efficacy when discovering his or her own ideas for solving a traffic problem are executed for communitywide benefit. Participants inside a "hot spot" feel the resonance of being a part of a winning team and experience a whole new sense of being in a community of kindred spirits.

In sum, we have seen in previous chapters that leaders need to craft inspiring visions, adopt constructive mental models, and manage complex change for sustainability management, but their efforts come into full flower only when they skillfully engage their employees. The concepts discussed in this chapter in the context of these exemplars of exceptional practice demonstrate how employee engagement can produce extraordinary results for the individual, the team, the organization, and the larger world.

▓ References

American Management Association (AMA). (2007). *Creating a sustainable future: A global study of current trends and possibilities 2007–2017*. New York: American Management Association.

Ashforth, B. E., & Pratt, M. G. (2002). Institutionalized spirituality: An oxymoron? In R.A. Giacalone & C. L. Jurkiewicz (Eds.), *The handbook of workplace spirituality and organizational performance* (pp. 93-107). Armonk, NY: M. E. Sharpe.

Bandura, A. (1997). *Self-efficacy: The exercise of control*. New York: Freeman.

Boyatzis, R., & McKee, A. (2007). *Resonant leadership: Renewing yourself and connecting with others through mindfulness, hope, and compassion*. Boston: Harvard Business School.

Cameron, K. S., Dutton, J. E., & Quinn, R. E. (2003). *Positive organizational scholarship: Foundations of a new discipline*. San Francisco: Berrett-Koehler.

Dychtwald, K., Erickson, T., & Morison, R. (2006). *Workforce crisis: How to beat the coming shortage of skills and talents*. Boston, MA: Harvard Business School.

Goleman, D., Boyatzis, R., & McKee, A. (2002). *Primal leadership: Realizing the power of emotional intelligence*. Boston, MA: Harvard Business School.

Gratton, L. (2007). *Hot spots: Why some teams, workplaces, and organizations buzz with energy – and others don't*. San Francisco: Berrett-Koehler.

Hall, A. (2006). Engaging employees in social consciousness at Eileen Fisher, *Journal of Organizational Excellence*, published online by Wiley InterScience, Autumn, DOI:10.1002/joe20111, 4552.

Human Resource Institute. (2000). *The future of attracting, retaining, and motivating key talent* (White paper). St. Petersburg, FL: Mark Vickers.

Kaye, B., & Jordan-Evans, S. (2005). *Love 'em or lose 'em: Getting good people to stay* (3rd ed.). San Francisco: Berrett-Koehler.

Knowles, R. N. (2002). *The leadership dance: Pathways to extraordinary organizational effectiveness*. Niagara Falls, NY: Center for Self-Organizing Leadership.

Knowles, R. N. (2006). Engaging the natural tendency of self-organization. *World Business Academy Transformation, 20*(15), 1-10.

Kouzes, J. M., & Posner, B. Z. (2007). *The leadership challenge* (4th ed.). San Francisco: Jossey-Bass.

Kowalski, R. (2005). Interview with James Johnson. Unpublished manuscript, Case Western University, Cleveland, OH.

Sacks, D. (2007, September). Working with the enemy. *Fast Company, 118*, 74-81.

Saks, A.M. (1995). Longitudinal field investigation of the moderating and mediating effects of self-efficacy on the relationship between training and newcomer adjustment. *Journal of Applied Psychology, 80*, 211–225.

Scott, L. (2005, October 24). Wal-Mart: Twenty-first century leadership (Speech). Retrieved December 21, 2007, from walmartstores.com/Files/21st%20Century%20Leadership.pdf.

Seligman, M. E .P., & Csikszentmihalyi, M. (2000). Positive psychology: An introduction. *American Psychologist, 55*, 5-14.

Willard, B. (2002). *The sustainability advantage*. New York: New Society.

Wirtenberg, J., Harmon, J., Russell, W. G., & Fairfield, K. D. (2007). HR's role in building a sustainable enterprise: Insights from some of the world's best companies. *Human Resource Planning, 30*(1), 10-20.

Wrzesniewski, A. (2002). "It's not just a job": Shifting meaning of work in the wake of 9/11. *Journal of Management Inquiry, 11*, 230-234.

Wrzesniewski, A. (2003). Finding positive meaning in work. In K. S. Cameron, J. E. Dutton, & R. E. Quinn (Eds.), *Positive organizational scholarship: Foundations of a new discipline* (pp. 296-308). San Francisco: Berrett-Koehler.

6

Sustainable enterprise metrics and measurement systems

William G. Russell, Shakira Abdul-Ali, Gil Friend, and David Lipsky

> Data is not information. Information is not knowledge. Knowledge is not understanding. Understanding is not wisdom.
>
> *anon.*

How does society, a nation, an enterprise, or an individual know if they are sustainable? Measures are a key ingredient to help move people from awareness to understanding and ultimately to action. While not the only tool, metrics are a powerful resource for allowing people to learn and teach, to journey from unconscious incompetence to conscious competence (T)(F) (Howell, 1982, pp. 29-33). Applying the **states of knowing model** (Atherton, 2003) to the matter of sustainability, it could be said that communities have been unconsciously incompetent (they haven't known that they haven't known). Governments, companies, groups, and individuals have been slow to realize that sustainable development is relevant. Wealthy people took for granted that water would flow when they turned on the tap. The poorest people presumed that the trees, birds, and fish that lived freely and profusely in their environments would continue to be there for their children, year in and year out. Figure 6.1 depicts the journey through which people will progress as they become aware and gain understanding about their current state of sustainability. The figure depicts two senses: awareness of self (represented by the vertical line in the diagram) and knowledge of the world (the horizontal

Figure 6.1 **States of knowing and not knowing**

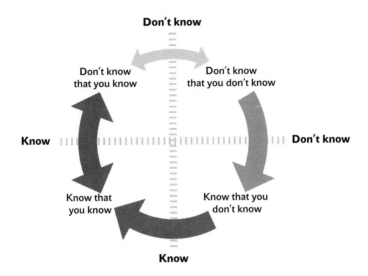

Source: J. S. Atherton (2003). Tools for thought: Knowing and not knowing. Retrieved January 2008, from www.doceo.co.uk/tools/knowing.htm. Copyright 2003, J. S. Atherton. Reproduced with permission.

line). Well-designed global, national, enterprise, and personal sustainability metrics will provide users with intelligence to fit their need to be conscious and know what they need to know in order to make informed decisions and take effective actions.

The sustainability measurement practices of hundreds of businesses were explored in *Creating a Sustainable Future* (American Management Association [AMA], 2007) and the *2007 AMA Sustainability Survey* on which it is based. Several insights emerged and helped focus the themes and content for this chapter. Using a 5-point scale ratings system, respondents indicated that measuring sustainability was important, scoring 3.9 out of 5 points. Lack of standardized metrics and benchmarks was ranked fourth in the top ten factors hindering companies from becoming more sustainable. These companies have reached the stage of conscious incompetence.

Sustainability is an ever-changing end state; "one knows that one doesn't know" what that end state will be. Acknowledging and accepting that no one knows definitively is an important part of designing and implementing sustainability metrics and measurement systems. Developing an integrated framework of ecosystems, social systems, and economic systems will allow businesses and individuals to develop the collective awareness and understanding to energize and enable global action. Business management systems with integrated sustainability metrics are powerful tools to inform leaders, employees, and stakeholders throughout the company lifecycle value chain. These measurement systems, along with a common vision of the desired future state, are the critical ingredients for a sustainable world.

This chapter provides overviews of the enormous progress being made on sustainable development indicators, measurement frameworks, and systems at the global, national, and enterprise levels. The outcomes of those systems, even knowing how much is still to be learned about them, allow an appreciation of the world's current condition.

Measures are also introduced for each of the relevant chapters in this book. These are intended to help leaders and managers more clearly appreciate how one can apply measurement tools to more qualitative sustainability attributes in order that they be tracked and managed within a holistic sustainability metrics and management program.

■ Global sustainable development indicators overview

The world is a living system, and, unless human systems inflict irreparable damage, a natural lifecycle of extraction, growth, development, and regeneration is inevitable. How do we ensure that this process is sustainable? We must create rigorous metric guidelines that will ensure a new, more sustainable approach to global development. As such, sustainable development[1] (SD) is an increasingly common goal among governments, nongovernmental organizations, and companies as more and more leaders are committing to focusing on the simultaneous well-being of people, the planet, and profits: the triple bottom line. Government leaders are acknowledging and facilitating the design and application of sustainable development indicators for national governments and the world at large. Some nongovernmental organizations have also self-organized multistakeholder collaborative initiatives to create and maintain highly useful metrics methodologies, scientific databases, research reports, and a variety of informative calculator applications. Corporations, too, are supporting the development of global and national sustainable development indicators and measurement systems as they see the need for policy and business leaders alike to progress from not knowing to knowing and supplying their organizations with the macro-level intelligence that inevitably will affect their businesses.

Sustainable development measurement frameworks

There is much debate about what to measure, how to measure, and how to develop goals and targets within specific time and location boundaries. There is also much debate about how to compare one entity (nation, region, resource, and so on) with another. A number of international agencies, nongovernmental organizations, and national governments have been identifying and defining the nature and type of indicator to be collected and evaluated. The United Nations Commission for Sustainable Development (UNCSD) has served an important role in taking on the challenge of bringing attention to the need for SD indicators at the national level. UNCSD offers a menu of indicators, but has not produced a common framework and a common set of influential SD indicators. Common frameworks have not automatically led to common measures, and common measures may not lead to coordinated action, but they are important elements for enabling a coordinated approach to designing sustainable development metrics and measurement systems and informing effective global actions for SD.

---

1 *Sustainable development* (SD) is used here when referring to global and national sustainability measurement efforts. *Sustainability* is used when referring to enterprise-level measurement efforts.

Sustainable development indicators

According to a recent UNCSD report, *Sustainable Indicators: Proposals for a Way* 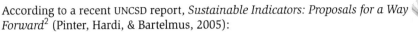 *Forward*[2] (Pinter, Hardi, & Bartelmus, 2005):

> Decision-makers demand indicators for SD that can be integrated into the relevant level of policy-making (regional, national, subnational, local). In cases where serious attempts to systematically implement SD are made, this brings up the challenge that indicators, including social and environmental indicators, usually without a known and accepted monetary value, are brought to bear on *economic* policy-making. These demands lead to the following preferences:
>
> - a small set of indicators
>
> - indicators that are linked to policy targets
>
> - environmental and social indicators that are compatible with macro-economic indicators and the budgeting process. (p. 6)

A sustainability performance indicator is a measurement that reflects the status of a social, economic, or environmental aspect or system over time. As a society, our understanding of sustainability is new and is coming into sharper focus. Table 6.1 (T) presents a framework and measurement set that was developed after a detailed review of national governments' experience implementing Agenda 21 indicators.[3] It was prepared for the UNCSD, and offers one example of a comprehensive list of indicators that can be collected and measured at the global and national, as well as regional and community, levels. Organizations collecting data used within this framework can benchmark their own performance against institutions using the same or similar frameworks.

Case. The ecological footprint

The ecological footprint has become a widely acknowledged measurement tool. According to the Global Footprint Network (Ecological Footprint Overview, 2007), the ecological footprint is a "resource accounting" tool that measures

> the extent to which humanity is using nature's resources faster than they can regenerate. It illustrates who uses how much of which ecological resources, with populations defined either geographically or socially. And, it shows to what extent humans dominate the biosphere at the expense of wild species.

Put another way, the ecological footprint is a resource management tool that measures how much land and water area a human population requires to produce the resources it consumes and to absorb its wastes under prevailing technology. Figure 6.2 shows the productive and nonproductive areas for the planet. Table 6.2 shows that, in 2003 (most recent data available), humanity's ecological footprint is more than 22% larger than the planet's capacity to regenerate: it now takes more than one year and two months for the

---

2   The entire UNCSD report can be viewed on the *Living Fieldbook* (L). See the Introduction, pages 7-8, for *Living Fieldbook* details.

3   Agenda 21, a plan of action also known as *The Blueprint for Sustainable Development*, and a set of principles called the Rio Declaration on Environment and Development, were adopted by more than 178 governments at the United Nations Conference on Environment and Development (UNCED) held in Rio de Janeiro, Brazil, June 3–14, 1992.

Table 6.1 **UNCSD theme indicator framework**

Social		
Theme	*Subtheme*	*Indicator*
Equity	Poverty (3)	Percentage of population living below poverty line
		Gini index of income inequality
		Unemployment rate
	Gender equality (24)	Ratio of average female wage to male wage
Health	Nutritional status	Nutritional status of children
	Mortality	Mortality rate under five years old
		Life expectancy at birth
	Sanitation	Percentage of population with adequate sewage disposal facilities
	Drinking water	Population with access to safe drinking water
	Healthcare delivery	Percentage of population with access to primary healthcare facilities
		Immunization against infectious childhood diseases
		Contraceptive prevalence rate
Education (36)	Education level	Children reaching grade 5 of primary education
		Adult secondary education achievement level
	Literacy	Adult literacy rate
Housing (7)	Living conditions	Floor area per person
Security	Crime (36, 24)	Number of recorded crimes per 100,000 population
Population (5)	Population change	Population growth rate
		Population of urban formal and informal settlements

Environmental		
Theme	*Subtheme*	*Indicator*
Atmosphere (9)	Climate change	Emissions of greenhouse gases
	Ozone layer depletion	Consumption of ozone-depleting substances
	Air quality	Ambient concentration of air pollutants in urban areas
Land (10)	Agriculture (14)	Arable and permanent crop land area
		Use of fertilizers
		Use of agricultural pesticides
	Forests (11)	Forest area as a percentage of land area
		Wood-harvesting intensity
	Desertification (12)	Land affected by desertification
	Urbanization (7)	Area of urban formal and informal settlements
Oceans, seas, and coasts (17)	Coastal zone	Algae concentration in coastal waters
		Percentage of total population living in coastal areas
	Fisheries	Annual catch by major species

(continued opposite)

Environmental (continued)		
Theme	*Subtheme*	*Indicator*
Fresh water (18)	Water quantity	Annual withdrawal of ground and surface water as a percentage of available water
	Water quality	BOD in water bodies
		Concentration of fecal coliform in fresh water
Biodiversity (15)	Ecosystem	Area of selected key ecosystems
		Protected area as a percentage of total area
	Species	Abundance of selected key species

Economic		
Theme	*Subtheme*	*Indicator*
Economic structure (2)	Economic performance	GDP per capita
		Investment share in GDP
	Trade	Balance of trade in goods and services
	Financial status (33)	Debt-to-GNP ratio
		Total ODA given or received as a percentage of GNP
Consumption and production patterns (4)	Material consumption	Intensity of material use
	Energy use	Annual energy consumption per capita
		Share of consumption of renewable energy resources
		Intensity of energy use
	Waste generation and management (19–22)	Generation of industrial and municipal solid waste
		Generation of hazardous waste
		Management of radioactive waste
		Waste recycling and reuse
	Transportation	Distance traveled per capita by mode of transport

Institutional		
Theme	*Sub-theme*	*Indicator*
Institutional framework (38, 39)	Strategic implementation of SD (8)	National sustainable development strategy
	International cooperation	Implementation of ratified global agreements
Institutional capacity (37)	Information access (40)	Number of Internet subscribers per 1,000 inhabitants
	Communication infrastructure (40)	Main telephone lines per 1,000 inhabitants
	Science and technology (35)	Expenditure on research and development as a percentage of GDP
	Disaster preparedness and response	Economic and human loss due to natural disasters

Source: F. Casado. (2003). SKN Worldwide: Aligning–integrating–automating sustainability indicators. PowerPoint presentation at International Sustainability Indicators Network annual meeting, Toronto, Canada. Copyright 2003, SKN. Reproduced with permission.

Figure 6.2 **Regenerative biocapacity of the Earth**

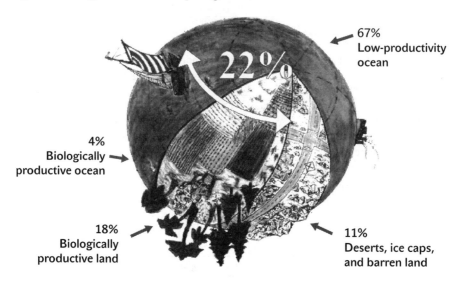

67%
Low-productivity
ocean

4%
Biologically
productive ocean

18%
Biologically
productive land

11%
Deserts, ice caps,
and barren land

Source: M. Wackernagel, Global Footprint Network. (2005). The ecological footprint: What's in it for you? PowerPoint presentation. www.footprintnetwork.org. Copyright 2005, M. Wackernagel. Reproduced with permission.

Table 6.2 **Global footprint accounts** (global hectares per person, 2003 data)

	Footprint	Biocapacity
Cropland	0.5	0.5
Grazing land	0.1	0.3
Fishing ground	0.2	0.1
Forest land	0.2	0.8
Carbon	1.1	–
Built-up land	0.1	0.1
Total	**2.2**	**1.8**

Source: Copyright 2008, Global Footprint Network. Reproduced with permission.

Earth to regenerate what humans use in a single year. Ecological footprints are available for every country and for specific footprint areas that are each critical to global sustainable development. (This connection is discussed further in Chapter 7, pages 221ff.)

Tool. Gapminder Trendalyzer: animated global sustainable development measurements

The Trendalyzer software (acquired by Google) turns complex global trends into animations, making decades of data come alive. Asian countries, as colorful bubbles, float across the grid — toward better national health and wealth. Animated bell curves representing national income distribution squish and flatten. This tool is a clear example of the convergence of technology, scientific, and government data collection, and visual animation graphics and video presentations of the results. An inspiring video presentation by Hans Rosling which uses the tool to present complex data and make global trends for life expectancy, child mortality, and poverty rates become clear, intuitive, and enjoyable, is available on the *Living Fieldbook* (**L**) and www.gapminder.org/video/talks/ted-2007---the-seemingly-impossible-is-possible.html.

Global sustainable development indicator networks

The following are a few examples of the many networks that have organized themselves to collaborate and advance a specific area of globally and nationally relevant sustainable development metrics and reporting standards and systems.

International Sustainability Indicators Network (ISIN)[4]

This network focuses on providing a vehicle for collaborative communication among members who are interested in sustainability. Key tools include listserv discussions, virtual and in-person meetings, and special programs and trainings. It has an excellent list of local, regional, national, and global communities that are currently working in this area as well as targeted writings and links.

International Society for Ecological Economics (ISEE)[5]

The International Society for Ecological Economics (ISEE) advances the understanding of the relationships among ecological, social, and economic systems for the mutual well-being of nature and people. It attempts to address some of the key questions in ecological economics, such as:

- How is human behavior connected to changes in hydrological, nutrient, or carbon cycles?

- What are the feedbacks between the social and natural systems, and how do these influence the services we get from ecosystems?

ISEE provides networking, conferences, a journal, Web tools, membership database, newsletters, job postings, and funding opportunities.

---

4 www.sustainabilityindicators.org (accessed January 29, 2008).
5 www.ecoeco.org (accessed January 29, 2008).

■ Enterprise sustainability metrics and management systems overview

This section provides an overview of sustainability measurement frameworks, metrics, and tools used at the enterprise level to design and implement integrated sustainability business metrics and management systems. Wirtenberg and her colleagues (Wirtenberg, Harmon, Russell, & Fairfield, 2007) reported that developing and using metrics appears to be central to efforts focused on managing in a sustainable fashion. One executive in their study said,

> It's in the business plans where we want to get things like metrics embedded, because it's done at the planning stage; it's not something that's constantly imposed . . . for me that's one of the best ways to align our structures and systems. (2007, p. 13)

Lifecycle-based framework for sustainable enterprise measurement

Bridges to Sustainability[6] worked with the American Institute for Chemical Engineers to define a sustainability measurement framework and a series of indicators relevant to a variety of industrial sectors and companies (Tanzil & Beloff, 2003). The enterprise sustainability measurement framework (Fig. 6.3) provides a three-dimensional lens through which organizations can look in order to ensure that they've considered all factors related to the triple bottom line. The y axis addresses the basic domains of the triple bottom line (people, planet, profit); the x axis incorporates the natural cycle for the sustainability of those domains. Ideally, the "fate" (waste, reuse) of all production activity should become the supply for other useful products and/or activities. The z axis incorporates other aspects, including time, location, values, and such resources as goodwill, reputation, and core competencies.

Each of the variables in the sustainability framework can provide a range of data points for assisting the enterprise in measuring its efforts to generate a zero footprint within a life-giving workplace. Once specified, these data points can help the organization uncover trends along both temporal (past, present, and future) and material (quantitative and qualitative) scales.

Enterprise sustainability measurement system qualities and technology

With advancement of business management systems and systems thinking, managing a business has become inextricably linked to data management and information technology. Today's business managers depend on real-time data and metrics management systems to inform their day-to-day operating decisions and long-term strategic plans. Companies are deploying a variety of technology solutions such as PC-based spreadsheets and risk analysis software to collect data, calculate metrics, and generate reports.

---

6 Bridges to Sustainability was a nonprofit institute designed to foster the implementation of greater sustainability through partnerships. The former Bridges to Sustainability was acquired by Golder Associates in 2005. The nonprofit continues to operate under the name Bridges to Sustainability Institute.

Figure 6.3 **Enterprise sustainability measurement framework**

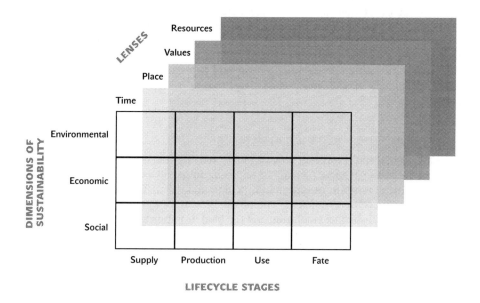

Source: Copyright 2000, Bridges to Sustainability. Used with permission.

Enterprise resource planning (ERP) systems automate and improve manufacturing processes and resource management, and support input–output evaluations and material-flow cost accounting. Enterprise databases, intranets, and Web-based portals are supporting metrics management systems such as balanced scorecards, a variety of environmental and social indicators, and financial and sustainability reporting.

While advancements in business management and technology systems were evolving, sustainability measurement and reporting also experienced rapid maturation. In the early 1990s there was the advent of environmental reporting including the early Ceres reports.[7] The Bhopal, India, chemical plant explosion led to the Community Right-to-Know legislation and the requirement for some corporations to publicly report their Toxics Release Inventories. In 1997, sustainability reports were advanced with the beginning of the Global Reporting Initiative (GRI). With Enron, and related market scandals, came the 2002 passing of the Sarbanes–Oxley Act. This required more stringent compliance functionality and better reporting capabilities to satisfy investor and other stakeholder demands for greater transparency.

Sustainability business management and reporting systems must leverage applications that link sustainability, knowledge management, and performance improvement. Traditional management systems were not designed for a balanced view of financial, environmental, and social metrics. They were developed to measure performance data

7 Ceres (pronounced "series") is a national network of investors, environmental organizations, and other public interest groups working with companies and investors to address sustainability challenges such as global climate change. In 1989, Ceres announced the creation of the Ceres Principles, a ten-point code of corporate environmental conduct that included the mandate to report periodically on environmental management structures and results.

for quality, risk, and cost control. Next-generation systems integrating sustainability go beyond compliance and risk management. New technologies promise clearer views of complex issues with more integrated functionality. They are influencing new thinking about the causal relationships of issues and are forcing a shift in decision-making and management behaviors in favor of reduced burden-shifting[8] and greater accountability.

Additional details on technology trends, software tools, and Web-based services for sustainability measurement and reporting are included in *Implementing Technology Applications for Sustainability Management and Reporting* (Russell, 2004) and "Real Time Regulation: A New Business and Policy Frontier" (Friend, 2005), available on the *Living Fieldbook* (**L**).

Sustainability performance indicators

There are specific indicators that provide timely, reliable, and cost-efficient information on the current state of social, economic, and environmental elements of sustainability. These may include **input**, **output**, and **outcome** indicators. Those indicators may be aggregated into a compressed set of **composite indicators** (total cost assessment, life-cycle assessment, ecological footprint, and the like). Composite indicators are useful in simplifying a long list of indicators to provide a visible indication of key trends. The def-

---

THE LANGUAGE OF INDICATORS

ESAT has learned the importance of word meanings for effective communication. The language of indicators has a history of misunderstanding and confusion. We offer this sidebar to provide more clarity on how these terms are interpreted by the authors.

Indicator. A measure of a key attribute or characteristic considered indicative of the state of a system — a business, an economy, an ecosystem — that is, a measure of public health & safety (mortality and morbidity, nutritional status), environmental quality (air quality, energy use), economic vitality (profit, job creation), and the like. Ideally, an indicator is a simple variable that can be measured objectively, such as population, revenues, and number of events. Indicators provide a basis for measuring change over time and, thereby, for understanding the relative condition of an entity — both to itself, and to other entities and groups of entities.

Index. An indicator, but more typically applied in a relative scale and often in combination with multiple indicators: for example, multiple indicators may be combined into a single index that is deemed to indicate the overall relative performance or con-

---

(continued opposite)

---

8 *Burden-shifting* refers to companies improving their own performance, not by eliminating the particular impact, but by moving outside their corporate systems' measurement boundary. This may be done by outsourcing, asking suppliers to assume a burden, or selling off currently "dirty" business units or product lines.

dition of an entity. Stock performance measurements are a classical example of indices. (See Dow Jones Sustainability Indexes on page 188.)

Footprint. A measurement of impacts on the environment and natural resources. An "ecological footprint" measures how much land and water area a human population requires to produce the resources it consumes and to absorb its wastes under prevailing technology. The ecological footprint metric presented earlier is one of the most well-regarded footprint measurement programs. A "carbon footprint" measuring human impacts on climate through greenhouse gas emissions, represented as carbon equivalents, is another rapidly growing footprint measure.

Inputs. Measures of the resources an organization uses to produce a product or provide a service, such as total dollars invested, raw materials purchased, number of people employed, amount of energy used.

Outputs. Indicators of the amount of product or service provided: for example, refrigerators manufactured, revenues or profits realized, amount of greenhouse gas (GHG) generated.

Outcomes. Measures that assess how well a product's or service's goals and objectives are accomplished. Outcome measures indicate the quality or effectiveness of a product or service: for instance, cleanliness ratings based on routine inspections could describe a city's success (or lack thereof) at cleaning its streets or parks. A business might track market share, share value, customer satisfaction, or progress toward mission.

Efficiency. Indicators that measure the amount of resources required to produce a unit of output or to achieve a certain outcome. These measures inform judgments about how well resources were used to achieve intended aims — the question of "bang for the buck" — by comparing input indicators with output and outcome indicators.

Input–output comparisons include energy use per unit of product, water use per gallon of product.

Input–outcome measures include tons of GHG per dollar of profit, tons of compost per acre of land reclaimed, dollars invested per percentage increase in market share.

Benchmarks. Performance comparisons to peers, best-in-class performers, and the like, which help identify leaders' and laggards' best practices and opportunities for performance improvement.

---

initions given in the sidebar represent concepts used throughout this chapter and by the growing number of sustainability metrics practitioners.

Tables 6.3 through 6.5 present examples of enterprise indicators for economic, environmental, and social domains.

Table 6.3 **Economic indicators**

Traditional indicators	Sustainability indicators	Emphasis of sustainability indicators
• Median income • Per capita income relative to the US average	• Number of hours of paid employment at the average wage required to support basic needs	• What wage can buy • Defines basic needs in terms of sustainable consumption
• Unemployment rate • Number of companies • Number of jobs	• Diversity and vitality of local job base • Number and variability in size of companies • Number and variability of industry types • Variability of skill levels required for jobs	• Resilience of the job market • Ability of the job market to be flexible in times of economic change
• Size of the economy as measured by GNP and GDP	• Wages paid in the local economy that are spent in the local economy • Dollars spent in the local economy that pay for local labor and local natural resources • Percentage of local economy based on renewable local resources	• Local financial resilience

Source: Sustainablemeasures.com./Indicators/TraditionalvsSustainable.htm. Reproduced with permission.

Table 6.4 **Environmental indicators**

Traditional indicators	Sustainability indicators	Emphasis of sustainability indicators
• Ambient levels of pollution in air and water	• Use and generation of toxic materials (both in production and by end user) • Vehicle miles traveled	• Measuring activities causing pollution
• Tons of solid waste generated	• Percentage of products produced that are durable, repairable, or readily recyclable or compostable	• Conservative and cyclical use of materials
• Cost of fuel	• Total energy used from all sources • Ratio of renewable energy used at renewable rate compared to nonrenewable energy	• Use of resources at sustainable rate

Source: Sustainablemeasures.com./Indicators/TraditionalvsSustainable.htm. Reproduced with permission.

Table 6.5 **Social indicators**

Traditional indicators	Sustainability indicators	Emphasis of sustainability indicators
⊛ SAT and other standardized test scores	⊛ Number of students trained for jobs that are available in the local economy ⊛ Number of students who go to college and come back to the community	⊛ Matching job skills and training to the needs of the local economy
⊛ Number of registered voters	⊛ Number of voters who vote in elections ⊛ Number of voters who attend town meetings	⊛ Participation in the democratic process ⊛ Ability to participate in the democratic process

Source: Sustainablemeasures.com./Indicators/TraditionalvsSustainable.htm. Reproduced with permission.

Setting goals and targets

The goals and impacts of sustainability can be hard to measure, which runs contrary to decision-makers' tendency to look for easy, clear methods to delineate progress and success. The sustainability challenge is daunting to many, in part because it seems so far away, and in part because the common formulation of it is so vague. The Brundt-land definition[9] is noble, but not testable; where's the target? Sustainability frameworks exist to define and produce powerful sustainability measures, but leave open the question of how aggressively to pursue them.

CASE. NASA AND APOLLO GOALS: STARTING WITH THE END STATE

Only the more courageous among us match the stretch goals standards of the Apollo mission. NASA realized that challenging technical achievements required for the moon mission would have to be supported by powerful social innovations. The first act of the Apollo project was to throw a victory party — at which the NASA organization celebrated the successful moon launch and return. After the party, they sat down and asked themselves, "How did we do it? What did we do at the end of the process

(continued over)

9 The Brundtland Commission (World Commission on Environment and Development, 1987), in a report often considered the beginning of the global dialogue on sustainability, recognized sustainable development as "a process of change in which the exploitation of resources, the direction of investments, the orientation of technological development, and institutional change are made consistent with future as well as present needs" (1987, p. 25; see also Chapter 4, pages 118-119).

that enabled us to fulfill this mission? What were the actions in the last year, and the year before that and the year before that?"

When the gap is big, and the pathway not clear, this reverse mental engineering can make it possible to see a path – from the goal to the start – that may be obscured by the dizzying permutations that exponentially multiply when looking from the start toward the goal, when the branching possibilities are too numerous to see clearly. (To deal with the challenge of apparent technical impossibility – or at least of large gaps between "need to" and "know how" – NASA created the department of "It Can't Be Done," which dispassionately turned impossible demands into design specifications that could be systematically invented and engineered into possibility.)

Most companies prefer to set reasonable goals that they are confident they will achieve. Others select aggressive and public goals that demand both technical innovation and organizational breakthroughs. The following are examples:

- **ST Microelectronics.** Cut GHG emissions by a factor of ten by 2010
- **DuPont.** Zero emissions, zero defects, zero injuries
- **Nike.** Eliminate chlorine
- **Interface.** "No smokestacks or sewer pipes"

A stretch sustainability goal[10] – such as 100% renewable energy portfolio within ten years – may seem equally outlandish. "Can we do it?" some will ask. "Is it even possible?" On the other hand, the more useful question to ask, given that people will need to trend in that direction at some rate in any case, may be "what would it take to achieve that goal (and not at the expense of business goals)?" Radical efficiency gains? A new kind of deal with an energy provider? Something we haven't thought of yet? It's in the stretch beyond the goals already within reach that "invention" comes into play. Not "can we?" but "how can we?"[11]

Collaborative networks for enterprise sustainability metrics and reporting

The following are two examples of the many networks that have organized themselves to collaborate and advance a specific area of enterprise sustainability metrics and reporting.

The Global Reporting Initiative (GRI) [12]

Some sustainability metrics might be derived from sustainability reporting standards. The Global Reporting Initiative, or GRI, launched by Ceres, has become recog-

---

10 Chapter 2 (pages 81ff.) contains an essay by Theresa McNichol discussing setting stretch goals via the use of Appreciative Inquiry.
11 This material is reprinted from Friend, 2004, with permission.
12 www.globalreporting.org (accessed January 29, 2008).

nized as a global standard in sustainability reporting and continues to evolve. Over 1,200 organizations disclose their sustainability performance with reference to the GRI guidelines. The standards provide guidance on the format and content of the reports as well as providing assistance on how to normalize and verify data. They contain a comprehensive set of organizational, management system, and performance parameters relating to a company's economic, social, and environmental performance. The guidelines encourage companies to set targets and commitments and then to report on the extent to which these are being met, providing reasons for any gaps or failures. The GRI strongly encourages the adoption of a stakeholder engagement process, with the aim of reporting on those issues of greatest relevance to stakeholders.

Greenhouse Gas Protocol Initiative[13]

The purpose of the Greenhouse Gas Protocol (GHG Protocol) Initiative is to provide an international accounting tool for government and business leaders to understand, quantify, and manage GHG emissions. These tools also provide a vehicle for developing countries' businesses to compete in the global marketplace and help their governments make informed decisions.

▨ Metrics applications for sustainable enterprises

Effective metrics are only as good as the positive change they can drive in strategy and execution. This occurs when employees understand where their organizations are headed, and how they can contribute and receive reinforcement for doing so. This is no easy task. Robert S. Kaplan and David P. Norton described these challenges as well as proposed solutions in the *Harvard Business Review* (1992) and in their book *The Balanced Scorecard: Translating Strategy into Action* (1996).

They found that:

- Only 5% of workers understand their organization's strategy

- Only 25% of managers have incentives linked to strategy

- 60% of organizations don't link budgets to strategy

- 86% of executive teams spend less than one hour per month discussing strategy

The following subsections will present two widely recognized enterprise-wide measurement methodologies — balanced scorecard and Baldrige — that have been successfully adapted to incorporate sustainability measurement metrics and sustainability-aligned goals and objectives. Enterprises are also implementing more specialized measurement programs. Four such specialized measurement aspects are introduced in case examples and tool summaries. Key performance indicators are identified using the Business Metabolics software tool. Energy and greenhouse gas metrics are discussed along with the OpenEco portal application. Building and product performance indicators are also presented.

---

13 www.ghgprotocol.org (accessed January 29, 2008).

Sustainability balanced scorecard

The **balanced scorecard** process is an example of an enterprise-wide measurement system that has been successfully adapted to support sustainability-aligned metrics and business management systems. The purpose of the balanced scorecard is to help organizations manage results more effectively with a balance of measures in four categories: financial, customer, internal processes, and learning/growth. Once developed, a balanced scorecard becomes an instrument for aligning organizational performance with strategy.

Broadening balanced scorecard measures to include environmental and social issues creates an effective tool for measuring enterprise sustainability. In their paper "The Sustainability Balanced Scorecard," Figge and colleagues provide a systematic approach for organizations to use when creating their own sustainability balanced scorecard (SBSC). (Figge, Hahn, Schaltegger, & Wagner, 2002). The authors suggest three methods for creating an SBSC to fit an organization's needs:

- Integrating environmental and social into the four pillars of the balanced scorecard

- Addition of a nonmarket perspective into the balanced scorecard

- Deduction of a derived environmental and social standard (p. 8)

To learn more about sustainability balanced scorecards and see more cases visit the *Living Fieldbook* (**L**).

Case. Sustainability balanced scorecard: Rio Tinto PLC

Rio Tinto PLC, a world leader in mining and processing the Earth's mineral resources, uses a sustainability balanced scorecard. Its products include aluminum, copper, diamonds, and coal. The company operates primarily in North America, Europe, Asia, Australia, and New Zealand.

To create its sustainable balanced scorecard, Rio Tinto created a sustainable development leadership panel. This group was tasked with developing a set of decision-making criteria to help Rio Tinto businesses and departments incorporate sustainable development in all of their initiatives.[14]

To balance financial metrics the company uses a sustainability framework that includes:

- **Social.** Enhancing human potential and well-being

- **Environment.** Maximizing resource efficiency and minimizing environmental damage

- **Economy.** Optimizing economic contribution[15]

The sustainability balanced scorecard connects Rio Tinto's overall sustainability strategy with project and initiative results.

---

14 www.accountingforsustainability.org.uk/output/page110.asp (accessed December 12, 2007).
15 Ibid.

Baldrige model for sustainability performance measurement

The current Baldrige award grew from the Malcolm Baldrige National Quality Award program supervised by the US Commerce Department's National Institute of Standards and Technology (NIST). The Baldrige criteria for excellence include:

- Leadership
- Strategic planning
- Customer and market focus
- Information and analysis
- Human resource focus
- Process management
- Business results

See the *Living Fieldbook* for more details on the Baldrige award, criteria, and cases (**L**).

Case. Baldrige Green Zia: the environmental Baldrige award

Baldrige is being adapted for sustainability in the Green Zia Environmental Excellence Program. This program was developed in 1998 by New Mexico's Environment Department. This award was based on the Baldrige award criteria and adapted to focus on sustainability.

The Green Zia program helps organizations achieve environmental excellence through continuous environmental improvement. The program is administered by the New Mexico Environmental Alliance, a partnership made up of state, local, and federal agencies, along with academia, private industry, and environmental advocacy groups. The program can drive significant positive organizational change and help organizations significantly improve their sustainable practices.

Table 6.6 presents the sustainability adapted value items and scoring weights. The noted program benefits include the following:

- All organizations (or components within an organization) can be directly compared with one another without the need for normalization of results
- A positive response to an item helps define a "best practice" for that item, and best practices can be shared by all organizations, no matter what their product or service
- Independent, third-party examiners are used to score applications
- The model works well with other environmental programs, and helps score the implementation of those programs
- The model systematically evaluates an organization's efforts to continually improve products, services, and delivery and support processes
- The model encourages an organization to integrate environmental efforts into its core business function

Table 6.6 **Baldrige model evaluation items**

1. Leadership

    1.1 Organizational leadership (75 pts)

    1.2 Community leadership (50 pts)

2. Planning for continuous environmental improvement

    2.1 Strategic planning for environmental improvement (50 pts)

    2.2 Action planning (50 pts)

    2.3 Integration and implementation (50 pts)

3. Customer, supplier and other interested party involvement

    3.1 Customer involvement (25 pts)

    3.2 Supplier involvement (25 pts)

    3.3 Other interested-party involvement (25 pts)

4. Information and analysis

    4.1 Information collection and management (60 pts)

    4.2 Analysis and decision-making (40 pts)

5. Employee involvement

    5.1 Employee education and skill development (50 pts)

    5.2 Employee involvement (55 pts)

    5.3 Employee satisfaction, value, and well-being (20 pts)

6. Process management

    6.1 Process characterization and control (50 pts)

    6.2 Process improvement (50 pts)

7. Results

    7.1 Environmental results (100 pts)

    7.2 Customer, supplier, employee, and other interested-party results (150 pts)

    7.3 Financial results (75 pts)

Source: The Organization and Overview, Green Zia Environmental Excellence Recognition Program.
www.nmenv.state.nm.us/Green_Zia_website/pdfs/Grn_Zia_App_Org_Overview-2006.pdf.

- The model does not score anecdotes or isolated incidents that are not driven by established and repeatable approaches

- Benchmarking and other comparisons of results are encouraged[16]

Case. Business Metabolics: key performance indicators

Intensive work on sustainability indicators using the Business Metabolics methodology and software tool have led to the finding that three key performance indicators (KPIs) consistently rise to the top of the list: return on resources (input–output metrics); product to nonproduct ratio; and the carbon footprint. There's a large universe of indicators possible, but these three — one simple, one sobering, one significant

16 Personal communications with R. Pojasek, 2001–2002.

— provide critical leverage for driving behavior toward improved environmental and economic performance.

● **Return on resources (ROR).** The ratio of profit, revenue, or intended result to energy, water, toxics, or other critical resource inputs. This indicator directly links economic and environmental performance: How much money is the organization making (or how much product is the organization shipping) per unit of critical resources used, or unit of environmental burden generated?

● **Product to nonproduct ratio (P2NP).** This ratio can be seen as a special case of ROR — the ratio of productive output to "nonproduct output" (NPO); all the waste that companies produce but can't sell and ship out by way of smokestacks, sewer lines and "waste" dumps

● **Carbon footprint (CF).** The GHG — commonly expressed in CO_2 equivalents — generated from a company's activities. This measure ties to global warming impacts and Kyoto Protocol targets, and has tradable economic value; more important, it will drive deep process and strategy innovation that can have significant impact on profit and future market share

Tool. Business Metabolics: real-time metrics[17]

Business Metabolics is an example of a key performance indicator (KPI) system that streamlines the collection, analysis, and reporting of an organization's environmental, social, and economic performance data. The Web-based system reduces data management costs and enables users to quickly generate visual analyses of productivity,

Figure 6.4 **Throughput pie**

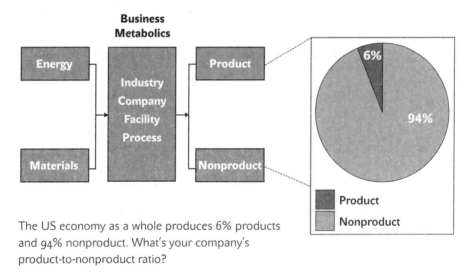

The US economy as a whole produces 6% products and 94% nonproduct. What's your company's product-to-nonproduct ratio?

Source: Natural Logic. Available from www.natlogic.com. Copyright 2007, Natural Logic. Reproduced with permission.

17 www.businessmetabolics.com (accessed January 29, 2008).

material flow, and footprint for both operational decision-making and corporate social responsibility (CSR), and sustainability reporting.

Figure 6.4 presents a schematic (in this case illustrating a P2NP analysis) showing how this tool can support an organization's measurement strategy. The *Living Fieldbook* (**L**) contains additional information about this and other metrics software applications.

Energy and greenhouse gas emissions measurements

The Greenhouse Gas Protocol Initiative, introduced above, has developed emissions measurement protocols and calculation tools that organizations can use to conduct energy audits, calculate their GHG emissions inventories and carbon footprint, prioritize their opportunities to reduce that footprint, and implement improvement programs. It has been put to use by companies and climate initiatives around the globe. Entities making use of the GHG measurement include reporting initiatives (e.g., the Carbon Disclosure Project, the GRI, the Ceres Sustainable Governance Initiative), industry initiatives (e.g., the International Forum of Forest and Paper Associations, the International Aluminium Association), and trading groups (e.g., EU Emissions Trading Scheme, the Chicago Climate Exchange).

Figure 6.5 presents an example of the calculation used to measure the activity data for a building without separate metering.

Figure 6.5 **Calculating building activity data**

$$\left(\frac{\text{Area of organization's space}}{\text{Total building area}} \right) \quad \begin{array}{c} \text{Total building} \\ \text{use of} \\ \text{electricity} \end{array} \quad \begin{array}{c} \text{Approx. kWh} \\ \text{used by} \\ \text{your organization} \end{array}$$

Activity data × emissions factor = CO_2 emissions

Source: Copyright 2008, OpenEco, www.openeco.org. Reproduced with permission.

Tool. OpenEco: energy and GHG measurement and benchmarking[18]

Organizations can access OpenEco to acquire free tools that are easy to use, to help participants measure, track, and compare energy performance, and to benchmark best practices to reduce GHG emissions and encourage sustainable innovation. Built by Sun Microsystems and based on the Business Metabolics model, OpenEco initially focuses on building energy performance, and plans extensions into vehicle fleet performance as well. Sun plans to open source OpenEco, enabling the participating community of users to jointly enhance the planet.

The *Living Fieldbook* (**L**) contains additional materials and tools pertaining to this topic.

18   www.openeco.org (accessed January 29, 2008).

LEED building sustainability performance ratings

One example of building performance standards is the Leadership in Energy and Environmental Design (LEED) green building rating system. The purpose of this system is to transform the building market by defining a common standard of measurement for integrated, whole-building design practices, environmental leadership, stimulate green competition, and raise consumer awareness of green building benefits.

LEED was first developed in 1994 by the Natural Resources Defense Council (NRDC) Senior Scientist Robert K. Watson. LEED has grown to encompass over 14,000 projects in 50 US states and 30 countries covering 1.062 billion square feet (99 km^2) of development area.

The rating system originally developed continues to be refined to stay current with new and emerging building technologies. Six major areas are covered by the system: sustainable sites, water efficiency, energy and atmosphere, materials and resources, indoor environmental quality innovation, and design process. Metrics have been developed for the full variety of building categories.

To get a building certified an organization submits its plans via an electronic automated system. The plans can then be reviewed by 10,000 membership organizations that currently constitute the US Green Buildings Council (USGBC). The process is transparent, allowing for continuous learning by the member organizations.

The system works on a series of "prerequisites" and a variety of "credits" in the six major categories listed above. Here is one example from the commercial buildings. In this area there are 69 possible points and four levels of certification:

- Certified: 26–32 points (noninnovation points)
- Silver: 33–38 points
- Gold: 39–51 points
- Platinum: 52–69 points

An example of a building that achieved gold status, 7 World Trade Center is considered New York City's first "green" office tower. Additional information on LEED and several more building case examples are available on the *Living Fieldbook* (L).

Product performance indicators

Product performance indicators are a growing trend and provide consumers with more transparent information that allows them to make informed purchasing decisions. What does it cost in money, work, and other resources for a tomato to travel to your plate? How many miles does it take the average tomato to get to your plate? Tomatoes are a product, and we live in a world of products. These products have enormous impact on the people and environment as they are produced, transported, consumed, and disposed of. How can we measure the impact on sustainability of the products we use every day? The following cases provide examples that point the way.

Case. Better World Handbook and Network: personal sustainability practices

One approach to providing measures that help educate and empower individuals is provided by the Better World Network.[19] The goal of the *Better World Handbook* (Jones,

---

19 www.betterworldnetwork.org.

Figure 6.6 **Better World product ratings aspects**

BETTER WORLD SHOPPER

✓	**Human rights**
✓	**The environment**
✓	**Animal protection**
✓	**Community involvement**
✓	**Social justice**

Source: Better World Shopper website, www.betterworldshopper.org. Copyright 2007, The Better World Network. Reproduced with permission.

Johnson, Haenfler, & Klocke, 2001) and its attendant website, the Better World Network, is to empower people to take simple, effective actions in their daily lives to help make the world a more just and sustainable place.

To accomplish this it focuses on seven key areas:[20]

- Economic Fairness
- Comprehensive Peace
- Ecological Sustainability
- Deep Democracy
- Social Justice
- Culture Of Simplicity
- Revitalized Community

It provides a measurement chart with rankings to help people shop for products from companies that support the five sustainability aspects listed in Figure 6.6.

Many other organizations are also joining in and providing measures of sustainability for their consumers.

Case. Automobile industry example: MPG standards

What does it cost the environment for an individual to get where he or she needs to go? At an average of 15 to 40 mpg, tomato travel is significantly contributing to global warming. Better World Network[21] says that the best way to combat this is to buy local produce. Looking at the larger picture and calculating total vehicle miles traveled times the impact per mile, yields a clearer and scarier picture of true sustainable end-state metrics that must be attended to. Miles per gallon can also be

20 www.betterworldnetwork.org (accessed December 28, 2007).
21 Ibid.

increased. In June 2005 in a joint project of ETH Zurich, with partners from academia and industry, the experimental Pac-Car II achieved 12,645 mpg during the Shell Eco-marathon in Ladoux, France. See the *Living Fieldbook* for changes in mpg standards.

Case. GE Ecomagination product performance measures

General Electric's Ecomagination program seeks to leverage the brand value in green business.[22] This program started because GE senior leadership saw that there were major trends creating increasingly intense environmental and growth challenges for customers across a majority of GE's businesses. Ecomagination was created as a business strategy in response to these challenges. (Also see GE case in Chapter 3, page 104.) The goal is to increase revenue by US$20 billion by 2010 while reducing greenhouse gas emissions. One effort as part of this initiative calls for doubling of investment in clean research and development.

To measure some of these intended outcomes, GE uses a rigorous, third-party-audited certification process to determine whether individual products and services deliver sufficiently differentiated financial and environmental performance to be "Ecomagination-certified." See the *Living Fieldbook* for more information about Ecomagination (**L**).

▓ Financial performance indicators

Financial performance indicators have enormous influence and affect the decisions of governments, companies, and investors. They include all the familiar, globally relevant economic indicators such as interest rates, inflation rates, and gross domestic product (GDP), which is discussed elsewhere in this chapter, and again in Chapter 7, pages 207-208, for its impact on sustainable globalization. They include indicators of enterprise costs, benefits, and profits. Activity-based costing, lifecycle costing, material-flow accounting, and economic value added (EVA) are all examples of methodologies used by enterprises to better measure, analyze, and understand their enterprise, product, and process financial performance. Not least of all of the financial indicators is the always elusive price per share.

This section cannot possibly cover the full spectrum of financial indicators. It attempts to show how traditional financial indicators are now being questioned and their unintended consequences explored. It lets readers know there are many consciously competent people, learning, teaching, and working hard to raise our collective awareness. Alternative and sustainability-enhanced financial indicators and tools are available. The *Living Fieldbook* contains all articles referenced and additional articles, case studies, and tools (**L**).

Global ecosystem services value measurement: US$33 trillion per year

Not every businessperson is going to go and invest in a tree, but this financial indicator is a powerful beginning. World-leading ecological economist Robert Costanza, director of the University of Vermont's Gund Institute for Ecological Economics, and his many colleagues and collaborators have been conducting complex database integration and

22 ge.ecomagination.com/site/index.html#vision/intro (accessed December 30, 2007).

analysis efforts to bring the world to at least a state of conscious incompetence regarding the unaccounted-for value of our global ecosystems. His seminal 1997 *Nature* article "The Value of the World's Ecosystem Services and Natural Capital" (Costanza, d'Arge, de Groot, Farberk, Grasso, & Hannon, 1997), is frequently cited. The full article is available on the *Living Fieldbook* (**L**). It states,

> The services of ecological systems and the natural capital stocks that produce them are critical to the functioning of the Earth's life-support system. They contribute to human welfare, both directly and indirectly, and therefore represent part of the total economic value of the planet. We have estimated the current economic value of 17 ecosystem services for 16 biomes,[23] based on published studies and a few original calculations. For the entire biosphere, the value (most of which is outside the market) is estimated to be in the range of US$16–54 trillion per year, with an average of US$33 trillion per year. Because of the nature of the uncertainties, this must be considered a minimum estimate. Global gross national product total is around US$18 trillion per year. (p. 253)

GDP alternatives: the genuine progress indicator (GPI)

> The gross national product does not allow for the health of our children, the quality of their education or the joy of their play. It does not include the beauty of our poetry or the strength of our marriages, the intelligence of our public debate or the integrity of our public officials. It measures neither our wit nor our courage; neither our wisdom nor our learning; neither our compassion nor our devotion to our country; it measures everything, in short, except that which makes life worthwhile.
>
> *Robert F. Kennedy, 1968*

The genuine progress indicator (GPI) is a solid example of a community well-being measure that is in use in several regions around the world. It is viewed by its supporters as a better measure of economic sustainability. The GPI includes everything the GDP measures. It then adds additional measures that represent costs of the negative effects related to selected economic activities such as war, crime, and drug and alcohol treatment. Looked at in terms of GDP, it is analogous to the difference between gross profit (GDP) and net profit (GPI).

The city of Alberta, Canada, uses a tool featuring 51 economic, social, and environmental indicators that assess how well it is doing "as individuals, families, communities and as a province" (Costanza et al., 2004). It and similar GDP alternatives are rapidly gaining in acceptance worldwide. (See Chapter 7, "Gross Domestic Product," pages 207-208, for more on how investors and organizations are rethinking and refining GDP.)

IMU: flow-cost management

Flow-cost management is a methodology adapted for sustainability objectives by the IMU-Augsburg in Germany. It provides an innovative solution that leverages information systems to systematically reduce raw materials and consequent ecological waste.

---

23 **Biome** is a living community characterized by distinctive plant and animal species and maintained under the climatic conditions of the region.

Flow-cost management can be performed using already installed enterprise resource planning (ERP) information systems and/or already established databases.

The University of Augsburg conducted a series of pilot applications. It found that material flows constitute a considerable cost factor, averaging 56% of total costs for the pilot companies. IMU first worked with the companies to develop their material flow diagrams (Fig. 6.7). Then IMU worked with the companies to configure their ERP system and related databases to better align with the material flows. The resultant process changes achieved an average material cost saving of 10 to 25% of total costs and resulted in an average profit increase of over 20% (Strobel, 2001).

Figure 6.7 **Material flow diagram**

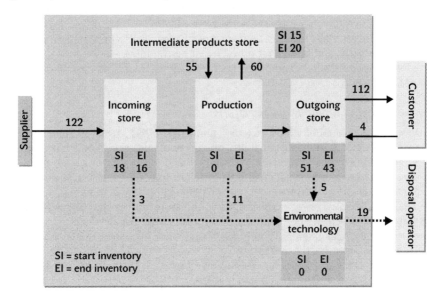

Source: Dr. M. Strobel, Institut für Management und Umwelt. (2001). *Eco-effizienz: Relieving stress on the environment by means of flow management: Flow cost accounting.* Augsburg, Germany: Institut für Management und Umwelt, p. 7 . Reproduced with permission.

Case. E+Co: sustainable performance measurement of investments[24]

E+Co is a nonprofit public investment company whose focus is to bring clean, affordable energy to the rural energy impoverished. E+Co is discussed in more detail in Chapter 7 (pages 212ff.), but is included here for its use of a Web-based data collection and dashboard metrics management system, and triple-bottom-line investment performance indicators used to measure the returns and impacts on capital invested.

E+Co uses a Web-based portal to cost-effectively collect data from each of more than 125 small rural investment companies two times a year. These data are reported into a dashboard with the ability to be aggregated and sorted to provide the entrepreneur, the investor, other stakeholders, and themselves a fully informed view of selected conditions.

24 www.eandco.net

E+Co has roughly US$60 million in capital and returns 1 to 2% to investors. Mainstream investors would see that as poor, but E+Co views its return through a triple-bottom-line lens. It sees value in bringing energy and an improved quality of life to millions of the world's rural poor.

Shareholder value ratings

Environmental, social, and governance indexes are discussed in both Chapter 3, because of their strategic importance, and Chapter 7, because of their influence on the worldwide flow of capital. Some investors are using this enhanced intelligence to simply continue to identify a few companies that have a better probability of outperforming their markets and their competitors. Others are using this information to inform entire markets generally; through more effective allocation of capital across the capital markets, these investors may raise the performance bar for all. Like other measurement systems, each investor has his or her own perspective on what is important to measure, how best to measure, and how to report on his or her findings.

The following are several example companies that are leaders as we travel this segment of the journey.

Dow Jones Sustainability Indexes (DJSI)[25]

The Dow Jones Sustainability Indexes (DJSI), launched in 1999, track the financial performance of selected leading sustainability-driven companies worldwide. It is a cooperative effort of Dow Jones Indexes, STOXX Limited, and SAM to provide asset managers with benchmarks to manage sustainability portfolios. It monitors industry-specific sustainability trends and evaluates corporations based on a variety of criteria including climate change strategies, energy consumption, human resources development, knowledge management, stakeholder relations, and corporate governance.

The Dow Jones Sustainability World Index (DJSI World) is one example of an investment product offered by the organization. It analyzes the biggest 2,500 companies worldwide and, using its criteria for measurement, captures the top 10% based on long-term economic, environmental, and social criteria.

Innovest Strategic Value Advisors[26]

Innovest Strategic Value Advisors is an internationally recognized investment research and advisory firm. Its Intangible Value Assessment platform combines more than 120 performance factors, including innovation capacity, product liability, governance, human capital, emerging market, and environmental.

Innovest provides the research services behind the Carbon Disclosure Project (CDP), a global survey of the top global companies, sponsored by investors representing over US$30 trillion of capital. A ratings product, Carbon Beta, has been developed, which complements this research and provides ratings measures to investors who wish to use climate change and GHG emissions to inform investment decisions.

Global Compact Assessment Service (GC+) is another innovative Innovest investment research product. This assessment tool measures companies' performance and strategies against the ten principles of the United Nations Global Compact.

Innovest also leverages Internet technology by delivering its vast body of research reports, company ratings, and profiles to its customers via its I-Ratings Research Portal service.

25 www.sustainability-indexes.com (accessed January 29, 2008).
26 www.innovestgroup.com (accessed January 29, 2008).

KLD[27]

KLD's research is designed for investors and money managers who integrate environmental, social, and governance factors into its investment process. KLD's research can be used for screening, company analysis, or fund creation. KLD rates a company's sustainability performance by analyzing key environmental, social, and governance (ESG) factors including environment, community and society, employees, supply chain, customers, governance, and ethics.

One example KLD index is the KLD Global Sustainability Index (GSI). This is a broadly diversified, sector-neutral global benchmark ratings approach. Ratings are based on ESG rankings. KLD believes that sector neutrality limits the financial risk associated with sector bias.

TruCost[28]

Trucost is an example of how new innovations in corporate risk ratings are working their way into analysts' and investors' measurement options. It measures companies on 700 environmental impacts and includes analysis of enterprise functions such as supply chain. It further differentiates itself by using environmental and carbon footprint measurements within its ratings. Its approach recognizes an end state of environmental sustainability as a lens to assess business opportunities and threats.

The journey toward an end state in which economic interests align and holistically integrate with social and environmental interests is now under way.

■ Measuring sustainable enterprise qualities

> Everything that can be counted does not necessarily count; everything that counts cannot necessarily be counted.
>
> *Albert Einstein*

The sustainable enterprise qualities presented within this book can be measured and their performance monitored to support management's need to be aware, to understand, and to act to improve these qualities within a context of sustainability. From this point forward, on a chapter-by-chapter basis, we provide indicators, indexes, and values that organizational leaders can use to evaluate and implement sustainability practices.

It is notable that the qualitative nature of many social and stakeholder-related issues lead to indicators that are most adaptive to surveys interpreted through Likert scales. Developed by Rensis Likert, the scale is a multi-item tool used to measure such intangible qualities as intensity (less, more), value (not important, extremely important), relativity (worst, best), and frequency (never, always).

Measuring through the prism of the Leadership Diamond

Chapter 1 presents the Leadership Diamond (see page 29), created by Daniel F. Twomey, which provides a full-bodied approach for determining leadership impact. The

---

27 www.kld.com (accessed January 29, 2008).
28 www.trucost.com (accessed January 29, 2008).

Leadership Diamond model can help heighten the leader's sense of awareness and level of engagement in ways that contribute to the organization's ability to attain goals for sustainability.

Many organizations currently use assessments to measure or predict leadership performance. There are assorted reliable, valid instruments that address a multiplicity of desirable qualities for new and emerging leadership. Organizations in pursuit of sustainability have generally two options: develop a customized instrument or acquire a tool that features a set of indicators that closely adapt to sustainability leadership.

One such tool, the *Leadership Practices Inventory* (LPI), developed by Jim Kouzes and Barry Posner (2007), is a widely used, valid, and reliable 360-degree assessment tool that would support a transition toward sustainability. This instrument measures what Kouzes and Posner refer to as "exemplary" leadership qualities comprising the following concepts:

- Model the way

- Inspire a shared vision

- Challenge the process

- Enable others to act

- Encourage the heart

Table 6.7 offers an example of a tool that draws on the Leadership Diamond as a framework, with indicators derived from Twomey's leadership domains and the listening-into-being leadership model presented by Shakira Abdul-Ali.[29] The competencies exhibited are most appropriate for more-senior executives, such as a chief sustainability officer. Versions adapted for different leader levels are available on the *Living Fieldbook* (**L**).

Incorporating these competencies into a Likert-scale-type assessment tool will permit organizations to measure both leadership potential and achievement. In order to track leadership learning curves over a specified period of time, it would be useful for the tool to include a progression of proficiency levels, as follows:

Proficiency level

1 = Little or no skill: I have little or proficiency in this area

2 = Minimum skill: I can perform this skill with help

3 = Adequate skill: I routinely perform this skill with little or no help

4 = Proficient skill: I am consistently proficient in this skill

5 = Expert skill: I am called on to train or coach others in developing this skill

Results from this kind of assessment, over time, will ensure that sustainability practices can be cascaded downward throughout the entire organization.

---

29 See Twomey's essay "Nature and domains of leadership for sustainable enterprise" (pages 30ff.) and Abdul-Ali's essay "New frameworks for leading sustainable enterprise" (pages 41ff.) in Chapter 1 as well as Table 1.1, "'Listening-into-being' leadership qualities and characteristics" (page 45).

Table 6.7 **Leadership quality indicators**

Relating and influencing Domain A leadership	Directed and energized by enterprise intent Domain B leadership	Guided and enabled by governing principles Domain C leadership
• Creates relationships to support sustainability • Influences decisions in favor of sustainability • Ability to embrace and harmonize diverse perspectives • Builds networks and interdependent relationships across organizational boundaries • Sees decision-making as a contributory process • Listens authentically • Anticipates conflict: accepts it as "part of everything"	• Demonstrates awareness of and has ability to influence events • Sees, understands, and influences trends • Identifies routines, patterns, and behaviors that support or hinder sustainability • Identifies sequences of events that impact, or are impacted by, sustainable practices • Demonstrates ability to think in nonlinear domains • Demonstrates ability to "trust the process"	• Recognizes global dynamics and trends that impact sustainability initiatives • Focuses on enterprise intent inside of sustainability paradigm • Ability to embrace paradox • Designs organization structure and processes focused on sustainability

Measuring mental models

Chapter 2 (pages 60ff.) presents John Adams's six dimensions of mental models, an exceptional framework for evaluating whether and how individuals and groups have successfully shifted toward more sustainable mindsets and behaviors. Organizations should survey their members regularly, to determine where the organization is experiencing success and which of the dimensions need more or slightly altered attention.

Other methodologies for measuring mental models could involve more complex processes. Researchers, according to the essays in Chapter 2, propose that mental models are formulated and acted on through imagery, conceptualization, and language, intertwined to produce meaning that is overwhelmingly symbolic in nature. To that end, concept maps, along with interviews and surveys, can enable organizations to uncover mental model patterns that either help or hinder sustainability. The *Living Fieldbook* offers several papers that describe these methodologies in greater detail (**L**).

Organizations might consider a customized survey to address prevailing mental models regarding sustainability. An example of such a survey tool, using John D. Adams's six dimensions, is available on the *Living Fieldbook* (**L**).

Measuring corporate sustainability strategy

Chapter 3 describes how sustainability metrics help leaders in measuring the gap between where the organization is and where it seeks to be at some identified point in the future. Infusing corporate strategy with sustainability-focused practices will be a turning point that will enable all stakeholders to move in unison toward the attainment of a life-giving workspace that generates a zero footprint.

Earlier in this chapter we presented both balanced scorecard and Baldrige methodologies as examples of how mainstream methodologies are being adapted to integrate and align the company's strategy and operations with sustainability.

A review of other efforts to measure the achievement of sustainability includes several initiatives to define triple-bottom-line indicators that are relevant to enterprise operations. One report compares five scoring systems that were applied to 40 of the largest global industrial companies operating in the sectors of motor vehicles and parts, electronics, petroleum refining, and gas and electric utilities (Morhardt, Baird, & Freeman, 2002). The full report describing the way the scoring procedures were developed and the number of items measured by each methodology is available for viewing on the *Living Fieldbook* (**L**).

Those scoring systems include:

* The Global Reporting Initiative (GRI) 2000 sustainability reporting guidelines

* The ISO 14031 environmental performance evaluation standard[30]

* The Davis-Walling and Batterman scoring system[31]

* The scoring system jointly developed by the UK consultancy SustainAbility and the United Nations Environment Programme (UNEP)

* The Deloitte Touche Tohmatsu scoring system[32]

These indicators, driven through the lens of either of the strategy development models presented in Chapter 3, offer a fairly powerful means for ensuring that all stakeholders are being led by, and contributing to, sustainability targets. The indicators presented in the **total sustainability management model** in that chapter mirror the factors assessed in the GRI scoring system; a broad construction of the **universal strategy formulation model** can find alignment with the ISO 14031 indicators. Figure 6.8 presents a model for measuring a sustainability strategy that uses a number of indicators related to these scoring systems. The competencies identified in Figure 6.8, which were presented above in the discussion on leadership, can be converted for use into strategy assessment tools (**T**).

Measuring sustainability change management practices

Transitioning toward sustainability will inevitably involve some degree of organizational change. Chapter 4 (pages 123-124) describes a robust process for implementing an organization-wide change management process that supports achievement of a triple bottom line. This approach recommends a four-dimensional effort, as follows:

* Framing

* Aligning

* Igniting

* Renewing

30   This is part of the ISO 14000 body of voluntary international environmental standards, offering a list of 197 topics from which companies may select metrics for environmental management.

31   This scoring system covers 29 topics identified in 25 environmental reports in 1996 by *Fortune* 50 US companies.

32   This system was largely derived as a subset of the SustainAbility–UNEP system.

Figure 6.8 **Sustainability drivers and measures**

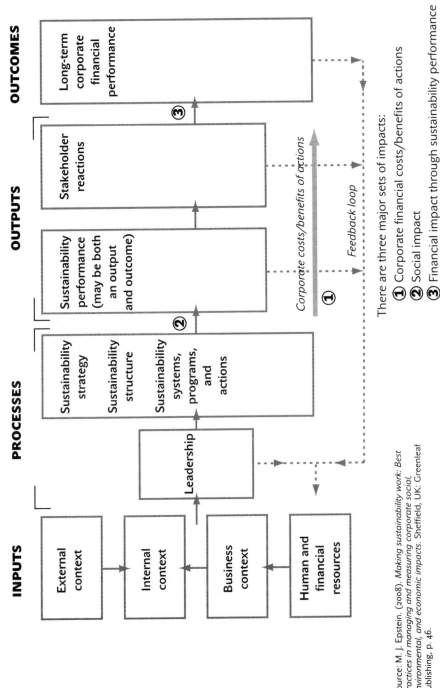

Source: M. J. Epstein. (2008). *Making sustainability work: Best practices in managing and measuring corporate social, environmental, and economic impacts.* Sheffield, UK: Greenleaf Publishing, p. 46.

The FAIR methodology can offer an ample menu of metrics to enable an organization to track the success of its change management process. Sustainability measures should be developed before the change, in order to establish baseline knowledge. Tables 6.8 and 6.9 are two useful strategy-focused sustainability indicators that record relevant data to monitor the effectiveness of a sustainability change management process. Table 6.8 is geared to project management and organizational tracking of 12 change implementation success factors; Table 6.9 is an easy way to self-track individual progress of the same 12 factors on the road to sustainability. Periodic review of the indicators included in these tables will enable the organization and individuals to measure sustainability changes over time. (See also Chapter 2 and the sidebar "Assess your organizational readiness to move to sustainable enterprise: Change readiness diagnostic tool" in Chapter 4, pages 128-129.)

Each of these tracking tools can record relevant data to monitor the effectiveness of a sustainability-focused change management process. Periodic review of the indicators included in these forms will enable the organization to measure sustainability changes over time.

Measuring sustainability-driven employee engagement

Chapter 5 presented cases that provide richly compelling and diverse examples of how engaged employees will, in response to an opportunity to contribute to the well-being of organization stakeholders, step up to the plate, and often go above and beyond the call of duty. Clearly, employee engagement is a powerful component of organization change.

Consulting firms and research outfits have long been engaged in the task of establishing employee engagement metrics and measuring both outputs (measuring frequencies of occurrences) and outcomes (measuring change toward stated targets). There are a number of valid and reliable instruments that can measure employee engagement, based on these and other criteria. Several instruments are referenced on the *Living Fieldbook*. The consulting firm, DecisionWise,[33] has concluded from its experiences that employee engagement can be represented by the following equation:

$$\text{Motivation} + \text{Satisfaction} + \text{Effectiveness} = \text{Engagement}$$

An effective practices guideline published by the Society for Human Resources Management (SHRM) identified the factors presented in Table 6.10 as reflective of positive employee engagement (T) (Vance, 2006). Table 6.10 offers an example of a framework that organizations can use when designing an employee engagement metric that supports and promotes sustainability practices.

Organizations seeking to operationalize these employee engagement drivers can refer to Chapter 5 to determine which sustainability factors can be best tied to these drivers. Relevant qualities can then be adapted, such as "Pride in employer's commitment to sustainability" or "Recognition and positive feedback for contributing to sustainable practices." In this way, the magnitude of sustainability-focused employee engagement can be measured over time.

---

33 decwise.com/contact-us.html (accessed December 28, 2007).

Table 6.8 **Change management factors**

Change success factor	Sample focuses of change project					
	Database software design	Database implemen- tation	Process design team A	Process design team B	Process design team C	Integra- tion
Understanding and acceptance of the need for change						
Belief that the change is both desirable and possible						
Sufficient passionate commitment						
Specific deliverable/goal and a few first steps						
Structures or mechanisms that require repetitions of the new pattern						
Feeling supported and safe						
Versatility of mental models						
Patience and perseverance						
Clear account- ability: visible, vocal, consistent, persistent sponsors and stakeholders						
Explicit "boundary management": the role of other people						
Critical mass in alignment						
Rewarding the new behavior and withdrawal of rewards for the old behavior						

Source: A version of this table appeared in J. D. Adams. (2003). Successful change. *OD Practitioner, 35*(4), p. 7. Copyright 2003, J. D. Adams. Reproduced with permission.

Table 6.9 **Change management measurement grid**

Change success factor	Assessment		
	Doing OK	Needs attention	Actions steps needed
Factors for deep individual pattern change and for organizational change			
1. Understanding and acceptance of the need for change			
2. Belief that the change is both desirable and possible			
3. Sufficient passionate commitment			
4. Specific deliverable/goal and a first few steps			
5. Structures or mechanisms that require repetitions of the new pattern			
6. Feeling supported and safe			
7. Versatility of mental models			
8. Patience and perseverance			
Additional factors for organizational change			
9. Clear accountability, visible, vocal, consistent, persistent sponsors and stakeholders			
10. Explicit "boundary management": the role of other people			
11. Critical mass in alignment			
12. Rewarding the new behavior and withdrawal of rewards for the old behavior			

Source: Personal communication with J. D. Adams, San Francisco, April 18, 2008. Copyright 2005, J. D. Adams. Used with permission.

Table 6.10 **Employee engagement drivers and measures**

Engagement drivers	Motivate	Satisfy	Effectiveness
Pride in employer	✓	✓	
Satisfaction with employer	✓	✓	
Job satisfaction	✓		
Opportunity to perform well at challenging work		✓	✓
Recognition and positive feedback for one's contributions	✓	✓	✓
Personal support from one's supervisor		✓	✓
Effort above and beyond the minimum			✓
Understanding the link between one's job and the organization's mission			✓
Prospects for future growth with one's employer	✓		
Intention to stay with one's employer	✓	✓	

Measuring sustainable globalization

Chapter 7 presents a comprehensive and tightly developed framework for examining the challenge of sustainable globalization. Leaders are challenged to consider what and how their organization initiatives impact and are impacted by globalization. Some of these include:

- **Gross domestic product.** Defined as: GDP = Consumption + Investment + Government spending + (Exports – Imports), this can assist organizations in approaching their own overall impact in the global community through an assessment of their own (microfocused) GDP. See the financial metrics section of this chapter (pages 185ff.) for more information on GDP and alternative metrics for sustainability

- **Environmental, social, and governance (ESG) index.** ESG indexes combine a host of environmental, social, governance, and so-called "controversial" business ratings to assist an organization in the development of its corporate responsibility report. See the financial metrics section (pages 185ff.) for more details

- **Carbon footprint.** Organizations can measure their impact on the environment in terms of the amount of greenhouse gases produced by their efforts, as measured in units of carbon dioxide. See the greenhouse gas metrics section (page 182) for more details

- **Ecological footprint.** The ecological footprint is a measurement of the land area required to sustain a population of any size. Organizations can apply the footprint measurement to their own initiatives, to "keep score" of their sustainability. See the ecological footprint section (pages 165ff.) for more details

● **Gini coefficient.** The Gini coefficient is used as a measure of the inequality in the distribution of income, such that a value of 0 means complete equality in wealth distribution, and 1 means one person owns all the wealth (World Bank, 2006)

These and other measurement frameworks offer macro-focused models for assessing how organizations can witness their overall impact in specific domains of sustainability. Yet, in order to examine organization impact in each of these domains, multiple sets of micro measurements are more helpful. Different metrics frameworks permit evaluation of different kinds of impact. A number of scholars, think tanks, and public policy analysts have constructed measurement frameworks from which organizations can adapt relevant indicators. Several are identified below.

Measuring transorganizational collaboration and networks for sustainability

Chapter 8 discusses the ways in which collaboration, social networks, and stakeholder engagement can support organizations in achieving sustainability. Jenny Ambrozek and Victoria Axelrod present an exercise (page 249) to enable individuals and organizations

Figure 6.9 **Alliance partner measurement example**

Question 1 (tie strength)
How frequently did people interact for issues related to the alliance on average over the past two years . . .

	Infrequently/ almost never				Very frequently/daily
. . . on the level of your firm?	☐	☐	☐	☐	☐
. . . on the alliance level?	☐	☐	☐	☐	☐

How frequently did people interact for social support (either for giving or receiving confidences about personal problems) on average over the past two years . . .

	Infrequently/ almost never				Very frequently/daily
. . . on the level of your firm?	☐	☐	☐	☐	☐
. . . on the alliance level?	☐	☐	☐	☐	☐

How close was the working relationship . . .

	Distant, like an arm's-length relationship		Fairly close, like discussing and solving issues together		Very close, practically like being close colleagues
. . . on the level of your firm?	☐	☐	☐	☐	☐
. . . on the alliance level?	☐	☐	☐	☐	☐

(continued opposite)

Question 2 (trust)

Please indicate your level of agreement with each of the statements below.

	Firm level					Alliance level				
	Strongly disagree				Strongly agree	Strongly disagree				Strongly agree
Other people can be trusted to make sensible alliance-related decisions	☐	☐	☐	☐	☐	☐	☐	☐	☐	☐
Other people would not be prepared to gain advantage by deceiving us	☐	☐	☐	☐	☐	☐	☐	☐	☐	☐
People can rely on each other to abide by the alliance management agreement	☐	☐	☐	☐	☐	☐	☐	☐	☐	☐
We are not reluctant to make alliance-related resource commitments even when specifications are ambiguous	☐	☐	☐	☐	☐	☐	☐	☐	☐	☐
People have a high level of mutual trust in various alliance activities	☐	☐	☐	☐	☐	☐	☐	☐	☐	☐
People always stand by their word even when this is not in their own best interest	☐	☐	☐	☐	☐	☐	☐	☐	☐	☐
People never use opportunites that arise out of alliance activities to profit at our expense	☐	☐	☐	☐	☐	☐	☐	☐	☐	☐
Other people are flexible when we cannot keep a specific alliance-related promise due to unexpected change in the business environment	☐	☐	☐	☐	☐	☐	☐	☐	☐	☐

Source: J. Walter. (2005). Collaboration within and between firms: Network structures, decision processes, and their impact on alliance performance. (Unpublished doctoral dissertation). University of St. Gallen, Graduate School of Business Administration, Economics, Law and Social Sciences, pp. 141-142. Reproduced with permission.

to "examine and learn from" their own networks. This exercise can lead to the discovery of metrics indicators that can be used to track sustainable practices among networked partners.

Collaborations and networks have been the subject of research for a number of years. Various methods have been designed to evaluate the effectiveness of those alliances. For example, through network mapping, discussed in more detail in Chapter 8 (pages 252-253), organizations can track "what key connections are missing, who are the leaders, who should be leading but is not, who are the experts, the mentors and the innovators, and where are collaborative business alliances forming?" (Marvin, 2006). Once these relationships and associations are revealed, organizations can pursue a more focused survey process to measure the effectiveness of these collaborations to contribute to sustainability (T). Jorge Walter (2005) includes an elegant example (an excerpt is shown in Fig. 6.9) of a survey to measure the effectiveness of collaborative alliances.

Referring to desirable transorganizational and stakeholder qualities found in Chapter 8, organizations can implement the networking mapping process to identify relevant and valuable relationships. They can then apply a Likert scale framework such as that presented above to measure the strength and quality of those relationships relative to sustainability practices.

■ Conclusion

Executives managing change have long acknowledged the importance of metrics to assess baseline conditions and progress toward goals. While the AMA survey (AMA, 2007) suggests that many companies say they don't know how to measure sustainability, there is, in reality, an abundance of information that provides guidance and tools to establish global sustainable development and enterprise-level sustainability metrics. We have presented such case examples as Rio Tinto, and its experience using the balanced scorecard. Tools such as Business Metabolics, OpenEco, Gapminder, and the many collaborating sustainable measurement and reporting networks are examples of how technology is advancing to make the management and analysis of large, complex data sets understandable and useful for strategic and real-time business decision-making. Organizations that have been residing in a state of conscious incompetence can be fully prepared to act.

Sustainability is an ever-changing end state; "one knows that one doesn't know" what that end state will be. There is one thing, however, that we now know for sure, and the ecological footprint metric will not let us forget. We have only one Planet Earth. Numbers alone cannot capture the deepest meanings of sustainability. Yet we have little choice but to relentlessly pursue, and rely on, those quantitative and qualitative measures that will empower us to preserve that which is beyond measurement.

> People are fond of counting their troubles, but they do not count their joys.
> If they counted them up as they ought to, they would see that every lot has
> enough.
>
> *adapted from Fyodor Dostoevsky*

References

American Management Association (AMA). (2007). *Creating a sustainable future: A global study of current trends and possibilities 2007–2017.* New York: American Management Association.

Atherton, J. S. (2003). Tools for thought: Knowing and not knowing. Retrieved December 25, 2007, from www.doceo.co.uk/tools/knowing.htm.

Casado, F. (2003, March 13–16). SKN Worldwide: Aligning–integrating–automating sustainability indicators. Powerpoint Presentation at International Sustainability Indicators Network annual meeting, Toronto.

Costanza, R., d'Arge, R., de Groot, R., Farberk, S., Grasso, M., Hannon, B., et al. (1997, May 15). The value of the world's ecosystem services and natural capital. *Nature, 387,* 253-260.

Costanza, R., Erickson, J., Fligger, K., Adams, A., Adams, C., Altschuler, B., et al. (2004). Estimates of the Genuine Progress Indicator (GPI) for Vermont, Chittenden County and Burlington, from 1950 to 2000. *Ecological Economics, 51,* 139-155.

Figge, F., Hahn, T., Schaltegger, S. & Wagner, M. (2002). The sustainability balanced scorecard: Theory and application of a tool for value-based sustainability management. Presented at Greening of Industry Network Conference, Gothenburg, Germany.

Friend, G. (2004, June 30). How high the moon: The challenge of "sufficient" goals. *New Bottom Line, 13*(3). Retrieved January 29, 2008, from www.natlogic.com/new-bottom-line/v13/25-v13/194-new-bottom-line-volume-13-3.

Friend, G. (2005, November 2). Real time regulation: A new business and policy frontier. *New Bottom Line, 14*(9). Retrieved January 29, 2008, from www.natlogic.com/new-bottom-line/v14/26-v14/209-new-bottom-line-volume-14-9.

Howell, W. S. (1982). *The empathic communicator.* University of Minnesota: Wadsworth Publishing.

Jones, E., Johnson, B., Haenfler, R., & Klocke, B. (2001). *Better world handbook.* Gabriola Island, BC, Canada: New Society Publishers.

Kaplan, R. S., & Norton, D. P. (1992, January–February). The balanced scorecard: Measures that drive performance. *Harvard Business Review,* 71-80.

Kaplan, R. S., & Norton, D. P. (1996). *The balanced scorecard: Translating strategy into action.* Boston, MA: Harvard Business School Press.

Kouzes J., & Posner, B. (2007). *Leadership practices inventory* (3rd ed.). New York: John Wiley.

Marvin, K. (2006). *Developing and nurturing multi-organizational networks.* Retrieved December 19, 2006, from marvincoach.com/NetworkDevelopment.pdf.

Morhardt, J. E., Baird, S., & Freeman, K. (2002). *Scoring corporate environmental and sustainability reports using GRI 2000, ISO 14031 and other criteria.* Claremont, CA: Roberts Environmental Center, Claremont McKenna College. Retrieved December 27, 2007, from www.interscience.wiley.com.

Pinter, L., Hardi, P., & Bartelmus, P. (2005). *Sustainable development indicators: Proposals for a way forward.* Prepared for the United Nations Division for Sustainable Development (UNDSD). Winnipeg, Manitoba: International Institute for Sustainable Development (IISD).

Russell, W. (2004). *Implementing technology applications for sustainability management and reporting.* Sustainability Knowledge Network, SKN Worldwide–USA, Inc.

Strobel, M. (2001, April). *Eco-effizienz: Relieving stress on the environment by means of flow management: Flow cost accounting.* Institut für Management und Umwelt, Augsburg, Germany.

Tanzil, D., & Beloff, B. (2003). Automating the sustainability metrics approach. Paper presented at the American Institute of Chemical Engineers Spring Meeting, New Orleans, November, 2003.

Vance, R. J. (2006). *Employee engagement and commitment: A guide to understanding, measuring, and increasing engagement in your organization.* SHRM Foundation, an affiliate of the Society for Human Resource Management. Retrieved December 27, 2007, from www.shrm.org/foundation/1006EmployeeEngagementOnlineReport.pdf.

Walter, J. (2005). *Collaboration within and between firms: Network structures, decision processes, and their impact on alliance performance.* Unpublished doctoral dissertation. St. Gallen, Switzerland: University of St. Gallen, Graduate School of Business Administration, Economics, Law and Social Sciences.

Wirtenberg, J., Harmon, J., Russell, W. G., & Fairfield, K. D. (2007). HR's role in building a sustainable enterprise: Insights from some of the world's best companies. *Human Resource Planning, 30*(1), 10-20.

World Bank. (2006). Poverty analysis: Measuring inequality. Retrieved December 30, 2007, from www.worldbank.org.

World Commission on Environment and Development (WCED). (1987). *Our common future.* Oxford, UK: Oxford University Press.

PART IV

Connecting, integrating, and aligning toward the future

7

Sustainable globalization
The challenge and the opportunity[1]

Victoria G. Axelrod, Joel Harmon,
William G. Russell, and Jeana Wirtenberg

> The major challenge — and opportunity — of our time is to create a form of
> commerce that uplifts the entire human community of 6.5 billion and does
> so in a way that respects both natural and cultural diversity. Indeed, that is
> the only realistic and viable pathway to a sustainable world. And business
> can — and must — lead the way.
>
> *Stuart L. Hart* (2007, p. 228)

Sustainable globalization presents at once the greatest challenge — and the greatest
opportunity — of our lifetime. We are being called on to alter our fundamental ways of
living on Earth as a human species. The Intergovernmental Panel on Climate Change
(IPCC)[2] comprising 2,500 scientific expert reviewers and 800 contributing authors from
130 countries, concluded its Fourth Assessment Report by asking this profoundly
important question: What changes in lifestyles, behavior patterns and management
practices are needed, and by when? (Pachauri, 2007, slide 15).

In this chapter and throughout the book, we attempt to address this question from
multiple perspectives. Each is vital to advance our readers' understanding and enable
us to come to workable and practical solutions. We focus on articulating the issues
through an overall lens we are calling *sustainable globalization*.

---

1 The authors gratefully acknowledge contributions to this chapter by Pam Hurley, Linda M. Kelley,
and Anna Tavis.

2 www.ipcc.ch/about/index.htm (accessed January 3, 2008).

■ What do we mean by 'sustainable globalization'?

Globalization is defined as "the rapid expansion and integration of business activities across borders in response to dramatic technology and government policy changes in the latter part of the 20th century" (Sullivan, 2002, p. 235). Globalization has integrated national economic systems through international trade, investment, and capital flows and has increased social, cultural, and technological interactions. World trade has been the engine of world economic growth in the last 50 years. But many poor countries have been left behind because rich countries have subsidized agriculture and blocked access to their markets. The growth in world trade has been unevenly spread. Some developing countries — many in Asia — have increased growth by producing more manufactured goods. But others — often in Africa — have fallen ever further behind.

Sustainable globalization represents a breakthrough and a fundamental transformation in how people approach doing business in a global world in the 21st century. It shifts from a zero-sum, selfish, win–lose approach to one that fully takes into account the short- and long-term impacts of people's actions on the larger ecosystem of which humans are a part, recognizes and values our use of precious natural resources, demonstrates respect for all people on the planet, supports local communities in creating the best possible future for themselves, and builds human, social, and financial capital at the local, national, and global levels. Sustainable globalization is principle-centered, operating on foundational values of service, collaboration, and the triple bottom line.

To deepen our understanding, we introduce here, and organize this chapter around, a "six lens" practical framework for thinking about sustainable globalization:

- Economic/financial
- Technology
- Poverty and inequity
- Limits to growth
- Movement of talent
- Geopolitical

We take a systemic and holistic view of these complex and interrelated issues to bring them together into an integrated whole that takes all six lenses into account. At the same time, from a practical perspective, we find value in systematically and sequentially looking at each individual lens, before attempting to integrate them into a holistic view of sustainable globalization (see Fig. 7.1).

As we have seen in other chapters, managers in every function can play a key role in shaping the future of their organizations around sustainability. How rapidly can the world advance management systems, structures, and processes so they can be sustainable for the next generation, and the next? The ability of people and businesses to act fast within these six converging arenas will be the perennial test of this and future generations of managers.

We are heartened to see that business is already beginning to address the environment in areas such as water pollution, alternative fuels, and carbon emissions. Clearly, much more remains to be done, and we have only scratched the surface considering the immense challenges before us. Although carbon emissions are emerging as a new, long-lasting priority, other topics on the sustainability spectrum remain a central field for

Figure 7.1 **Six lenses for sustainable globalization**

Source: Copyright 2007, V. G. Axelrod, J. Harmon, W. G. Russell, and J. Wirtenberg. Used with permission.

influencing how business can begin to adjust, shift, and remake itself to manage every day and every decision based on a more complete and sustainable model of success.

◼ Looking through the economic and financial lens

The world's largest enterprises, the Global 1000, have the economic power to exert enormous influence over their own sustainable future as well as that of others. They have the power to convene NGOs (nongovernmental organizations), government leaders, policy think tanks, and professional and trade associations for horizontal collaboration to address global issues. And recently, with the support of such alliances and organizations as the UN Global Compact, the World Resources Institute, the Clinton Foundation, and many others, they have begun to make major strides in expanding their influence and their role for the mutual benefit of all. Two issues stand out in stark relief as we look at sustainable globalization through an economic and financial lens. First we see the need to look at economies in general, and companies in particular, through an environmental, social, and governance (ESG) framework, and second we see the need to fundamentally redefine what we mean by gross domestic product (GDP).

Environmental, social, and governance (ESG) framework

The ESG framework is rapidly becoming a new reference point for financial analysis and decision-making. Increased focus on long-term value creation is bringing ESG issues into the mainstream of business. The realization that sustainability is an economic and business issue is changing companies' behavior globally. The UN Principles of Responsible Investment are frequently used as a framework for developing ESG practices.[3]

Gross domestic product (GDP)

From an international trade perspective, globalization is traditionally looked at primarily in terms of growth in GDP. A few highlights show the addressable imbalances from financial globalization as reported by Garth le Pere, executive director, Institute for Global Dialogue, Midrand (le Pere, 2007).

In GDP terms, some 54 countries were poorer in 2003 than in 1990 (and 20 of these were in sub-Saharan Africa). Other illuminating figures include the following: between 1988 and 2000, the world's poorest 5% lost almost a quarter of their real income and, for the same period, the top 5% gained 12% of theirs; for every US$100 in world exports, US$97 goes to high- and middle-income countries and only US$3 to low-income countries; if Africa, East Asia, and Latin America were to increase their world exports by just 1%, it could lift 130 million people out of poverty; and a 1% increase of Africa's share of world trade would generate US$70 billion or five times what the continent has received in aid and debt relief over the last five years.

Continuing to grow globally is inevitable; however, the consequences for sustainability as measured only by financial wealth are unacceptable.

Rethinking and redefining GDP

At the same time as we see such clear global trends based on the traditional concept of GDP, we note that the notion of GDP as we know it is being redefined. In particular, Wall Street is increasingly acknowledging the need to pay attention to and include all five capitals in the GDP equation: human, social, natural, manufactured, and financial. This redefinition of GDP requires quantification of what previously were considered "externalities": positive and negative unintended consequences of growth such as the impacts on and use of the natural environment, as well as what were historically considered to be independent social or ethical issues of national "well-being," reputation of organizations in the eyes of consumers or stakeholders, and health.

What if China follows in the United States' footsteps?

Imagine the following picture posed by Lester Brown of a China that is pursuing a GDP unfettered by sustainability measures. Brown (2006) develops the example of China's economic development as an illustration of the unsustainability of the consumerism mental model, by projecting the use of resources necessary for Chinese citizens to become consumers at the level of US citizens in 2004:

> What if China catches up with the United States in consumption per person? If the Chinese economy continues to grow 8% a year, by 2031 income per person will equal that of the United States in 2004. If we further assume that consumption patterns of China's affluent population by 2031, by then 1.45

---

3 www.unpri.org/principles (accessed January 30, 2008),

billion, will be roughly similar to those of Americans in 2004, we will see some startling outcomes.

At the current annual US grain consumption of 900 kg per person, including industrial use, China's grain consumption in 2031 would equal roughly ⅔ of the current world grain harvest. If paper use per person in China in 2031 reaches the current US level, this translates into 305 million tons of paper — double existing world production today of 161 million tons. (Say goodbye to the world's forests.) And if oil consumption per person reaches the 2004 US level by 2031, China will use 99 million barrels of oil a day. The current world is producing 84 million barrels a day and may never produce much more. This helps explain why China's fast expanding use of oil is already creating a politics of scarcity.

Or consider cars. If China one day should have three cars for every four people, as the US now does, its fleet in 2031 would be 1.1 billion vehicles, well beyond the current world fleet of 800 million. Providing the roads, highways, and parking lots for this fleet will require an area equal to China's land in rice growing, its principle food staple.

The inevitable conclusion to be drawn from these projections is that there are not enough resources for China to reach US consumption levels . . . If the fossil-fuel based, automobile centered, throw-away economy will not work for China in 2031, it will not work for rapidly developing India either, which in 25 years is projected to have even more people than China. Nor will it work for the other 3 billion people in developing countries who are also dreaming the "American dream." (pp. 10-11)

The indicator that will replace the GDP is currently evolving, but has not yet been fully developed. If it is to achieve widespread adoption, it should be as useful and easy to use as GDP. Some of the factors to be considered fall under the rubric of social well-being, or socioeconomics, such as health, environment, security and terrorism, energy, and climate change.

In summary, sustainable globalization requires a number of profound and critical shifts in the thinking and behavior of global corporations. This affects both the way companies assess and plan for their own sustainable future and the way the investment community at large evaluates, invests in, and communicates about companies from a sustainability perspective. ESG will become an additional lens for evaluating companies, as the very concept and notion of GDP as we know it will continue to evolve.

▓ Looking through the technology lens

Technology as a driving force for global growth and democratization: One Laptop for Every Child

One Laptop for Every Child[4] has accepted the challenge to level the playing field for learning, self-expression, and exploration for the nearly 2 billion children of the developing world with little or no access to education. As we were wrapping up the writing of this book, children in the developing world were clicking, tapping, and typing on

4 laptop.org.

their new specially designed XO computers provided for US$100 each by One Laptop for Every Child,[5] a nonprofit dedicated to bringing the world, its knowledge, its games, and its opportunities for creativity and productivity, to children who had likely never before seen, much less touched, a computer.

The global future rests on the continuing democratization of information. Efforts by multinational companies such as IBM, AMD, News Corp., Google, Red Hat, and eBay are under way to offer future generations access to information and knowledge, the "capital" of a sustainable future, from the bottom up.

Laptop Giving, the nonprofit founded by Nicholas Negroponte, states its vision as follows:

> By giving children their very own connected XO laptop, we are giving them a window to the outside world, access to vast amounts of information, a way to connect with each other, and a springboard into their future. And we're also helping these countries develop an essential resource — educated, empowered children.[6]

C. K. Prahalad in *The Fortune at the Bottom of the Pyramid* (2006) reframes the assumptions commonly held of those who live in poverty as the gap between those at the top and those at the bottom widens. Prahalad (2006, pp. 169-185) shows examples of large enterprises driving initiatives with profitable outcomes for the poor, with particular emphasis on the role of technology in leveling the playing field.

ITC, a US$4 billion Indian multibusiness conglomerate, needed to improve its supply chain of soy crops (ITC e-Choupals, 2008). By providing 2,000 Internet information kiosks to subsistence farmers who previously had no access to even such basic information as weather, ITC increased both its yield and that of the farmers. e-Choupals (a form of cooperative) were created by ITC to enable individual farmers to aggregate for better buying power for farm supplies, negotiating, selling, and connecting electronically. (For more on e-Choupals, see the *Living Fieldbook* (🔗).)

Technology is driving inequality between rich and poor more dramatically than financial globalization or trade alone, according to IMF researchers Jaumotte and colleagues in the *IMF Survey Magazine* article, "Technology Widening Rich–Poor Gap" (Jaumotte, Lall, Papageorgiou, & Topalova, 2007). The study began with the IMF researchers asking themselves such questions as, What is contributing to the widening of the income gap within countries? Is globalization the main driving force, or have other factors such as skill-biased technological progress also contributed to inequality?

After analyzing a wide variety of data (Jaumotte et al., 2007), the researchers determined that the main factor driving the recent increase in inequality across countries has been technological progress. This factor alone explains most of the increase in the Gini coefficient[7] from the early 1980s, supporting the view that new technology, in both advanced and developing countries, increases the premium on skills and substitutes for relatively low-skill inputs. Interestingly, among developing countries, the effect of technological progress is stronger in Asia than in Latin America, possibly reflecting the greater share of technology-intensive manufacturing in Asia.

---

5 "Vision," www.laptopgiving.org/en/vision.php (accessed January 30, 2008).

6 Ibid.

7 Gini coefficient is a wealth equality ratio. 0 equates to an equal distribution of wealth, 1 equates to all wealth held by one person. A curve is figured to depict the balance of wealth along a continuum (en.wikipedia.org/wiki/Gini_coefficient [accessed January 30, 2008]).

We are a networked world, which may be a benefit for the checks and balances required for global sustainability. The velocity of Internet communication via such mechanisms as blogs, podcasts, YouTube, and the like enables misdeeds to be exposed and enterprises to form collaborative forums to share best environmental social practices across industries (CSR: Leadership for Sustainability in a Networked World, 2007).

According to Hans Rosling of Gapminder, the world is undergoing major social change as more children survive, healthcare improves and the countries move to market economies.[8] When this improvement of the world is viewed in a highly contextualized manner, rather than by region or continent, it is clear that as GDP rises so does Internet use. In 2007, India had a middle class of 400,000,000 — already more than the total population of the United States and soon to surpass that of the European Union.

These rapidly increasing, globally oriented cohorts of Internet-savvy middle class in India (Internet in India, 2006) and China are joining social networking sites and virtual worlds. Leaders and managers of today's enterprises, as power players around the world are learning, will find social networks are extremely useful and effective tools for beginning to engage with these emerging markets and collaborating in ways that truly support global sustainability.

▧ Looking through the lens of poverty and inequity

> Currently, more than eight million people around the world die each year because they are too poor to stay alive. Our generation can choose to end that extreme poverty by the year 2025.
>
> *Jeffrey D. Sachs* (2005, p. 1)

Today we face extreme contrasts between extraordinary levels of material wealth in much of the developed world, on the one hand, and extreme poverty for most of the rest of the world, on the other. And the trends are going in the wrong direction. During the past 40 years, the gap between the richest and the poorest people in the world has been widening. For example, in 1960, the richest 20% accounted for 70.2% of global GDP, while the poorest 20% controlled 2.3%, representing a ratio of 30 to 1. By the year 2000, the gap had widened drastically, such that the richest fifth controlled 85% of global GDP, while the poorest controlled only 1.1%, representing a ratio of 80 to 1 (Hart, 2007, p. xxxviii).

The Fortune at the Bottom of the Pyramid [9]

In their seminal article "The Fortune at the Bottom of the Pyramid," C. K. Prahalad and Stuart L. Hart (2002) made a strong case for the enormous opportunities to bring prosperity to the poorest people of the world — that demographic sector they refer to as "the

---

8 To view a data animation video in which Rosling walks the viewer through global change, "debunking third-world myths with the best stats you've ever seen," go to www.gapminder.org/ video/talks/ted-2007---the-seemingly-impossible-is-possible.html (accessed January 30, 2008) (▦).

9 The "bottom of the pyramid" refers to the world's 4 billion poorest people who live on less than two dollars a day — representing two-thirds of the world's population (Prahalad & Hart, 2002, p. 15).

bottom of the pyramid." The fortune opportunity is to be found by multinational corporations changing their view and seeing through a new, more inclusive lens:

> Low-income markets present a prodigious opportunity for the world's
> wealthiest companies — to seek their fortunes and bring prosperity to the
> aspiring poor. This is a time for multinational corporations (MNCs) to look
> at globalization strategies through a new lens of inclusive capitalism. For
> companies with the resources and persistence to compete at the bottom of
> the world economic pyramid, the prospective rewards include growth, prof-
> its, and incalculable contributions to humankind. (p. 1)

Furthermore, they describe the opportunities and the business case that lie ahead for
companies that are willing to grapple with the enormity of the challenge and put their
toes in the water:

> Collectively, we have only begun to scratch the surface of what is the biggest
> potential market opportunity in the history of commerce. Those in the pri-
> vate sector who commit their companies to a more inclusive capitalism have
> the opportunity to prosper and share their prosperity with those who are
> less fortunate. In a very real sense, the fortune at the bottom of the pyramid
> represents the loftiest of our global goals. (Prahalad & Hart, 2002, p. 15)

Bottom of the pyramid (BoP) 2.0

More recently, in his book *Capitalism at the Crossroads* (2007), Stuart Hart deepened
understanding of sustainability and globalization: "Constructively engaging these challenges [international terrorism, the backlash against globalization, global-scale environmental change] will be the key to ensuring that capitalism continues to thrive in the
coming century — to everyone's benefit" (Hart, 2007, p. xxxix). Hart argues that a sustainable global enterprise *must move beyond greening* (pollution prevention and product
stewardship), *beyond clean technology* and *base of the pyramid,* to "becoming indigenous," harnessing the native capabilities of all peoples, built on foundations of creativity, respect, co-development, and the reinvention of industry (Hart, 2007, pp. 228-230).

'New market creation'

The preferred new approach for the BoP protocol, Hart (2008) now argues, is **new market creation**, characterized by three key interrelated components: "Opening Up,"
"Building the Ecosystem," and "Enterprise Creation" (slide 6). In this new paradigm,
"co-generated business concepts" are "opened up" by launching a nonbusiness-specific
immersion guided by two-way dialogue and humility to catalyze the generation of new
business concepts. **Building the ecosystem** is accomplished by deepening the commitment among the company, community, and other partners in order to construct the
business model. **Enterprise creation** builds locally embedded businesses by evolving
the business structure and building the market base through staged and flexible
resource commitments (Hart, 2008, slide 6). (We note that this perspective is consistent
with the discussions about the application of a local business SWOT analysis in Chapter
3 and about the leader's mindset in Karen Davis's essay in Chapter 1, pages 37ff.)

Indigenous business development

According to Dorette Steenkamp, executive director, Uthango Social Investments, South
Africa,

Sustainable development and related enterprise growth in communities will only be possible if we prioritize true engagement of communities. Listening in an active, responsive way to community members requires putting aside own agendas and often asks for organizational courage to innovate existing processes. The fears and aspirations of communities have a direct influence on the sustainable practices embedded in their enterprises and actions — especially at a micro-enterprise and local economic level. Globalization is not the greatest threat at grassroots, but lack of engagement on authentic indigenous solutions disrespects community building principles and perpetuates non-sustainable development practices. Endorsement of any form of development starts with listening and engaging communities through appropriate technology and relationship economics.[10]

Alvarez and Barney (2006) distinguish two dimensions of business development in the new global sustainable paradigm: discovery-based versus creation-based. In the **discovery-based** paradigm, businesses "target" the unmet needs in the BoP, estimate the size of the market, "deploy" new technologies, extend their current business model via structural innovation, and then "scale up." In contrast, in **creation-based** business development, the process begins with humility and an open mind. Competitive imagination is sparked, and something new is co-developed. A new business model is built based on trust and social capital. Rather than "scaling up" it is "scaled out."

An excellent example of indigenous business development is the inspiring story of E+Co, a company that is creating a new energy paradigm for universal energy in energy impoverished developing countries.

E+Co: a 'new energy paradigm — universal sustainable energy in developing countries'

E+Co is a nonprofit public investment company whose focus is to bring clean affordable energy to those who lack access, the rural energy-impoverished. By providing loans and entrepreneurial development services, E+Co has provided clean energy access to well over 2 million people and businesses in 35 developing countries (Farias, Harmon, Russell, Farias, & Twomey, 2006).

E+Co serves as an "intermediary financing" organization that assembles money from a blend of foundations, governments, and private investors, lends it to entrepreneurs in Latin America, Asia, Africa, and Eastern Europe, and provides specialized professional and administrative services to help them start and grow their businesses (see Fig. 7.2; Farias et al., 2006).

E+Co has roughly US$60 million in capital and returns 1 to 2% to investors, which may not appear to be substantial unless measures other than pure profit are included in the return — such as **triple-bottom-line** measures of economic, environmental, and social returns. A few highlights of E+Co's accomplishments over the 14 years since its inception are the following (Farias et al., 2006):

- Mobilized over US$120 million of capital for clean energy enterprises

- Supported 125 enterprises to provide modern energy services to over 2.2 million people

10 Personal communication with L. Kelley/Delia Lake in Second Life, January 9, 2008.

Figure 7.2 **E+Co's enterprise-centered model**

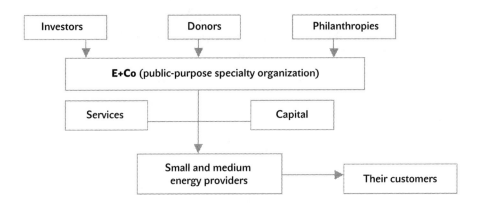

Source: Pioneering a new energy paradigm: Alleviating "energy poverty" in the world. Proceedings of the Eastern Academy of Management International, Amsterdam, June 2006. Copyright 2006, G. Farias, J. Harmon, B. Russell, C. Farias, and D. Twomey. Reproduced with permission.

- Created over 2,000 new jobs
- Produced 44 million liters of clean water
- Saved 76 million kilograms of firewood and 28 million barrels of oil
- Offset 1.1 million metric tons of CO_2
- Generated more than US$1.2 million for enterprises by selling carbon under the Kyoto Protocol

Highly effective ventures such as E+Co represent the possibilities that can be generated by investors willing to effect environmental, social, and governance (ESG) change through nonprofits with the microfinance expertise.

North–South perspectives and issues

Many believe that there is a need for new and different perspectives for global and regional problems, processes, and solutions. Currently most firms and executives from affluent, developed countries are stuck in a perspective from the Northern Hemisphere that is so predominant that some are not even aware there are other perspectives. On the other hand, the developing countries, mostly located in the Southern Hemisphere, not only experience a different set of problems but also provide a different perspective about global issues, which are typically misunderstood by the North. A vibrant North–South dialogue is crucial, since successful global programs rest heavily on the people and institutions of the South for implementation. Many of the grand, well-intentioned programs developed from the Northern perspective have failed miserably, in part because of their less-than-positive assumptions about the motivation and capabilities of the South. Neither the problems nor the opportunities in developing countries can be clearly understood from a Northern perspective alone. In fact, people must learn to develop processes and cultures that enable dynamic and creative collaboration between the South and the North in defining issues, establishing collaborative decision-making, and implementing new endeavors. Table 7.1 depicts some of the key shifts in thinking required to incorporate North–South differences in service of sustainability.

Table 7.1 **Shifts in thinking required to incorporate North–South differences in service of sustainability**

Issue	From	To
Who sets the agenda?	The most powerful	The most knowledgeable and affected
Whose cultural norms prevail?	Those of the North (e.g., developed)	The people whose behaviors are important to implementation
Method of negotiation?	Advocating unilaterally formed positions	Inquiring together (South–North) to define problem
Who benefits?	Our (North) firm/nation benefits	The most needy must benefit (world must benefit)

Note these continua are consistent with and expand on John Adams's discussion of mental models in Chapter 2 (pages 6off.). See especially Tables 2.1 through 2.4.

Source: Copyright 2007, D. F. Twomey. Used with permission.

North–South cultural differences and economic power shifting have significant long-term sustainability implications. Several South American countries (primarily Ecuador, Peru, and Venezuela) are rethinking their core legal and economic systems to better align with environmental and social values. President Chavez in Venezuela disrupted the oil supply chain when he nationalized the oil and renegotiated the extraction and refining contract terms. The government of Ecuador is looking at rewriting the constitution to diminish the legal standing of corporations so that they are not at the same standing as a person. It is also suggesting giving legal standing to the environment (Martinez, 2007).

Corporate social responsibility, reporting, and disclosure

An increasing plethora of literature on corporate social responsibility centers on the obligation of organizations, especially corporations, to address societal problems and ills (Wirtenberg, Abrams, & Ott, 2004; Margolis & Walsh, 2001). Research in all sectors (Wirtenberg et al., 2004) demonstrates the following:

- Corporate social responsibility is increasing
- Accountability for business ethics and governance is on the rise
- Corporate role in human rights and economic gaps are widening
- Accountability for the use of natural resources is becoming more prevalent
- Need for enhanced sustainability of enterprises is increasingly urgent
- Business and government partnerships creating more challenges and opportunities

- New organizational models are emerging across traditional sectors (public–private)

> Business must be run at a profit, or else it will die. But when anyone tries to run a business solely for profit . . . then also the business must die, for it no longer has a reason for existence.
>
> *Henry Ford*

Now at the beginning of the 21st century, policy, formal and informal, is expanding rapidly to address corporate social responsibility. New organizations and industries, as well as many kinds of program, are being established to deliver on sustainability. This includes the formation of international bodies such as the World Economic Forum to convene on policy. It also includes the investment sector where socially responsible investment research, analyst relations, and institutional houses and indexes, such as the Dow Jones Sustainability Index, rate companies on their triple-bottom-line performance. Corporate social responsibility reports and audits have been developed and their production and use is increasing.

Corporations, individuals, NGOs, and international policy groups are making many advances in the area of corporate social responsibility (CSR). The transformation of CSR from a movement into a viable industry and job function is now here. CSR, socially responsible investing (SRI), and sustainability, like the quality movement, have become businesses in themselves. CSR alone is a US$37 billion business according to Business for Social Responsibility (BSR),[11] a nonprofit trade association with 250 member companies and Global 1000 enterprises.[12] BSR's mission is to build sustainability into the business strategy. Enlightened companies understand the power that cross-sector collaboration can have in driving their CSR efforts.

One recent example is Google's RechargeIT, which works on three levels to reduce CO_2 emissions:

- **The individual drivers of its fleet of cars.** The company is working with A123 and Hymotion to convert its hybrids to plug-in cars

- **The grid.** The company is demonstrating vehicle-to-grid technology and funding research

- **The planet.** The company has a 1.6 MW solar installation

Reframing the financial conversation around sustainability and the environment is best done by holding individual managers with areas of large energy consumption accountable in their departmental budgets. "A lot of changes aren't technology, but are institutional and people changes," says Jonathan Koomey, project manager at Lawrence Berkeley National Laboratory in an *Information Week* article by M. K. McGee. McGee adds that, in the second of two 2007 reports on reducing the energy use of rapidly expanding technologies, Koomey suggests "combining the budgets of IT and facilities expenses of data centers so that IT leaders have more incentive to deploy energy-saving technologies and processes" (McGee, 2007).

There have been many developments in recent years in response to the growth of ethical consumerism in Northern and Western markets. Corporations have responded to concerns over environmental impacts, labor relations, and efforts such as social

---

11 www.bsr.org (accessed December 21, 2008).
12 www.bsr.org (accessed January 30, 2008).

auditing, independent monitoring, social certification, and social label programs. So what do the firms with headquarters in developed economies do when they start manufacturing in developing countries? Are domestic firms in developing countries displaying any social responsibility through their own policies and actions? Attitudes and approaches to corporate environmental reporting, CSR, and sustainability are shaped by history and culture; however, emerging countries are slowly adopting sustainable approaches to be competitive (French, 2007).

■ Looking through a limits-to-growth lens

> Every natural system in the world today is in decline . . . We are drawing down resources that took millions of years to create in order to supplement current consumption . . . As a consequence, habitats are destroyed, species become extinct, and in the process, the productive health of the environment is compromised and decreased.
>
> *Paul Hawken* (2005, p. 23)

Although our book is on sustainability for business leaders, the reality is that all businesses operate in a dynamic context of multiple perspectives. Sustainable globalization in the 21st century must seek a balance — there are "limits to growth" (Meadows, Meadows, & Randers, 2004), which enlightened enterprises, some 300+ years old (de Geus, 1997), have known for centuries.

Ecosystems under stress

As Paul Hawken describes in his chapter "The Death of Birth" in *Ecology of Commerce* (2005, pp. 19-36), every single ecosystem of our planet is under profound stress. For example:

- Fisheries are facing collapse
- There is a huge loss of land for food production
- The effects of climate change are all too evident

"Traditional business risks have been fires, floods, and dangers related to employee health & safety — risks to tangibles. There is a growing, daunting list of mega-issues that threaten both tangible assets and intangible assets like reputation" (Willard, 2005, p. 93).

Currently, there are over 6.2 billion people on our planet Earth and that number increases by 200,000 more people each day, which adds up to another 74 million people per year. Increased population causes amplified stress in many natural and social resources that enterprises depend on for their livelihood. The following section is an overview of some of the mega-issues that have potential to seriously disrupt future sustainability.

Climate change

Among the key findings from the recent Intergovernmental Panel on Climate Change (IPCC) Fourth Assessment Report (Pachauri, 2007):

Warming of the climate system is unequivocal

Climate change is a serious threat to development everywhere.

Today, the time for doubt has passed. The IPCC has unequivocally affirmed the warming of our climate system, and linked it directly to – human activity. (slide 3)

Slowing or even reversing the existing trends of global warming is the defining challenge of our ages. (slide 3)

Projected sea level rise at the end of the 21st century will be 18 to 59 cm. Furthermore, the partial loss of ice sheets we are already seeing at an alarmingly accelerating rate will cause meters of sea level rise, major changes in coastlines and inundation of low-lying areas, great effects on river deltas and low-lying islands. (slides 7–8)

Approximately 20% to 30% of species on our planet are facing the risk of extinction. (slide 8)

The large scale and persistent changes will impact the productivity of marine ecosystem, fisheries, and vegetation on land. (slide 8)

Health issues

Climate changes compound health issues. From global warming to extreme weather events the changes in disease patterns is evident. In the "Climate Change Futures" (2005) report by Harvard Medical School's Center for Health and the Global Environment with the United Nations Development Programme (UNDP), malaria, West Nile virus, Lyme disease, and airborne allergens each represent significantly changed disease patterns. Heat exacerbates growth cycles of such disease vectors as mosquitoes and some microbes themselves, floods force movement of people while improving breeding grounds, and global travel advances the spread of disease. The socioeconomic losses are far-reaching, ranging from lives lost to restrictions in travel and tourism. No part of our ecosystems remains untouched.

Equity issues

We are facing unprecedented challenges on a global scale due to climate change which will affect people in every country in the world, and will have its greatest impact on developing countries. Equity issues and challenges stand out and are being significantly exacerbated by the impacts of global warming. (Pachauri, 2007, slide 14)

Africa by 2020:

Between 75 and 250 million people are projected to be exposed to increased water stress. In some countries, yields from rain-fed agriculture would be reduced by as much as 50%. (Pachauri, 2007, slide 14)

Asia by 2050s:

Freshwater availability is projected to decrease substantially. Coastal areas, especially heavily-populated large delta regions will be at greatest risk from sea flooding. (Pachauri, 2007, slide 14)

Small Island States:

> Sea level rise is expected to exacerbate inundation, storm surge, erosion and other coastal hazards threatening vital infrastructure. By mid-century there will be significantly reduced water resources in many small island states. (Pachauri, 2007, slide 14)

The IPCC (Pachauri, 2007) urgently called on governments and industries around the world to work collaboratively together to mitigate the human and economic impacts of these unequivocal trends. Every major sector of business and society will be affected; the key ones are energy, transportation, buildings, industry, agriculture, forestry, and waste.

Water

The world is going to depend on the rapidly developing economies for one of our most important natural resources — freshwater. Over the last 100 years, water needs have increased tenfold. Worldwide, the biggest user of freshwater is agriculture, which still represents 70% of all water used, with industry consuming about 21%, and individuals the remaining 10% (United Nations Environment Program, 2006). There is a widespread view that the wars of the future will be waged to secure water sources rather than oil or gas. A small number of countries make up the world's largest freshwater reservoir, accounting for 60% of resources — and these include two of the four BRICs.[13] Brazil has the world's greatest water reserves, most of which are in the Amazon River, followed by Russia, which claims 20% of the world's "total unfrozen, freshwater reserve," in Lake Baikal.[14] The BRICs' attitude to sustainability will impact the entire world.

Food

According to Jacques Diouf, head of the UN Food and Agriculture Organization (paraphrased in Rosenthal, 2007), "the world food supply is dwindling rapidly and food prices are soaring to historic levels." The changes are creating, warned Diouf, "a very serious risk that fewer people will be able to get food." The changes are attributed to the early effects of global warming, which has decreased crop yields in some crucial areas, and to a shift away from farming for human consumption toward crops for biofuels and cattle feed. "Demand for grain is increasing with the world population, and more is diverted to feed cattle as the population of upwardly mobile meat-eaters grows" (Rosenthal, 2007, p. 1). So, ironically, as the world becomes more prosperous, based on current consumption patterns, there will actually be less food in the world to eat. This is because as more people in the world eat meat, grains are being diverted from people to livestock.

Another major factor is that many farmers in the United States are now selling their corn to make subsidized ethanol. Thus, as seen in Chapter 2, people are trying to solve one problem but creating other, unintended, effects that could actually be worse than the original problem.

---

13 BRICs is a term coined by Goldman Sachs to represent Brazil, Russia, India, and China (Goldman Sachs, 2007).

14 UNESCO World Heritage Centre website, whc.unesco.org/en/list/754 (accessed March 22, 2008).

Ecosystems services

Can we put a price on the services all of us reap from the environment? What is the price of a day without air pollution or watershed land or rain forest? Robert Costanza, director and founder of the Gund Institute for Ecological Economics at the University of Vermont and cofounder of the International Society for Ecological Economics, estimated the biosphere's worth at around US$33 trillion (Harris, 2003).

Ecosystem services are the benefits we derive from our Earth's "natural capital" or collective natural resources. Biodiversity costs are incurred when these resources are destroyed or degraded to such a degree that they become significantly less available for use.

> It is a strange fight, Montana ranchers say. Raising cattle here in the parched American outback of eastern Montana and Wyoming has always been a battle to find enough water.
>
> Now there is more than enough water, but the wrong kind, they say, and they are fighting to keep it out of the river.
>
> Mark Fix is a family rancher whose cattle operation depends on water from the Tongue River. Mr Fix diverts about 2,000 gallons per minute of clear water in the summer to transform a dry river bottom into several emerald green fields of alfalfa, an oasis on dry rangeland. Three crops of hay each year enable him to cut it, bale it and feed it to his cattle during the long winter.
>
> "Water means a guaranteed hay crop," Mr. Fix said.
>
> But the search for a type of natural gas called coal bed methane has come to this part of the world in a big way. The gas is found in subterranean coal, and companies are pumping water out of the coal and stripping the gas mixed with it. Once the gas is out, the huge volumes of water become waste in a region that gets less than 12 inches of rain a year. (Robbins, 2006)

Manufacturing and agribusiness sector

Manufacturers are keenly aware of losses to natural resources such as platinum, oil, and the massive consumption of cement and steel in China to build the infrastructure (Kahn & Landler, 2007). Holcim Cement[15] has been ranked a "Leader of the Industry" by Dow Jones Sustainability Index in each of the past two years. Knowing that over 70% of the world population will be living in urban environments by 2030, which produce 40% of CO_2 emissions, Holcim has made a commitment to reduce CO_2 emissions through a more sustainable approach to property construction. Using its position as the world's largest producer of cement, it set up the Holcim Foundation for Sustainable Construction in 2003. Its aim is to promote dialogue on sustainable construction among architects, planners, construction engineers, and investors throughout the world.

The global food basket is under equal pressure. As Michael Pollan notes, in the United States the honeybee needed for pollination is succumbing in large numbers to colony collapse disease for unknown reasons. One possibility that has been suggested is overuse in the US$14 billion agriculture industry (Pollan, 2007).

---

15 www.holcim.com (accessed January 10, 2008).

■ Looking through the movement-of-talent lens

Migration and urbanization

Nearly all future world population growth will take place in less-developed countries. Over half of world population growth will occur in Asia, but one-third will be in Africa, which today accounts for only about 13% of the world's population (Population Reference Bureau, 1999, p. 2).

The burden for growth will fall mainly to women for child bearing and rearing. Women's lives are improving in less-developed countries, but only with access to education, healthcare, and paid employment. Women make up more than one-third of the informal labor force in many countries, selling goods in local markets or working for themselves or family members in cottage industries.

However, in moving to urban areas, although other problems arise, women find greater access for their children's education, better work possibilities, and healthcare.

WOMEN UNIONIZE IN INDIA

The Self-Employed Women's Association (UN Population Fund, 2007), a trade union of 700,000 members in six Indian states, has set up facilities that provide healthcare, childcare, insurance services, research, training, communication, and marketing, as well as housing and infrastructure for poor urban women working in the informal economy.

Movement of people in general is projected to be increasing by anywhere from 2 million to 4 million people per year, and in 1998 more than 145 million lived outside their native countries. Migration is driven by labor flow, family reunification, asylum, and illegal migration. By 2030, more than 75% of the world's population will be living in urban areas — centers with over 2,000 residents or national or provincial capitals. Over one-half of urban dwellers worldwide at that time will reside in Asia (Population Reference Bureau, 1999, p. 11).

Although less-developed countries' populations are moving to more urban areas, technology is quickly "flattening" the world, enabling those in rural areas to accrue some benefits.

Just how flat is the world?

The World Is Flat, argues thought leader and *New York Times* columnist Thomas Friedman (2005), when he popularized globalization's most recent center-stage role. According to Friedman, cheap, ubiquitous telecommunications have finally obliterated all impediments to international competition, and the dawning "flat world" is a jungle pitting "lions" against "gazelles," where "economic stability is not going to be a feature" and "the weak will fall farther behind." The flat world sees the further outsourcing of the service sector (telemarketing, accounting, computer programming, call centers, research, and the like) to the English-speaking abroad; manufacturing will continue to be off-shored to China.

Or is it round, as Larry Prusak argues? He thinks it's unrealistic to imagine that work will continue to flow outward from today's more developed nations to the less-developed ones enabled by the virtual nature of the Internet and other communication technologies (Prusak, 2006).

It's spiky, claims Richard Florida (2005). Florida, who wrote *Flight of the Creative Class*, mapped innovation against the major cities of the world. Innovation is agreed by most to be the engine of sustainable growth. What he found were three types of place that made up the "economic landscape," and it was far from flat or round.

First are the cities that generate innovations. These are the tallest peaks; they have the capacity to attract global talent and create new products and industries. They are few in number, and difficult to topple. Second are the economic "hills" — places where people manufacture the world's established goods, take its calls, and support its innovation engines. These hills can rise and fall quickly; they are prosperous but insecure. Some, such as Dublin and Seoul, are growing into innovative, wealthy peaks; others are declining, eroded by high labor costs and a lack of enduring competitive advantage. Third, there are the vast valleys — places with little connection to the global economy and in which people have few immediate prospects.

The implications are that talent is flooding into the major cities worldwide leaving vast valleys of disenfranchised. These geographic flatlands are of concern as gaps create disparate "tribalisms" of thinking and political backlash. Another reason to pay attention to the bottom of the pyramid or in this case the bottom of the spikes.

▓ Looking through a geopolitical lens

Most commentators agree that globalization diminishes the power of the nation state — for good or bad. Some argue that it drives homogenization — Coca-Cola and McDonald's everywhere; others argue it inspires communities to value, preserve, and share with others the jewels of their own cultures. A third view is that it has exploded into tribalism in certain parts of the world — the Middle East, South and Southeast Asia, and Africa, for example. The populations of many countries in the developing world identify much more readily with their "tribes" or communities than with the artificial concept of "nation states."

Geopolitical issues affecting sustainability include, among others, governance; terrorism and security; nationalism and tribalism; and new emergent forms of democratic capitalism.

Governance issues: regulations rule the day

Government and intergovernmental regulation and agreements are key in shaping the overall global face of sustainability of individual companies. In the worldwide AMA sustainability study, "effectively addressing regulatory restrictions wherever we operate" was rated as one of the top four sustainability-related factors driving key business decisions today and was projected to be among the top six in ten years as well (American Management Association [AMA 2007], p. 12 [Fig. 1]).

Ecological footprint implications on global trade agreements

The ecological footprint previously introduced and described in Chapter 6, answers two critical questions:

- How much of the regenerative capacity of the biosphere is used by human activities?

- How much is available within a region?

As of 2003, the total global ecological demand was at 2.2 hectares per person; the total global supply based on the Earth's biocapacity is 1.8 hectares per person.[16] This means the world has already surpassed its ability to meet current demands. At the same time, the world ecological footprint has been steadily increasing, to the point that it would require approximately one and a quarter Earths to satisfy current demand, and four Earths and more to satisfy the biosphere demands as population increases, assuming that persons currently living in poverty are able to elevate to a middle-class lifestyle and follow a consumption pattern that is the same as their developed-country counterparts.

Figure 7.3 provides a depiction of the world in terms of ecological creditors and debtors. This suggests a new, more eclectic view of the world. Today we tend to create a false separation between developing nations and developed nations or its close analogy of Northern and Southern Hemisphere national alliances. If ecological footprint trends continue toward potential depletion of the global ecological resources, a tragedy of the commons–type shift in national behaviors could be expected. One could anticipate ecological creditor nations becoming more protectionist in regard to resource sharing. These creditor nations are becoming more aware of the rising demand for the ecosystem services they are providing to debtor nations and are already exploring market mechanisms to more appropriately monetize and trade these currently undervalued ecological assets and economic externalities. It is also feasible that, acting in their societal self-interests, nations would resort to military conflicts should weaker, but more ecologically viable, nations either refuse to "share" or attempt to politically and economically assert themselves.

The Human Development Index and ecological footprint of nations are plotted in Figure 7.4. An HDI rating of greater than 0.8 is considered to be a sustainable quality of life or social system value. An ecological footprint of less than 1.8 hectares per person is considered to be a sustainable consumption level of biologically reproductive resources and ecosystem services. Using these indicators, the lower-right quadrant would represent nations that are both environmentally and socially sustainable. Looking at the sustainability of specific nations around the world, one can gain several insights. While the United States currently has a high HDI rating, it has the second worst ecological footprint and is severely overshooting its use of biologically reproduced resources and services. The African nations are all experiencing extremely poor qualities of life, but are at the moment ecologically sustainable. The European nations are achieving a sustainable HDI rating, but are still overshooting their ecological footprints, but at a lesser rate than North American nations. It is particularly interesting to observe the positioning of South American nations. A few of these nations appear to currently be achieving both sustainable social and ecological performance; several more are within a reasonable range of achieving this objective. It should be noted that the AMA sustainability survey (AMA, 2007) observed that employees from these same nations rated themselves highest among all employees as to the sustainable performance of their companies. They were aware of sustainability issues and are demonstrating leading intentions and practices in sustainable governance, human rights, and production practices.

In an interconnected world, there are few firewalls left. These risks have associated consequences for enterprises.

---

16 Personal communication with N. Freeling, via e-mail, April 22, 2008.

Figure 7.3 **Ecological creditors and ecological debtors**

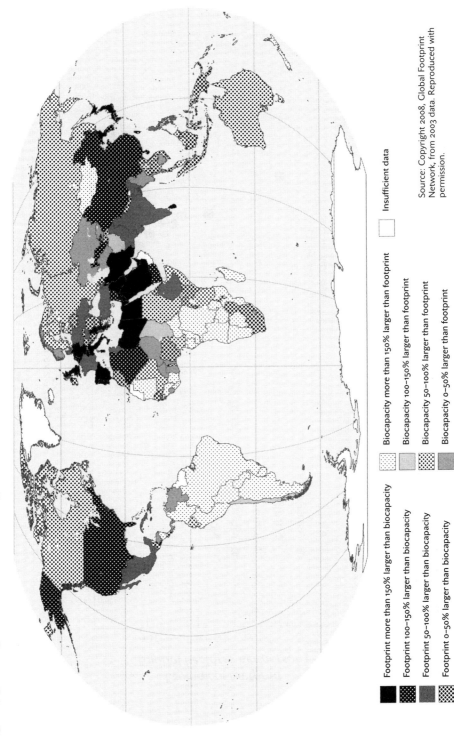

Footprint more than 150% larger than biocapacity

Footprint 100–150% larger than biocapacity

Footprint 50–100% larger than biocapacity

Footprint 0–50% larger than biocapacity

Biocapacity more than 150% larger than footprint

Biocapacity 100–150% larger than footprint

Biocapacity 50–100% larger than footprint

Biocapacity 0–50% larger than footprint

Insufficient data

Source: Copyright 2008, Global Footprint Network, from 2003 data. Reproduced with permission.

Figure 7.4 **Sustainable development: where are we today?** Human Development Index and ecological footprint of nations

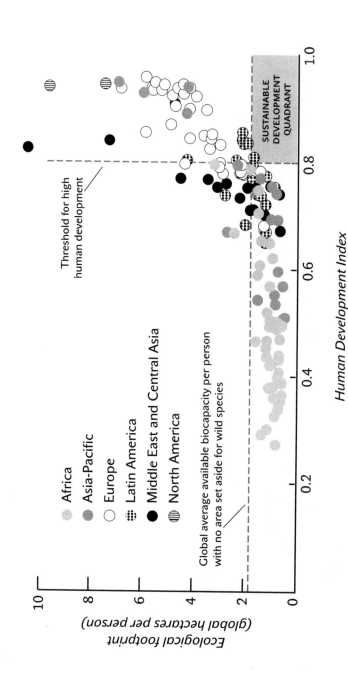

Source: Copyright 2008, Global Footprint Network. Reproduced with permission.

Prudence dictates that the sustainable enterprise account for these risks in both strategic and financial plans. As Mark Haynes Daniell says in *World of Risk*, "A new and more comprehensive model of solutions will need to respond to the full impact of future crises, and to manage risks as well before they become expensive, and avoidable catastrophes" (Daniell, 2004). The precautionary principle, established in the 1970s, is an example voluntary risk management ethic. It was embodied in several European Union laws in the 1980s and is often considered a "risk prevention" policy. Applied either voluntarily or within a regulatory compliance mode, the principle responds to concerns about managing potential risks before their consequences are irreversible. It is a decision process or rule that says if an action or policy might cause significant harm to public health or the natural environment, even in the absence of a scientific consensus on the exact nature or extent of the harm, then the burden of proof falls on those who advocate the action or policy, and all reasonable alternatives (including the alternative of doing nothing) should be formally considered (Montague, 2008).[17] As well as being foundational to one of the principles of the UN Global Compact, it has been foundational to many policies of the EU, such as the WEEE (ewaste) Directive and has been formally adopted by the city and county of San Francisco.

Nationalism vs. tribalism

Harvard Business School professor Michael Porter wrote in 1990 that in a world of increasing global competition, nations have become more, not less, important. "Differences in national values, culture, economic structures, institutions, and histories all contribute to competitive success . . . Ultimately nations succeed in particular industries because their home environment is the most forward-looking" (Porter, 1979–1998, p. 155).

Alfons Trompennaars (1993), who examined seven advanced economies from the lens of national culture, found that, "in any culture, a deep structure of beliefs is the invisible hand that regulates economic activity. These cultural preferences, or values, are the bedrock of national identity and the source of economic strengths — and weakness" (1993, p. 4) So we can open up a wider range of opportunities for wealth creation by understanding that we base economic decisions on values or beliefs. To homogenize capitalism to an Anglo-American approach limits creativity and innovation.

To further the ability to leverage the strengths and opportunities of the rich diversity of cultures around the world, we recommend an approach of inquiry and learning. In particular, the comprehensive *Globe Study of 62 Societies* (House, Hanges, Javidan, Dorfman, & Gupta, 2004) is a good starting point for managers seeking to build their base of knowledge and cultural understanding.

17 Precautionary principle definition from Wikipedia, en.wikipedia.org/wiki/Precautionary_principle (accessed March 22, 2008).

THREE SCENARIOS FOR THE FUTURE OF SUSTAINABILITY

In *Creating a Sustainable Future*, the AMA (2007) report based on the AMA sustainability survey, conducted by a number of the authors of this book, we described three scenarios of how sustainability could evolve over the next ten years: 2007 to 2017, which could portend and determine, in a very real sense, the future of humanity for centuries to come. Scenarios are fictional stories about possible futures. They are not intended to predict the future. Rather, they are intended to help readers challenge their own hidden assumptions about how the future may turn out, and are based on ideas and trends that already exist. The future most likely will be a combination of these scenarios plus events and trends that we cannot begin to foresee at this juncture. The three scenarios are described in detail in AMA, 2007, and are briefly described here.

Scenario one: things fall apart

By the year 2017, most organizations have given up on trying to be "sustainable," which is now seen as a passé business buzzword from a decade before. Most businesses just want to survive in an increasingly anarchic world, one plagued by what is becoming a global war for natural resources, especially oil and water.

Scenario two: muddling toward sustainability?

In 2017, sustainability is, at best, a mixed bag and, at worst, an utter mess. Countries keep trying to create global agreements on everything: fisheries, greenhouse gases, water conservation, pandemics, the reduction of global poverty, and so on. But the agreements are usually based on unchallenging consensus targets that, even when missed, are seldom punished by the larger community. Moreover, as with the Kyoto Protocol, many of these agreements don't include the nations that have the largest impact on the problems. In other words, most of the agreements have symbolic value but no real teeth.

Scenario three: a global sustainability culture

In 2017, a global sustainability culture seems to have taken root. Some believe that a cultural "tipping point" has been reached. Many issues have shaped it: alarming scientific findings, changes in climate patterns, geopolitical conflicts, global media networks, innovations in the marketplace, the success of "green" business, and many other factors. The bottom line, however, is that the confluence of these factors has created what some experts call a global "sustainability culture" or "preservation mindset."

Our conclusion is still the same as when we wrote the AMA report in early 2007:

> Time will tell which of these scenarios comes closest to the truth. Much will depend on the actions that business, governments, educational institutions, NGOs, and others take today. If these entities can work together to align their values and organizational processes around sustainability principles, then our global society has a greater chance of addressing, ameliorating, and sometimes even solving a range of social and environmental problems (p. 51).

AMA global sustainability survey: highlights of regional results and analysis

Joel Harmon

The worldwide AMA sustainability survey (AMA, 2007) data from 1,365 respondents in over 50 countries enabled us to explore differences across geographic regions in the degree to which sustainable development strategies and practices are being embraced, an issue not examined in *Creating a Sustainable Future*, the report based on the 2007 survey. Based on the demographic data that respondents provided, we aggregated them into the six regional groupings shown in Table 7.2.

Table 7.2 **Response frequencies**

	Frequency	Percentage
Latin America (e.g., South and Central America, Caribbean, Mexico)	67	4.9
All Asian (e.g., India, China, Japan, Korea, Oceana)	160	11.7
Africa–Middle East	71	5.2
Europe (both Eastern and Western)	144	10.5
Canada	75	5.5
United States	848	62.1
Total	1,365	100.0

Cross-regional comparisons

The survey found a number of significant differences across regions. In general, sustainability appeared to have taken significantly stronger hold outside the United States and Canada. For example, respondents from Latin American, African, and Asian regions reported that their organizations were implementing and seeing benefits from sustainable development strategies to a significantly higher degree than did those from the United States and Canada. But even the more progressive regions appeared to be implementing sustainability only to a moderate degree. We also found the regions were significantly different with regard to the degree to which organizations within them were perceived to exhibit the seven qualities necessary to effectively implement sustainability strategies:

- Having top management's strong support
- Making sustainability central to organizational strategy

(continued over)

- Deeply ingraining values consistent with sustainability
- Aligning organization systems
- Developing rigorous metrics around sustainability
- Engaging a broad range of stakeholder groups
- Holistically integrating the various organization functions working on sustainability

As Figure 7.5 shows, organizations from the Latin American and Asian regions generally were seen as the strongest in exhibiting these qualities, and in fact had significantly stronger ratings than did the United States and Canada in the areas of alignment and metrics. Better progress seems to be being made generating top-management support, embedding values, and making sustainability a central part of strategy than with aligning systems, engaging stakeholders, and integrating organization activities.

Further, there was a similar pattern in regard to the degree to which organizations were seen to be implementing specific practices related to the environmental or social (people, communities) aspects of sustainability — highest for Latin America and Asia, lowest for the United States and Canada, with Africa–Middle East and

Figure 7.5 Extent to which qualities to effectively implement sustainable development strategies are exhibited

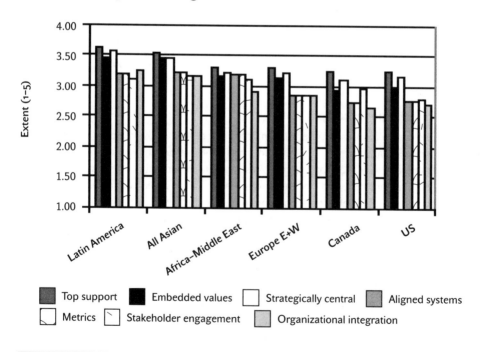

(continued opposite)

Figure 7.6 **Extent to which sustainability-related practices are being implemented**

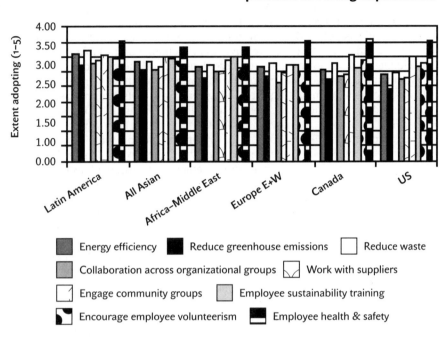

Energy efficiency   Reduce greenhouse emissions   Reduce waste

Collaboration across organizational groups   Work with suppliers

Engage community groups   Employee sustainability training

Encourage employee volunteerism   Employee health & safety

Europe in between. Figure 7.6 shows those practices for which there were the strongest differences across regions.

Practices to ensure employee health & safety were being adopted the most across the regions, and practices to reduce greenhouse gases the least, with Latin American and Asian organizations apparently making significantly more progress than US organizations in reducing emissions. In regard to energy and waste efficiency, and working with suppliers and getting groups across the organization to work collaboratively to improve sustainability, Latin American organizations were reported to be significantly ahead of those from the United States and Canada.

Note: Joel Harmon created the table and figures in this sidebar based on AMA sustainability survey (AMA, 2007) results.

■ Holistic integration

The world is truly at a crossroads in defining and determining the future of humanity. Viewing the current domestic and worldwide situation from a single lens is no longer an option. Each of our six lenses for sustainable globalization — **Economic/financial, Technology, Poverty and inequity, Limits to growth, Movement of talent**, and **Geopolitical** — is a necessity as the challenges confronting humanity are complex and interwoven. As we have seen, seemingly intractable problems abound, including to name only a few: resource depletion in energy, food, and water; global warming; widening economic gaps and entrenched poverty; insurmountable healthcare crises such as SARS and AIDS; skyrocketing healthcare costs; drug abuse; leadership vacuums and lack of ethics in business; racial, religious, and ethnic divisions; terrorism and war. The "solutions" we have known in the past, which stem from a single discipline (e.g., economics, politics, or the environment), sector (public/private/nonprofit), industry, or region, are inadequate to cope with complex challenges. Systemic, multicausal, long-standing problems require systemic, long-term solutions that engage all the key constituencies in a deep inquiry into both their source and their solutions. The Belfer Center at Harvard,[18] whose mission is to "provide leadership in advancing policy-relevant knowledge about the most important challenges of international security and other critical issues where science, technology, environmental policy, and international affairs intersect," is just one of many resources using a multidisciplinary approach.[19]

As stewards of the planet, it is incumbent on individuals and businesses to develop new interdependent and interdisciplinary/cross-functional models of collaboration to address climate change, which is rapidly approaching a "point of no return." With a growing world population and increased demands for planetary resources, people must begin to think globally while acting locally in communities and businesses. Wherever an individual is is the place to start. Take positive actions at an individual as well as an organizational level.

Six lenses for sustainable globalization tool

Every organization needs to ask questions and assess where they are in relation to the six lenses for sustainable globalization. Much like the premise of the balanced scorecard, one set of questions is not suitable for all organizations; questions need to be appropriate to your industry, global reach, resource constraints, size, business competencies, external networks, and the like. But at a minimum the following questions, by each lens, will begin the dialogue that needs to take place when longer-term, macro-business strategy is the topic at any organizational level. Include in your discussion how much you want the results to influence business decision-making: that is, 20%, 40%, and so on. Conversely, if you do nothing, how much are you impacted by negative results in any of the six lenses?

Economic/financial

- Do we look at ESG as an organization? If, yes what is our ESG framework?

- To what degree do we use GDP to forecast? What other sustainability indexes can we use which are more inclusive of ESG?

---

18 "Mission Statement," belfercenter.ksg.harvard.edu/about (accessed January 10, 2008).
19 belfercenter.ksg.harvard.edu/about (accessed January 10, 2008).

Technology

- How environmentally sustainable are the technologies we use?
- How much "social media" do we use to connect all levels of the organization?

Poverty and inequity

- What bottom-of-the-pyramid opportunities have we explored?
- What is our understanding of the role we play in North–South collaborations?
- What is our CSR approach?

Limits to growth

- How much does our supply chain mask environmental pollution?
- What environmental impacts does our organization create?
- What is our "carbon footprint" compared with the most ecologically friendly organizations?

Movement of talent

- How much do we contribute to the movement of talent to urban areas?
- How well do we understand the global talent pools? Do we create new centers of talent?

Figure 7.7 **Six lenses for sustainable globalization: sample results**

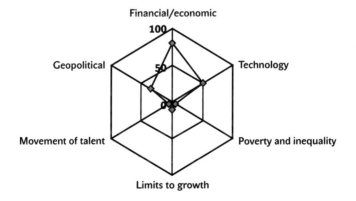

Source: Copyright 2007, V. G. Axelrod, J. Harmon, W. G. Russell, and J. Wirtenberg. Used with permission.

Geopolitical

● To what extent do we use our "power to convene" our business networks to address macro ESG issues that cut across national borders?

● How well do we incorporate the national cultures and values of the countries in which we operate our enterprise?

By plotting your responses in each of the six lenses, it is possible to see just how well integrated and holistic your organization is with regard to sustainable globalization (see Fig. 7.7).

■ Conclusion

We conclude our chapter with our opening question posed by the IPCC (Pachauri, 2007, slide 15). To create sustainable globalization what changes in lifestyles, behavior patterns, and management practices are needed, and by when?

It is up to each of us to relentlessly ask this question of ourselves, our business partners, our politicians, scientists, technologists, academics, and educators.

We believe we have outlined the major issues of globalization and the means by which organizations can begin to ask questions of themselves about their role in formulating solutions through the six lenses for sustainable globalization. There is no magic bullet; the process takes hard and collaborative effort.

Given the current momentum surrounding the need for more sustainable solutions, and the directions that are being proposed, there is reason for optimism. Real change can be strategically nurtured and implemented. As long as business, governments, NGOs, and the collective people that engage with them holistically monitor the condition of the world in the complementary context of these six highly interconnected global lenses, we are confident that good informed decisions can be made and necessary changes to the current global vision and the course of progress will occur.

In our view, solutions must come simultaneously from several different realms and all involve fundamental and profound transformations or paradigm shifts in what we think we know (i.e., "the way it is") and what actions we take. These fundamental transformations in our mindsets and behaviors will inexorably lead to fundamental transformations in some of most cherished and unquestioned concepts of consumerism, economic systems, and management systems, and profoundly leverage our uses of natural resources, technology, innovation, and the unleashing of human potential around the world. This is sustainable globalization.

■ References

Alvarez, S., & Barney, J. B. (2006). *Toward a creation theory of entrepreneurial opportunity formation.* Retrieved January 30, 2008, from www.cefe.net/forum/Creation_Theory.pdf.

American Management Association (AMA). (2007). *Creating a sustainable future: A global study of current trends and possibilities 2007–2017.* New York: American Management Association.

Brown, L. R. (2006). *Plan B 2.0: Rescuing a planet under stress and a civilization in trouble.* New York: W. W. Norton & Company.

Climate change futures. (2005, November). *Health, ecological and economic dimensions.* A project of The Center for Health and the Global Environment, Harvard Medical School. Sponsored by Swiss Re and United Nations Development Program.

CSR: Leadership for Sustainability in a Networked World. (2007, September). Advertising section sponsored by BSR. *Business Week.* Retrieved January 10, 2008, from www.businessweek.com/adsections/2007/pdf/09242007_corporate_2.pdf.

Daniell, M. (2004). *World of Risk.* River Edge, NJ: World Scientific Publishing Co.

De Geus, A. (1997). *The living company.* Boston, MA: Harvard Business School Press.

Farias, G., Harmon, J., Russell, B., Farias, C., & Twomey, D. (2006, June). *Pioneering a new energy paradigm: Alleviating "energy poverty" in the world.* Amsterdam: Proceedings of the Eastern Academy of Management International.

Florida, R. (2005). The world is spiky. *Atlantic Monthly.* Retrieved January 10, 2008, from www.leessummit.org/pdf/spikey.pdf.

French, H. W. (2007, November 24). Far from Beijing's reach, officials bend energy rules. *New York Times.* Retrieved January 9, 2008, from www.nytimes.com/2007/11/24/world/asia/24evaders.html?_r=1&pagewanted=all&oref=slogin.

Friedman, T. L. (2005). *The world is flat: A brief history of the 21st century.* New York: Farrar, Straus, & Giroux.

Goldman Sachs Group Inc. (2007, June 22). *GS Sustain.* New York: The Goldman Sachs Group.

Harris, L. (2003, April 8). At what cost? Biological economist Robert Costanza puts a price tag on nature. *Grist.* Retrieved January 10, 2008, from www.grist.org/news/maindish/2003/04/08/what.

Hart, S. L. (2007). *Capitalism at the crossroads: Aligning business, Earth, and humanity* (2nd ed.). Upper Saddle River, NJ: Wharton School Publishing.

Hart, S. L. (2008, March 12). *Business at the crossroads: Aligning commerce, Earth and humanity.* PowerPoint presented as part of an American Management Association webcast.

Hawken, P. (2005). *The ecology of commerce.* New York: Collins Business.

House, R. J., Hanges, P. J., Javidan, M., Dorfman, P. W., & Gupta, V. (2004). *Culture, leadership, and organizations: The Globe Study of 62 societies.* Thousand Oaks, CA: Sage Publications.

Internet in India (2006, September 19). India: Social networking. Retrieved January 8, 2008, from internetinindia.com/2006/09/19/india-social-networking.

ITC e-Choupals. (2008). ITC's rural development philosophy at work. Retrieved January 9, 2008, from www.itcportal.com/ruraldevp_philosophy/echoupal.htm.

Jaumotte, F., Lall, S., Papageorgiou, C., & Topalova, P. (2007, October 10). Technology widening rich–poor gap. *IMF Survey Magazine: IMF Research.* Retrieved January 9, 2008, from www.imf.org/external/pubs/ft/survey/so/2007/RES1010A.htm.

Kahn, J., & Landler, M. (2007, December 21). China grabs West's smoke-spewing factories. *New York Times.* Retrieved January 10, 2008, from www.nytimes.com/2007/12/21/world/asia/21transfer.html.

Le Pere, G. (2007) The positive and negative consequences of globalisation. Ministry of Foreign Affairs, Norway. Retrieved January 9, 2008, from www.regjeringen.no/en/dep/ud/campaign/refleks/innspill/engasjement/pere1.html?id=492843.

Margolis, J. D., & Walsh, J. P. (2001). *People and profits? The search for a link between a company's social and financial performance.* Mahwah, NJ: Lawrence Erlbaum Associates, Inc.

Martinez, N. (2007, Summer). Democracy rising. *Yes! Magazine.* Retrieved January 9, 2008, from www.yesmagazine.org/article.asp?ID=1730.

McGee, M. (2007, December 12). Computer servers in the US, Europe and Japan are power hogs. *Information Week,* Retrieved January 9, 2008, from www.informationweek.com.

Meadows, D. H., Meadows, D. L., & Randers, J. (2004). *Limits to growth: The 30-year update* (Paperback ed.). White River Junction, VT: Chelsea Green.

Montague, P. (2008, January 21). *The precautionary principle in the real world.* Environmental Research Foundation. Retrieved March 18, 2008, from www.precaution.org:80/lib/pp_def.htm.

Pachauri, R. K. (2007, November 17). *IPCC Fourth Assessment Report, Synthesis Report.* PowerPoint presentation given at the 27th session of the Intergovernmental Panel on Climate Change. Retrieved January 6, 2008, from www.ipcc.ch/graphics/presentations.htm.

Pollan, M. (2007, December 16). Our decrepit food factories. *New York Times Magazine*. Retrieved January 10, 2008, from www.nytimes.com/2007/12/16/magazine/16wwln-lede-t.html?scp=3&sq=%22Colony+Collapse+Disorder%22.

Population Reference Bureau. (1999). *World population more than just numbers*. Retrieved January 10, 2008 from www.prb.org/pdf/WorldPopMoreThanNos_Eng.pdf.

Porter, M. E. (1979–1998). *The competitive advantage of nations*. Boston, MA: Harvard Business School Publishing.

Prahalad, C. K. (2006). *The fortune at the bottom of the pyramid* (Paperback ed.). Upper Saddle River, NJ: Wharton School Publishing, pp. 169-185.

Prahalad, C. K., & Hart, S. L. (2002, 1st quarter). The fortune at the bottom of the pyramid. *Strategy + Business, 26*, 54-67. Retrieved February 3, 2008, from www.cs.berkeley.edu/~brewer/ict4b/Fortune-BoP.pdf.

Prusak, L. (2006, April). The world is round. *Harvard Business Review*. Retrieved January 10, 2008, from harvardbusinessonline.hbsp.harvard.edu/hbsp/hbr/articles/article.jsp?ml_action=get-article&articleID=F0604A&ml_issueid=null&ml_subscriber=true&pageNumber=1&_requestid=110327.

Robbins, J. (2006, September 10). In the West, a water fight over quality, not quantity. *New York Times*. Retrieved January 10, 2008, from www.nytimes.com/2006/09/10/us/10river.html?_r=1&scp=1&sq=In+the+West%2C+a+Water+Fight+Over+Quality%2C+Not+Quantity+&oref=slogin#.

Rosenthal, E. (2007, December 17). World food stocks dwindling rapidly, UN warns. *International Herald Tribune*. Retrieved January 7, 2008, from www.globalpolicy.org/socecon/hunger/economy/2007/1217stocks.htm.

Sachs, J. D. (2005). *The end of poverty*. New York: Penguin Books.

Sullivan, J. J. (2002). *The future of corporate globalization: From the extended order to the global village*. Westport, CT: Quorum Books.

Trompennaars, A. (1993). *Seven cultures of capitalism: How America wins and loses the unconscious war of capitalism*. New York: Doubleday.

United Nations Environment Program (UNEP). (2006). *Challenge to international waters: Regional assessment in a global perspective*. Nairobi, Kenya: UNEP. Retrieved March 24, 2008, from www.giwa.net/publications/finalreport/giwa_final_report.pdf.

United Nations Population Fund. (2007). *State of the world population 2007: Unleashing the potential of urban growth*. Chapter 2: Women's empowerment and well-being: The pillars of sustainable cities. Retrieved January 10, 2008, from www.unfpa.org/swp/2007/presskit/pdf/sowp2007_eng.pdf.

Willard, B. (2005). *The next sustainability wave. Building boardroom buy-in*. Gabriola Island, BC, Canada: New Society Publishers.

Wirtenberg, J., Abrams, L., & Ott, L. (2004). Assessing the field of organization development. *Journal of Applied Behavioral Science. 40*(4), 465-479.

8

Transorganizational collaboration and sustainability networks[1]

William G. Russell, Jenny Ambrozek, Victoria G. Axelrod, Jane Carbonaro, and Linda M. Kelley

What does it mean to be a holistically integrated enterprise fully aligned for sustainability? First and foremost, it means improving core abilities to collaborate, engage stakeholders, and work effectively in the context of a larger social and industrial ecology[2] networked system. In contrast, most enterprises today are focused primarily on issues of control, secrecy, competition, and unilateral success regardless of their externalities, or impacts on the environment, communities, and society at large. To be truly sustainable, enterprises must evolve toward cultures of trust, transparency, collaboration, and service. Ultimately this will optimize their own long-term financial viability, while contributing to solving complex problems, fulfilling the desires of the world's growing population, and avoiding overshooting our planet's ecosystem capacity.

One leading sustainable enterprise executive stated (Wirtenberg, Harmon, Russell, & Fairfield, 2007):

---

1 The authors gratefully acknowledge contributions from Anna Tavis to this chapter.
2 **Industrial ecology** is the shifting of industrial processes from linear (open-loop) systems, in which resource and capital investments move through the system to become waste, to a closed-loop system where wastes become inputs for new processes.

> I don't think sustainability is necessarily a competitive advantage. How do we get sustainable? [We] can get more and more sustainable in our business practices only by being part of a sustainable ecosystem. I can't be a lone sustainable company, [while] the ecosystem is going down the tubes. There's no way . . . It's truly like the Internet. The more people that get on the network, the more powerful they become. So that's why competition [doesn't] even exist in this discussion; it's more *"coopetition."* You've got to partner to build the ecosystem. A healthy economic ecosystem creates more value for everyone. (p. 14)

Our objective for the chapter is to present some critical themes, a few representative best practices, case examples, and implementation tools associated with the topics of collaboration, stakeholder engagement, and the view of the enterprise as if it were a living system. We then review how second-generation Web applications such as social-networking applications and wikis,[3] referred to as Web 2.0, can be used to assess and purposefully engage human, industrial, and natural system networks to facilitate creativity, collaboration, and sharing among users. Information technology and Internet applications provide exciting opportunities for innovation and the ability to design and evolve sustainable management systems uniquely appropriate for each enterprise.

The first part of the chapter provides some best-practice insights for effective organizational collaboration. No single individual, enterprise, community, or nation can meet its needs and desires alone. Individuals and enterprises must collaborate with others to achieve their own objectives and so that others may achieve theirs. We examine core collaboration concepts and natural tensions such as trust, control, competition, and network communities. Special attention is paid to stakeholder engagement, as this is a core component of any enterprise seeking to become more sustainable.

The next part of the chapter explores how enterprises act as if they are living systems. Individual and enterprise actions are connected to and interact with the cumulative global flow of goods and services and their associated consumption and production of natural, human, and economic capitals. Sustainable enterprises can learn to architect participation in these globally connected systems by identifying, assessing, and engaging their existing interconnected personal and industrial ecology networks. Applying systems thinking, industrial ecology, and collaborative cultures to an enterprise allows the enterprise to make sense of extremely dynamic and complex real-world events. Network analysis, both personal and enterprise, can support such practical organization-wide objectives as knowledge management, recruiting, employee retention, and supply chain management, critical to sustainability.

The next part of the chapter addresses how the Internet is evolving into a second generation, or Web 2.0, for connecting people within social network communities of interest. These new Internet applications and services improve the ability to efficiently collaborate, create, and interact within large networks of people with aligned interests, accelerating the objectives of a sustainable enterprise. Selected network mapping and assessment tools are presented and social networks with sustainability-aligned user groups are introduced. We — ESAT, Enterprise Sustainability Action Team, the 29 authors of this book — are proactively engaging with these groups with the intention that they may choose to connect with the *Living Fieldbook* workspace and contribute their own innovations to our work (**L**).

---

3 A wiki is a website or similar online resource that allows users to add and edit content collectively.

▪ Transorganizational collaboration and stakeholder engagement

The following section summarizes the roots and best-practice resources for collaboration and stakeholder engagement and presents a few example cases of sustainability-related multidisciplinary stakeholder-engaged collaborations. Awareness of these practices is not new; however, their application is still not commonplace. Organizational development publications are a rich resource of practical application and case examples that long predate the Internet. There is, however, still a need for more cross-discipline knowledge sharing; many technology developers designing the social web or interactive Web tools and sustainability practitioners seeking to effect change using these tools are either not familiar with critical collaboration practices or are not practicing them sufficiently to achieve their objectives. Innovation and sustainable solutions emerge from these holistically integrated systems.

Organizational collaboration

Organizational collaboration, **stakeholder engagement**, and **social networks** as the backbones of organizations are far from new concepts. Marvin Weisbord in *Discovering Common Ground* (1992) provides the genealogy of his future-search model for collaborative stakeholder engagement, presenting it as stemming back to Gestalt psychologists from the 1920s and the later work of Fred Emery and Eric Trist.

Although the roots for stakeholder engagement and collaboration are deep, establishing and maintaining an organization with collaborative behavior is still one of the more difficult challenges for any enterprise (Wirtenberg et al., 2007).

Transorganizational collaboration has not evolved into a common practice in spite of much-acclaimed corporate partnerships/alliances and networks. *The Firm as a Collaborative Community: Reconstructing Trust in the Knowledge Economy*, by Charles Heckscher and Paul Adler (2006), offers rich cases of firms grappling with redefining organizational trust in a highly interconnected and competitive environment.

There are some early examples of important collaborative efforts that have informed the world's understanding of global trends and environmental risks. The most notable is that of the Intergovernmental Panel on Climate Change (IPCC). The IPCC is a scientific intergovernmental body set up by the World Meteorological Organization (WMO) and the United Nations Environment Program (UNEP) to provide decision-makers and others with an objective source of information about climate change. Hundreds of scientists all over the world contribute to the work as authors, contributors, and reviewers. Its reports are intended to be policy-neutral. They adhere to high scientific and technical standards, aim to reflect a range of views and expertise, and provide wide geographical coverage.[4]

Stakeholder engagement

Stakeholder engagement represents organizational collaboration involving employees, suppliers, customers, NGOs (nongovernmental organizations), government, investors, and communities. It represents one of the most critical aspects of a company's efforts to operate effectively and more sustainably. Respondents to the *2007 AMA Sustainabil-*

---

4 www.ipcc.ch/about/index.htm (accessed December 21, 2007); for more on IPCC, see Chapter 7, pages 204 and 216ff.

ity Survey recognized the importance of stakeholder engagement, rating it a 3.9 on a 5-point scale (4.0 for high-performing firms) (American Management Association [AMA], 2007, p. 30).

The first stakeholder process took place in 1960. Weisbord (1992) tells the story of the forced merger of two British companies, Armstrong–Siddeley, maker of piston engines, and jet pioneer Bristol Aero Engines. Eric Trist and Fred Emery facilitated a five-day workshop. Unique at the time was CEO Sir Arnold's desire to bring the two companies together "to create teamwork across the conflicting cultures . . . to study together the world at large to which the industry, and he as CEO, was exposed" (Weisbord, 1992, p. 21). He wanted "great minds" from outside the two companies (today's external network) to be invited into the workshop, not to lecture but to dialogue with the group at critical points.

Weisbord quotes Trist in *Discovering Common Ground*:

> Dealing with the wide world first breaks participants away from their daily concerns and centers the process on "search" and "appreciation" rather than decision-making. The problems of the industry are then looked at in a wide context. Their own company comes last. Its future will take place in these wider contexts, the full reality of which is not always taken into account. Any proposals for the company are future-oriented. (1992, p. 25)

Sir Arnold's "future search" approach to transorganizational collaboration continues to evolve. Many people and organizations are working to formalize the stakeholder engagement process. For example, the Clarkson Principles of Stakeholder Management represent a statement of principles by which corporate citizens should operate (Post, 2002, p. 82).

■ CORE: Core Organizational Renewal Engagement

Victoria G. Axelrod

Chapter author Victoria Axelrod and her business partner Bill Becker have built on the "future search" approach and developed CORE (Core Organizational Renewal Engagement),[5] a tool that drives innovation, growth, and ultimately organizational sustainability. It incorporates social network analysis (SNA) to identify key stakeholders or participants (internal and external to the organization) and their impacts on the core business competencies.

Purpose

The primary purpose is to create a common understanding and appreciation of which key relationships most support the host organization's people, products, processes, and systems to allow its sustainability in the marketplace. CORE leverages those relationships and potential new relationships to improve the way the organization does things now as well to prepare it for future demands of the marketplace.

---

5 The CORE process is copyright 2002, Bill Becker and Victoria G. Axelrod.

All organizations, for-profits as well as nonprofits, operate in a marketplace; they compete for resources, talent, time, and attention. By drawing in their stakeholders for a future-oriented business dialogue, they are able to capitalize on untapped opportunities and understand multiple perspectives or challenges that may not be apparent from an internal view.

Each CORE process summarized below and on the *Living Fieldbook* (L) shares common principles for mapping the networks and convening the stakeholders, sharing the outcomes, and implementing the actions; however, each process is highly customized for the organization.

Several levels of outcomes can be realized

- All the key stakeholders necessary to carry out action plans developed in the conference are present in the room

- Volunteer action teams with leaders, champions, and mentors are established, with target dates for meeting short- and long-term objectives

- The discovery of the core organizational competencies provides a road map for functional and individual competencies analyses, training and development needs analysis, and organizational and individual performance management measures, as well as a foundation for reengineering. It also leads to the discovery of new core products and services within the range of the organization's core competencies, while offering the opportunity to identify to-be-acquired competencies

- The conference is a whole-system community-building process that creates trust and appreciation for the individual, and collective expertise of the total stakeholder group

Conditions

Some of the primary conditions that *must* be present to successfully implement a CORE conference are:

- A clearly committed top manager of the host organization and a clear understanding and consensus by her or his direct reports and other key influencers to proceed with the conference — in other words the leader must be willing to put in the "sweat equity" and resources to follow through

- An energized workforce — that is, a workforce that is not so beaten, disillusioned, and oppressed that they are lacking the level of trust in management needed to participate honestly, and/or are basically just "pairs of hands" and have little belief in their own abilities or little experience realizing their full abilities or empowerment

- An understanding that, whether it is a department, division, or total organization using the process, it has an organizationally systemic impact; it will require the involvement of other functions and additional stakeholders not present in the conference; and as a result of the conference new challenges and opportunities will appear

Process

Each process shares common principles for mapping the networks and convening the stakeholders (two days), sharing the outcomes and implementing the actions (several months); however, as mentioned above, every process is highly customized for the individual organization.

A detailed matrix outlining the CORE process is provided on the *Living Fieldbook* (**L**), as are stakeholder engagement case details and additional examples.

Examples

The CORE process has been used to:

- Ensure organizational sustainability with a global yogurt manufacturer to identify new products with inherent health benefits years before the market took off — 65 stakeholders

- Generate US$23 million in new-venture revenue for a professional educational association — 120+ stakeholders

- Bring a nuclear power plant back online — 40+ stakeholders

- Identify earned income opportunities for a pacesetter nonprofit in universal design for living — 25+ stakeholders

Changed organizational context requires new approaches

Although decades of work have ensued since the first use of stakeholder engagement with Emery and Trist, the fundamental causes of slow and limited adoption have been individuals' inabilities to trust and to relinquish control and supremacy of a hierarchical bureaucracy as the preferred model of organization (Hamel & Breen, 2007). Collaborative processes by their nature tend to be emergent, which can be unsettling for individuals and groups who have low tolerance for the unexpected or have been overschooled in static planning models.

The global interconnected context of organizations and the issues of sustainability for the future have forced organizations to rethink both their process of operation and the nature of the services and products they provide. Customers are demanding solutions to meet complex issues as off-the-shelf standard products and services no longer meet their needs or are too resource-intensive and cannot continue long-term. Examples of these trends are surfacing daily. Richard Heinberg (2007) summarizes an example of this for the global food system:

> Our global food system faces a crisis of unprecedented scope. This crisis, which threatens to imperil the lives of hundreds of millions and possibly billions of human beings, consists of four simultaneously colliding dilemmas, all arising from our relatively recent pattern of dependence on depleting fossil fuels.
>
> The first dilemma consists of the direct impacts on agriculture of *higher oil prices*: increased costs for tractor fuel, agricultural chemicals, and the transport of farm inputs and outputs.
>
> The second is an indirect consequence of high oil prices — the *increased demand for biofuels*, which is resulting in farmland being turned from food production to fuel production, thus making food more costly.

The third dilemma consists of the impacts of *climate change and extreme weather events* caused by fuel-based greenhouse gas emissions. Climate change is the greatest environmental crisis of our time; however, fossil fuel depletion complicates the situation enormously, and if we fail to address either problem properly the consequences will be dire.

Finally comes the *degradation or loss of basic natural resources* (principally, topsoil and freshwater supplies) as a result of high rates, and unsustainable methods, of production stimulated by decades of cheap energy.

Each of these problems is developing at a somewhat different pace regionally, and each is exacerbated by the continually expanding size of the human population. As these dilemmas collide, the resulting overall food crisis is likely to be profound and unprecedented in scope.

The idea that organizations are whole systems with inclusive participatory practices and the network view of organizations have been developing over a long period with enormous external pressures from changing technology, new ways of understanding human behavior, and a complex global economic environment. Although it seems as if stakeholder engagement, collaboration, and networks are new practices, they have been unfolding over decades of small steps and explorations.

A new form of trust for open contexts

Trust has reemerged as a critical component for collaboration. The Introduction to the book *The Firm as a Collaborative Community: Reconstructing Trust in the Knowledge Economy* by Charles Heckscher and Paul Adler (2006) nicely frames its re-emergence:

> Complex knowledge-based production requires high levels of diffuse cooperation resting on a strong foundation of trust. Contrary to the claims of neoliberal approaches, neither markets nor hierarchies are sufficient for coordination in such conditions: bonds of trust are essential. Yet the old corporate communities based on a culture of loyalty, which have been the basis for commitment for a century now, have been taken apart by three decades of economic turbulence, downsizing and restructuring. These developments raise the fear that the foundations of organizational trust are eroding when they are most needed.
>
> A growing group of theorists has been exploring the possibility of a new form of trust that would enable interdependent activity in the more fluid, open contexts characteristic of knowledge production, reconciling choice with community. The past few years have seen a proliferation of work on non-traditional forms of trust: "studied," "deliberate," "swift," and "reflective."
>
> And an emerging body of research focuses on new forms of organization among professionals and in "post-bureaucratic" firms and markets. (p. 2)

Open or collaborative systems hinge on the abilities of the members of those systems to trust one another, to share information, respect and value differences, adapt to the environment, learn, and follow through on commitments.

■ Case. 'Sustainable Uplands': learning to manage future change

Victoria G. Axelrod

The Uplands represent a critical ecological resource in the UK. This case shows how the "Sustainable Uplands" project researchers were able to collaborate using a multistakeholder-engaged process to develop a sustainable land use strategy acceptable to the parties (Dougill et al., 2005).[6]

Background: land use has global and local sustainability consequences

As the planet's more than 6.2 billion inhabitants collectively seek to use land for shelter, farmland, timber, recreation, watershed, and a host of other purposes, what was only seen as a local issue of sustainability is now global. People face the challenge of managing trade-offs between immediate human needs and maintaining the capacity of the biosphere to provide goods and services in the long term (Foley et al., 2005, p. 570).

Although there is global impact, it still falls to many local areas to develop comprehensive land use plans.

Every local area has multiple stakeholders with very different agendas. When tapping stakeholders' understanding of the limits and balances, the local knowledge is critical to developing a long-term land use plan, acceptable to all.

In the UK, the Uplands represents Britain's most significant carbon store. It is a source of potable water and is vital for biological conservation, extensive livestock farming, tourism, recreation, forestry, game, and fishing. Widespread degradation is occurring in response to current land use and management (e.g., fire, grazing regimes, and land drainage) and historic atmospheric deposition of pollutants.

Unique to the Sustainable Uplands: Learning to Manage Future Change research project, led by the University of Leeds, UK, through a joint task force, are two points relevant to this chapter.

First, the need to have a multidisciplinary group of researchers — local stakeholders, social and natural scientists, and policy-makers — was acknowledged during the initiation of the research project. The advantage is a diversity of knowledge and perspectives for a rich dialogue as well as comprehensive analysis. Most projects of this nature tend to bring in groups with a stake in the outcomes in a serial or linear fashion rather than involving a multistakeholder group from the onset. The possible unintended consequences of linear methods are missed data points, misunderstandings, time delays, duplicating explanations, and lack of shared commitment to or ownership of addressing issues.

Second, social network analysis (SNA) was used to determine the critical stakeholders. Using SNA (Dougill, et al., 2005), one can get such information as:

6 Unless otherwise noted, all information in this case study was taken from Dougill et al., 2005 and the Sustainable Uplands website, homepages.see.leeds.ac.uk/~lecmsr/sustainableuplands/documents.htm. Information from the Sustainable Uplands website was retrieved in November and December 2007.

- Who are the central actors that everyone knows and trusts?

- Which people share similar views, trust each other, work together?

- Are there certain groups that are particularly isolated or poorly connected?

This information can be used to target certain individuals for future research, especially if you want them to diffuse information and attitudes through their networks. Related to this, the Uplands project wanted to explore relationships between different institutions involved in the area. (slide notes, slide 19)

The objectives of the study are:

- Identify sustainable rural futures that are desired by different stakeholders

- Identify drivers of change and model likely future scenarios

- Develop innovative adaptive management and policy options that could facilitate multiple sustainable rural futures under different scenarios

- Model the environmental, economic, and social implications of these options

- Develop sustainability indicators to monitor and further adapt management and policy to achieve sustainable multiple land use

The Sustainable Uplands project's models show that the Peak District National Park is releasing carbon from its soils into the atmosphere. This is likely to be exacerbated by future climate change, and, since the majority of UK carbon is stored in peats, this could fuel further climate change.

However, if the Sustainable Uplands project could restore damaged and eroding peats to pristine condition, this area could save an amount of carbon equivalent to 2% of car traffic in England and Wales every year. The easiest way to do this is blocking drainage ditches created in the 1950s to improve land for agriculture. But the costs are still prohibitive. The researchers have now shown that it is possible to finance this through the sale of carbon credits, and, in the long term, possibly even provide a new revenue stream for the Uplands. In addition to the climate benefits, this would restore biodiversity and function to degraded ecosystems, reduce accidental fire risk, prevent the sedimentation of salmon spawning beds, save water companies millions in removing color from the water, and reduce the chance of flash flooding downstream.

Key learnings

The importance of this case is primarily the methodology of the study: that is, the detailed exploration the researchers are conducting behind the scenes on the intricacies of sustainability indicators and local stakeholder inclusion in the research.

- Sustainability indicators, as they report, can have two ideological paradigms: one that is expert-led and top-down, and one that is community-based and bottom-up. By combining both of these processes, top-down and bottom-up, in the Uplands project they reach a "holistic" approach, which is our point in this chapter about engaging the entire organizational ecosystem to identify collaborative solutions. In the Uplands project, multiple scenarios are formulated by such processes

● The entire project is also regarded as an ongoing learning project, one that iterates as the scope of the research project and conversation or dialogue among researchers, policy-makers and local stakeholders unfolds

Additional case details may be found on the *Living Fieldbook* workspace (**L**).

■ Putting networks to work: architecting participation

Like collaboration and stakeholder engagement from the previous section, understanding that value is created through resource and human networks and interactions is also not new. The ancient Silk Road provides an early example of a value network (Meredith, 2007).

> Until 1600, India and China combined accounted for more than half the globe's economic output, sending everything from silk, porcelain, tea, furniture, spices and wallpaper — a Chinese invention — overland via the Silk Road or via ship on the Spice Route. Until the late 19th century, India and China remained the world's two largest economies.
>
> But protectionism and world wars intervened, then India and China shut themselves off from the world. By 2003, India and China together accounted for just 20% of the global economy, despite their vast populations.
>
> After a century-long hiatus, India and China are moving back toward their historic equilibrium in the global economy, and that is producing tectonic shifts in economics as well as geopolitics.

In the 21st century, trade is no longer geographically defined. Traveling by land, sea and air, Chinese-manufactured goods flow to every part of the world. Enabling this process is information technology (India has become the backoffice to the world) — connecting people so they can collaborate across time zones, mostly virtually. "Before our eyes, two giant nations — India and China — are simultaneously embracing both capitalism and globalization. The world economy is being transformed as a result" (from Forbes.com's Introduction to Meredith, 2007). And, although considerable economic effort remains focused on producing goods, increasingly greater value is produced through relationships, knowledge creation, and services.

Silk Road traders confronted extreme temperatures, dust storms, robbers, wars, thieves, and other forms of economic and political turmoil.[7] Two thousand years later, economic and political uncertainties and conflicts remain. Concerns about local weather conditions have given way to global climate and environmental preservation concerns. Demands on individuals have progressed from enduring extreme physical conditions to operating effectively while confronted with an exponentially growing sea of computing technology-enabled information and people connections.

How do businesses organize to operate as sustainable enterprises in this connected, 21st-century, global business environment? What are the available tools and technologies to support them? What are the keys to putting human networks to work, architecting, and engaging participation?

This section proposes the key to sustainable enterprise begins with understanding organizations as complex network webs. Human networks, built on interactions and

---

7   encarta.msn.com/encyclopedia_761579956_2/Silk_Road.html (accessed December 21, 2007).

knowledge sharing, operating not just inside organizations but extending beyond. Networked enterprises are co-created through relationships with customers, suppliers, partners, competitors, industry groups, and government bodies. Such enterprise network ecosystems are dynamic, reflecting the ability of the computer systems that support knowledge sharing and collaboration to aggregate and diffuse exponentially growing information about business conditions and technology developments.

Organizations as complex network webs

Critical to any discussion of a stakeholder engagement or of a collaborative organization is the understanding of an organization as a system — that is, the organization does not operate in a vacuum; rather, it is a part of a larger system or environment of markets, regulators, government, customers, suppliers, vendors, partners, alliances, and more in a global 24/7 economy. In an industrial age it was convenient to think of organizations and operating processes as linear, but it is not so any longer.

Seeing organizations as systems or networks is a biological rather than a mechanical view of an organization, giving it a "living" rather than a static quality. It also implies that the environment and the entity interact. One influences the other dynamically, which has tremendous relevance for sustainable systems. Death or dysfunction of either has significant consequences for the whole.

Fritjof Capra, a physicist, has written extensively on systems thinking and the importance of seeing organizations as living systems. He provides the following lessons (Capra, 2007) for the management of organizations:

Lesson #1
A living social system is a self-generating network of communications. The aliveness of an organization resides in its informal networks, or communities of practice. Bringing life into human organizations means empowering their communities of practice.

Lesson #2
You can never direct a social system; you can only disturb it. A living network chooses which disturbances to notice and how to respond. A message will get through to people in a community of practice when it is meaningful to them.

Lesson #3
The creativity and adaptability of life expresses itself through the spontaneous emergence of novelty at critical points of instability. Every human organization contains both designed and emergent structures. The challenge is to find the right balance between the creativity of emergence and the stability of design.

Lesson #4
In addition to holding a clear vision, leadership involves facilitating the emergence of novelty by building and nurturing networks of communications; creating a learning culture in which questioning is encouraged and innovation is rewarded; creating a climate of trust and mutual support; and recognizing viable novelty when it emerges, while allowing the freedom to make mistakes.

People often refer to the "organization" as a whole, which is driven by a legal definition of an entity (Sharp Paine, 2003). We often fail to realize that, in day-to-day operation, organizations are made up of hundreds or thousands of individuals interacting in groups or networks of interactions. To understand why collaboration will or will not succeed it is necessary to focus on the collective social relationships undergirding the individual interactions. Individuals collectively are constantly acting out strongly held values and beliefs,[8] usually not explicitly stated, about who they will trust, how much they will participate, to whom they will make commitments, and what they will, or will not, gain by choosing to interact — a dance between control and freedom.

Today, computer networks can track resource flows and connect people. Linear thinking and geometric views of organizations are no longer adequate. Consider Figure 8.1, which depicts the complex web of networks underlying a 21st-century organization. Although engaging employees and mobilizing their talents in a competitive, fast-moving business environment is increasingly critical, it is only part of making enterprises sustainable. Vital too in relationship-based, shrinking-core, expanding-periphery organizations (Gulati & Kletter, 2005) is engaging customers, partners, suppliers, external advisors, and industry groups to co-create the enterprise. For "individuals and groups, networks that span structural holes are associated with creativity and innovation, positive evaluations, early promotion, high compensation and profits" (Burt 2001/2006, p. 45).

Figure 8.1 **Organizations as complex network webs**

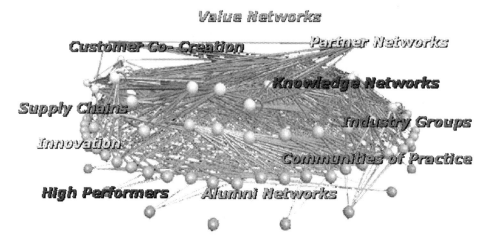

Source: Adapted by J. Ambrozek from foodwebs.org, 2007, with permission. thecity.sfsu.edu/~wow/index_page/wow2.html. Image produced with FoodWeb3D, written by R. J. Williams and provided by the Pacific Ecoinformatics and Computational Ecology Lab (www.foodwebs.org, I. Yoon, R. J. Williams, E. Levine, S. Yoon, J. A. Dunne, & N. D. Martinez, 2004).

8 For more on the mental models that generate these values and beliefs, see Chapter 2. Chapter 2 of this book and the *Living Fieldbook* (L) provide sample cases of people and organizations bringing to consciousness their mental models. See the effect this can have on businesses and the communities in which they are situated.

Analyzing networked organizations

Research and understanding about how human interactions, industrial ecology systems, and networks impact organizational performance — the way resources flow and work really gets done — is flourishing. David Krackhardt's seminal 1993 *Harvard Business Review* article "Informal Networks: The Company Behind the Chart" was one of the early influencers of this work. Today organizational network analysis (ONA) is an emerging discipline helping organizations operate as network ecosystems, connecting resources and people in and across organizations and beyond for sustainable performance. It's also providing insight into how individual effectiveness is related to personal network structures.

Organizational networks can also be understood using technology-based tools examining data flows through e-mail, contact databases, and document archives to map social networks, showing who is connected to whom and where expertise and individuals' interests lie throughout the enterprise.

Steps to a survey-based ONA

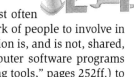

Network analysis begins by defining a business problem, most often about less-than-effective communication. Consider the network of people to involve in the study. Develop a questionnaire to determine how information is, and is not, shared, and discover where valuable knowledge lies. Then use computer software programs such as Inflow or UCINET, and NetDraw (see "Network mapping tools," pages 252ff.) to analyze the findings and create network maps and metrics to communicate the results. Finally, with follow-up interviews investigate and validate particularly important study findings, communicate the results back, and create intervention plans to influence network operation and improve organizational effectiveness.

A rich variety of sample network maps can be found on the *Living Fieldbook* (**L**).

Architecting participation

Understanding how an organization operates as a human network ecosystem is a starting point. Architecting interactions and ensuring participation so knowledge is shared and ideas are implemented to create value is required. Paying attention to organizational structures, supporting a collaborative open culture that rewards sharing (Bryan & Joyce, 2007), and a technology platform that enables easy connectedness are all keys.

Sustainable enterprises: 'People are the Company'

In the inaugural *Fast Company* magazine, John Seely Brown and Estee Solomon Gray (1995) reminded us that "People are the Company" and observed, "Organizations are webs of participation. Change the patterns of participation, and you change the organization" (p. 78).

Personal networks: assets to manage

Sustainable enterprises need to be engaged and effective and encourage employees to be engaged and effective as well. Network analysis helps organizations understand and facilitate networks inside and outside enterprise walls to improve operating effectiveness. The methodology also helps individuals enhance performance by considering the networks in which they participate. Interest in how individuals can network to improve their position has flourished since Mark Granovetter's classic 1973 "Strength of Weak

Ties" article alerted people to the value of acquaintances in tasks such as finding jobs. Decades of work by thought leaders including Ron Burt have grown our understanding of how "social capital," the notion that "the people who do better are somehow better connected" (Burt, 2001/2006, p. 32), actually works.

Recent research suggests that "as much as 90 per cent of the information employees take action on comes from people in their network. As such, the quality and scope of an employee's network has a substantial impact on his or her ability to solve problems, learn when transitioning into new roles and implement plans of any substance" (Cross, Thomas, & Light, 2006, p. 2).

Steve Borgatti (2004) summarizes current understanding of human networks:

- Human networks are often clumpy — ideas and behavior are more homogeneous within groups

- Weak ties (at least those that are local bridges) connect the clumps

- Cosmopolitans bridge social worlds

- Structural holes increase chances of bridging

- Bridging creates value (slide 9)

Research by Cross et al. (2006) translates the theory into how high performers apply network dynamics by:

- Positioning themselves at key points in a network and better leveraging their network when implementing plans

- Investing in relationships and extending expertise to help avoid learning biases and career traps

- Valuing networks and building high-quality relationships, not just big networks

In a world of burgeoning "social" networking, connecting and sharing platforms from LinkedIn to Facebook and YouTube, consumers are experiencing the power of connecting with others sharing similar interests, discovering new connections, and reconnecting with people from the past. Network analysis teaches that taking that insight to work, and managing one's network as an asset to bridge groups, grow, and learn is key to a person's performance. In the process, changing one's pattern of participation can contribute to changing one's organization.

To get started try the following personal network drawing exercise.

▨ Tool. Personal network drawing exercise[9]

Jenny Ambrozek and Victoria Axelrod

Goal

Examine and learn from one of your personal networks

Tasks

1. **Think** about either your regular job or a project you are currently working on and the people with whom you are involved

2. **Draw that network** of people with whom you interact by addressing the following questions:
   - Who do you go to for information to get your work done?
   - Who comes to you with questions to get their work done?
   - Who stands in the way of your getting work done?
   - Would you be more efficient if you had more access to some people?
   - Who do you go to for personal and professional support?

Use arrows to connect you to people in your network. Show which way the communication flows: toward or away from you. Can be both ways.

Adjust the thickness of the lines to reflect the volume of information flow.

Annotate your drawing using this key to show the nature of the communication flow:

   YW: Your work
   TW: Their work
   RB: Roadblocks
   WIHA: Wish I had access
   S: Support

3. **Analyze your network**. Consider actions you can take to make your network more efficient

Add notes to your drawing.

4. **Take action.** Turn your thinking into improving your network and your performance at work. Who has knowledge that would be helpful to you? To what groups are you not connected but should be? Is there a conversation that needs to happen to reduce a roadblock? Network

Putting human networks to work

It is no surprise that innovative organizations are taking advantage of the power of networks to innovate new business models and opportunities for sustainability. A case example from Eli Lilly shows how that company has tapped external networks to create value from "crowdsourcing" (Burge, 2007).

---

9 Adapted from an exercise developed by Joe Cloonan, knowledge management research coordinator. First published in *Knowledge Tree* eJournal, 2007.

■ InnoCentive: sustainable enterprise through ideagoras

Jenny Ambrozek

Talking about networked organizations as new models for sustainable enterprise is one thing. Putting networks to work is another. Eli Lilly's InnoCentive, a self-described "Open Innovation Marketplace," which Tapscott and Williams called an *ideagora* in a 2007 *Business Week* article (Tapscott & Williams, 2007), shows how it's done.

In the late 90s pharmaceuticals company Eli Lilly realized the limits to its internal research-and-development capability and decided on a bold initiative (Burge, 2007). It would create a business incubator, e.Lilly, whose first company was InnoCentive, the brainchild of former Lilly R&D executive Alpheus Bingham. Through InnoCentive, Lilly would reach beyond the walls of its internal laboratories and "crowdsource" its research needs.[10] By 2007 InnoCentive[11] had become a global scientific network operating as a marketplace by connecting:

> commercial, academic, and nonprofit organizations (Seekers)[12] who post Challenges spanning a wide spectrum of industries and disciplines to Solvers.[13] The Solver who submits the solution best meeting the Seeker's Challenge requirements receives a cash award ranging from $5,000 to $1,000,000. Challenges are offered in physical sciences, life sciences, engineering/ design, chemistry, math/computer science and business/ entrepreneurship.

Soon after its inception, InnoCentive's Seeker community began to grow far beyond Lilly; as of early 2008, InnoCentive (2007, 2008) could boast "135,000 Solvers, 175 countries, [and] 40 Industry Disciplines and Growing," making it clear that the notion of tapping the wisdom of the crowds had taken root in the global business community.

One of the Seekers benefiting from the Solvers scattered across the globe is Colgate-Palmolive. As Jeff Howe reports, in his 2006 *Wired* magazine article "The Rise of Crowdsourcing," by posting a "challenge" on InnoCentive, Colgate-Palmolive found a solution to a problem that had long eluded its in-house researchers — how to inject fluoride powder into a toothpaste tube without it dispersing into the surrounding air — and a self-styled problem solver walked away with a $25,000 fee.

> [Solver] Melcarek knew he had a solution by the time he'd finished reading the challenge: Impart an electric charge to the powder while grounding the tube. The positively charged fluoride particles would be attracted to the tube without any significant dispersion . . . Melcarek earned $25,000 for his efforts. Paying Colgate-Palmolive's R&D staff to produce the same solution could have cost several times that amount — if they even solved it at all. (Howe, 2006, p. 3)

InnoCentive's challenges are not limited only to for-profit problems. Since December 2006 a partnership with the Rockefeller Foundation has opened the doors to addressing

---

10 Crowdsourcing definition from Wikipedia, en.wikipedia.org/wiki/Crowdsourcing (accessed October 8, 2007).
11 InnoCentive, www.innocentive.com/solvers.php (accessed October 8, 2007 and March 9, 2008).
12 www.innocentive.com/seekers.php (accessed February 1, 2008).
13 www.innocentive.com/solvers.php (accessed February 1, 2008).

not-for-profit issues by funding a nonprofit area on InnoCentive specifically designed to spur science and technology solutions to pressing development problems (Rockefeller Foundation, 2006).

Researchers investigating InnoCentive idea marketplace dynamics are shedding light on the factors contributing to InnoCentive's success in solving challenges that have defeated in-house researchers. Lakhani and colleagues (Lakhani, Jeppesen, Lohse, & Panetta, 2007) highlight the dynamics of open innovation and the factors in successful problem solving. Notably:

> Problem-solving success was found to be associated with the ability to attract specialized solvers with a range of diverse scientific interests. Furthermore, successful solvers solved problems at the boundary or outside of their fields of expertise, indicating a transfer of knowledge from one field to others. (p. 2, abstracts)

The lessons from InnoCentive: the promise of ideagoras

InnoCentive is a high-profile open-idea marketplace, but it is not alone. Similar ventures range from yet2.com,[14] which brings technology buyers and sellers together to maximize investment returns, to Eureka Medical,[15] which links medical professionals and talented independent inventors with medical device and healthcare product ideas to innovation-seeking companies, to TopCoder,[16] a marketplace that allows custom software developers to compete for opportunities.

Although the idea of open innovation and marketplaces that connect inventors to organizations with specific problems is growing, according to Tapscott and Williams in a chapter on ideagoras (pp. 97-123) in their 2006 book *Wikinomics*, implementing such innovations demands careful thought and preparation for change. Recommendations include:

- Setting realistic expectations and realizing that idea liquidity needs to be built to generate real benefits

- Changing the culture and breaking down deep-rooted biases that inhibit seizing new opportunities

- Harvesting external ideas starts with a keen sense of what you are looking for

- Developing an optimal ratio of internal to external innovation that is right for your organization

- Pushing the envelope. "Ideagoras lower the costs of communicating, collaborating, and transacting and could very well revolutionize the way firms conduct R&D." It allows divesting noncore activities and conserving resources for "cutting-edge challenges and opportunities" (Tapscott & Williams, 2006, p. 121)

In today's dynamic, networked world, organizations must constantly adapt to engage talent and partners beyond their own boundaries, if they are to co-create a sustainable future.

14 www.yet2.com/app/about/home (accessed October 8, 2007).
15 www.eurekamed.com (accessed January 3, 2008).
16 www.topcoder.com (accessed January 4, 2008).

▪ Collaboration and networking technology

The complex product designs and progressively ambitious product and service life-cycles of a sustainable enterprise depend on effective collaboration and networking to succeed. These products and processes would not have been feasible without rapid advancements in information technology tools, global access to shared information, and the evolution of self-organized socio-technical networks and network assessment insights and tools. This section introduces some key collaboration and network technology concepts and tools for collaboration, network mapping and assessments, and emergent social networks. These second-generation Web 2.0 applications are connecting a rapidly growing community of users with common sustainability interests and the shared objectives of sustainable enterprises worldwide.

Web 2.0 technologies supporting connectedness

A rapidly developing suite of low-cost, easy-to-implement-and-use tools and services, including wikis and social network services and collectively referred to as Web 2.0, supports connectedness and working collaboratively in organizations (O'Reilly, 2005). What distinguishes Web 2.0 from the less-interconnected initial Internet applications is its ability to turn the World Wide Web into a seamless connecting and publishing platform. The user is at the center, empowered to have a voice. Blogs, wikis, social tagging, user reviews, and social networking platforms are now extremely popular and powerful "social media" tools that are now finding their way into organizations.

Web 2.0 technologies are powerful because they leverage "network effects." Platforms become more powerful as the number of users grows: for example, the more team members contributing and sharing insights to a group wiki, the more diverse the perspectives and the greater the opportunities for new insights to emerge.

The power of technology to support connecting groups in organizations will increase with future Web generations. The next Internet generation, Web 3.0, foresees "a place where search engines and software agents can better troll [sic] the Net and find what we're looking for" (Metz, 2007).

Network mapping tools

Social network maps and related network assessment techniques reinforce and inform stakeholder engagement programs as well as the enterprise sustainability strategy in general (Krebs & Holley, 2006). Social network analysis (SNA) is the mapping and measuring of relationships and flows among people, groups, organizations, computers, websites, and other information/knowledge processing entities. The nodes in the network are the people and groups while the links show relationships or flows between the nodes. SNA provides both a visual and a mathematical analysis of human relationships. Management consultants use this methodology with their business clients and call it organizational network analysis (ONA) while others are using network mapping to evaluate material resource flows and economic transactions.

The following are examples of network mapping tools and their applications. See the *Living Fieldbook* (**L**) for example maps using these leading tools.

Mind maps[17]

Mind maps were developed in the late 1960s by Tony Buzan as a way of helping students make notes that used only key words and images. They were much quicker to make, and, because of their visual quality, much easier to remember and review. The nonlinear nature of mind maps makes it easy to link and cross-reference different elements of the map. Futurist Peter Russell has developed a full list of mind map software tools as well as some relevant applications for sustainability.[18]

TouchGraph[19]

TouchGraph was founded in 2001 with the creation of the original visual browser for Google. Since then millions of people have used TouchGraph's tools to discover the relationships contained in Google, Amazon, wikis, and most recently Facebook. TouchGraph offers both free, open-source and commercial software applications.

InFlow[20]

InFlow software was developed by leading network consultant Valdis Krebs for social and organizational network analysis. InFlow maps and measures knowledge exchange, information flow, emergent communities, networks of alliances, and other connections within and between organizations and communities. It has been used on several stakeholder engagement and sustainability-related projects. InFlow 3.1 is being used by ESAT to map, assess, grow, and put to work our own *Sustainable Enterprise Fieldbook* network community.

UCINET[21]

UCINET, published by Analytic Technologies, is a comprehensive package for the analysis of social network and related network data. The software can handle networks with more than 5,000 nodes. Social network analysis methods include centrality measures, subgroup identification, role analysis, elementary graph theory, and permutation-based statistical analysis.

Social networks and sustainable enterprises

Technology linking computers into networks has delivered the means to share information between individuals across the globe cost-effectively and with time-independence. Applications facilitating social networking have advanced from the simple UseNet bulletin boards, to today's latest, Internet-based, feature-rich multimedia communication tools.

The attraction of social networks often stems from a singular interest or avocation providing a commonality that leads individuals to join one or more networks in the professional realm. Social network features include file sharing, calendar management, messaging, e-mail, text chat, voice chat, video chat, blogging, and discussion groups, and comprise some of the fundamental tools available to members. As individuals and organizations become increasingly focused on sustainability issues, leveraging the

---

17 www.imindmap.com.
18 They can be found at www.peterrussell.com/MindMaps/MMSoft.php.
19 www.touchgraph.com.
20 www.orgnet.com/inflow3.html.
21 www.analytictech.com/ucinet/ucinet.htm.

Table 8.1 **Social networking sites**

Network	Total members	Noteworthy functionality	Number of sustainability forums	Comments
Primary sites				
Facebook	40 million+	Robust feature set and provides RSS* feeds	500+	ESAT group established
MySpace	200 million+	Ease of use, broad functionality	95	
YouTube	100 million+ (users per month)	Video content	85	
Professionally focused				
Second Life	9 million+	Rich 3D interface	35	ESAT group established (see case study, pages 257ff.)
Spoke	13 million+	Large-scale professional networking	n/a	
LinkedIn	35 million+	Large-scale professional networking	n/a	
Sustainability-focused				
WiserEarth	<5,000	Robust content, "wiki"-style authoring, editing	All	Public site
Rethos	<5,000	100% UGC (user-generated content)	All	Public site with sponsors
Xigi	<5,000	Facilitates investor due diligence	All	Public site
Treehugger	<5,000	Active discussion forums	All	Public site
GaiaSpace	<5,000	Collaborative project workspace	All	Private use only
Sustainability Knowledge Network (SKN)	<5,000	Collaborative project workspace and rich library resource	All	Public and private users; home of the *Sustainable Enterprise Living Fieldbook*

* RSS (Really Simple Syndication) is a family of Web feed formats used to publish frequently updated content such as blog entries, news headlines, and podcasts.

knowledge capital available in online communities has presented itself as a new opportunity for success. Although social networks for business communication were initially leveraged by small business entrepreneurs who sought to economically broaden their business reach, large corporations such as Eli Lilly (see InnoCentive case on pages 250-251) have come to understand how using these tools can improve productivity as well as extend their influence to opinion leaders.

For the purposes of this chapter, Table 8.1 delineates social networking sites in three tiers: traditional social networks, networks with a professional focus, and finally, to the heart of this chapter, networks that are focused on sustainability and collaboration. The matrix introduces each of these sites and their respective features. The list presented reflects those sites that, at the time of publication, enjoy the greatest subscription base.

Facebook[22]

Facebook has become a huge-impact player in the social network space. Although once the domain of students — until summer 2006, its focus was exclusively university students — it has become recognized as a leading choice for professional networking. One of the distinctive features is that users can take advantage of RSS feeds for key information, allowing them to keep abreast of their Facebook realm without logging in. Facebook has also made a strategic decision to allow its source code to be open for the world of public application developers so it can tap into their creativity and innovation potential.

MySpace[23]

The biggest player in the social networking space, MySpace membership in 2007 was said to be increasing at a rate of 5 million per month. It is very easy for users to locate and connect with one another, and use a robust feature set that includes blogs, announcements, instant messaging, e-mails, group interactions, video content management, and more.

YouTube[24]

YouTube is a content-rich site, with approximately 100 million clips viewed per day in 2007. Content creators are registered users; their number is much smaller than the audience. Known as the leader in alternative media, YouTube provides users with not only an interactive library of original video content but also excerpts from broadcast and cable television.

Second Life[25]

With a rich, visual approach, Second Life offers a slick interface enabling a 3D virtual world interface for individuals and groups seeking both social and business relationships. It is billed as a new venue for collaboration, training, distance learning, new media studies, and marketing.

22 www.facebook.com.
23 www.myspace.com.
24 www.youtube.com.
25 www.secondlife.com.

Spoke[26]

One of the original social network platforms geared toward the professional enterprise, Spoke has been in the vanguard providing integration with enterprise tools such as Microsoft Outlook as well as customer relationship management packages.

LinkedIn[27]

The goal of LinkedIn is to be the world's largest business network, allowing users to find jobs, connect with people, and locate service providers through their existing business networks. Taking an approach of separation degrees, users are able to obtain "introductions" of up to three degrees away, and reasonably expand their circle of contacts.

WiserEarth[28]

WiserEarth is a community directory and networking forum that maps and connects nongovernmental organizations and individuals addressing such critical issues as climate change, poverty, the environment, peace, water, hunger, social justice, conservation, human rights, and more.

Rethos[29]

Rethos is a new media portal and online community working to address social and environmental issues. Motivated individuals, forward-thinking nonprofits, and socially conscious corporations are brought together in an environment designed to foster intellectual debate and discovery.

Xigi[30]

Xigi is a professional social networking site providing market intelligence, news, research, and analytical tools. Its premier feature, Xigi-maps, provides a social network visualization tool that, at its most basic, graphically articulates the social networks of its individual users and organizations. Xigi's intent is to provide its users with a means to make sense of the capital market for good, or rather, to track the emerging market for social capital, including fair trade, microfinance, social enterprise, independent media, and clean technology.

Treehugger[31]

Treehugger bills itself as the leading media outlet dedicated to sustainability. In essence, Treehugger is a straightforward, green website featuring constantly updated content. Its goal is to first educate people, then facilitate interaction, and finally enable individuals to take action. The community is facilitated via its Treehugger discussion forums.

26 www.spoke.com.
27 www.linkedin.com.
28 www.wiserearth.com.
29 www.rethos.com.
30 www.xigi.net.
31 www.treehugger.com.

GaiaSpace[32]

GaiaSpace is a private online community that was created to support a major multi-national company's need for a collaborative tool to coordinate knowledge and project tasks for a large and dispersed group of employees. Currently it offers a private space in which business professionals can share and develop ideas. The goal is to further business profitability, social change, and the ability of its users to create new markets.

Sustainability Knowledge Network[33]

The Sustainability Knowledge Network is a collaborative workspace designed to facilitate topical research on a broad range of sustainability issues, to identify and learn about the efforts of major sustainability-engaged stakeholders, to allow members to self-organize sustainability project teams with customized private and public workspaces, and to build social networks of organizations, institutions, and people driving sustainability. Features include a dynamic sustainability reference library, blogs, discussion forums, collaborative project workspaces, and partner and stakeholder network channels. This network was used by the contributors of *The Sustainable Enterprise Fieldbook* and hosts the *Sustainable Enterprise Living Fieldbook*, which is described in more detail in the Introduction (pages 7-8).

Using the virtual world of Second Life to promote real-world sustainability

Linda M. Kelley/Second Life avatar,[34] Delia Lake

> "The 3-D Internet may at first appear to be eye candy," [Sam] Palmisano writes in an e-mail interview, "but don't get hung up on how frivolous some of its initial uses may seem." He calls 3-D realms such as Second Life the "next phase of the Internet's evolution" and says they may have "the same level of impact" as the current Web version has had on people around the world. (David Kirkpatrick, 2007)

Metaverse[35] pioneers are creating business and nonprofit interfaces between virtual worlds and the real world. Virtual worlds such as Second Life, with user-defined and -developed content, produce a real experience of "being there" for the participants. The virtual systems are immersive, graphical 3D, massively multiuser (many tens of thousands "inworld"[36] at any one time), synchronous, interactive, collaborative spaces with shared content. They are also rich, versatile, and powerful ways of connecting, communicating, and collaborating among people from all corners of the real world.

---

32 www.gaiaspace.com.
33 www.sknworldwide.net.
34 **Avatar** is the term used in virtual reality and cyberspace interfaces to represent an icon or representation of a user in a shared virtual reality.
35 The term **metaverse** comes from Neal Stephenson's 1992 novel *Snow Crash* (Bantam Spectra), and is now widely used to describe the vision behind current work on fully immersive 3D virtual spaces.
36 A person is **inworld** when he or she is connected to or "visiting" a virtual space.

As of 2007, there are a variety of flexible, adaptive virtual-world platforms including Second Life, HiPiHi (based in China and in beta testing only at the time of writing), Entropia Universe, Kaneva, There, and Active Worlds, to name a few. In addition, the military is using proprietary, firewalled worlds — often Forterra-based — developed to simulate various scenarios of war. Early adopters have already populated Second Life's virtual community, the public metaverse, individually and with their enterprises. The numbers are growing exponentially.

The Grundfos Second Life virtual space

The Grundfos Group, a major international manufacturer of pumps, decided to explore the opportunities offered by the virtual world of Second Life and to focus its virtual space on sustainable development (Grundfos Group, 2007). Since its founding, Grundfos has been committed to environmental, social, and ethical responsibility. Its virtual island (slurl.com/secondlife/Grundfos/132/167/35) displays information about Grundfos and its products. It also has interactive stations where visitors can learn ways to reduce their energy consumption and a booth to buy trees to plant both virtually and actually. It also has two models of rural African villages. The first has no safe water supply and the second has a Grundfos solar-and-wind-powered water pump. At the end of the village's path is a booth where people in Second Life can purchase virtual water pumps. The money from sales of virtual pumps is used toward installing real-world-donated water pumps. To be consistent with its values, the company has also purchased, through the Green Islands Project, a year's worth of carbon offset credits for the amount of energy the site's Second Life server uses.

Following the company's motto "be > think > innovate," the Grundfos Group takes a proactive approach to developing its presence in Second Life. To attract people to Grundfos's virtual site, Grundfos hosts a variety of events that underscore the company's commitment to environmental and social responsibility in ways that are educational and entertaining. Events typically combine education, music, and visual arts. The goal is to raise awareness of Grundfos's work in sustainability, engage with people from around the world, and encourage people to get involved.

In the natural world, it would be both difficult and costly to run these events with expert presenters and entertainers from around the globe. Virtually, though, it is relatively easy to gather experts and artists from different real-life countries to come together for an hour or two, without ever leaving home. No travel costs or time away. Event summaries can be reviewed on the *Living Fieldbook* (**L**).

Other Second Life company examples

Grundfos is not alone in its company venture into Second Life. Many well-known companies and agencies are engaged there with innovative approaches to business in a world with virtual components. IBM has a significant presence and supports multicultural arts in this virtual world as it does in the real world.

PA Consulting is using Second Life to invent a new way of doing global business sustainably for itself and for its clients. The company has built a demonstration island with simulations of business applications using virtual environments, including an airport to use for emergency and disaster training and a model of an interactive smart home that produces more energy (solar, wind, and heat pump) than it uses. These virtual builds are part of its client product design and process. In addition, PA Consulting is using Second Life as part of its company new-hire interview and orientation process, saving on travel costs and conserving energy.[37]

Philips Design is using its Second Life location not only to promote its green Climate products, but also to gather a self-organizing group of people interested in contributing ideas to the next generation of Philips products. The NGO OneClimate brought broadcasts from the 2007 United Nations Climate Change Conference from Bali into Second Life and provided a forum for people in that virtual world to converse with representatives to the conference. In addition, it broadcast the first live policy speech by a US politician in Second Life when Congressman Ed Markey spoke from Virtual Bali to the real-world conference (OneClimate, 2007).

The future?

Social networking and particularly virtual environments can contribute significantly to enterprise sustainability. Leaders and managers of today's enterprises need to understand and reach out to this globally connected population. Customary channels for gathering information, discerning rising concerns, and building alliances are neither broad enough nor fast enough to allow today's enterprises to take optimal actions. Social media, and particularly online virtual environments, can be very effective channels for decision-makers to get a sense of emerging trends from the collective activities of these millions of people from around the globe, who are also connecting individual to individual. The social media might be thought of as a socially collaborative corollary to mass customization.

> Paradoxically, people are more independent and atomized than ever by virtue of their being so pervasively connected. Connectivity enables you to seize more independence while independence motivates you to become ever more connected [so] independence blurs with interdependence. (Stan Davis and Christopher Meyer, 1998, pp. 48-49)

The metaverse is changing so rapidly that writing about virtual worlds requires more than a bit of intuiting the future for what will be long-past history for our readers. In October 2007, Linden Labs, makers of Second Life, formed a partnership with IBM and nearly 30 other companies to work on creating a layer of interoperability across all online virtual worlds. As technically challenging as this task is, it is an inevitable next step. With portability, avatars would truly be digital alter-egos that could move intact from one virtual world to another, as a means of conducting business from anywhere, with anyone, anywhere. "Everything is running at warp speed. You need to get out there and get ahead in your thinking . . . What you have to do is be part of inventing the future" (Robert L. Dilenschneider, 2007, p. 57).

Immerse yourself

Words alone are not sufficient to give readers a true sense of these 3D virtual spaces. Although Second Life may be a bit disorienting in the beginning and may cause people to stretch their comfort boundaries, it is contagious and provides a wonderful example of how technology and sustainability are aligning.

---

37 Personal communication with C. Nehmzow at PA Second Life consulting offices, slurl.com/secondlife/PAconsulting/116/137/27, September 13, 2007.

Social technologies challenge organizational culture and structures

While the latest generations of Web technologies are impressive for their ease of use and low-cost information-sharing capabilities, even more significant are the mindset changes they promote, which challenge organizations' traditional top-down control. These Internet-enabled tools are reshaping the enterprise mental models, strategies, and change processes described in earlier chapters.

Rapid adoption of "open" Web 2.0 tools by consumers carries over into workplaces. To be sustainable in the 21st century, enterprises need also adapt to the changed locus of control, to consumers given voice by low-cost social media tools, and employees expecting to be more active in creating the environments in which they work.

■ Conclusion

The ancient Silk Road provides an early example of a network emerging out of geographic, industrial ecology, and socially integrated systems. It was natural-capital-based and leveraged the technology and knowledge of its time. Collaboration and stakeholder engagement were essential survival skills. The silk-fueled economy connected the world as it had never been connected before.

Today the Internet is the dominant emergent network. People connect virtually and are finding new ways to engage and collaborate with each other. Stakeholder-engaged collaborative commerce is an emerging business model, but companies are challenged to make such ideals operational. Through greater use of information technology tools and through engaging in social networks with millions upon millions of people with shared interests and values, people are working to build a shared global culture that values trust and reciprocity. Information and connections of human and social capitals are the silks fueling the economy now, and Web 2.0 technologies are connecting the world as never before.

Along the journey, people continue to self-organize and evolve. Technology-enabled natural, human, social, manufactured, and financial capitals will be holistically integrated with a new "DNA" of core values of trust, "coopetition," sharing, and community service. Sustainability will emerge as the dominant network. Each capital will be its own specialized silk and the sustainability-aligned web will again mimic nature.

Ultimately work is social and people make organizations. Business runs on relationships and interactions that continually demonstrate the enterprise's respect for the individual, invite individuals' participation, and establish trust. Individuals collectively are constantly acting out strongly held values and beliefs, usually not explicitly stated, about who they will trust, how much they participate, to whom they make commitments, whether there are gains to be made in any specific venture — the dance between control and freedom.

The future of the sustainability movement may, in fact, largely depend on whether collaboration becomes well integrated into the larger global culture and whether organizations are able to effectively align their stakeholders and organizational processes around sustainability principles. To the degree that organizations of all sorts (private, public, governmental, NGOs, and others) align with sustainability ideas and integrate them into the larger society, the global society will or will not become more sustainable. Specifically, much will depend on whether a collaborative win–win style of addressing these issues becomes more common or whether a more confrontational approach becomes the norm. Holistic integration and sustainability alignment are the keys to the future.

References

American Management Association (AMA). (2007). *Creating a sustainable future: A global study of current trends and possibilities 2007–2017*. New York: American Management Association.

Borgatti, S. (2004). Burt's "Social origin of good ideas" paper. PowerPoint presentation, MB 814 Fall 2004 Schedule. Retrieved October 9, 2007, from www.analytictech.com/mb814/slides/Burt.pdf.

Bryan, L., & Joyce, C. (2007). *Mobilizing minds: Creating wealth from talent in the 21st century organization*. New York: McGraw-Hill.

Burge, R. (2007). InnoCentive: Crowdsourcing diversity. Assignment zero. Retrieved October 8, 2007, from zero.newassignment.net/filed/drowdsourcing_diversity.

Burt, R. S. (2006). Structural holes versus network closure as social capital. In K. S. Cook, R. S. Burt, & N. Lin (Eds.), *Social capital: Theory and research* (pp. 31-56). New Brunswick, NJ: Aldine Transaction, Transaction Publishers. (Original work published 2001).

Capra, F. (2007). Life and leadership: A systems approach (Executive summary). Retrieved December 21, 2007, from www.fritjofcapra.net/management.html.

Cross, R., Thomas, R. J., & Light, D. A. (2006). How top talent uses networks and where rising stars get trapped (Research report). Network roundtable at the University of Virginia. Retrieved October 9, 2007, from https://webapp.comm.virginia.edu/NetworkRoundtable/Portals/0/Public/Research/High_Performer_Networks_and_Traps_Roundtable_Final.pdf.

Davis, S. M., & Meyer, C. (1998). *Blur: The speed of change in the connected economy*. Reading, MA: Addison-Wesley.

Dilenschneider, R. L. (2007). *Power and influences*. New York: McGraw-Hill.

Dougill, A. J., Reed, M. S., Hubacek, K., Burt, T., Chapman, P. J., Fraser, E.D.G., et al. (2005, May). Managing uncertainty in dynamic socio-environmental systems: An application to UK Uplands. Presentation at Rural Economy and Land Use Programme Workshop: Scoping the Research Agenda, Kings Rooms, York, UK. Retrieved February 1, 2008, from homepages.see.leeds.ac.uk/~lecmsr/sustainableuplands/York%20Presentation%20%28Dougill%20&%20Reed%29.ppt.

Foley, J. A., DeFries, R., Asner, G. P., Barford, C., Bonan, G., Carpenter, S. R., et al. (2005, July 22). Global consequences of land use. *Science, 309*(5734), 570-574.

Granovetter, M. S. (1973). The strength of weak ties. *American Journal of Sociology, 78*(6), 1360-1380.

Grundfos Group. (2007, September 10). Grundfos sets a new agenda in Second Life (Press release). Retrieved November 10, 2007, from www.grundfos.com/web/grfosweb.nsf/Webopslag/HMTE-76VR9V.

Gulati, R., & Kletter, D. (2005). Shrinking core — expanding periphery: The relational architecture of high performing organizations. *California Management Review, 47*(3), 77-104.

Hamel, G., & Breen, B. (2007). *The future of management*. Boston, MA: Harvard Business School Press.

Heckscher, C., & Adler, P. (2006). *The firm as a collaborative community: Reconstructing trust in the knowledge economy*. Oxford, UK: Oxford University Press.

Heinberg, R. (2007, December 3). What will we eat as the oil runs out? *Global Public Media* (MuseLetter #188). Retrieved January 4, 2008, from globalpublicmedia.com/richard_heinbergs_museletter_what_will_we_eat_as_the_oil_runs_out.

Howe, J. (2006, June). The rise of crowdsourcing. *Wired, 14*(6) (Electronic version). Retrieved October 8, 2007, from www.wired.com/wired/archive/14.06/crowds.html.

Kirkpatrick, D. (2007, January 23). Second Life: It's not a game. *Fortune*. Retrieved October 6, 2007, from money.cnn.com/2007/01/22/magazines/fortune/whatsnext_secondlife.fortune/index.htm.

Krackhardt, D. (1993). Informal networks: The company behind the chart. *Harvard Business Review, 71*(4), 104-111.

Krebs, V., & Holley, J. (2006). Building smart communities through network weaving. Retrieved January 4, 2008, from www.orgnet.com/BuildingNetworks.pdf.

Lakhani, K. R., Jeppesen, L. B., Lohse, P. A., & Panetta, J. A. (2007). The value of openness in scientific problem solving (Working paper). Retrieved January 8, 2008, from www.hbs.edu/research/pdf/07-050.pdf.

Meredith, R. (2007, July 30). Geopolitics, oil and water. *Forbes.com*. Retrieved January 9, 2008, from www.forbes.com/opinions/2007/07/27/elephant-dragon-meredith-oped-cz_rm_0730dragonnine.html.

Metz, C. (2007, March 14). Web 3.0. *PC Magazine*. Retrieved October 4, 2007, from www.pcmag.com/article2/0,1759,2102852,00.asp.

OneClimate. (2007, December). OneClimate Virtual Bali event. Retrieved January 8, 2008, from www.oneclimate.net/virtualbali.

O'Reilly, T. (2005, September 30). What is Web 2.0? Design patterns and business models for the next generation of software. Retrieved January 3, 2008, from www.oreilly.com/pub/a/oreilly/tim/news/2005/09/30/what-is-web-20.html.

Post, J. E. (2002). *Redefining the corporation: Stakeholder management and organizational wealth*. Palo Alto, CA: Stanford University Press.

Rockefeller Foundation. (2006, December 18). The Rockefeller Foundation to extend InnoCentive's online, global scientific platform for technology solutions to global development problems. (Press release). Available from the Rockefeller Innovation for Development website: www.rockfound.org/about_us/press_releases/2006/121406rf_innocent_pr.pdf.

Seely Brown, J., & Solomon Gray, E. (1995, October). The people are the company. *Fast Company, 1*, 78. Retrieved March 21, 2008, from www.fastcompany.com/magazine/01/people.html.

Sharp Paine, L. (2003). *Value shift*. New York: McGraw-Hill.

Tapscott, D., & Williams, A. D. (2006). *Wikinomics: How mass collaboration changes everything*. New York: Penguin Group.

Tapscott, D., & Williams, A. D. (2007, February 15). Ideagora: A marketplace for minds. *Business Week*. Retrieved October 8, 2007, from www.businessweek.com/innovate/content/feb2007/id20070215_251519.htm.

Weisbord, M. (1992). *Discovering common ground: How future search conferences bring people together to achieve breakthrough innovation, empowerment, shared vision, and collaborative action*. San Francisco: Berrett-Koehler.

Wirtenberg, J., Harmon, J., Russell, W. G., & Fairfield, K. D. (2007). HR's role in building a sustainable enterprise: Insights from some of the world's best companies. *Human Resource Planning, 30*(1), 10-20.

PART V
When it all comes together

9

A new beginning
When it all comes together

Jeana Wirtenberg, David Lipsky, and William G. Russell

No river can return to its source, yet all rivers must have a beginning.

Native American proverb

We have now arrived at a new beginning. This beginning contains the crucial possibilities of creating a sustainable future; success is our only option. As this moment passes, the flywheel of sustainability is moving in the wrong direction. We are depleting our natural resources, neglecting our people, and leaving less for the next generation. Collectively we must work together to accelerate the journey from awareness to understanding and, most important, to action. Factual awareness alone will not slow our regress; global understanding has the potential to stop the wheel, and collective global action will move us in the right direction.

This moment, the moment we are in together, is our greatest opportunity to forge a new beginning.

We have learned that the term *conclusion* may not be the best way to describe the ending of this physical book on sustainability. Each thing we collectively learned and shared in our team makes us see even more clearly how much more information there is to learn and how many more insights and perspectives there are to explore if we are to have a lasting deep impact on the future of sustainability. In this chapter, we share what we have learned to this point and lay the foundation for a path forward that will provide for continued learning and sharing with the larger social network of sustainability we have chosen to contribute to. And as members of this network, we hope to continue to contribute, engaging with others on the collective global journey to a sustainable world.

There are all kinds of ways to read a book. Many of the ESAT (Enterprise Sustainability Action Team) authors have a habit of going straight to the conclusion as a test to decide whether to read the entire book. So for those of you who are reading this chapter first, we hope to entice you to explore further. Since this is intended to be a fieldbook that is used as an ongoing tool, we suggest you read the Introduction first and then dive right in to the subject you're the most interested in or have a pending opportunity to impact.

So how did we do?

In the beginning of the book, we clearly stated our purpose: to help forge a path to a better world and a more sustainable future by supporting employees, managers, and leaders at every level and in every function, sector, and industry in three key ways:

- Increasing readers' understanding and awareness of the meaning of sustainability on a conceptual, practical, and personal level

- Energizing and expanding readers' commitment to building sustainable enterprises that will contribute to enhancing the sustainability of the world and its ecosystems for generations to come

- Providing readers with the tools and techniques needed to individually and collectively take appropriate actions that will improve their personal and enterprise sustainability performance in the short and long term

All major change efforts require audacious leaders who have their sights set on future challenges and opportunities. Those at the forefront have to face not only opportunities but also responsibilities. Each of us has enormous potential to contribute to collective sustainability. How will you choose to spend your energy to drive sustainability individually and in the groups and enterprises you belong to? Our hope is that these collective efforts will ultimately contribute to a global change.

Common threads

There are threads that run through the book that hold some keys to accelerating the progress of sustainability. As Jim Collins (2001) discovered in *Good to Great*, the object is not to find the one right strategy, but rather to select appropriate strategies and move the flywheel of collective focused efforts so the flywheel spins faster and faster. Here are some of the key threads that tie these efforts together and require our collective efforts to achieve sustainable success.

What have we collectively learned about sustainability?

Our intended hopes for our readers are the same hopes we have for ourselves. As a result of writing this book and your reading it, we hope that each of us:

- Is energized to make an individual and collective difference as an early adopter of sustainability

- Is prepared to take action on an individual, group, enterprise, and global basis

- Has a clear and realistic understanding of the tensions and challenges we will face

- Has a higher level of comfort to face these challenges and turn them into opportunities by utilizing the tools and learnings from the cases we presented as well as the increased power of connection we now have as part of the larger sustainability network

Tensions of sustainability

Should anything last forever? Is the very idea of sustainability in conflict with the natural laws of the universe of birth, life, demise, and rebirth? There are big theoretical tensions such as this that must be addressed, and there are more practical ones whose answers require practical research. Our work has amplified the tensions that lie in the different views of the causes and cures of sustainability. We are at greatest risk when we think we have the only correct answer for anything. One example of this is the use of biofuels as a solution for reducing the negative environmental impacts of our current fuels, without considering the impact on global food production (Kleiner, 2007). We believe that the opportunities for progress lie in our ability to expose these tensions and come up with solutions that accelerate rather than compromise sustainability. We highlight more examples of tensions in our learnings section below.

Discovering and facing up to tensions is only one of the many valuable lessons we have learned in the process of co-creating this book. Our lessons have come from many sources including:

- Important sustainability work done by others around the globe

- The *2007 AMA Sustainability Survey* (American Management Association [AMA], 2007) and other foundational work done by our authors

- The cases we have been a part of or shared

- Stories of sustainability each of us has had the privilege of collecting through our experiences with powerful and passionate citizens around the world who are committed to sustainability

■ The Sustainability Pyramid

We recognize that learning is a vehicle to accelerate action. Sustainability's progress will be accelerated to the extent we learn from each other and look for the intersections of value among our diverse values, knowledge, and actions. In the beginning of the book (pages 11-12), we shared the **Sustainability Pyramid**, which was developed as part of a study of the world's most sustainable companies (Wirtenberg, Harmon, Russell, & Fairfield, 2007). This model has provided us with a more specific map of efforts we must take to increase our sustainability. It represents the learnings shared with us from these best-practice companies and will provide a context to share what we have collectively learned from our experience of writing this book. The three stages of the pyramid are **Foundation, Traction,** and **Integration.**

Foundation stage learning accelerators

Deeply held shared values were the key foundational attribute that allowed leading organizations to make progress on their sustainability efforts. We found this was true for our team as well. As we worked through the many challenges that arise when 29 sets of individual minds, opinions, and approaches try to agree on anything, we came up with a common set of principles that drove our efforts. These included:

- Holistic, emergent view
- Collaborative, sharing inclusive, open approach
- Inquiry–action–inquiry . . .
- Act with integrity and help each other; be respectful
- Win–win–win
- Listen deeply – for understanding – and create the space for conversations
- Work in the in-between space and across boundaries
- Stay present to our intention, focus on improving the world
- Be attractors
- Be careful that we understand what we mean
- Seek to discover and serve mutual interests
- Walk in others' shoes
- Be committed and accountable
- Create room for the difficult conversations
- Live what we want to become; pay attention to our "way of being"
- Develop tangible actions and short-term successes

These shared values provided the foundation for our collective work and allowed us to leverage our differences to come up with a better product. Here are some of our other learnings for the foundation stage:

Meaning and higher purpose are driving forces

People will offer their commitment to sustainability when they can connect it with their own passions, interests, and legacy desires. Ask someone how they would like to leave the world as a better place than they found it, and you will be surprised and impressed with the committed deep answers you will get back. In Chapter 5 on employee engagement, we highlight the importance of employees having a clear sense of why and where their enterprises choose to focus their sustainability energies.

Requires new state of being/new ways of seeing

We learned from the AMA sustainability survey (AMA, 2007) that our core values are critical in determining the actions we take individually as well as enterprise-wide. In Chapter 2, on mental models, John Adams shows us that the way we think impacts how we act.

Seeing an organization as if it were a living system, a natural system — not as a machine

When looking at any organization, increase the magnification and you will find that the living cells are the people who provide the energy and direction. So when you want to change an organization, you must account for each individual within this system, often more organic than organized in nature. This concept is highlighted in Chapter 8, in which we show the importance of seeing organizations as systems or networks that are biological rather than mechanical: "living" rather than static.

Respect

We learned the importance of one of the first ingredients needed to accelerate sustainability: respect. It provides a foundation of the values and thinking required to generate creative solutions and move people to committed action. Respect occurs as an individual experience but can also be seen as part of a culture that values its people, as highlighted in the DuPont case in Chapter 5 (pages 146ff.).

Inclusion and diversity

Ingredients for generating commitment to, as opposed to compliance with, sustainable efforts are inclusion, a respect for diversity, and the opportunity for people to make valuable contributions. Respect for diversity is clearly illustrated in the "Mental models in civil society" case in Chapter 2 (pages 77ff.) and is beautifully described in the essay by Shakira Abdul-Ali, "New frameworks for leading sustainable enterprise" in Chapter 1 (pages 41ff.).

Way of being: integrity, mutuality (genuinely connecting with others), and sustainability

One early morning the five-year-old son of one of the authors kept asking him to stop e-mailing and look out at front of the house. After resisting so one more e-mail could get done (and one more and one more), exasperated, our author followed the son outside. The son proudly pointed out a beautiful red, orange, and purple sunrise. We are so often caught up with the less important things at the expense of what is most important. We see the beauty of sunrises as inspiration for all of us to contribute to sustainability so that the beauty of our planet and people can continue to be appreciated by generations to come.

New transformational paradigm is needed

We have discovered that a new transformational paradigm for sustainability will require a common set of deeply held values, a new set of mental models, and a new level of discipline for action associated with the potential possibilities and impacts of our current and future practices. A singular focus of profit, people, or planet skews our understanding of sustainability and prevents us from seeing the enormous value of the intersections. In this intersection lies the possibility of synergistic and viral progress.

- A singular focused question might be: How can we recycle more? This only gets to the symptom of our current wasteful practices

- A question focused at the intersection is: How can we unleash the enormous intelligence, energy, and passion of our next generation of leaders so they may identify ways to build products that take less away from the environment and still generate value for all stakeholders?

Trust

We learned that making progress in sustainability requires trust throughout the enterprise and across business sectors, countries, and governments. It all starts with one individual choosing to trust another. We must start by seeing differences as opportunities to create better solutions. Trust will be generated if we give each unique person the opportunity to feel valued and to contribute.

Tension of idealism vs. practicality

Tensions are engendered by differences, and both are ingredients for better results. As we worked on the different sections of the book, we learned that, while we all had a shared passion for impacting the field of sustainability, we also had many diverse perspectives on how to accomplish this. One example of this has been the ongoing challenge of idealism versus practicality. As we shared our diverse views, both perspectives appeared equally powerful. We shifted our focus from choosing one or another to creating the best balance of both — a balance that would provide a diverse set of readers with access to ideal theories and approaches as well as practical tools and cases.

Prevailing mental models

We learned that mental models are strong and difficult but not impossible to change. Ask yourself how your own mental models have shifted as you read this book or learned more about the field from other sources.

Traction stage learning accelerators

The **Traction** stage of the Pyramid focuses on engaging employees, developing sustainable metrics, and aligning the formal and informal organization. Some of our key learnings at this stage include the following:

Leaderful organizations

The leader's role as well as the act of leadership is critical in the shift to sustainability. As we learned in the leadership chapter, Chapter 1, an organization is **leaderful** when the information flow is open, relationships are healthy, employees are involved in decision-making, and initiative is encouraged. If an employee in the organization, regardless of level, sees something that needs to be done, she or he steps forward to meet the need and is supported in that effort by upper management.

Top-management support is necessary but not as a top-down, command-and-control style of management

Leaders who generate commitment as opposed to compliance have the potential to make significant steps toward increased sustainability. We learned in the mental models chapter (Chapter 2) that a leader generates commitment through clarity of vision and mission. In his essay in Chapter 2 (pages 60ff.), John Adams shows us that the articulation of these in mission and vision statements — or in "the Bowl" as Richard N. Knowles would say (pages 27, 51, and 143) — together with related goals and objectives, strategies and tactics, are critical because they clarify what an organization feels it is in business to do, define what success looks like, and lay out the steps necessary to achieve it.

Alignment inside and outside

The number of supporters you gain for sustainability efforts is directly related to how inclusive and open your early discussions were. Ask: Have we taken the time and effort to be inclusive? The resulting level of alignment will tell the truth.

Respect for human needs and future generations

We all have connections to the next generation. What legacy do you choose to leave? What is our opportunity and responsibility for this legacy? Will we choose to stop some of our current wasteful practices to leave a better world for the next generation? For example, if everyone consumed at current US rates, we would need three to five planets to support us (Wackernagel & Rees, 1996). But we only have one. Taking this to its ultimate extreme, in Chapter 7, "Sustainable Globalization," we include Lester Brown's (2006) extrapolation of what would happen to the world if the billions of people in China consumed at the same rate as those in the United States (pages 207-208).

Hope

When organizations, communities, and enterprises get up each morning, what is their hope for the day, week, year, and decade? Sounds like a funny analogy, but it does get you thinking: What is the collective hope of an enterprise? It is made up and spread across the populations of stakeholders that make up that enterprise. If individuals have been engaged and asked what is most important to them and feel heard, you will achieve results. The "Appreciative Inquiry case study: executive MBA candidates," by Theresa McNichol in Chapter 2 (pages 81ff.), gives us tools and processes to bring forth people's deep-seated hopes and dreams.

Importance of informal conversations and group interactions

- The Latin root for the word *converse* is *to turn together*. This is a valuable explanation of how we produced this book, as well as our hope for the *Living Fieldbook*. We felt much stronger as a group than we did on our own. Writing can be a lonely business, especially for those of us who prefer group discussion to individual contemplation. As a result of getting our group together, we were re-energized and revitalized, reminding each other of the importance of our efforts and contribution. This is also why we have such a strong commitment to the *Living Fieldbook* and portal at www.TheSustainableEnterpriseFieldbook.net (**L**)

- We realize the value and importance of the power of creating a space for informal conversations and group interactions. You can also measure and use the patterns of informal relationships to accelerate change. In Chapter 8, "Transorganizational collaboration and sustainability networks," we share how social network analysis was used to determine all of the critical stakeholders in a major UK land use sustainability project

It's all about effectiveness — not good or bad

We discovered that there are many effective approaches to address sustainability. These are often different across cultures. The less we judge with an eye toward right and wrong, the more open we will be to the possibilities of appreciating and leveraging diverse approaches. In Chapter 7, "Sustainable globalization," we introduced six lenses for systematically assessing a company's situation: Economic/financial; Technology; Poverty and inequity; Limits to growth; Movement of talent; and Geopolitical. Only by holistically integrating across all six lenses can we fully appreciate the opportunity and the challenges of creating a sustainable global enterprise. As we stated in the mental models chapter, our definition of effectiveness or success will continue to shift as the bar is raised by our sustainability progress.

Authentic conversations, listening and sharing ideas

The ingredients for authenticity in sustainability will come from honestly sharing the facts and realities of our sustainable challenges, maintaining an openness and willingness to understand diverse views, and working to come up with better solutions. In the PSE&G case in Chapter 5 (pages 148ff.), we highlighted the importance of authenticity and transparency in the development of a robust, transparent safety communications system.

Integration stage learning accelerators

Integration requires broad stakeholder engagement and holistic integration. We faced some of these same opportunities and challenges with ESAT. We conducted consistent calls, worked hard to be open to feedback as we approached deadlines, and even found a little time to celebrate our progress. As we attempted to integrate our work across our chapter teams, we were faced with the many challenges of diverse approaches, perspectives, and styles. ESAT learned that our efforts were just beginning with the completion of this physical book. Our next challenge is to integrate these learnings into our own individual and organizational lives. Here are some of our other learnings for the integration stage:

Sustainability is a never-ending journey

Time and vigilance are both required ingredients for a successful sustainability recipe. As we learned from Chapter 2 (mental models) and Chapter 3 (sustainability strategy), long-term thinking and planning are critical. Zero-sum games teach us that pursuing short-term isolated profits will yield very different results from those attained by following long-term sustainable practices. We learned that there is a discipline of vigilance required at an individual and enterprise-wide level — from asking our children to separate the plastic and cardboard in their holiday presents for recycling to ensuring a living wage in developing-world countries. All of these efforts, micro and macro, require long-term commitments.

Learning in the intersection

As each of us contributed to this work, we began to realize that one of the greatest opportunities for significant contribution to sustainability lay between the white spaces or intersections of our work. In the vast potential of the intersection of people, social systems, and the environment lay unique solutions that result in great improvements.

Culture of blaming vs. doing it

To the extent that we focus on what we are for (more sustainability) as opposed to what we are against (business interruption) we will be able to make progress in our efforts. In addition to its negative impacts, blaming creates a wasteful effort that takes us away from our most important purposes. It is far more productive to search for common ground and move from there than it is to try and resolve differences. Acknowledge differences but move from common ground. A great example of a positive and "can do" approach to a fundamentally unsustainable situation is demonstrated in the case by Sangeeta Mahurkar-Rao, in Chapter 5 on employment engagement, in which everyone stepped up to the challenge at T-Systems in Pune, India (pages 157ff.).

Zero footprint

Each of us will have an impact on the world. Will we leave it in a state that is better, worse, or the same as when we found it? What can each of us do to collectively move ourselves toward a more sustainable world? How will we go beyond zero footprint so that collectively we can reverse the effects of our practices and regenerate and replenish the natural resources of our planet? What role can each of us play in creating and implementing the strategies to effect the changes that can be mutually beneficial to our organizations, companies, nations, and the world? These issues are explored in depth in Chapters 3 and 7.

Learning–action cycles, not knowing

Margaret Mead said, the difference between civilizations that survived and failed was just one thing: the ability to tolerate new ideas. To the extent we can do this and accept the fact that we do not currently have the "truth" of the impacts of our actions and the solutions associated with sustainability, we will survive. To be open and prepared for new ideas and learning is critical for the success of any sustainability project. In Chapter 8, we highlight the importance of setting up sustainability projects in such a way that reviewing and using learning are key continuous drivers for project success.

Can we get there incrementally?

Must we travel from A to B to C or do we require a fundamental and transformational A to XYZ approach to sustainability? Does awakening to the opportunities and consequences of sustainability require cataclysmic events such as oil spills, extreme weather shifts, or pending enterprise failures as we are already starting to witness around the world (Pachauri, 2007)? In Chapter 4, on change, we shared an approach for effecting positive sustainable change in any enterprise through the use of iterative pilot studies. This approach can provide broad engagement and yield the natural tipping points for converting skepticism and resistance into enthusiasm.

Knowledge creation

Knowledge creation and sharing were highlighted especially in the mental models (Chapter 2), change (Chapter 4), employee engagement (Chapter 5), and trans-organizational collaboration and sustainability networks (Chapter 8) chapters, but we explored and examined these notions throughout the entire book. Sustainability efforts will require a higher and deeper level of these efforts as we move from the early-adopter phase of gaining a common foundational base and seek alignment of all sectors of our world needed to gain traction and alignment of our common efforts. To help forge these deeper relationships and networks, try the personal network drawing exercise in Chapter 8 (page 249).

Emergence

Being open to and patient with the emergence of new ways of being and acting is a key ingredient to the recipe of sustainability success. Answers are not always discernible at the surface of our awareness, but lie in the connections at deeper levels of understanding. Karen Davis's essay on global wisdom organizations and leadership, in Chapter 1 (pages 37ff.), points us toward a very different way of being that is rooted in ancient and indigenous cultures and traditions, and in the wisdom of the Earth. In a global wisdom society with global wisdom organizations, we trust the dynamics of self-organizing and collective consciousness to evoke creative responses and initiatives that ethically serve society and Earth in life-affirming, sustainable ways.

Starting from within; self-transformation; willingness to confront barriers

A thousand starfish lay washed up on the beach for what looked like miles. The little girl walking with her grandmother reached down each step and began to throw one starfish at a time back into the ocean. The grandmother said, "It will not make a difference because you can not save them all." The little girl said after each lifesaving throw, "It will make a difference to this one." Sustainability is not one huge starfish; it is millions and millions of them. We must first overcome the barrier of believing we cannot make a difference through our individual efforts: they will make all the difference collectively.

Self-organizing leadership

"Let's restructure" is the common answer and the cure-all "chicken soup" of solutions for many enterprise problems. We have learned that allowing self-organization as opposed to putting a different structure on similar behavior, challenges, and opportunities usually results in the new behavior. People know how to get things done, satisfy customers, save money, and contribute to sustainability. The important question is: How can we help our leaders be more secure and dance the dance that enables and fully engages their people in ways that maximize each individual's contribution?

Empowerment vs. leadership support

If leaders are leaders for their functional expertise of running organizations, then what happens when "organizations" change? If we will require new forms of self-organized enterprise in the future, what will be the requirements to lead these? These issues are explored deeply in Chapter 1. In his essay (pages 29ff.), Daniel Twomey shows us that there is no particular leadership model that will carry us successfully into the future because leadership will change as people and organizations learn and evolve. Leaders are critical in bringing together the right people, creating the conditions, and reframing the conversation for self-organizing at the unit or cross-unit levels. Leaders infuse the enterprise with a clear and compelling intent, as well as with values and principles about how people within the enterprise self-organize.

Emergent vs. expert models

We learned in the chapter on change (Chapter 4) that, although it may be easier to hire an "expert" consultant, it may not be the most effective way to create long-term sustainable change, especially because the changes need to be owned by the entire organization. This applies as well to the current theories regarding sustainability, including those presented in this book. We feel confident that we are presenting some leading-edge concepts, but they only become real and useful to people when they try them on their own, adapt, learn, and achieve real, sustainable results.

Importance of public–private partnerships, collaboration, and multistakeholder perspectives

Another accelerator of sustainability efforts will continue to be partnerships across stakeholders, sectors, and geographies. As we saw from the multiple examples of stakeholder engagement presented in Chapter 8, and wonderfully illustrated by the Sustainable Uplands case in that chapter, the more we can get diverse perspectives and enterprises working together, the more sustainable results we will achieve.

Time orientation

You have heard the phrase "learn from the past, live in the present, and plan for the future." This represents a valuable sustainability lesson. The mental model of time orientation significantly impacts the actions we take today and the consequences we will face in the future based on these actions. Although many organizations in our investment community are driven by short-term thinking and profits, companies such as Innovest Strategic Value Advisors have begun to help focus people's attention on current sustainability practices and their long-term implications.

Congratulations! You have now reached a new beginning . . .

A beginning is only the start of a journey to another beginning.

anon.

What we call the beginning is often the end. And to make an end is to make a beginning. The end is where we start from.

T. S. Eliot

▧ References

American Management Association (AMA). (2007). *Creating a sustainable future: A global study of current trends and possibilities 2007–2017*. New York: American Management Association.

Brown, L. R. (2006). *Plan B 2.0: Rescuing a planet under stress and a civilization in trouble*. New York: W. W. Norton & Company.

Collins, J. (2001). *Good to great: Why some companies make the leap and others don't*. New York: HarperCollins.

Kleiner, K. (2007). The backlash against biofuels. *Nature Reports Climate Change*. Retrieved February 5, 2008, from www.nature.com/climate/2008/0801/full/climate.2007.71.html.

Pachauri, R. K. (2007). *27th Session of the Intergovernmental Panel on Climate Change* (Fourth Assessment Report). Valencia, Spain: IPCC.

Wackernagel, M., & Rees, W. (1996, October 11). Our ecological footprint: Reducing human impact on the Earth. *Much Ado About Nothing*. Retrieved September 9, 2007, from www.buynothing.biz/blog/index.php?itemid=13.

Wirtenberg, J., Harmon, J., Russell, W. G., & Fairfield, K. D. (2007). HR's role in building a sustainable enterprise: Insights from some of the world's best companies. *Human Resource Planning, 30*(1), 10-20.

Coda
An invitation to participate with us in the *Living Fieldbook*
www.TheSustainableEnterpriseFieldbook.net

Sustainability starts with each and every person on the planet. We must make the right choices and work together to improve the way we treat each other and our planet. We must also create sound businesses that can continue to increase the standard of living and provide a place where people can contribute their best.

We invite you to be a part of our *Living Fieldbook* (**L**) at www.TheSustainable EnterpriseFieldbook.net. This vehicle will provide our readers with the opportunity to continue to learn and contribute to sustainability efforts across the globe through the Sustainability Knowledge Network (SKN) Portal. The *Sustainable Enterprise Living Fieldbook* will build on and support the hard-copy book by providing an ongoing mechanism for the social sustainable network to continue to share best practices and energize global sustainability efforts.

Each of us must look inside himself or herself to find what personally gives us energy, and we must continually seek opportunities to use our energies and skills toward sustainable ends. This book represents our attempt to help ourselves and our readers together unleash our energy, direct it using what we have learned about good sustainable practices, and ensure we leave the legacy we want to leave on this planet.

Now we want to invite *you, personally*, into the conversation that we have been having for two or more years and that culminated in this book. To do this, we share with you some of our authors' thoughts about what we have learned and what we are taking away from the rich process of thinking together and working collaboratively to produce this book over the past few years.

John Adams:

- The future isn't what it used to be — by a long shot!

- This work is not about quick fixes! Bigger pictures and longer timeframes are essential

- Learning about deep systems-level change is everyone's job #1

- The age of the consumer is just about over no matter what we collectively decide about creating a sustainable future

Shakira Abdul-Ali:

- Sustainability lives within a cyclical realm, and therefore requires practices that are oriented within a nonlinear framework. Linear thinking, by itself, will surely break the process of sustainability

Greg Andriate:

- Sustainable transformation is fundamentally about changing intangible components of any enterprise: the way people perceive their roles, approach their jobs, and make choices on a daily basis
- Sustainable enterprise goals improve value propositions for all stakeholders (employees, customers, local community, government, and shareholders), while simultaneously engaging the minds and hearts of people working to deliver increased value to all constituencies
- Creating "sustainable enterprise cultures" may require behavior change from every person at every level of the organization

Beth Applegate:

- We must understand the nature of privilege; often neither the recipients of biased privilege nor the "target" of such biases are consciously aware of the discrimination inherent in culture structures
- Capacity building moves us beyond personal behavior change to systemic change
- Keep asking questions to raise your awareness of your own mental models

Doug Cohen:

- In the not-too-distant future, society will applaud the bold "leadership acts" of those who steered their organizations into becoming sustainable enterprises. For leadership is and has always been an experiment in *reality creation*
- The time is *now* and we make the road by *walking together*

Karen Davis:

- We must focus on:
  - Seven-generation thinking and action
  - Rediscovering the answers we have from Nature's wisdom
  - Trusting multiple ways of knowing
- One by one each can make a difference

Orrin Judd:

- The time to act is now

- Every individual can make a difference

Linda Kelley:

- The need for individuals and enterprises to move to a path that generates world sustainability is *urgent*!

- A sustainable enterprise is possible to achieve and can be profitable

David Lipsky:

- People are the key. Living the beautifully simple idea of leaving things better than we found them requires we also leave every person a little better for every interaction, every conversation. Feeling better understood and more valued, each person is more capable of making a powerful and unique contribution to the journey toward a sustainable world.

Sangeeta Mahurkar-Rao:

- Understanding that addressing sustainability is not merely "good to do" but it is what will essentially define a successful corporation in the 21st century: a key success factor

- Twentieth-century organization/business models will not be adequate to address the challenges (of sustainability) of the 21st century. They will require radical change

Terri McNichol:

- Change is good

- I have a dream

- Imagine!

- Inspire invention

Govi Rao:

- What got us here will only sink us faster and deeper!

- We need a "systems approach": *Many systems*! *Not one*!

- Think big! Start small! & Scale fast!

Bill Russell:

- A new global culture that promotes collaboration ahead of competition and service to others ahead of self is both possible and sustainable

- Every business has a responsibility and unique role to play in the journey to this new "target" state of sustainability

- Sustainability can only be achieved if a tipping point (majority?) of individuals change current mental models of what they need and what they desire in order to survive and be fulfilled

- Knowledge is more precious than stuff

Dan Twomey:

- We are bounded by powerful destructive forces, which, in large part, we fail to comprehend

- The well-being of future generations is being compromised, and the threat of grave consequences looms over the horizon

- We must think radically, act decisively, and learn rapidly, with faith that these monumental challenges can be met and paths to a better world may be found

Jeana Wirtenberg:

- The world is truly at a crossroads. We must see that we are all interconnected and choose the path to a brighter future for us all . . . when it all comes together!

Glossary of terms

Action research
Coined by Kurt Lewin in the mid-40s, this has developed into a number of methodologies designed to progressively solve problems by planning, taking actions, measuring results, and taking new actions in an iterative fashion based on those results.

Agenda 21
Also known as *The Blueprint for Sustainable Development*, a program for action on all aspects of sustainable development, Agenda 21 was adopted by more than 178 governments at the United Nations Conference on Environment and Development (UNCED) in Rio de Janeiro, Brazil, 1992. See www.unep.org/Documents. multilingual/Default.asp?DocumentID=78& ArticleID=1163.

Agribusiness
An umbrella term for industrialized food production, or the business and industry of agriculture. For some, this term has a negative connotation because "agribusiness" is the opposite of the family or local farm.

AI (Appreciative Inquiry)
A collaborative process of discovery, envisioning, dialogue, and creating new options regarding important issues. Its hallmark is a focus on the positive: what works well rather than what doesn't work.

AMA (American Management Association)
An association dedicated to professional development and advancing the skills of individuals to drive business success. Many *Fortune* 500 companies, as well as business and government workers, are members. See www.amanet.org.

Avatar
The term (originally for incarnations of divine beings in Hindu philosophy) representing a user in a shared virtual-reality world (e.g., Second Life).

Biodiversity
The variety of living organisms from a single cell to fully developed, complex species, peoples, or ecosystems — in an individual habitat, particular geographic region, or on the planet as a whole.

Biome
A living community characterized by distinctive plant and animal species and maintained under the climatic conditions of the region.

BoP (bottom of the pyramid)
Coined by C. K. Prahalad and Stuart L. Hart, this refers to the world's 4 billion poorest people who live on less than two dollars a day — representing two-thirds of the world's population, as of 2004. For more on BoP 1.0 and 2.0, see www.amanet.org/editorial/webcast/2008/business-crossroads.htm.

Bowl
A metaphorical reference for an organization's mission, vision, standards, principles, and expectations co-created by those in the organization at all levels. This provides guidance in organizations committed to using self-organizing leadership principles.

BSC (balanced scorecard)/SBSC (sustainability balanced scorecard)
A concept for measuring whether the smaller-scale operational activities of a company are aligned with its larger-scale objectives in terms

of vision and strategy. It helps managers focus on performance metrics while balancing financial objectives with customer, process, and employee perspectives. Measures are often indicators of future performance. A sustainability balanced scorecard expands the typical BSC approach and objectives to include additional objectives and indicators for environmental and social perspectives and to represent a broader set of stakeholders.

Burden-shifting
A company's improving its performance, not by eliminating a particular impact, but by moving outside its corporate system's measurement boundary. This may be done by outsourcing, asking suppliers to assume a burden, selling off currently "dirty" business units or product lines, or buying carbon credits.

Carbon credit
A unit of measure for the emission of carbon dioxide and other equivalent greenhouse gases. One carbon credit is equal to one metric ton of CO_2. Carbon credits are used to encourage reduction of emissions, in accordance with the Annex to the Kyoto Protocol of 1997 (see unfccc.int/resource/docs/2005/cmp1/eng/08a02.pdf), and can be sold through trading companies by facilities whose emitted CO_2 is below their agreed-upon targets and purchased by those who are exceeding their targets.

Carbon footprint
A measure of the atmospheric carbon dioxide produced, directly or indirectly, by sets of specific carbon-producing human activities such as the energy used to run a household, business, or mode of transport over a period of time.

CAS (complex adaptive system)
This consists of autonomous agents continuously interacting and producing a constantly evolving and changing order. A flock of geese flying in formation with a constantly changing lead goose is an example of a CAS.

CDP (Carbon Disclosure Project)
A nonprofit organization that provides information to investors and other stakeholders regarding the opportunities and risks to commercial operations presented by climate change. See www.cdproject.net.

Change management
A planned approach to transitioning from state A to state B using a systematic method for building buy-in, engagement, and support at multiple levels of the organization. A proactive approach to handling challenges and responding to resistance encountered when adapting to alterations at organizational and individual levels. Often used for installation of new work procedures and technologies or implementing new cultures.

Corporate governance
The structure and systems that officially allocate power within organizations and manage the relationships between the owners or shareholders and managers and employees of the business.

Corporate sustainability
The goal of a business organization to make a profit and, in the course of operations, not deplete, pollute, or degrade the environment or the communities in which it operates and that it serves.

Crowdsource
Coined by Jeff Howe in 2006 to describe a process of using a diverse group of people outside an organization to generate ideas, solutions, products, or services. These people are paid if their inventions or ideas are accepted. InnoCentive is a company that manages this type of process.

CRP (complex responsive process)
This consists of all people's interactions through conversations and gestures. Everything that takes place in an organization begins with and flows through conversations; they are the pathways of all activities.

CSR (corporate social responsibility)
A concept that holds that businesses are more than profit-seeking entities and have an obligation to benefit society and the environment. CSR extends the definition of whom a corporation serves from customers and shareholders to communities, NGOs, employees, and the environment. Some companies use the term CR, or corporate responsibility, instead of CSR.

DILO assessments
An acronym for "Day in the life of": a tool for tracking target opportunities from the beginning to the end of a process; may be applied to a person, object, form, sample, order, or other unit of analysis.

DJSI (Dow Jones Sustainability Index)
Established in 1999; the first global index tracking the financial performance of the leading sustainability-driven companies worldwide. See www.sustainability-index.com.

Ecological economics
A transdisciplinary field of academic research that addresses the dynamic and spatial interdependence between human economies and natural ecosystems. Its main focus is the "scale" conundrum: how to operate an economy within the ecological constraints of the biosphere.

Ecological footprint
A resource management tool that measures how much land and water area a human population requires to produce the resources it consumes and to absorb its wastes under prevailing technology.

Ecosystem
A community of living organisms and nonliving things (rocks, built environment) that are interdependent for survival within a given area. Areas may be as small as a pond or as large as a watershed of thousands of acres or more. Cities are urban ecosystems.

Ecosystem services
The benefits humans derive from the Earth's "natural capital" or collective natural resources. Biodiversity costs are incurred when these resources are destroyed or degraded to such a degree that they become significantly less available for use.

Enterprise
As used in this book: any organization (for profit, not-for-profit, nongovernmental, public, community, and so on) created to meet a stated purpose.

ESOP (employee stock ownership plan)
A mechanism for organizations to allow employees to purchase stock in the company so that they have a share of ownership and an investment in its future.

FAIR model
An acronym, coined and copyrighted by Organization Innovation LLC in 2008, for the essential elements required for transformational change: **Framing** enterprise mindsets to develop fresh mental models of what we are and what we can become; **Aligning** economic models, physical infrastructure, and workplace processes to achieve a competitive level of performance; **Igniting** growth and innovation through market focus, new business models, and technologies changing industry rules of competition; and **Refreshing** the enterprise to foster creativity, generate energy, and reinvigorate *esprit de corps.*

Five capitals model
Increasingly the investment world is considering the "five capitals" — human, social, natural, manufactured, and financial — and acknowledging their importance to GDP.

GDP (gross domestic product)
The value of all final goods and services produced in a country in one year. GDP can be measured by adding up all of an economy's incomes (wages, interest, profits, and rents) or expenditures (consumption, investment, government purchases, and net exports [exports minus imports]).

Geopolitical
A dynamic relationship between geography (a region of the world) and politics, which may have economic and foreign policy consequences.

GHG (greenhouse gas)
GHGs are components of the atmosphere that come from natural sources and human activity and contribute to the "greenhouse effect." These include water vapor, carbon dioxide, methane, nitrous oxide, ozone, and chlorofluorocarbons.

Gini coefficient
A measure of the inequality in the distribution of income, such that a value of 0 means complete equality in wealth distribution, and 1 means one person owns all the wealth.

Global warming
The increase in the average temperature of the oceans and the air near the Earth's surface, which is thought to be causing more severe floods and droughts, increasing the prevalence of insects and related diseases affecting human health, causing the sea levels to rise, and redistributing the Earth's precipitation.

Globalization
The process by which organizations have transcended national boundaries in their communi-

cations and operations spurred on by rapidly developing technology and changing government policy; often refers to an increasingly integrated global economy marked especially by economic, finance, trade, and communications in an interconnected and interdependent world with the transfer of capital, goods, and services across national frontiers.

GPI (genuine progress indicator)
An indicator that attempts to measure whether a country's growth, increased production of goods, and expanding services have actually resulted in improvement of the welfare of the people in the country. See www.rprogress.org.

Greenhouse Gas Protocol
A widely used international accounting tool for government and business leaders to understand, quantify, and manage greenhouse gas emissions. See www.ghgprotocol.org.

Greenwashing
The act of misleading or overstating to the public the environmental practices and impacts of an enterprise or the environmental benefits of a product or service. For more information, see www.greenwashingindex.com.

GRI (Global Reporting Initiative)
Started in 1997, a multistakeholder institution whose mission is to develop and disseminate globally applicable Sustainability Reporting Guidelines. More than 1,200 organizations disclose their sustainability performance with reference to GRI guidelines. The standards provide guidance on the format and content of the reports and assistance in normalizing and verifying data. See www.globalreporting.org.

HDI (Human Development Index)
A metric of a country's accomplishments on dimensions of human development, including health, knowledge, and standard of living. See hdr.undp.org/statistics.

High involvement process
Any process or procedure that actively engages people in the functions or activities in which they are involved.

Holistic integration
A systemwide or systemic approach that acknowledges that each part of an issue relates to another and can't be resolved in isolation.

Ideagoras
Places on the Internet where large numbers of people and businesses gather to exchange ideas and solutions.

IMF (International Monetary Fund)
An international organization that promotes monetary cooperation and exchange among member countries and provides financial and technical assistance and surveillance.

Industrial ecology
The shifting of industrial processes from linear (open-loop) systems, in which resources and capital investments move through the system to become products and waste, to a closed-loop system in which the wastes become inputs for new processes.

Interdependencies
In the context of business or organizational operations, refers to the interlinking of tasks that cannot occur or progress without the other.

Inworld
Refers to being present, in avatar form, in one of the immersive, 3D, interactive virtual-reality software platforms such as Second Life, There, Active Worlds, Entropia Universe, HiPiHi and others.

IPCC (Intergovernmental Panel on Climate Change)
A scientific body established in 1988 by the World Meteorological Organization (WMO) and UNEP, two United Nations organizations, tasked with evaluating the risk of climate change caused by human activity. See www.ipcc.ch.

ISO 9000 procedures
Standards developed and published by the International Organization for Standardization, including standards for the development, manufacture, and supply of products, systems, machinery, devices, and services. ISO is a network of the national standards institutes of 157 countries. See www.iso.org/iso/home.htm.

ISEE (International Society for Ecological Economics)
ISEE facilitates understanding between economists and ecologists and the integration of their thinking into a transdiscipline aimed at developing a sustainable world. See www.ecoeco.org.

Knowledge management

A process to systematically identify, collect, save, and share what an organization considers valuable documents, resources, knowledge (both explicit and tacit), and competencies of individuals.

KPI (key performance indicator)

An essential metric or target by which an organization measures, manages, and monitors how well it is doing in a specific area; such as health & safety, diversity, energy consumption, revenue and profitability.

Leaderful

A property of an organization in which people, at all levels, are fully involved and encouraged to take the initiative and responsibility to work on a problem when they find one that is within their skills and knowledge.

LEED (Leadership in Energy and Environmental Design)

A green building rating system developed by the US Green Building Council (USGBC); provides a suite of standards for environmentally sustainable construction.

Likert scale

Developed by Rensis Likert, the scale differentiates responses to a multi-item tool used to measure such intangible qualities as intensity (less, more), value (not important, extremely important), relativity (worst, best), and frequency (never, always).

Mental models

Personal operating systems that shape and structure the way a person thinks, feels, moves, behaves, and sees the world.

Metaverse

Coined by Neal Stephenson in *Snow Crash* (1992); now refers collectively to all the 3D immersive, software-generated, virtual-reality worlds where people interact with each other in the form of avatars.

NGO (nongovernmental organization)

An organization that is not part of the local, state, or federal government and that pursues social good exclusively rather than profits or the political requirements of government, although many activities conducted by an NGO might be government programs or receive government funding.

Nonprofits

Legally designated organizations that do not distribute profits to owners, are restricted in the extent of allowable commercial enterprise, and are usually granted exemptions from taxes; the preferred structure of organizations whose missions are to address nongovernmental societal concerns and needs.

OD (organization development)

Planned processes by which human resources are identified, used, and developed to strengthen overall organizational and system effectiveness. Covers such areas as managing culture and organizational change; building organizational learning; organization structure/design; improving an enterprise's ability to adapt and transform; knowledge management; leadership development; teambuilding; and more. The focus is primarily on groups, but individual growth frequently occurs during OD processes.

ONA (organizational network analysis)

A methodology for determining informal relationship networks in an organization through questionnaires, statistical analysis of results, and software to draw network maps.

Opportunity map

A methodology that engages key process stakeholders in identifying improvement opportunities for target work process flows; a collaborative effort to create visual representations of "real-world processes," typically using small, color-coded notes to capture data about what does or does not work well in a process flow diagram.

Organizational core competencies

Areas of specialized expertise that are key to an enterprise's success and often differentiate it from its competitors.

Organizational culture

The shared values, beliefs, and work styles that define what is important to a specific organization; influences acceptable behaviors and practices.

Organizational DNA

The fundamental principles and beliefs determining enterprise behaviors, decisions, and performance. These core elements, deeply embedded in processes and procedures, are so central to enterprise identity (who we are and how we work) that changes generate widespread consequences.

P2NP (product-to-nonproduct ratio)
This ratio can be seen as a special case of ROR — the ratio of productive output to "nonproduct output" (NPO): all the waste that companies produce but can't sell and ship out by way of smokestacks, sewer lines, and "waste" dumps.

Process Enneagram
A model developed and copyrighted by Richard N. Knowles that diagrams the relationships and sequences among actions in order to facilitate common understanding and coordinated accomplishments within a group. It is used so members of a group or enterprise can organize, study, and learn from their activities. Every accomplishment arises from the activities that went into making it happen, yet most of the time these activities are lost from memory. This action-symbol provides a mechanism for the activities to be captured and remembered for future reference.

Renewable energies
Energies that effectively use natural resources and do not involve the consumption of exhaustible resources, such as fossil fuels and uranium. They are based on sources that are naturally replenished, such as sunlight, wind, rain, tides, and geothermal heat. Sometimes referred to as "clean" energy, as a consequence of producing fewer or no hazardous emissions or pollutants, and having minimal impact on fragile ecosystems. See www.eere.energy.gov.

Rio Declaration on Environment and Development
A set of 27 principles for sustainable development adopted at the Rio Conference, the UN Conference on Environment and Development, in 1992 (see *Agenda 21* above).

ROR (return on resources)
The ratio of profit, revenue, or intended result to energy, water, toxics, or other critical resource inputs.

RSS (Really Simple Syndication)
A Web-based technology through which users publish frequently updated content such as blog entries, news headlines, and podcasts and individuals receive only the content they want.

Self-organization
A powerful, natural, pervasive property of the universe in which things organize themselves spontaneously; seen everywhere, in galaxies, rivers, and the way people choose to interact.

Self-organizing leadership
Relates to the insights and skills needed by leaders to effectively and purposefully engage with the natural tendency of people to self-organize.

SNA (social network analysis)
Same as ONA but often applied to networks that extend beyond traditional organizational networks: for instance, assessing and mapping large online social network communities.

SRI (socially responsible investing)
An investment strategy that uses societal concerns such as environmental sustainability, social fairness, and community well-being along with assessments of economic profitability to inform investment decisions.

Stakeholders
Those who have an effect on or are affected by a firm's actions. Stakeholder groups range from clearly defined consumers and customers, owners or stockholders, employees, suppliers, creditors, and regulating authorities to other constituents such as local communities and the environment.

Strategic corporate social responsibility
The idea that corporate social responsibility should be integrated into the firm's strategic perspective and operations because of the long-term or sustainable value that it brings to the organization and its stakeholders.

Strategic management process
The process of developing an organization's strategic goals, objectives, courses of action and allocation of its resources (e.g., people, money, tasks). From an action perspective, it is the process of leveraging organizational strengths and addressing weaknesses to exploit opportunities and neutralize threats in its external environment. In the adaptation used in this book, it is the integration of sustainability goals into the broader strategic planning process.

Strategy Formulation Process Model
An approach or concept that emphasizes a firm's proper identification of objectives, out-

comes, and planning for future time periods. Here it is defined around a triple bottom line of return on investment and return on value for the health of the environment and society as opposed to a strict for-profit business concept emphasizing consumer needs and wants, shareholder value, and profitability regardless of impacts and unintended consequences.

Stretch goals
Targets that are highly desirable yet not easily attainable, requiring extraordinary effort or organizational and individual commitment or resources to achieve.

Supply chain
The set of organizations that provide critical inputs to a firm's internal value-creating activities.

Sustainable enterprise culture
A deep-rooted enterprise mindset valuing and balancing the sustainable development elements of economic viability, environmental responsibility, and social equity.

SWOT/SWOT Framework (strengths, weaknesses, opportunities, threats)
An analytical process framework involving gathering information on the internal and external environments to assess the firm's current strengths, weaknesses, opportunities, and threats, which can impact its goals and objectives.

Systems thinking
Seeks understanding by taking into account the inherently complex relationships and interdependencies among people, situations, issues, and actions within a functional whole.

TBL (triple bottom line)
An evaluation of businesses by comprehensively assessing their financial, environmental, and social performance.

Transformation map
A single-page communication tool illustrating major strategy elements, specific milestone goals, metrics, critical success factors, and high-level actions plans in a multiyear journey to sustainable enterprise (often presented in large poster format).

Transformational change
A major shift fundamentally altering perspectives, priorities, tools, and working conditions throughout an organization or enterprise.

Transorganizational
Refers to connecting through and across the boundaries of individual enterprises to further commonly shared interests.

Transparency
The extent to which organizational decisions and operating procedures, business, nonprofit, government, or individual are open and visible to insiders and outsiders.

UNCSD (United Nations Commission for Sustainable Development)
Promotes and facilitates sustainable development, providing support in the form of technical assistance and capacity building as well as measures of progress at international, national, and regional levels. See www.un.org/esa/sustdev/csd/review.htm.

UNDP (United Nations Development Program)
Provides resources and knowledge to 166 countries to address inequities in democratic governance, social well-being, health, poverty, crisis prevention, energy, and empowerment of women. See www.undp.org.

UNEP (United Nations Environment Program)
Provides a forum for nations to participate and receive scientific, technical, and financial support in various aspects of environmental challenges to improve quality of life. See unep.org.

USGBC (US Green Buildings Council)
A nonprofit community of leaders working to make green buildings accessible to everyone within a generation. See www.usgbc.org.

Value chain
The series of departments within an enterprise as well as external partners and subcontractors that carry out value-creating activities to design, produce, market, deliver, and support a product or service offering.

Way of being
Relates to one's deep, inner way of relating to the world.

Web 2.0

The second generation of World Wide Web technologies, such as social networking sites, wikis, blogs, and virtual-reality worlds, most of which are designed to facilitate conversations and discussions within self-selected communities of interest.

Wiki

Web-based tool that allows for immediate collaboration by individuals to create and edit Web pages and other documents.

Workscape

The broad environment impacting overall enterprise working conditions. The entire range of variables governing physical environment, workplace tools, work–life balance, and personal relationships that variously affect employee morale, engagement, and discretionary effort, which in turn determine individual and team contributions to the larger organization.

World-wisdom traditions

Collectively, the ancient philosophies and historical religions whose truths have withstood the test of time and continue to be relevant to people in addressing and wrestling with life's larger issues.

Zero footprint

Having no lasting detrimental impact on the environment, especially in terms of pollutants and degraded or consumed resources.

About the contributors

Shakira Abdul-Ali, MSOD, PHI, New York, NY, USA
Abdul-Ali is an organization development specialist, trainer, and coach. As a Training and OD Specialist for PHI (www.phinational.org), Abdul-Ali functions to improve the lives of people receiving home or residential healthcare by improving the workplace of the individuals who provide that care.

Prior to joining PHI, Abdul-Ali provided consulting and training services through her company, Alchemy Consulting (www.alchemyconsultingllc.com). Her clients included New Jersey Transit; University of Minnesota; Head Start; Cornell University Management Development Program; Merck; Girl Scouts USA; Union, Middlesex, Essex, and Atlantic Cape county colleges; Right Management; and America Speaks. Before starting her own firm, Abdul-Ali held a number of public-sector roles, including Chief, New Jersey Office of Minority Business Enterprise; Administrator, New Jersey Small Business Division Office of Technical Assistance; and Assistant Director, New Jersey Governor's Study Commission on Discrimination in Public Sector Contracting.

Abdul-Ali received a BA in Economics and Urban Studies from Wellesley College, and an MS from the American University/NTL Organization Development program. She is an MBTI-qualified facilitator and a certified leader for the National Coalition Building Institute.

John Adams, PhD, Organizational Systems PhD Program, Saybrook Graduate School, San Francisco, CA, USA
Adams is Professor and former Chair of the Organizational Systems Program at Saybrook Graduate School. The program emphasizes sustainability research and implementation.

His work focuses on understanding the psychology of successful sustainability initiatives. He is author of *Thinking Today as if Tomorrow Mattered* (Eartheart Enterprises, 2000) and numerous articles and book chapters on mental models for sustainability. Adams is also a faculty member at the Bainbridge Graduate Institute's Green MBA program, and a guest lecturer at the Sri Sathya Sai University MBA Programme in Puttaparthi, India.

Adams is Founder and Director of Eartheart Enterprises (www.eartheart-ent.com), which offers sustainability, health and stress, and successful change implementation support.

Formerly he was Manager, Integrated Work Environments at Sun Microsystems, an interdisciplinary team designing workplace scenarios that optimized team success factors.

Adams has published 10 books and over 50 articles on topics including sustainability, organizational transformation, change implementation, and workplace health and stress management. He serves on the editorial boards of *The Organization Development Practitioner* and the *Journal of Social Change*. He has two degrees in mathematics and received his PhD in Organizational Behavior at Case Western Reserve University.

Jenny Ambrozek, BA DipEd, SageNet LLC, Hastings-on-Hudson, NY, USA
Ambrozek is Founder of SageNet (www.sageway.com) a consulting practice helping businesses create value by applying collaboration and participatory media tools to connect with customers, partners, and employees. Ambrozek's work in online interaction began in the mid-1980s with Edutel, an Aus-

tralian Caption Center–supported educational content service delivered on Prestel standard Videotex and captured in *The Edutel Book: A Guide to Videotex in Education.*

Coming to the United States in the 80s, she joined Prodigy Services. In eight years at Prodigy, Ambrozek brought together a wide range of member-engagement components across a range of content areas. As Director, Community Development, she learned firsthand the importance of day-to-day operating practices in minimizing the cost of supporting interaction.

Since 1996 Ambrozek has helped clients implement successful online network and collaboration efforts to engage customers and promote internal knowledge sharing. With Joe Cothrel, she conducted the *Online Communities in Business 2004* study and contributed to the communities of practice organizational network survey instrument for the Network Roundtable, University of Virginia. Ambrozek is a Co-founder and author of the "21st Century Organization" blog and provides her participatory media expertise to the University of Warwick Knowledge Innovation Network. She earned her BA DipEd at Macquarie University.

Gregory S. Andriate, EdD, Organization Innovation LLC, Palm Coast, FL, USA

Andriate is Executive Director of Organization Innovation, a consulting firm partnering with clients to develop sustainable enterprise capabilities for the 21st century. An expert in business innovation and transformational change, he helps organizations reframe, restructure, revitalize, and renew capabilities securing business value for customers and shareholders.

Since 1985, Andriate has led over 30 organizational transformation interventions in Europe and North and South America. His experience includes financial reporting/insurance savings plan conversions, agricultural/pharmaceutical product development cycle improvements, and workscape revitalization initiatives in 22 petrochemical manufacturing sites. His executive coaching experience includes reinventing corporate functions in engineering, communications, ecology/health/safety, finance, human resources, IT, logistics, and procurement.

Previously Andriate was Manager, Executive Development for BASF, responsible for executive competency and high-performance business capabilities development. Earlier, he was Assistant Dean, University of Bridgeport Metropolitan College, responsible for adult degree programs, and a faculty member at Bridgeport, Hartford, New Mexico, and West Virginia universities.

Andriate has published book chapters in *Information and Behavior* and *Communication Yearbook 6* and articles in such journals as *Communication*, *Communication Quarterly*, and *Communication Research Reports*, and has served on editorial boards of two academic journals. He earned his Bachelor's and Master's at Rutgers University and his Doctorate in Educational Psychology at West Virginia University.

Beth Applegate, MSOD, Applegate Consulting Group, Takoma Park, MD, USA

Applegate is President of Applegate Consulting Group (www.applegateonline.com), which has provided consulting services for over 18 years. She brings a rich and diverse portfolio of experience and a solid grounding in theory pertaining to organizational behavior, management, political science, and grassroots organizing.

Applegate is known as an insightful, forthright, and compassionate person who holds a deep concern about racial equity and social justice. She approaches her work and life with a sense of inquiry, possibility, and purpose. While working with each client system, Applegate supports the client in evaluating whether the espoused core values — those deeply held views we hold as a compass for ourselves, regardless of whether or not we are rewarded — are congruent with the behavior and actions of the organization as a whole.

Applegate earned an MS in Organization Development at the American University/National Training Laboratory, Institute for Applied Behavioral Sciences where she was inducted into the Phi Alpha Alpha national honor society. She is a recipient of the Hal Kellner Award, presented to a student whose characteristics include being "challenging, thoughtful, humorous" and who "holds a deep concern about social justice."

Victoria G. Axelrod, MA, Axelrod Becker Consulting, New York, NY, USA

Axelrod is a management consultant and organization strategist. She has extensive experience developing, integrating, and executing company strategy. She is a Principal of Axelrod Becker Consulting (axelrodbecker.com), which develops sustainable growth by identifying new revenue opportunities based on untapped internal strengths through the power of stakeholder networks. Clients are start-ups to *Fortune* 500 companies, nonprofits, and government agencies.

Axelrod is a former Senior Vice President and Head of Global Best Practices for the American Management Association where she doubled the revenue to $300 million in four years. She is also a Partner of Norman N. Axelrod Associates (a technology planning and solutions consulting firm).

She co-founded both the blog "21st Century Organization Group," to address issues in today's interconnected technology-driven global business environment, and c21org.typepad.com.

She has published and made frequent presentations to groups such as US National Security Agency, Bausch & Lomb, Baruch College MBA Program, New School, Human Resource Planning Society, and the US Chamber Institute. Board member service includes eSight and Organization Development Network of Greater New York. She has a BA from the University of Michigan and an MA from Columbia University.

J. Flynn Bucy, PhD, The Bucy Group, McLean, VA, USA

Bucy is Founder and Principal of The Bucy Group, a consulting network providing business, civil society, development agencies, and academic institutions with effective strategies for moving toward sustainability — primarily through multistakeholder partnerships. He also serves as a strategy consultant.

Bucy is a social entrepreneur and catalyst for multisectoral partnerships bringing business firms, government agencies, multilateral development institutions, civil society organizations, and academic institutions together to forge creative solutions to global challenges. He has an entrepreneurial approach to creation of effective sustainability strategies and partnerships. Engagements included working with ChevronTexaco to develop a global community engagement program, the Clinton Foundation on climate change, World Vision International to develop a strategy for harnessing emerging carbon offset markets to benefit the poor in developing countries, the TCC Group, Citizens International, Earth Council Foundation, and various technology start-ups.

Prior to founding The Bucy Group, Bucy was Assistant Director of the Center for Entrepreneurship at Baylor University, Vice President of Sales for the Government Systems Division of EDS, and a staff consultant for Arthur Andersen Consulting.

Bucy earned a BA in economics and an MBA in International Business at Baylor University and a PhD in Organizational Behavior at George Washington University.

Jane Carbonaro, BS, Four Corners International, Half Moon Bay, CA, USA

Carbonaro is Director of Collaborative Services for Four Corners International, where she is responsible for client and partner development. In this role, she also serves as technology liaison, having been deeply involved in ERP software development and deployment efforts for more than a decade.

Carbonaro's background includes work in information management for sustainability and environmental health & safety. Additionally, she has managed customer support and business development organizations with responsibility for all client, partner, and development interfaces.

Since 2002, Carbonaro has been involved in the development and support of online communities and collaborative work environments. Since 2006, Carbonaro has been an advisor to SKN Worldwide–USA on the design and functionality of the Sustainability Knowledge Network collaborative workspace portal. She has contributed to an extensive review of social network platforms currently being used to advance sustainable development objectives and technology tools used to support transorganizational collaborative efforts. She has a BS in Public Relations from San Jose State University.

Douglas Cohen, MA, The Leadership Center, Maplewood, NJ, USA

Cohen is Founder of The Leadership Center; Chair, Resource Council, National Youth Initiatives, US Partnership for Education for Sustainable Development (www.uspartnership.org); and Founder, Inspired Futures Global Campaign–Inter-Generational Partnerships for Livable Futures, New York/Wellington, New Zealand. His cross-sector efforts focus on designing large-scale change campaigns to achieve generational solutions in human systems. Cohen leads "At the Edge of Emergence" retreats worldwide, inviting change agents on seven continents into collaborative efforts to bring about an inspired, healthy, and sustainable future culture.

Through youth-focused Leaders of the Next Generation programs, Cohen emphasizes leadership development, sustainability literacy, and systemic change literacy for tomorrow's leaders. He consults to emerging green economy clients and is developing green jobs for at-risk youth through his consultation to the New York State Office of Children and Family Services. Cohen consults to the New Zealand Department of Conservation on leadership for the learning organization.

Cohen's writing appears in *Einstein's Business* (St. John, 2006). He co-authored *Who's Minding the Future?* with Holly English (Leadership Excellence, 2001); and wrote a vignette in *Shaping the Learning Organization* (Marsick, Watkins, 1990). Cohen received his BA in Psychology from the Evergreen State College, Olympia, WA, and his Master's in Applied Behavioral Science from The Leadership Institute, Seattle/Spokane, WA.

Karen J. Davis, MA, New York, NY, USA

Davis has consulted with organizations globally for over 35 years. Her life's work is in the spirit of Earth wisdom, and her values and practices are grounded in multiple ways of knowing.

Davis (kdavis@globetrotter.net) is dedicated to building a global community and sustainability by working and learning with colleagues and groups worldwide. She is on the postgraduate faculty in Organizational Behavior and Development at the Universidad Diego Portales in Santiago, Chile. She is a board member of Open Space Institute, is active in the International Organization Development Association, and has been a Trustee of the Organization Development Network. Karen serves on the board of a large healthcare company and on boards of various community and cultural organizations.

Karen's educational background includes specializations in chemistry, counseling psychology, and social psychology. Her music training and experience are significant influences in her work and life. When not traveling or working around the world, she lives in New York City, returning regularly to her native Arizona. Summers, she is on her farm in rural Quebec, Canada, with her virtual office. Karen describes herself as a "global citizen and gardener." The Earth is her playground and lifelong teacher.

George-Thérèse Dickenson, BA, New York, NY, USA

Dickenson has been a poet, writer, and editor for 30 years. Her work focuses on language, the environment, and peace-and-justice issues. Recently she was editor of two community-based newspapers and the daily news compendium *Garden State EnviroNews*. She was Managing Editor at two Ziff-Davis magazines and Senior Editor at *New York* magazine.

She founded Incisions: Prison Arts, which became a model for prison arts programs. Dickenson directed the foundation, taught in prisons, edited a magazine of prisoners' writings, and performed their work at museums and arts and literary venues, and on the radio. *Candles Burn in Memory Town* is an anthology of writings from Incisions workshops.

Dickenson's books of poetry include *Striations* and *Transducing*. She is featured in a number of anthologies including *UpLate: American Poetry Since 1970* and *American Poets Say Good-bye to the Twentieth Century*, both edited by Andrei Codrescu. She has given poetry readings, performances, and lectures in venues ranging from the NuYorican Poets Café to Harvard University and the Whitney Museum (NYC). Dickenson has an honors BA from Wellesley College, where she was a Durant Scholar and a member of Phi Beta Kappa.

Tom Drucker, MA, Consultants in Corporate Innovation, Marina Del Rey, CA, USA

Drucker is President of Consultants in Corporate Innovation (www.corporateinnovation.com). His work is unique because he integrates the principles of positive psychology and advances in neuroscience with the methods of process improvement and change management. Drucker serves as a trusted advisor and a business consultant to owners, professional partnerships, and leaders of every size business and is proud to be partnering with Jeana Wirtenberg in www.whenitallcomestogether.com, focusing on building sustainable enterprises through improving leadership, culture change, collaboration, and learning.

Xerox Corporation recruited Drucker from his doctoral program, and he began his business career working directly for the chairman of Xerox. In his 15-year career with Xerox, he developed practical and cost-effective methods for designing and implementing new strategies and sustainable organizational changes. He left Xerox in the early 80s to start Consultants in Corporate Innovation. Drucker serves on the board of the Otis College of Art and Design in Los Angeles where he has started a mentoring program for young artists.

Drucker received his MA in Clinical Psychology from UCLA while working with and being mentored by Abraham Maslow and Viktor Frankl. He pursued a PhD at UCLA's business school where he combined operations research, anthropology, linguistics, and behavioral science.

Kent D. Fairfield, PhD, MBA, Silberman College of Business, Fairleigh Dickinson University, Madison, NJ, USA
Fairfield is Assistant Professor of Management at the Silberman College of Business, Fairleigh Dickinson University. Formerly a Vice President at the Chase Manhattan Bank, he later founded Kent Fairfield Associates, consulting on teams, leadership development, and change management. His current research concerns interdependence between employees and managers, between groups, and between organizations. He also explores the factors underlying sustainability management, including individual differences in how people carry out decision-making, leadership, and employee engagement.

His publications have appeared in the *Journal of Applied Social Psychology, Human Resource Planning, Nonprofit Management and Leadership, Journal of Healthcare Management,* and *Journal of Management Education.* He has made presentations at scores of academic and professional conferences in the United States and abroad.

He emphasizes learning from experience in his teaching, including requiring students to conduct community service projects and carry on mentor relationships with executives. He earned an MA and PhD in Organizational Psychology from Columbia University and an MBA in Finance from the Harvard Business School.

Alexis A. Fink, PhD, Microsoft Corp., Redmond, WA, USA
Fink works in the People and Organization Capability function at Microsoft. Currently, she is Group Manager, Culture and Talent Transformation. In this role, she is responsible for execution of and deriving insights from Microsoft's suite of employee engagement research programs, for driving enterprise-wide culture change, and for building out an enterprise-wide talent strategy and framework. In prior roles at Microsoft, she had responsibility for Microsoft's assessment strategy and portfolio for executive assessment, for leadership competency research, and for the enterprise-wide competency research strategy.

Prior to joining Microsoft, Fink spent eight years at the global chemistry giant BASF, leading through acquisition integrations, driving curriculum design, and leading large-scale organizational change initiatives. In addition to her industry experience, her academic talents led her to conduct research for the US Navy and NASA, and to teach at the doctoral level.

Fink received her doctorate from Old Dominion University, in Norfolk, VA. A productive scholar as well as an accomplished practitioner, she has over 30 publications and academic presentations to her credit.

Gil Friend, MS, Natural Logic, Berkeley, CA, USA
Friend is President and CEO of Natural Logic (www.natlogic.com) (CEO blog: blogs.natlogic.com/friend), a strategy and systems development company that helps companies and communities prosper by embedding the laws of nature at the heart of enterprise. He develops "generative feedback" systems, including Business Metabolics and OpenEco.org, which evaluate and track the sustainability performance of businesses, communities, and organizations. *Tomorrow* magazine called him "One of the country's leading environmental management consultants — a real expert who combines theoretical sophistication with hands-on, in-the-trenches know-how."

He has served on San Francisco Mayor Gavin Newsom's Clean Tech Advisory Council; was a founding board member of the Sustainable Business Alliance and Internet pioneer Institute for Global Communications; and co-founded the Institute for Local Self-Reliance, a pioneering sustainability "think-and-do tank," more than 35 years ago.

Friend writes "The New Bottom Line," a column on business strategy; "The Week in Carbon" column for WorldChanging.com; and a blog on strategic sustainability at blogs.natlogic.com/friend. He is also writing the forthcoming book *Risk, Fiduciary Responsibility and the Laws of Nature.* He holds an MS in Systems Ecology from Antioch University and a black belt in Aikido. He is a seasoned presenter of "The Natural Step" environmental management system.

Joel Harmon, PhD, Institute for Sustainable Enterprise, Fairleigh Dickinson University, Madison, NJ, USA
Harmon is a Professor of Management in the Silberman College of Business at Fairleigh Dickinson University, a Distinguished Faculty Fellow of its Center for Human Resource Management, and Director of Research for its Institute for Sustainable Enterprise. During his 24-year academic career, he has

served as Department Chair, President of the University Faculty Senate, President of the Eastern Academy of Management, co-leader of the Sustainable Practices Action Research Community workshop series (1997–2007) at the Academy of Management, and founding member of the Academy's Theory-to-Practice Executive Steering Committee. Before joining academia, he held several management positions in industry.

He specializes in organization strategy and transformation, focusing on linkages between people, learning, and sustainability practices and corporate performance. He has published widely in a variety of leading academic and practitioner journals including *Health Care Management, Case Research, Human Resource Planning, Cost Management, Group Decision & Negotiation,* and *Organization Behavior & Human Decision Processes.*

Harmon earned his PhD in Organization Communication and Change from the State University of New York at Albany and an MS in Environmental Policy and Planning from Rensselaer Polytechnic Institute.

Pam Hurley, MA, TOSCA Consulting Ltd., St. Albans, Hertfordshire, UK

Hurley is Founder and Managing Director of TOSCA (www.toscagroup.com), an international consultancy with particular interest in the implications of the changing nature of the world of work for strategy. TOSCA helps organizations in all sectors develop sound strategy, build internal commitment to driving it forward, and put in place the necessary processes to ensure effective implementation. Together with a range of well-known client companies, TOSCA has developed a new thought leadership model that combines practical insights with leading-edge ideas and research to help understand what the future may hold and how to address its challenges and capitalize on its opportunities.

Hurley's previous roles cover both public and private sectors. In central government her policy and operational responsibilities included health, social security, and criminal justice as well as an efficiency scrutiny for the UK Prime Minister's Office. She also held HR and Planning Director posts in the National Health Service. Private-sector roles included leading research on societal change and values and their implications for strategy development with the Shell Global Scenarios Team and change management with the Shell International leadership group.

Hurley is an Associate Fellow, University of Oxford, and received her MA, with honors, in English Literature, from Edinburgh University.

Orrin D. Judd, MDiv, Judd Performance Consulting, Denville, NJ, USA

Judd is President of Judd Performance Consulting. He has over 20 years of independent and corporate professional human resource development experience, both domestic and international, with "blue-chip" companies from a variety of industries, as well as with public agencies. He has worked successfully with all levels of management and employees in developing skills, improving organizational climate and productivity, creating a vision, and achieving corporate objectives. Judd has a life-long commitment to employee involvement, the triple bottom line, and respect and caring for our environment.

Client assignments cover a broad spectrum of industries including telecommunications, flavor and fragrances, pharmaceutical, and retail, and both public-sector and nonprofit organizations. Orrin has been awarded the FDA Commissioner's Special Citation, the President's Quality Award from Hoffmann-LaRoche, and the Human Resources Diamond Award from AT&T. He is a certified Future Search facilitator and a member of the Future Search Network. He is also a member of the New Jersey Organizational Development Network and the NJ Human Resource Planning Group. Judd earned his BA in Psychology at Tufts University and his MDiv at Colgate Rochester Divinity School.

Linda M. Kelley, BA, Trans-Form, Boston, MA, USA

Kelley is Principal of Trans-Form, and certified practitioner of Applied Human Systems, Walking Your Talk (www.CultivatingExcellence.com), Boston, MA, and Second Life (avatar, Delia Lake, slurl.com/secondlife/Neufreistadt/33/114/127).

Kelley's focus is on professional and personal development. She uses a holistic approach to learning that integrates thinking, feeling, and moving for fast, genuine results. She works with individuals and teams to develop the mindset, presence, actions, and culture of leadership and effective teamwork for enterprises building a sustainable world.

Kelley brings to her consulting and coaching a practical, hands-on perspective from her 30 years of business experience coupled with an artist's sense of invention, play, and design, and an amateur naturalist's powers of observation. She has worked for and consulted to both businesses and government — from multinational corporations to small, closely held companies, civilian, military, and non-governmental agencies. Her business experience includes sales and marketing, systems analysis, project management, strategic planning, and training. Recently, she led a successful turnaround, and then negotiated the sale, of a century-old, family-owned company.

Kelley serves on the board of the Sustainable Business Network/Boston and the steering committee of the OD Learning Group, and is a member and former chair of the board of Extras for Creative Learning. She earned her BA in Sociology at Bucknell University.

Richard N. Knowles, PhD, the Center for Self-Organizing Leadership, Niagara Falls, NY, USA

Knowles is Co-founder and Director of the Center for Self-Organizing Leadership. His work is focused on helping organizations become much more effective through the use of Self-Organizing Leadership.

He served in the DuPont Company for over 36 years beginning as a research chemist (40 patents), then in a variety of manufacturing assignments at Repauno, NJ, Chambers Works, NJ (as Assistant Plant Manager), Niagara Falls, NY (Plant Manager, 1983–87), Belle, WV (Plant Manager, 1987–95), and finally as Director of Community Awareness, Emergency Response and Industry Outreach. In 1995 he received the EPA Region III Chemical Emergency Planning and Preparedness Partnership Award.

His leadership work is featured in Tom Petzinger's *The New Pioneers* (Simon & Schuster, 1999) and Roger Lewin and Birute Regine's *The Soul at Work* (Simon & Schuster, 2000). He is author of *The Leadership Dance: Pathways to Extraordinary Organizational Effectiveness* (Center for Self-Organizing Leadership, 2002).

He has discovered and developed a unique approach to using the Process Enneagram, a highly effective tool for organizational transformation. It cuts to the heart of the key variables in dynamic situations enabling people to more successfully move forward through complex challenges. Knowles earned a PhD in Organic Chemistry at the University of Rochester and a BA in Chemistry at Oberlin College.

David Lipsky, PhD, Conversant, Highland Mills, NY, USA

Lipsky is a senior consultant with Conversant. He has over 20 years of experience in building organizational and leadership capabilities that contribute to business success and personal growth. He has accomplished this by focusing on the potential and possibilities of the people and businesses he has worked with and using his extensive experience in strategic alignment, leadership development, and organizational transformation.

Lipsky has had the opportunity to work with many organizations in a variety of industries, including Sony, Unilever, United Technologies, Bank of America, Alpharma, KPMG Peat Marwick, and Merrill Lynch.

Lipsky is also an Associate Professor at Manhattanville College. He has lectured and authored articles and book chapters on internal consulting, organizational development, and sustainability. Lipsky received his undergraduate degree from Cornell University in Human Ecology and received a PhD in Applied Psychology from Hofstra University, focusing on leadership effectiveness and success.

Sangeeta Mahurkar-Rao, PhD, ProCelerité LLC, Clifton, NJ, USA

Mahurkar-Rao is Co-founder and CEO of ProCelerité (www.procelerite.com), an enterprise focusing on business process transformation for global businesses needing to align themselves with rapidly evolving market forces.

Mahurkar-Rao's business orientation and work in organization development has deep roots in systems thinking. She sees organizations consisting of numerous interrelated systems and believes that for a company to be sustainable it is imperative to understand both the whole and the interrelationship of the parts.

Formerly, Mahurkar-Rao was Global Head of HR and OD at Persistent Systems where she focused on aligning HR with business and led a strategic realignment to a role- and competency-based organization, while driving aggressive growth in the employee base. She has been retained by global companies to successfully lead strategic value-adding initiatives including organizational restructuring, visioning, and process alignment. She has been associated with NVIDIA, Winphoria Networks, Philips Software, and Tata Consultancy Services.

Mahurkar-Rao is on the leadership team of the Global Community on the Future of OD. Her research has been published, and she co-edited and co-authored *Roots of Reason: Science and Technology in the Ancient World* (Quest Publications, 2002). She received her PhD in Cognitive Science from the Bulgarian Academy of Sciences, Bulgaria.

Theresa McNichol, MA, Ren Associates, Princeton, NJ, USA

McNichol is President of Ren Associates, and a former museum director and curator. She is a Chinese culture scholar and an award-winning artist who has both exhibited her paintings and taught nationally and internationally. With her unique combination of skills and experience, she looks at trends in management and leadership issues from a unique vantage point. McNichol's publications and presentations at Asian, European, and American conferences reflect her interests in aesthetic leadership, cultural capital, intangible assets, and reflective practice.

McNichol, who has held adjunct posts at several universities, is currently adjunct Associate Professor at Mercer County Community College. She is a member of the Innovation in Education seminar at Columbia University and of several advisory boards including the Institute for Sustainable Enterprise at Fairleigh Dickinson University, NJ. Looking ahead to emerging fiscal and cultural legacy issues baby-boomers face as they move into retirement, she is instituting a philanthropy division at a New Jersey senior healthcare facility.

McNichol majored in Chinese language and Asian cultural studies at Brooklyn College, where she received a BA She received her MA in Interdisciplinary Studies from New York University. Her paintings are included in many private and public collections.

Susan Nickbarg, MBA, SVN Marketing, Silver Spring, MD, USA

Nickbarg is Principal of SVN Marketing, a respected organizational improvement firm that provides hands-on strategic planning, corporate responsibility training, and integrated communications and program development services assisting global companies, start-ups, and nonprofits succeed at becoming sustainable enterprises.

Credited with creating cutting-edge sustainability initiatives, she has enabled companies to meet or exceed expectations for sustainability. Her articles have appeared in *Business for Social Responsibility Weekly, Greenbiz, PR News, The Corporate Ethics Monitor,* and the *US Chamber of Commerce Business Civic Leadership Center.* Her writings demonstrate how to conceptualize and implement strategies and tactics that improve performance and promote sustainable growth. Topics include the environment, climate change, governance, PR, branding, communications, partnerships, CSR strategy, and CSR reporting. She also serves as a judge for the *PR News* Corporate Social Responsibility communications awards competition.

Formerly, Nickbarg was a Director at Discovery Communications and held marketing management roles at Edmark, an IBM subsidiary, Grafica Group, Novartis, and Sara Lee, where her efforts built strong brands, new businesses, and successful teams and partnerships.

Nickbarg earned an MBA at the University of North Texas, a BA at the State University of New York at Stony Brook, and a Certificate in International Relations at New York University.

Govi Rao, MA, Lighting Science Group Corp., Princeton, NJ, USA

Rao is Chairman and CEO of Lighting Science, a leader in energy-efficient LED lighting, offering digital lighting solutions for highly customized projects as well as ready-to-use, plug-and-play applications. Rao also serves as an Operating Advisor for Pegasus Capital Advisors, LP, a private equity fund manager that provides capital to middle-market companies across a wide variety of industries.

Previously, Rao was Vice President and General Manager of the Philips Solid State Lighting business in North America. He also held several other leadership roles at Philips, including Vice President of Business Creation & Brand, in which he was responsible for product management, strategic marketing, branding, and sustainability.

Prior to joining Philips, he spent over a decade with specialty chemicals leader Rohm & Haas in various leadership roles across a range of businesses and geographies.

Born and raised in India, Rao is an advisor to the US–China Center for Sustainability and a founding member of the Institute for Sustainable Enterprise at Fairleigh Dickinson University. He also serves on the board of the Alliance for Solid-State Illumination Systems and Technologies (ASSIST) and the board of educator programs at Villanova University. Rao earned his MA in Human Resource Development at Villanova University.

William G. Russell, President, SKN Worldwide–USA Inc., Leonia, NJ, USA

Russell is a leader in advancing sustainable development-aligned strategies and management systems. He has worked with a broad range of worldwide clients including small and large corporations, government and intergovernmental organizations, NGOs, nonprofits, and universities. In 2003, he founded SKN Worldwide–USA (www.sknworldwide.com), a sustainability consulting and technology services company. In 2004, he founded the Sustainability Knowledge Network (SKN; www.sknworldwide.net), a collaborative workspace portal to educate and integrate diverse communities of people and engage stakeholder organizations working to implement collaborative projects and programs that advance sustainability.

Russell is also affiliated with the Generation Consulting Group and the Institute for Sustainable Enterprise and Sustainable Business Incubator at Fairleigh Dickinson University where he works to support start-up companies with strategic advice and funding. Prior to founding SKN, he served as the US leader for environmental services at PricewaterhouseCoopers.

Russell is on the advisory boards of Innovest Strategic Value Advisors, an environmental and intangible-value risk ratings company and Four Corners International, a company specializing in developing new technologies that address climate change, sustainability, and globalization issues. He is also an external board member emeritus of the University of Michigan's Erb Institute for Global Sustainable Enterprise. He received his BS in Chemical Engineering from the University of Maryland and his MBA from Rutgers University.

Anna Tavis, PhD, American International Group Inc., New York, NY, USA

Tavis is Vice President of Organizational Development for American International Group, responsible for talent management, organization development, and learning.

Before joining AIG, Tavis was Director of Learning and Development at United Technologies, responsible for servicing over 215,000 employees in more than 70 countries. Prior to that, she led the organizational development function in Europe, Middle East, and Africa regions for Motorola, based in England and then was the Head of Talent Management for Nokia based in Finland. In academia, Tavis served on the faculty at Williams College, Fairfield University, and Columbia University.

Tavis serves on the board of the Princeton Alumni Association, published a book on Rainer Maria Rilke (1997, Northwestern University Press), and has authored over 30 articles in international journals. She is currently on the editorial board of HRPS and is a frequent presenter at international talent management and learning and development forums.

Tavis was born in St. Petersburg, Russia, and graduated from Herzen Pedagogical University with a degree in Linguistics and Education. She also studied at Bradford University, UK, and Dartmouth College, USA. She earned her MA and PhD in Comparative Literature from Princeton University and later received an advanced certificate in Business Administration from the University of South Carolina.

Daniel F. Twomey, DBA, Institute for Sustainable Enterprise, Fairleigh Dickinson University, Madison, NJ, USA

Twomey is Director, International Partnerships for the Institute for Sustainable Enterprise at Fairleigh Dickinson University (FDU). He teaches leadership and sustainability at FDU. Dan previously was Professor of Management at West Virginia University. He has consulted for many large and small organizations and published more than 40 articles in national and international journals.

Twomey was a founder and director of four outreach organizations that link business with academia and teaching and research with practice, including co-establishing a two-day Academy of Management Workshop: The Practitioner Series. He has played a substantive role in forwarding FDU's mission "global leader in education" by working with international universities and developing programs for both Executive MBA and undergraduate students. Recently he co-developed an innovative course that includes a stay in a small village in Costa Rica.

Prior to getting his doctorate, Twomey had a successful career in business, which he has continued as an academic, author, and consultant. Two of his recent publications include *Designed Emergence as a Path to Enterprise Sustainability*, *Emergence: Complexity and Organization* (E+CO, 2006), and *Democracy and Sustainable Enterprise* (Global Forum, 2006).

Jeana Wirtenberg, PhD, Institute for Sustainable Enterprise, Fairleigh Dickinson University, Madison, NJ, USA

Wirtenberg is Co-founder and Director, External Relations & Services, Institute for Sustainable Enterprise (ISE; www.fdu.edu/ise) in the Silberman College of Business at Fairleigh Dickinson University. Her work at the Institute focuses on bringing people together to learn how to develop and lead thriving, sustainable enterprises that are "in and for the world." She was a lead author on the recent worldwide study *Creating a Sustainable Future: A Global Study of Current Trends and Possibilities 2007–2017*, sponsored by the American Management Association. With ISE colleagues, Wirtenberg is principal designer of the three-day manager workshop Green Leadership: Implementing Sustainability Strategies for the American Management Association.

Wirtenberg is President of Jeana Wirtenberg & Associates, a consulting firm that focuses on building sustainable enterprises through leadership, culture change, collaboration, and learning (www.whenitallcomestogether.com). Formerly, she was HR Director at Public Service Enterprise Group (PSEG), where she was responsible for a variety of initiatives designed to transform the firm and build organizational capacity.

She held positions in AT&T Human Resources and Marketing, and led research programs at the National Institute of Education and the US Commission on Civil Rights.

Wirtenberg co-edited *Sex Role Research: Measuring Social Change* (Praeger, 1983) and a special issue of *Psychology of Women Journal: Women and the Future*. Her articles have appeared in numerous journals including *Human Resource Planning*, *Organization Development*, and *Journal of Applied Behavioral Science*. She serves as the Organization Effectiveness Articles Editor for *People & Strategy Journal* and is on the leadership team of the *Global Community for the Future of OD*. Wirtenberg received her PhD with honors in Psychology at the University of California at Los Angeles.

Index